ANDREW JACKSON, SOUTHERNER

Southern Biography
Andrew Burstein, Series Editor

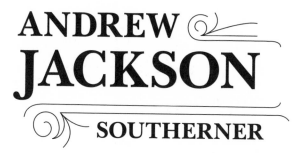

ANDREW JACKSON

SOUTHERNER

MARK R. CHEATHEM

Louisiana State University Press

Baton Rouge

PUBLISHED BY LOUISIANA STATE UNIVERSITY PRESS

Copyright © 2013 by Louisiana State University Press
Manufactured in the United States of America
First Printing

Designer: Hannah Allyce McClure
Typeface: Baskerville
Printer: McNaughton & Gunn, Inc.
Binder: Dekker Bookbinding

LIBRARY OF CONGRESS CATALOGING-IN-PUBLICATION DATA

Cheathem, Mark Renfred.
  Andrew Jackson, southerner / Mark R. Cheathem.
    pages cm. – (Southern biography)
  Includes bibliographical references and index.
  ISBN 978-0-8071-5098-6 (cloth : alk. paper) – ISBN 978-0-8071-5099-3 (pdf) – ISBN
978-0-8071-5100-6 (epub) – ISBN 978-0-8071-5101-3 (mobi) 1. Jackson, Andrew, 1767–
1845. 2. Presidents–United States–Biography. 3. United States–Politics and govern-
ment–1829–1837. I. Title.
  E382.C45 2014
  973.5′6092–dc23
  [B]
                                                    2012049695

For Amber

CONTENTS

ILLUSTRATIONS

ACKNOWLEDGMENTS

In a break with academic tradition I want first to thank my family for keeping me grounded in the real world. Balancing work and home can be difficult for me at times, so I am grateful that Amber, Laney, Allison, and David remind me that being a husband and a dad is more important than any scholarship that I produce. My sister, Lisa, and my aunt, Wanda, have been my consistent supporters. I hope that I have expressed sufficient gratitude to my parents, Danny and Brenda, for their hard work and sacrifices over the years.

Any scholar will tell you that having a support network outside of academia is important to living a well-rounded existence. For me and my family that could not be truer. Justin and Laura Sharp have provided laughs, friendship, and good food for longer than we probably want to remember. Andy and Christie Moore were our southern comfort during long New England winters. We've walked through many joys and trials with our friends at Broadmoor, NTCF, and NJF. Thank you for letting us help you as you have helped us.

I appreciate the support of my friends and colleagues at Southern New Hampshire University and Cumberland University, specifically Paul Barresi, Annabel Beerel, Bob Begiebing, Rick Bell, Allison Cummings, Laurie Dishman, Eleanor Dunfey-Freiburger, Karen Erickson, Kathy Growney, Fred Heifner, Jackie Hickox, the late Terry Holcomb, Nicholas Hunt-Bull, Natalie Inman, Diane Les Becquets, Andrew Martino, Bill McKee, Pete Peterson, Diana Polley, Monty Pope, Curtis Smith, Katie Smith, Susan Youngs, and Debbie Wilcox. President Harvill Eaton has been an unwavering supporter of the study of history in general and my scholarship in particular, as has Ed Thackston, Chair of the Board of Trustees. The following librarians at Vise Library were a cheerful bunch who never complained (at least not to me) about my many book orders and interlibrary loan requests: Rick Brown, Eloise Hitchcock, Clare Nathan, Jenny Stout, Ashli Thomas, Claire Walker, and Amber Woodard. Trey Woodard was a dutiful work-study assistant, while Emme Taylor patiently tended to my many requests for photocopying, transcription, and numerous other responsibilities. I hope that my love of history is obvious to my students, who indulge my numerous Jackson references ("And the connection to Andrew Jackson is . . ."). Tellingly, none of them have gone on to study Jackson in graduate school.

A number of friends and scholars deserve thanks for sharing their thoughts on, and criticisms of, this project in its various forms, including conference presentations: Nicholas Cox, Daniel Dupre, Lorri Glover, Catherine Kelley, Cynthia Kierner, Andy Moore, Lydia Plath, Kathryn Tomasek, and Tim Williams. Others, including Don Cole, Emma Lapsansky-Werner, and Ann Toplovich, wrote letters of support for various grant applications, for which I am grateful. I especially want to thank the members of the League of Literary Gentlemen–Tom Hilpert, Michael Kosser, and Rob Shearer–for their gentle prodding to write more accessible prose. They may not have succeeded in their efforts, but they gave it a good go. Three friends read the manuscript in its entirety: Marsha Mullin, an invaluable and underutilized resource for anyone who studies Jackson's life and one who knows far more about Jackson's life than she probably cares to admit; John Belohlavek, who is one of the kindest scholars I have ever met; and John Marszalek, my mentor and role model.

In addition to those already listed, many others have assisted me, sometimes unknowingly, with this project and the professional life of a historian. I tried to leave Dan Feller alone so that he could finish more volumes of the Jackson papers. He was a gracious mentor during my early career and remains a source of valuable advice. Connie Lester is still an important sounding board for career decisions. Jim Broussard and Gene Smith inducted me into the longest-running poker game in the profession; glad I could help fund your trips to Society for Historians of the Early American Republic meetings. During his visit to our campus as a conference keynote speaker, Mark Smith gave me valuable advice on publicizing history at a small liberal arts university. Kevin Levin, Sarah Pierce, and Heather Whitney inspired me to embrace social media for professional purposes. I am especially thankful to Darrell Dow for providing technical and creative assistance with my blog, jacksonianamerica.com.

Archivists and librarians at the following repositories were immensely helpful: the Filson Historical Society, the Library of Congress, and the

Tennessee State Library and Archives. I especially appreciate the assistance of Jim Holmberg at the Filson and Jeff Flannery at the Library of Congress. This book was generously funded with research support from Southern New Hampshire University, Cumberland University, the White House Historical Association, and the Filson Historical Society, which graciously gave me permission to quote from its collections.

Finally, Rand Dotson, Andrew Burstein, and the staff at LSU Press have made the publishing process much easier than I ever imagined. Rand has been a steady supporter, which I very much appreciate. Andy's optimistic critique of this project was helpful in focusing my arguments. My thanks to Elizabeth Gratch for her dutiful and thorough copyediting. Along those lines, to retain the sense of nineteenth-century written communication, I chose not to correct errors or use [sic] unless necessary for the reader's clarity.

ANDREW JACKSON, SOUTHERNER

Introduction

The 1828 presidential election was one of the nastiest in United States political history. Andrew Jackson's campaign accused the incumbent, John Quincy Adams, of being a pimp and spending the people's money to fund gambling in the White House. Adams was many things—stiff, dour, pious, the son of a president, an accomplished diplomat—but a betting whoremonger he was not.

The Adams campaign fought back by charging Jackson with numerous criminal acts: He had fought illegal duels that resulted in the death of a prominent man and ignored the pleas of several of his soldiers when they faced execution for desertion. Foreigners had also suffered from his wrath, as Jackson and his army had waged a war of extermination against the southeastern Indians and their British allies in the 1810s. Jackson's private life was not exempt during the 1828 campaign either. He stole another man's wife, critics claimed, and brazenly lived with her before she was divorced. He was a "trafficer in human flesh," buying and selling slaves and turning a blind eye when his overseer stabbed to death one of the slaves at Jackson's Hermitage plantation. The Adams men warned that voters would regret making a president of this murdering, home-wrecking, slave-trading, southern dictator.

Political protocol dictated that Jackson could not directly counter these attacks, but he did not sit by idly as they came his way. Jackson organized his political network to justify his actions as honorable, and its members offered an aggressive defense. He had fought duels to protect his and his wife's reputations. He had allowed the execution of his soldiers because to do otherwise invited mutiny and the destruction of his army. He had prosecuted the war against Native Americans and their allies because the United States needed the southeastern lands to secure its borders. Even his marriage to Rachel was honorable. Jackson had saved her from an abusive husband, and they had believed, wrongly it turned out, that her divorce was final before they married.

1

Other accusations, such as the slave-trading charge, were dismissed simply as deliberate attempts to manipulate the truth for political benefit.

In many ways the political arguments used by both presidential campaigns in 1828 centered on Jackson's southern identity. From the first scholarly treatment of Jackson by James Parton in the early 1860s, however, historians of the Jacksonian period and biographers of Old Hickory himself have consistently portrayed the seventh president as a frontier westerner. Frederick Jackson Turner's assessment of Jackson as "the very personification" of the American frontier, the "embodiment of the tenacious, vehement, personal West," summarized this interpretation. "He was born in the backwoods of the Carolinas . . . and he grew up in the frontier State of Tennessee," Turner argued.[1]

Turner was wrong. While the Waxhaws region into which Jackson was born was considered the backcountry, it was closely tied to the lowcountry region of Charleston, not the trans-Appalachian West. The American Revolution unified backcountry and lowcountry South Carolinians even more, creating a distinct American identity even as the war tore apart many families, including Jackson's. Turner was also mistaken in his claim that Jackson "grew up" on the Tennessee frontier. There is no question that Jackson faced the frontier and its many challenges, but the core of his identity had already been formed by the time the twenty-one-year-old lawyer arrived in Nashville in October 1788.

Historical scholarship has either ignored or minimized the reality that Jackson possessed all of the characteristics attributed to his western identity—his independence, violent temper, and hatred of Indians—before he arrived on the Tennessee frontier. Biographer John Spencer Bassett remarked that Jackson's "ideals were absorbed from the frontier environment . . . He voiced the best thought of the frontier . . . His Western ideals were for him the only ideals." Frederick A. Ogg called him "the untrained, self-willed, passionate frontier soldier." Historian Thomas P. Abernethy concluded that gambling, not a desire to emulate the elite society that he had witnessed in the Carolinas, led Jackson to "play the part" of a gentleman upon his arrival in East Tennessee. John William Ward's analysis of Jackson's symbolic significance centered on his western identity, while

Arthur Schlesinger Jr. failed to address his background at all. Richard B. Latner, whose study of Jackson's presidency explicitly linked Old Hickory to the West, acknowledged that "one would be hard-pressed . . . to fit slaveholding, tough-minded politicians like Jackson . . . into Turner's conception of western democratic idealism," yet he failed to elucidate from where Old Hickory's views on slavery originated and how they influenced his political decisions.[2]

More recent scholarship has also failed to explain how Jackson assumed the characteristics of the southern gentry. Lorman Ratner's compendium of short biographical sketches of Jackson and his closest allies offered a promising argument that the Tennessean emulated a Scottish thane, or clan leader, as he entered the gentry, but his analysis was brief and superficial. Along similar lines Andrew Burstein's study of Jackson's passions also centered on his relationship with the men with whom he surrounded himself, but his analysis was informed by literary theory and did not concern itself with southern cultural practices such as kinship and slaveholding. Likewise, Jon Meacham's Pulitzer Prize–winning biography of Jackson as president failed to place Old Hickory's outsized character in a social context that made him understandable. The two most recent surveys of the Jacksonian period fell into the same pattern of skimming over Jackson's transformation into a southern planter. Sean Wilentz's mammoth survey of American democracy in the early republic paid scant attention to Jackson's slaveholding and land speculation, both of which marked his entry into the planter class. While recognizing the importance of slavery to Jacksonian Democrats, Daniel Walker Howe's equally behemoth examination of the Jacksonian period treated Jackson's southern identity with similar brevity.[3]

There have been notable exceptions to the above trend. Robert Remini's three-volume biography discussed extensively Jackson's various business dealings, including land speculation and slaveholding, but that information was secondary to the frontier's influence on Old Hickory. William J. Cooper Jr. clearly elucidated Jackson's importance to southern politics, while Bertram Wyatt-Brown brilliantly explained his embodiment of southern honor. More recently, Bettina Drew's unpublished dissertation examined "Master Andrew Jackson" and the influence of his southern identity on his removal of the southeastern Indians, Matthew Warshauer offered an overview of Jackson as a chivalric slave owner, and Hendrik

Booraem's study of Jackson's early life made a convincing case that he had been exposed to, and influenced by, the southern gentry in the Carolinas.[4]

Although most scholars describe Old Hickory as a westerner, as representative of the trans-Appalachian frontier, Jackson was truly a southerner. He was born and raised in the Waxhaws region of the most southern of states, South Carolina, where he learned that the path to success included building an influential social network, choosing a career in law, and acquiring land and slave property. In Tennessee, Jackson worked toward becoming a southern planter and gentleman, although his enemies would have disputed the latter. His desire to live as part of the gentry was ever present, even as he defeated the British at New Orleans in 1815, ascended to the presidency in 1828, and built the Democratic party in the 1830s and 1840s. Jackson's propensity toward violence, defense of honor, enslavement of African Americans, embrace of kinship, and pursuit of Manifest Destiny created a southern identity to which many contemporary white southerners, elite and nonelite, could relate.

One of the greatest ironies of Jackson's life was that his identification with the South laid the foundation for the Civil War. Even though the idea of Indian removal preceded him, his actions as general and president accelerated the process, opening up southeastern lands to white settlers intent on making money from cotton. Jackson opposed disunion in 1832 and 1833, yet his longtime pursuit and support of Manifest Destiny helped drive a wedge between northerners and southerners and exacerbated the slavery debate. He supported the annexation of Texas, which, when accomplished, set off a chain of events that made slavery the crucial issue in the congressional debates over westward expansion and led to the nation's division.

Although Jackson died without witnessing the bloody conflict that began in 1861, his influence as the "patriot slaveholder" was obvious during the secession crisis of 1860–1861. Both northerners and southerners appealed to his example to make the case for and against secession. Abraham Lincoln's first inaugural address drew on Jackson's 1832 Nullification Proclamation, which denied South Carolina's right to nullify federal law and dismember the Union, to argue that "the central idea of secession is the essence of anarchy." In the end Old Hickory not only helped create the South that precipitated the nation's greatest crisis, but he also provided the model for Lincoln's opposition to the Confederacy's formation.[5]

I

"His Very Soul Was Grieved"

Like many settlers who came to the southern British colonies in the mid-eighteenth century, Andrew Jackson's family were Ulster Scots, Scottish immigrants who moved into northern Ireland in the late seventeenth and early eighteenth centuries because of the internal political and religious strife in England. Jackson's immediate ancestors lived in the Irish county of Antrim, in or near the town of Carrickfergus. Not much is known about the family of his father, whose name was also Andrew Jackson, except that Hugh Jackson, the future president's paternal grandfather, was supposedly "a company officer at the siege of Carrickfergus" in 1760. The family of his mother, Elizabeth Hutchinson, likely was involved in the linen trade. Linen weaving was an important segment of the economy of eighteenth-century northern Ireland, where many people also focused on farming to supplement their household income. The growth of the Irish linen industry led to more competition for land, which in turn increased rents. When the linen industry faltered for even a short period of time, there was a risk of losing one's land or living in poverty. With this increasing economic instability, many Ulster Scots chose to take their chances in the British colonies of North America.[1]

The Jacksons were one of the Ulster Scots families to seize this opportunity. When Andrew and Elizabeth Jackson, with their two sons, Hugh and Robert, made the voyage in the mid-1760s, they were undoubtedly looking to improve their economic opportunities. According to an early Jackson biographer, their "condition in life though not opulent or exalted, was a[mple] and independent." Having the assurance of a kinship network awaiting them made the trip across the Atlantic easier. Between 1763 and 1766 four of Elizabeth's sisters and their families took up residence along the North Carolina–South Carolina border. The presence of family promised that the adjustment to a new environment would be less challenging, and it reduced the risk of poverty and loneliness.[2]

The Jacksons' experience was not unique. Between 1717 and 1776 approximately 250,000 Ulster Scots emigrated to the American colonies in two large waves of immigration that occurred in 1754–1755 and 1771–1775. Many eventually settled in the Carolinas due to financial inducements. In the 1760s the colony of South Carolina offered land bounties to attract white settlers, ostensibly to help fight Native Americans for control of the frontier. Heads of households were promised one hundred acres of land and an additional fifty acres for every member of their family. Additionally, they would not have to pay taxes for a decade. Using the revenue from taxes placed on the importation of slaves, South Carolina also promised to pay for immigrants' voyage across the Atlantic and to give them forty shillings upon arrival in the state. This money the newcomers could then use to buy tools and other supplies needed to establish their households on the land grants.[3]

The Waxhaws region, where the Jacksons settled, was located between the confluence of the Broad and Catawba Rivers on the west and Twelve Mile Creek on the east. In the early eighteenth century the area had been inhabited by the Waxhaw, probably part of the Cofitachiqui people who had settled the Piedmont region prior to 1400 C.E. In 1716 the Waxhaw were vanquished by the Catawba, a conglomeration of several Native American communities located on the Catawba River northwest of Charleston. By the mid-1700s the Catawba were surrounded by American settlers moving into the region. Within a thirty-mile radius of the Catawba nation, which probably numbered around fifteen hundred members, nearly five hundred white families had settled. In defining the boundaries of property, land surveyors imposed a previously unknown geographic order to the Catawba's land. Farmers also constructed homes and other buildings to support their cultivation of the land. In doing so, white settlers created new communities in what they considered to be a frontier wilderness but what the Catawba regarded as their homeland. Linking these interior communities were roads to the coast, particularly to Charleston, and to the North. By 1767, the year of Jackson's birth, Reverend Charles Woodmason wrote that the Waxhaws, which was on the outer fringe of these settlements, was "most surprisingly thick settled beyond any Spot in England of its Extent."[4]

Unsurprisingly, the Catawba and the American settlers frequently clashed. The Catawba resented the changes being made to their environment, their land, and their culture. The free roaming of white settlers' cattle was a particular irritant, as was the settlers' damming of waterways. Without nearby governmental oversight Catawba protests over disputes that arose between the two groups were often dismissed. In fact, however, Catawba chiefs appeared to have just as little control over some members of their clans as did white leaders. Catawba trespassed on property marked off by white settlers, killed their unfenced livestock for food, and rode off with their horses, all without any obvious rebuke from their own leaders. The pervasive use of alcohol in both societies made the most innocuous quarrels potentially explosive.[5]

In 1759 open conflict between the Catawba and their white neighbors erupted. In the Waxhaws groups of Catawba conducted raids. They stole and killed horses and livestock, robbed homes, and murdered a widow. "If there be no means used to put a stop to such proceedings," angry settlers wrote South Carolina governor William Henry Lyttelton, "we will be obliged to Com[e] to blows." An epidemic of smallpox among the Catawba later that year ensured that the threatened "blows" never came. The Catawba population declined to only around five hundred individuals, and the survivors abandoned most of their towns to avoid further decimation. The following year the remaining Catawba agreed to cede a large portion of their land for a reservation to be located on Twelve Mile Creek, a tributary of the Catawba River. While the tension between the Catawba and the American settlers had not disappeared by the time of Andrew Jackson's birth, the relationship had largely stabilized.[6]

Into this environment the Jackson family arrived in America. The senior Andrew Jackson acquired two hundred acres on Twelve Mile Creek. The land was in an area along the colonies' borders that had not been clearly surveyed; it probably lay within North Carolina, several miles from claims settled by the families of the other Hutchinson sisters. Jackson may actually have squatted on the land. Elizabeth and her brother-in-law, James Crawford, paid neighbor Thomas Ewing for the deed to the land after her husband's death, suggesting that the acreage was not legally theirs. Whatever his claim to the real estate, which was larger than the average farm in the region, Jackson worked to carve out a place for his family. He built a cabin, cultivated the land, and maintained ties to family and friends by attending services at the Waxhaw Presbyterian Church. His efforts were short-lived, however. He died around the time a third son, his namesake, was born on 15 March 1767.[7]

According to his own account, the younger Andrew Jackson was born in South Carolina at the home of James and Jane Crawford, his uncle and aunt, his mother having moved there in anticipation of the impending arrival of a child. Now a widow, Elizabeth remained to tend to her invalid sister's household, including the eight Crawford children, in addition to her own three boys. Thus, Jackson grew up in a blended family. James Crawford served as a father figure to Jackson and his brothers. Crawford's brother, Robert, was also a strong male role model for the young boys. By 1774 he had bought and sold over sixteen hundred acres of land, making a great deal of money in the process. He also served in the British army and used the new circuit courts in the South Carolina backcountry to assert his social position in the community.[8]

Robert Crawford also owned slaves. While slaves likely only constituted 10 percent of the total backcountry population, they were present and spoke to the reality that while the South Carolina lowcountry and backcountry were divided by geography, culture, and religion, by the time Jackson was born, the Waxhaws were part of a trading community tied to Charleston. In nearby Pine Tree Hill, soon to be called Camden, Joseph Kershaw, a merchant with ties to Charleston and Philadelphia elite, established a store that "served as a magnet for millers and other craft specialists, as well as merchants, wagoners, and those involved in trade." The Catawba Path that ended in the Waxhaws passed through Camden on its way to Charleston, linking it to the transatlantic economy, where slaves and other goods were imported from Africa, the Caribbean, and Europe. Jackson's world, in other words, faced toward the Atlantic seacoast, not the interior.[9]

While the Crawford men were important male influences, Jackson's mother, Elizabeth, was an even more significant figure during his childhood. She was a woman highly regarded for her "virtue and piety," characteristics she tried to pass on to her sons. Surprisingly, Elizabeth appeared infrequently in Jackson's correspondence, but she was always a strong presence. Publications later authorized by Jackson for his political career referred to Elizabeth to craft his public image of love of country and sympathy for the common person. According to Jackson's earliest authorized biographers, for example, she "instilled into the minds of her sons lessons of early patriotism." "Often would she spend the winter's night," another authorized biographer wrote, "in recounting to them the sufferings of their grandfather, at the siege of Carrickfergus, and the oppressions exercised by the nobility of Ireland, over the laboring poor; impressing it upon them, as their first duty, to expend their lives, if it should become necessary, in defending and supporting the natural rights of man." At the age of seventy-one Jackson recalled a piece of advice that his mother had given him: "'indict no man for assault and battery or sue him for slander.'"[10]

Elizabeth may also have influenced her son in another important way. According to the recollections of Susan Alexander, a North Carolina resident who was probably a relative of the Jacksons, Elizabeth and her youngest son were "inveterate haters of the Indians on account of their barbarities." Jackson was, in her estimation, "a preserver . . . upon the frontier against the Indians; and his very soul was grieved when he could not get men to help him. Oh! we all suffered by those horrid Indians." In fact, by the time Andrew Jackson was born, the threat of widespread conflict between Native Americans and white settlers had dissipated. There was still isolated violence between the groups, however, and any child growing up in the South Carolina backcountry would have been aware of the potential danger that his or her family and community faced.[11]

Jackson also absorbed the community norms of Waxhaws society. Ulster Scots emphasized "individualism and a desire for a better life." Those who came to the American colonies helped to break down social standing accorded by family lineage. Instead, they recognized social status based on individual achievement; "one's own strength of will, self-control, inward determination, [sic] were now the primary factors determining status in a community." Consequently, community leaders—church elders, justices of the peace, and militia officers—emerged because of personal characteristics of strength, determination, and courage. The Crawford men were recognized for these virtues, as was Jackson's father, who was an elder in the Waxhaw Presbyterian Church. For the young Jackson these social expectations proved important as he entered adolescence.[12]

The Ulster Scots also valued education. For some it was an opportunity to prepare their young men for the ministry and give the ordinary layperson the ability to read the Bible. Ministers were usually in charge of formal education; informal education in the home centered on the Bible and the catechisms. Jackson's mother supposedly intended him to become a minister, so when her son was around age ten, she sent him to the local school, Waxhaw Academy. Jackson, along with his cousin William Crawford and neighbors William Smith and James White Stephenson, studied Greek, Latin, reading, and mathematics. After three years of attendance, Jackson may have studied at Queens College in Charlotte, North Carolina, for a short time. Established in 1771, the college was "the first institution of higher learning south of Virginia." It and similar schools incorporated "Latin, Greek, Hebrew, Philosophy and Theology in their course of instruction," building on the basic learning that the Waxhaw Academy provided.[13]

The Revolutionary War interrupted Jackson's schooling, but it gave him a different kind of education. His childhood had already witnessed significant disruption, but life in the Waxhaws became increasingly more difficult as the focus of the war shifted to the southern theater in the late 1770s. In May 1780 Charleston fell to British forces, and the king's army moved into the South Carolina upcountry, including the Waxhaws. Fear and chaos consumed the residents there; they had to be prepared to flee at a moment's notice.[14]

The Jacksons and Crawfords supported the Patriots in the fight against the British. The Crawfords, one of the more prominent families in the Waxhaws, were unusual among their neighbors in offering their early assistance. Robert Crawford joined the Revolution in 1776 and rose to the rank of major; many of the other men in the area waited to join until after the British launched their southern campaign in 1779. Poor and geographically isolated on the edges of the Waxhaws, the Jacksons, through the Crawfords, "were integrated into, even nurtured by, the established families in the core community." These kinship ties to the Patriot cause led Hugh, the eldest Jackson son, to sign up for service when he was only sixteen.[15]

Jackson's role in the war was minimal, but the Revolution still influenced him in several ways. First, Jackson had the opportunity to observe the training and mobilization of the militia. At his first battle, Hanging Rock, Jackson's duties were inconsequential and did not include engaging the enemy. He studied Colonel William Richardson Davie's approach to war and his treatment of subordinates, which served as models for his own future military career. Second, like many of their neighbors, Jackson and his family suffered loss. Hugh died following the Battle of Stono Ferry in June 1779. That Hugh had been "overcome by heat & fatigue at the battle" and not killed by a British bullet did not lessen his death's effect on Jackson. In March 1781 Jackson's uncle, James Crawford, was wounded during a Tory attack on Captain John Land's cabin; he died later that summer.[16]

Following Hugh's death, Jackson and his brother Robert continued to help the Patriots resist King George's forces. During a British attack on the Waxhaw meetinghouse in early April 1781, the two brothers hid themselves in a relative's cabin. A Tory neighbor discovered their presence and alerted the British dragoons. The soldiers ransacked the cabin, and one of the officers ordered Jackson to clean his boots. He refused, leading the officer to attempt to strike him with his sword. Jackson deflected the blow, but as he recalled decades later, "the sword-point reached my head and has left a mark there as durable as the scull, as well as on the fingers." Robert was similarly assaulted. Then the two boys, along with a number of other Patriots, were marched forty miles to Camden, where they were imprisoned for over two weeks. Conditions were deplorable. By the time the two brothers were released via a prisoner exchange, Robert had contracted smallpox and was also suffering an infection from the head wound he had received during their capture. He died shortly thereafter, while Jackson, who by that time had contracted smallpox himself, suffered its lingering effects for several months after returning to the Waxhaws.[17]

While Jackson was recovering, his mother left for Charleston to help tend to prisoners of war being held there by the British; two of her nephews were of particular concern. While on board a prison ship tending to her nephews and others, Elizabeth contracted ship fever, or typhus, and died in June 1781. She was buried in the city, although Jackson was never able to locate her grave. The American Revolution thus cost Jackson the remaining members of his immediate family and left him scarred physically and emotionally.[18]

At an early age, then, life in the Waxhaws had significantly formed Andrew Jackson's character and personality. Historian Peter Moore has argued that Jackson was the "antithesis" of the Waxhaws, a deeply religious, agricultural community held together by familial kinship. As a young man, Jackson disliked farming, lived a worldly, not religious, life, and, after his mother's death, had no immediate family in the community. Yet while Jackson never became a yeoman farmer, he valued land and the independence that it provided; the success of his "farms," or plantations, consumed much of his free time throughout his public career. Because of internal dissension, the Waxhaw Presbyterian Church lacked a pastor for much of Jackson's childhood, which undoubtedly weakened religion's pull on his life. When his future wife, Rachel, became extremely pious during their marriage, however, Jackson built her a church and often peppered his letters to her and others with biblical references. He even joined the church after his presidency. Orphaned and alone, Jackson replaced the family he had lost with a kinship network composed of his wife's extended family and his political allies. He valued these political and familial kin because they gave his world economic and emotional stability. Despite his seeming rejection of the place of his birth and childhood, the Waxhaws inextricably shaped Jackson's life.[19]

II

"A Person of Unblemished Moral Character"

The next few years saw Jackson struggling to create a new identity for himself. By age fourteen he had lost his father, mother, and two brothers. He was an angry young man. Jackson discovered the kinship ties that had brought his family to the Waxhaws and given it stability loosening. Finding a suitable replacement for his immediate family became a necessity if he wanted to overcome his orphanhood. Choosing a career also proved crucial as Jackson made a successful transition from the Waxhaws to Middle Tennessee.

After his mother's death, Jackson remained at the home of Major Robert Crawford, where his uncle ran a "public station," or commissary, to supply the local Patriot army. He soon quarreled with Captain John Galbraith, whom Crawford had placed in charge of the commissary. Galbraith, who was "of a very proud and haughty disposition," according to Jackson, "threatened to chastise" him for some unknown reason. Jackson told the older man that he was old enough "to know my rights" and that if he tried to discipline him, then the teenager "would most assuredly Send him to the other world." Scholar Henrik Booraem has noted that Jackson's response was out of proportion to the perceived slight and unwarranted given Galbraith's Quaker disposition. His analysis suggests strongly that Jackson's health and grief were taking a toll on the young man. Not surprisingly, Crawford sent his nephew to live at the home of another relative, Joseph White, a saddler.[1]

Jackson lived as an apprentice with White and his family for a few months in 1782. This period stimulated Jackson's lifelong love of horses. He not only learned how to make saddles, but he also came into contact with men who knew a horse's importance, both as a practical tool and as a status symbol. Residents of the Waxhaws possessed "a love of fine horses as well as a respect for those who owned them." Horse owners in the region engaged in quarter racing, a form of entertainment that often elicited gambling. For members of the southern gentry a horse showed a man's independence as well as provided a way for him to demonstrate prowess in "competitive encounters" that allowed him to "legitimately claim gentility." Jackson absorbed what he learned about using horses for both practical and symbolic purposes and put this knowledge to good use in the future.[2]

While Jackson was living with the Whites, Robert Crawford and Galbraith parted ways over a financial dispute, leading Jackson to move back in with his uncle. Over the next eighteen months Jackson made at least one, and possibly two, trips to Charleston. The first journey may have been to accompany Major Crawford as he made claims to the government for its use of his property during the war. The second seems to have been a solitary one. Jackson had recently received a small inheritance from an unknown relative, part of which he used to purchase a horse worth at least two hundred pounds. In Charleston he spent the rest of his inheritance in pursuit of entertainment, leaving himself nearly destitute. He took up gambling, a sport to which he increasingly turned to distract himself from his personal losses. A throw of the dice in a game called rattle and snap netted him two hundred dollars and saved his horse from having a new owner.[3]

Jackson's time in Charleston also provided him with a different perspective on African Americans. The Waxhaws contained a slave population that constituted roughly 10 to 12 percent of the community's total population. Slaves in the Waxhaws were property, bought for economic purposes, but backcountry ministers encouraged their integration into whites' religious communities. In Charleston, Jackson encountered a different racial environment. In 1790 the city's population numbered 8,089 whites, 7,684 slaves, and 568 free blacks. (The South Carolina lowcountry, which included the state's coastal districts and the city of Charleston, had a population of 28,644 whites and 78,000 slaves.) A resident of Charleston had occasion to witness slaves brought off of slave ships from Africa and the Caribbean and auctioned in public, as well as to hear Charlestonians arguing for the protection of slavery. Coupled with his experience with prominent men in the Waxhaws, such as Major Crawford, owning slaves, Jackson's exposure to slavery in Charleston reinforced the importance of owning human chattel. Ownership of a slave indicated economic prosperity and provided an important status symbol for a young man on the make.[4]

In December 1784 Jackson left the South Carolina backcountry for good to study law in North Carolina. His first attempt to pursue legal study was unsuccessful. Waightstill Avery, a Princeton graduate and former state attorney general who lived in Morganton, North Carolina, declined to take him on as a student. Jackson then moved, with his cousin William Crawford, to nearby Martinville, where he studied with local lawyer Charles Bruce. Bruce was a large landowner and a former member of the state legislature. He spent more time on the lucrative business of land surveying, however, than he did in practicing law. Bruce may have seen Jackson as a protégé, the two men sharing a love of horseracing and approval of the recently concluded Revolution. By 1786 Jackson had moved to Salisbury, North Carolina, to study law with Spruce Macay, another local lawyer who later became a noted judge. Macay was socially well connected. His wife, Frances, was the daughter of Judge Richard Henderson, who founded the Transylvania Company that had funded Daniel Boone's exploration and settlement of Kentucky; Macay's brother-in-law was Archibald Henderson, later a U.S. representative from North Carolina. Jackson was no doubt expected to copy legal documents in order to learn the language and form that lawyers used to present their arguments to the court. Jackson's mentors would also have made the aspiring attorney read law books, which provided him with a foundation and guide for making legal arguments.[5]

While studying law with Macay, Jackson roomed with William Crawford and John McNairy. Five years Jackson's senior, McNairy also read law under Macay and had opened his own practice in 1784. Jackson's social circle included the aforementioned Charles Bruce and also Tom Henderson and Tom Searcy. Henderson was the younger brother of Judge Henderson and the clerk of the court in Guilford County. Tom was a wealthy man in his own right, owning half the real estate in Martinville. Searcy was Tom Henderson's nephew as well as his partner in a store that they co-owned. While not a member of Jackson's social circle, one other individual was part of his extended network. Alexander Martin had served a term as North Carolina's governor and had been a senator in its legislature on two separate occasions. His brother-in-law was Tom Henderson, and his private secretary was Pleasant Henderson, Tom and Richard's younger brother. Martin was a wealthy land speculator and slave owner for whom Martinville had been named. All of these men were important in helping Jackson make the transition from a poor, backcountry youth into an accepted member of upper-class society, and their connections provided him with the model for his own kinship network.[6]

In early 1787 Jackson moved to Montgomery County, North Carolina, to complete his legal study under the supervision of Colonel John Stokes. When the lawyer believed that his student was prepared, Jackson appeared before two North Carolina justices, Samuel Ashe and John F. Williams, to be examined for entrance to the bar. Ashe and Williams granted him his law license, acknowledging that he was "sufficiently recommended to us as a person of unblemished moral character" and that he "[appeared] to possess a competent degree of knowledge in the Law." For the rest of the year and throughout most of 1788, Jackson sought opportunities to practice but found very few.[7]

When not studying or practicing law during these years, Jackson lived a life of revelry. Residents in Salisbury later recalled that he "played cards, fought cocks, ran horses, threw the 'long bullet' (cannon ball, slung in a strap and thrown as a trial of strength), carried off gates, moved outhouses to remote fields, and occasionally engaged in a downright drunken debauch." He ran a footrace against a friendly rival, Hugh Montgomery, who was given a substantial head start but had the handicap of carrying another young man on his back; Jackson won the race. He also infamously invited Molly and Rachel Wood, a mother and daughter "of ill repute," to a local ball, which caused a predictable uproar. Legal trouble found Jackson as well. In August 1787 he and two friends—William Cupples and Montgomery—had a warrant issued for their arrests. The exact charge was described as "trespass," which was defined as the loss of property. With the help of two other friends, Daniel Clary and Henry Giles, the three men posted a recognizance bond that guaranteed their appearance before the court in Rowan County. No further records exist, suggesting that the case was settled out of court or dismissed.[8]

With his prospects for practicing law in North Carolina looking dim, Jackson found relief from a member of his social network. In December 1787 the North Carolina legislature elected John McNairy superior court judge of the state's Western District, renamed the Mero District in 1788. This district extended to the Mississippi River, encompassing present-day Middle Tennessee. At the time Davidson and Sumner Counties constituted its political divisions. Alexander Martin's role as speaker of the North Carolina senate influenced McNairy's appointment. The legislature did not explicitly authorize the appointment of a prosecuting attorney, but McNairy chose one anyway: Jackson. The two men left in April 1788, joined on the journey westward across the Appalachian Mountains by several others, including Tom Searcy's brother, Bennett, and David Allison, another North Carolina lawyer, who had been in business with the prominent North Carolina Blount family since at least the early 1780s.[9]

In May 1788 Jackson and his fellow lawyers arrived in Jonesborough (or Jonesboro), in present-day East Tennessee. At the time Jonesborough had fifty to sixty family residences and a new courthouse. Its citizens had been part of an attempted secession movement in 1784–1785 to create a new state, named Franklin, after the North Carolina government failed to heed requests for protection from Native Americans as well as other grievances. By 1788 the Franklin movement had lost momentum, and its governor, John Sevier, left office before an elected replacement had been established. Realizing that making the journey to Nashville in time for the upcoming court session was impossible, the party took up residence in town for several months. Jackson passed the time by racing horses. He must have made money from the sport, as during this time he also bought from Micajah Crews a slave woman named Nancy. The reason for the purchase, witnessed by David Allison, is unclear. Jackson may have wanted female companionship or someone to cook his meals and wash his clothes, but buying a slave also marked his social advancement. Several of his wealthy North Carolina friends and mentors owned slaves, and this purchase, in conjunction with his budding legal career, identified him as a potential member of their gentry class.[10]

It was not that simple, however. Being a member of the gentry required more than a law license and a slave. In the Ulster Scots tradition the key to entering the gentry was owning enough land to be independent from others. It also "involved following a lifestyle, a code of behavior." On the southern frontier in the early American Republic, membership was not quite as strictly defined, but the general requirements of land, independence, sociability (good manners), honorable conduct, and recognition by the community remained. Jackson needed to look, live, and act like a member of the elite in order to ally with prominent men who could help him gain his desired place in life.[11]

The stay in Jonesborough was not without incident, however. In mid-August Jackson issued a challenge to Waightstill Avery, the attorney under whom he had attempted to study in 1784. The origins of the dispute are unclear, although most accounts mention that the two men were on opposing sides of a legal suit. Jackson's letter of challenge mentioned that Avery had "injured" his character and that he had "insulted me in the presence of a court and a larg audianc." Jackson demanded "satisfaction" from the older lawyer. Within a short time the two men met after sundown to fight a duel. Neither man's shot hit flesh, so they shook hands and parted ways without further animosity.[12]

This episode, shrouded as it is in mystery, once again demonstrates that others were beginning to see Jackson as a member of the southern gentry. Avery was a wealthy, well-regarded attorney in North Carolina. Accepting a challenge from Jackson required him to view the young lawyer as a social equal because only men of similar status dueled. This acknowledgment was important for Jackson's reputation. In the early United States dueling separated the upper class from the lower class, whose members tended to engage in less-sophisticated forms of violence, such as eye gouging and fisticuffs. It also "provided an opportunity for the parties to prove they deserved a reputation as honorable men." In fact, honor and reputation were synonymous. Honor included "the inner conviction of self-worth . . . the claim of self-assessment before the public . . . and the assessment of the claim by the public, a judgment based upon the behavior of the claimant." Much like owning a slave and racing horses, dueling gave a gentleman the opportunity to ensure public recognition of his social standing. For Jackson it also gave him private satisfaction that he was considered worthy enough to take the dueling grounds.[13]

Jackson's party, accompanied by guards to protect them from Native American attack on the two hundred–mile journey to Nashville, left Jonesborough in the early fall of 1788. Jackson was in the company of men—including John McNairy and Bennett Searcy—who had accepted him as one of their own. They were lawyers from the East looking to make a name and a fortune on the southern frontier. On October 26 they arrived in Nashville, a small community that as recently as the previous year had had only about forty residents. Over the next few years Nashville grew in size and importance and served as Jackson's base of political power and economic opportunity.[14]

III

"Gentlemanly Satisfaction"

The Nashville that Jackson first saw in 1788 was a community under constant threat from Native Americans. Middle Tennessee had first been opened to widespread white settlement during the American Revolution. In 1775 Judge Richard Henderson of North Carolina and his associates, via their Transylvania Land Company, purchased approximately twenty million acres from the Cherokee, including most of Kentucky and all of Middle Tennessee. Buying the land was one thing; settling it was another. Between 1775 and 1777 the Cherokee, incited by British officials, fought against white settlers in East Tennessee. This violence, which continued sporadically until the Treaty of Hopewell of 1785 legitimized Henderson's claims in Middle Tennessee, stifled white settlement of the Transylvania purchase. The state of Virginia also thwarted attempts to make the Transylvania landholdings a separate colony. These obstacles induced Henderson to push ahead with the settlement of the Cumberland River area in Middle Tennessee.[1]

In 1779 James Robertson explored the Cumberland region and declared it ready for habitation. Henderson, Robertson, and Colonel John Donelson, a Virginia surveyor, put together two groups from East Tennessee to travel to, and settle on, the Cumberland River. Robertson's group moved overland through present-day Kentucky by way of the Cumberland Gap, reaching French Lick on 25 December 1779. Donelson's contingent, consisting of thirty to forty boats, left Fort Patrick Henry on December 22, hoping that the cold weather would protect them from native attacks. Their plan was to follow the Tennessee River until it met the Ohio River, which would then connect them to the Cumberland River and eventually take them to Nashborough, the original name of the Cumberland settlement until it was changed to Nashville in 1784. The Donelson voyage ended successfully in April 1780.[2]

The Donelsons, therefore, were one of the pioneering, prominent white families in Middle Tennessee. Colonel Donelson initially settled his family at Clover Bottom, just east of Nashville. Native attacks convinced him to relocate to Mansker's Station, a better-protected settlement several miles north. By the end of 1780 Colonel Donelson had moved his family and slaves near Harrodsburg, Kentucky, to better provide for their needs. His death in 1785 compelled his widow, Rachel Stokley Donelson, to move the family back to the Nashville settlement.[3]

Jackson, along with several other young men, took up residence at the widow Donelson's as boarders. His roommate was John Overton, an aspiring lawyer. While living there, the two men witnessed a family crisis that shaped Jackson's personal and political future. The youngest Donelson daughter, Rachel, was living at her mother's house with her husband, Lewis Robards, a member of a prominent Virginia family. Lewis and Rachel had married in Kentucky in 1785; the newlyweds stayed behind when the Donelsons moved back to Nashville. On the surface their marriage appeared to make sense; both came from prominent, wealthy, slaveholding families. It suffered, however, from Lewis's fits of jealousy, which were exacerbated by Rachel's flirtatious nature. After one incident of perceived impropriety in 1788, in which Lewis suspected that Rachel was having an affair with Peyton Short, a boarder living in the home of Robards's widowed mother, Lewis demanded that Rachel return to Nashville. Rachel's brother Samuel traveled to Kentucky and escorted her back to Tennessee. After some negotiating among family members, the Robards agreed to reconcile and moved in together at the widow Donelson's, but their marriage continued to be volatile.[4]

Jackson's presence exacerbated an already deteriorating situation. He and Rachel quickly grew attracted to one another. Rachel was described as "the best story-teller, the best dancer, the sprightliest companion, the most dashing horsewoman in the western country." She was "gay and lively," just the type of woman who would draw the attention of a young, energetic man. Rachel reciprocated Jackson's interest. She may have been attracted to his "reddish-sandy" hair, his six-foot one-inch frame, or his "deep blue" eyes that penetrated those at whom he looked. Almost certainly, his assertiveness and leadership appealed to her.[5]

Looking to protect Rachel, Jackson attempted to speak to Robards about the way he treated his wife. Robards responded by accusing Jackson of having an illicit relationship with Rachel and threatened to "whip" him, a sign in southern society that Robards did not consider his competitor an equal. Jackson declared that he was innocent of any impropriety and refused to fight him but that if Robards insisted on continuing his haranguing, then he would demand "gentlemanly satisfaction," an indication that Jackson considered himself part of Robards's social class. Later Robards mentioned in Jackson's presence that his rival "was too intimate with his wife." Jackson threatened to "cut his ears out of his head." In response Robards swore out a warrant for Jackson's arrest. While the constable, guards, and Robards were accompanying him to jail, Jackson asked to borrow a guard's knife, with the promise that he "would do no harm with it." Jackson gave Robards a knowing look while playing with the knife then began chasing him with it. Robards disappeared, and the charges against Jackson were dismissed. Shortly thereafter, Robards moved back to Kentucky in disgust. He petitioned the Virginia legislature for a divorce in late 1790, receiving its permission to sue for the action that December. The specific accusation given in the legislative act was that Rachel had "deserted" her husband and had "lived in adultery with another man since such desertion." Almost three years later, on 27 September 1793, the legislature granted the divorce on the grounds of desertion and adultery.[6]

In the meantime, in January 1790, Jackson and Rachel traveled with a large party to Bayou Pierre, just north of the Natchez settlement, a prominent trading community located on the lower Mississippi River in Spanish territory. Ostensibly, the trip was made to protect Rachel from Robards's threats to force her return to Kentucky. Staying near her brothers and other male family members was the more logical decision, and Jackson's role as her protector suggests that their relationship was more than platonic. Both Jackson and Rachel had friends living at Bayou Pierre, including Thomas Green, who had previously resided in the Nashville area and served as an American administrator in Natchez. Jackson and Rachel claimed that they were married in Natchez during the summer of 1791. Despite lore that Green married the two lovers at his home, Richland, no documentary evidence for the marriage exists. Nevertheless, the couple presented themselves as married and expressed shock when they discovered that the divorce from Robards had not been completed until late 1793. After first denying the need for a wedding ceremony, Jackson eventually relented to the pressure that his good friend John Overton placed upon him and agreed to "remarry" Rachel. That union, conducted by Rachel's brother-in-law, Robert Hays, took place on 18 January 1794.[7]

The two Jackson marriages and the circumstances surrounding them have plagued historians since James Parton's multivolume biography of Jackson appeared in the mid-nineteenth century. For a long time historians relied on depositions made during the 1828 presidential campaign to support Jackson's claims that he and Rachel were innocent of immorality prior to their first marriage. Supporters contended that the marriage only took place after the couple mistakenly believed that Robards had been granted a divorce. Recent historians have argued convincingly that while the exact chronology may never be known, three things seem clear: Andrew and Rachel were almost certainly having an "emotional affair" before Robards left his wife in 1789; defenders of the Jacksons later manipulated the dates and chronology to protect Jackson's presidential prospects; and by living openly in adultery, the Jacksons provoked Robards into suing for divorce.[8]

What is telling about the disputed Robards-Jackson marital imbroglio is that it revealed not only changing values in the early republic but also the fluid social and legal relations existing on the southern frontier. After the American Revolution state legislatures, reflecting a more egalitarian political and social climate, enacted divorce laws that made marital separation if not easier to obtain, then at least more accessible to both parties. The Virginia legislature, which held jurisdiction over the state's Kentucky County, had only granted one divorce petition since changing its laws in 1786, however, so Robards's success was not guaranteed. One also has to understand that Jackson came from a southern community in which marriage was, at times, informally pursued and sporadically solemnized. Blindingly mad love may have precipitated his actions, but so did the marital examples that he had witnessed growing up in the Waxhaws.[9]

Despite the questionable circumstances surrounding the Jackson marriage and the accompanying trouble that would haunt his public career, Jackson benefited greatly from his marriage into the Donelson clan. It provided him with an extensive kinship network that was politically and economically powerful. In the early American South "family groups rather than public institutions served most of the needs of individual citizens . . .

the family maintained its power at the top of the social, political, and economic hierarchy" of southern society. Kin loaned money, bought and sold property, and connected political aspirants. This kinship network, however helpful, was nevertheless not a guarantee of success. Jackson still had to prove himself.[10]

Jackson made his successful entrée into genteel Nashville society by practicing law. He received appointment as prosecutor for Davidson County, and in February 1791 Governor William Blount officially named him attorney general for the Mero District. The approximately eighty-five cases in which he represented the government involved primarily minor property cases, with only a handful of instances of major crimes, such as murder and rape. Additionally, Jackson had his own private practice, representing clients in approximately four hundred cases. The focus of Jackson's private legal career is not surprising. He represented the vast majority of clients in disagreements over economic transactions, usually involving land. Some of his cases also addressed legal disputes over slave ownership, slave identity, and compensation for the loss of slave labor.[11]

Practicing law furthered Jackson's desire to construct a social network that would benefit his career. As a lawyer, he came into contact with prominent men in the community, either as clients or as supporting or opposing attorneys in the courtroom. Large landowners and prominent politicians, including a future mayor of Nashville and a future sheriff of Davidson County, asked for Jackson's legal expertise; those connections paid off monetarily in coming years. Two fellow lawyers, Howell Tatum and John Overton, partnered with him in land speculation and other business transactions. Along with Tatum and Overton, Jackson's old friend Bennett Searcy and another lawyer, Josiah Love, argued most of the court cases in the county, solidifying their influence on Tennessee's legal system. The lawyers and clients with whom Jackson fraternized were crucial to his advancement in Tennessee.[12]

Jackson also acquired independent wealth in his move up Nashville's social ladder. Land speculation was one important avenue to making money, and Jackson took full advantage of it. Looking around him, he had reason to be confident in that choice. Successful land speculation required influential politicians and frontiersmen who were experts not only at surveying boundaries but also at negotiating with politicians. Many of his family and friends in Tennessee had followed that formula and become successful. After the death of his father in 1785, one of Rachel's brothers, John Donelson III, took over his post as land surveyor in Middle Tennessee. Another brother, Stockley, also served as a surveying commissioner in East Tennessee and partnered with Jackson in several transactions. Daniel Smith, the future father-in-law of a third brother, Samuel, had helped Richard Henderson survey the western boundary between Kentucky and Tennessee in 1779 and 1780. Over the next several years Smith acquired thousands of acres of land as a surveyor for North Carolina in Middle Tennessee. Most significantly, the governor of the old Southwest Territory and Jackson's future patron, William Blount, along with his brother, John, acquired ownership of millions of acres in the Southwest Territory. They were able to do so with the help of the Donelson clan and Nashville co-founder, James Robertson.[13]

Jackson learned well from these examples. Between 1789 and 1803 he was involved in 129 land transactions totaling over 500,000 acres. Jackson and John Overton established a trading post at Chickasaw Bluffs, for example, the site of modern-day Memphis. Over the years Jackson sold off parcels of this land until his one hundred–dollar original investment netted him a profit of over fifty-five hundred dollars. Other sales and purchases involved notable established and up-and-coming members of Nashville and Tennessee society: David Allison, Martin Armstrong, John Donelson, Thomas and Nicholas P. Hardeman, Archibald Roane, James Robertson, Bennett Searcy, and Howell Tatum, to name the most prominent. The land transactions provided Jackson with fluid capital, while these men gave him significant political and economic associations that he used to better his social standing.[14]

Native Americans in the region did not welcome such expansive land grabs, but Jackson's involvement in the wars between Americans and the native inhabitants appears to have been limited. Near the end of his life he recounted that he had once saved a group of whites who were being tracked by Indians. While Jackson no doubt participated, as did other frontier settlers, in the protection of their homes from attacks, other stories about his courage in fighting Native Americans during this period are either apocryphal or exaggerated. That does not mean that Jackson was unaware of the tension between the two groups nor that it did not affect him. In a twenty-two-month period in 1791 and 1792, Native American attacks claimed 97 white casualties in the Mero District; the total population of Middle Tennessee was only 7,042. One white settlement northeast of Nashville, Ziegler's Station, was virtually wiped out in June 1792. That September, a multi-tribal attack on Buchanan's Station, four miles east of Nashville, failed only because of a lack of organization by the Native Americans and fierce resistance by the settlers. Jackson criticized the government's treaties with the Indians, asking, "Why do we attem[pt] to Treat with [a Savage] tribe tha[t] will neither ad[here to] Treaties, nor the law of Nations?" The constant threat to the security of the Nashville settlement undoubtedly reminded Jackson of stories that he had heard from Waxhaws residents during his childhood and reinforced his belief that Native Americans were duplicitous and, in his words, "barbarians."[15]

Jackson also diversified his economic situation with other business ventures. He engaged in extensive trading with merchants and farmers in Natchez, exchanging a wide range of goods: cotton, lime, tobacco, fur, lumber, horses, and slaves, just to name a few. Natchez was an important trading post, and Jackson's connection to it had begun even before his questionable travel there with Rachel in 1790. In the 1780s Americans had taken up residence in Natchez because of its location on the Mississippi River and proximity to New Orleans. By 1788 Spanish Natchez had a population of 2,449, with only a handful of Spanish residents. To induce more American settlement and to promote economic activity, Spain had issued a proclamation that Americans could stand on equal economic footing in Spanish America if they took an oath of allegiance to Spain. Still new to Middle Tennessee, and with few prospects for affluence, Jackson took the oath on 15 July 1789.[16]

In 1795 Jackson opened a store with Rachel's brother Samuel with the intention of using its proximity to the Cumberland River to expand his trading operations. This enterprise failed the same year. Jackson later partnered with two other relatives, John Hutchings and John Coffee, and a friend, Thomas Watson, in attempts to operate mercantile businesses in Clover Bottom, Gallatin, Hunter's Hill, and Lebanon, Tennessee, and Tuscambia, Alabama. Jackson learned an important lesson from these ventures: at that time in Nashville's development, storekeeping was a difficult business enterprise. While the settlement's location on the Cumberland

River was ideal for shipping goods to the Mississippi River, not until the Louisiana Purchase of 1803 was free navigation on the Mississippi guaranteed by the United States. Most store merchandise had to be shipped either by land from the East or by a circuitous land-water route, via the Ohio River, from Pennsylvania. Transportation expenses simply made it too costly to run a store.[17]

Despite these setbacks, Jackson became wealthy. His ownership of a growing number of slaves marked his financial prosperity in the "plantation complex," created by Great Britain and Spain at the end of the Seven Years' War in 1763, that connected the southern frontier to the transatlantic slave economy. Slaves on the southern frontier, including in Tennessee, were essential to the economic success of their owners. In the 1790 census slaves constituted 19 percent of the total population in Davidson County; in 1795, the year before Tennessee gained statehood, the slave population in the county had risen to nearly 28 percent. (Free blacks were almost nonexistent: a total of eighteen in 1790 and only six in 1795.) "Slaves were the property most sought after the land was secured," according to Tennessee historian Anita Goodstein. Most of the seven hundred slaves sold in Nashville between 1784 and 1803 were part of individual transactions; a large number were also children under the age of sixteen.[18]

Between the purchase of his first slave, Nancy, in 1788 and the end of 1803, Jackson was a party to no fewer than twenty transactions involving at least twenty-four slaves. Most were individual sales, and a good number were children. By 1790 Jackson had expanded his slave ownership from one female to at least two females and four males. A few years later a tax enumeration listed seven slaves belonging to Jackson, leading him to hire an overseer in November 1795. Three years later Jackson owned at least fifteen slaves and probably more.[19]

Like other contemporary southerners, Jackson treated slaves as property to be bought and sold, at times receiving a slave in lieu of cash. In 1791, for example, Rachel's brother Stockley offered to repay a loan from Jackson with "one likely Country born Negro boy or girl." Jackson also saw slaves as an avenue for making a profit. That was the case in 1803, when Jackson agreed to sell a "Negro boy," Bird, for his business associate Mark Mitchell. Jackson had stood as security for a five hundred–dollar debt that the latter had accrued. When Mitchell was unable to pay the debt, he contracted Jackson to sell Bird, with hopes that the sale would produce enough money to satisfy his creditor.[20]

The Mitchell transaction also highlights Jackson's involvement in the domestic slave trade. Historians have interpreted James Mountflorence's gratitude for Jackson having accompanied a shipment of "Swann Skins" to Natchez in 1790 as an indication that he had transported slaves for sale on the Mississippi. At least six of the slaves that Jackson bought between 1790 and 1803 were purchased from men listed as being residents of other states; a number of his slave transactions also occurred outside of Tennessee. His correspondence with William C. C. Claiborne and John Hutchings from 1801 and 1802 indicates that he sent slaves to Natchez to be sold as well. Jackson's involvement, however minor, in an interregional slave trade at this point in the frontier economy suggests that the market revolution was well under way in the new republic. It also reinforces historian Steven Deyle's argument that "the failure to account for the local [slave] trade misses the magnitude of the domestic slave trade and what a significant role it played in everyday life—not to mention that, essentially, every owner was a trader in slaves."[21]

Jackson's successful transition from an aspiring lawyer in the Carolinas to a member of the gentry in Middle Tennessee required significant work. Pursuing legal work, speculating in land, buying slaves—all were hallmarks of a man on the make. Most important, he married into the influential Donelson family. Jackson learned well the success of kinship networks from his family and community in the Waxhaws and his friends and allies in North Carolina. This marital union gave him the business and political contacts to support his claim to be part of Nashville's elite and provided him with a core kinship network for his public career.

IV

"As Members of Civilized Society"

Jackson's family connections, his business enterprises, and his contributions to the defense of Nashville were important in helping him cultivate ties to leading politicians. He had begun this process of social networking before moving to Tennessee, but new surroundings required new relationships. The most significant bond that he made in Tennessee was with William Blount. The former North Carolina delegate to the Continental Congress and Constitutional Convention and state legislator was also a land speculator and intriguer, conspiring with other prominent North Carolina leaders to explore uniting the western region of Tennessee with Spain. Blount's objective was to force North Carolina's cession of its western lands to Congress, allowing Tennessee to apply for statehood.[1]

Territorial status for Tennessee came first. In December 1789 North Carolina passed a cession act, which Congress ratified the following April. In May Congress enacted legislation forming the Southwest Territory, which included Tennessee. Blount was appointed territorial governor and, in turn, placed associates in influential positions. Jackson's friends benefited from this patronage. Donelson relative Daniel Smith was the territory's secretary and land surveyor. Archibald Roane, who may have been part of the Jackson party that traveled from North Carolina to Jonesborough in 1788, was attorney general of the Washington District in East Tennessee, and David Allison was Blount's business manager. John McNairy's appointment as superior court judge in the Mero District also brought Jackson to Middle Tennessee as prosecuting attorney.[2]

With Blount exercising unquestioned control of the Southwest Territory, Jackson knew that cultivating a friendship with the governor was indispensable to his ambitions. Upon becoming acquainted with Jackson, Blount immediately recognized him as a man who could help maintain stability on the Tennessee frontier. In February 1791 Blount appointed him attorney general of the Mero District; nineteen months later he made Jackson judge advocate for the Davidson County militia, a commission that was significant to the future success of Jackson's military career. Along with kinship networks the militia was one of the most important social institutions on the frontier. Officers received land grants as part of their first year's pay, which fit Jackson's speculative interests. The near universal requirement of service for Tennessee males was also crucial to linking him more closely to many men who could further his ambitions. Militias created social networks that bound elites to one another and enabled them to exert control over militia members who were eligible to vote. They also produced bonds of camaraderie, as Jackson had witnessed during his time as a courier during the Revolution.[3]

Jackson made other moves to strengthen his gentry membership as well. In 1791 he was elected a trustee of Davidson Academy, Middle Tennessee's first school. This position enabled him to mingle and make connections with the prominent members of the Nashville community, such as Thomas Craighead, the founder and president of the institution. Jackson also joined the Masonic order, although exactly when is unknown. He may have become a Mason before leaving North Carolina, but more likely it was after his move to Nashville. By the late 1790s he was a member of first Masonic lodge in Nashville. William R. Davie, the military commander whom Jackson had admired during the Revolution, was the lodge's grand master. Many of Jackson's closest friends in North Carolina, including Charles Bruce, Tom Henderson, and Bennett and Robert Searcy, and at least two of his earliest Tennessee colleagues, Robert Hays and John Overton, were Masons. The tight-knit Masonic brotherhood appealed not only to Jackson's desire to advance his career but also to his need for familial and fraternal support. It offered stability in "a society that was experiencing greater mobility." Lastly, it marked Jackson as a man of enlightenment as well as a man of republican character. "Post-revolutionary Masons saw their fraternity as profoundly connected to the utopian dreams of the revolution, as a peculiarly republican organization," according to Steven Bullock, the foremost historian of the fraternal organization. "Freemasonry, they argued, would exemplify, teach, and spread these ideals, with Masons serving as priests, teachers, and missionaries of liberty, virtue, and true religion."[4]

The ideals that Freemasons were supposed to "exemplify, teach, and spread" fit neatly within the political ideology termed "classical republicanism," which shaped the character of the early republic as well as of Jackson. Classical republicanism emphasized self-sacrifice, liberty, virtue, and territorial expansion. Americans were expected to be virtuous, which meant sacrificing their personal desires in order to benefit the larger community. For politicians this meant setting aside self-interest to enact the people's will, which was the only way to protect the nation's liberty. Territorial expansion was also key to the nation's future success. As James Madison argued in *Federalist* No. 10, a geographically large republic "[made] it less probable that a majority of the whole will have a common motive to invade the rights of other citizens." Conspiratorial thinking also pervaded classical republicanism. A powerful national government, a permanent army, restrictions on liberty—all were to be feared. Southern adherents to republicanism added a regional twist to the ideology. Politicians such as Thomas Jefferson came to believe that slavery was essential to maintaining the independence and liberty of the white citizenry; therefore, abandoning the institution was anathema to most whites living in the region. In their view the enslavement of African Americans represented freedom for whites.[5]

Jackson received the opportunity to exercise his political ideology in 1796, when he won election as one of the five Davidson County representatives to the state constitutional convention, which was held in Knoxville in the first two months of that year. Governor Blount had been compelled to call the convention in response to Tennesseans' demands that he address the constant conflict with Native Americans. A census revealed that Tennessee had the minimum number of residents (sixty thousand) to apply for statehood; a plebiscite showed that nearly 72 percent of those participating approved of the transition from territory to state. Based on this support, Blount called a constitutional convention and worked to ensure a pro-statehood delegation. Davidson County voters sent Jackson, Thomas Hardeman, Joel Lewis, John McNairy, and James Robertson to Knoxville as their delegates. Jackson and McNairy were selected as Davidson County's representatives to the constitution-drafting committee. Jackson opposed a proposed profession of faith for state officeholders and spoke out against a ban on clergy from holding civil, military, and other positions of trust in the state government. He supported property and resi-

dency requirements for legislators and a residency requirement for free-
men who wanted to vote. His stance on major constitutional issues was in
line with Blount's expectations.[6]

With Blount and fellow East Tennessean William Cocke selected as the
state's two senators, electing someone from Middle Tennessee to act as the
sole representative to the U.S. House made sense. Jackson was the choice,
giving him a post that provided another step up in society. Once Congress
convened in Philadelphia in December 1796, Jackson immediately made
clear his stance on the direction of the national government under George
Washington. A House committee, which included Jackson, was charged
with writing a response to the president's farewell address. Jackson voted
with the minority in refusing to issue Washington a declaration of thanks
for his service as chief executive. He found disconcerting the Virginian's
sympathy with England, which was presently embroiled in a war with
France and impressing American sailors into His Majesty's service. "From
the president['s] speech it would seem that the British were doing us no injury, Committing no Depredations, that all the Depredations on our Commerce was done by the French Nation," he wrote his brother-in-law, Robert Hays. To John Sevier he observed that the French "are now struggling
to obtain for themselves the same B[l]essings (liberty) that we fought and
bled for, we ought to wish them success if we could not aid them." Jackson
believed that a president, even one as esteemed as Washington, who could
not see the difference between French liberty and British despotism did
not deserve his thanks.[7]

In addition to criticizing Washington, Jackson worked to ensure that
Congress compensated Tennesseans for tamping down the threat by Native Americans to frontier settlements. Following attacks on the Cumberland settlements in 1793, John Sevier led seven hundred men in an attack
on Cherokee and Creek towns in northern Georgia. The Washington
administration had not authorized the military expedition, however, and
refused to reimburse Sevier and his men for their expenses. In December 1796 Hugh Lawson White, one of Sevier's men, petitioned the House
for compensation after President Washington rejected the initial request.
When other representatives balked at paying the claim, Jackson wanted
to know how Tennesseans could have responded differently. "When it
was seen that war was waged upon the State, that the knife and the tom-

ahawk were held over the heads of women and children, that peaceable citizens were murdered," he argued, "it was time to make resistance." Robert Rutherford of Virginia agreed with Jackson that the expedition was "a necessary one," but several representatives wanted more information. Finally, Virginia representative James Madison interjected that the expedition seemed constitutional to him; thus, the men should be paid. A select committee, composed of Jackson, Thomas Blount (William's brother) of North Carolina, and three other southerners, was appointed to review the documentation. In February 1797 it produced a report calling for the House to compensate Sevier's men, which it agreed to do. "I have got Seviers Claim passed through the house," Jackson proudly announced to Robert Hays.[8]

This second session of Congress adjourned in March 1797, and Jackson left for home. He had proven to be a representative who would speak his mind, however unpopular his views, and fight for his constituents. Historian Robert Remini argued that Jackson was influenced politically by Nathaniel Macon of North Carolina and Henry Tazewell of Virginia, two Jeffersonian Republicans. Macon was a former Anti-Federalist who feared a strong centralized government and a large standing army, hallmarks of classical republican ideology. He, like Jackson and other Republicans, opposed the passage of Jay's Treaty. This agreement with Great Britain attempted to resolve economic and diplomatic issues lingering since the Revolution, but Republicans denounced it for many reasons, including John Jay's unwillingness to force the issue of reparations for slave owners who had lost slave property during the Revolution. The two men were collegial, with Macon attempting to help Jackson receive compensation for his service as the Mero District's attorney general. Tazewell was president pro tempore of the Senate during Jackson's time in Congress. He also voted against Jay's Treaty and supported Jackson's opposition to taxation to expand the military during the Quasi-War with France.[9]

Most analyses of Jackson's political thought neglect to address his early ideological views, which reflected the classical republican view of American politics. Jackson adhered to a strict interpretation of the Constitution. He opposed direct taxation by the federal government, for example, especially when it would be used to establish a permanent army, one of the obvious measures of a despotic government. His view of the states' role in the federal government emphasized their sovereignty "in forming the federal Constitution." This sovereignty "never ought on any account to be Surrendered to the General Government, or its officers," he wrote John Sevier. President Washington "has Ever Since the Commencement of the present Government, been Grasping after power, and in many instances, Exercised powers, that he was not Constitutionally invested with." If the national government, via the chief executive, ever "overwhelmed" the states' sovereignty, "we may bid adieu to our freedom." The Washington administration also actively rid the national government of officials who differed with Federalist policies. Jackson found the expulsion of men of "republican principles" repulsive and "more dangerous than the establishment of religion." It was an "execrable system" that sought to strengthen the "executive patronage." "It is time that the American mind should be awakened from its Lethargy" and become aware of the danger posed to American liberty. Finally, Jackson denounced the fractious nature of partisan politics in Congress, where, he told John Overton, one could "see all constitutional Principles, violated and mataphorphist [metamorphosed] to Suit Party Purpose." For him naked political partisanship was anathema.[10]

Despite his cynicism about the political environment in Philadelphia, Jackson was undoubtedly pleased with his own service in the House. That pleasure would be tempered over the next few months, however, as political turmoil in Tennessee, accusations of political corruption against his mentor, Senator William Blount, and his personal financial debt all threatened to derail his career.

During the process of Tennessee applying for statehood in 1796, voters had elected John Sevier as governor. To prevent a conflict of interest as the state's commander-in-chief, Sevier stepped down as major general of the Tennessee militia, and an election was held. Jackson was a candidate for the position, but whether because of Jackson's youth or simply out of jealousy, Sevier opposed his bid. Instead, he threw his support to the eventual winner, George Conway. Sevier even went so far as to send letters to friends voicing his opposition to Jackson, calling him "'a poor pitifull petty fogging Lawyer'" whose "'scurrilous Expressions'" were "'treated . . . with Contempt.'" Jackson demanded that the governor explain his actions. Sevier replied that he based his view of Jackson on a misunderstanding that had since been cleared up. He had come to realize that Jackson was not a "private enemy"; therefore, Sevier had employed "friendly language" in corresponding with him since the November 1796 militia election. Jackson accepted his explanation, and the men's reputations, which both had mentioned as crucial to their disagreement, were safe. Tension between the two remained, however.[11]

The friendship between Jackson and John McNairy, which dated to their time together in North Carolina, also cooled during this period. McNairy heard rumors that Jackson had told others that he "did not like" his longtime friend and did not want him elected to the Tennessee constitutional convention. Additionally, Jackson had supposedly opposed his election to the state superior court. McNairy found support for these allegations in Jackson's comment to him that his *"conduct appeared to me in a manner that I could never have that real friendship for you that I once had."* He also pronounced himself "hurt" that Jackson had taken an opposing side in a lawsuit. Jackson replied that McNairy's conduct had demonstrated to him that he was "not capable of true principles of friendship." Additional pointed remarks in Jackson's letter suggested that he was willing to confront McNairy in a manner other than the written word. McNairy refused to back down. "Sir if any of my words or actions have made me responsible," he informed Jackson, "I am ready to answer for them as honor may direct." Jackson concluded the episode by acknowledging that the two men may have misunderstood one another. "Let the matter drop here," he wrote. "As members of civilized Society, I indulge the idea that we shall pass through life in an easy manner; with the help of those rules and forms of politeness which such a state ought to impose upon every man." He nevertheless made sure that McNairy knew that his "feelings in regard to the violation of our once intimate friendship" had not yet been healed. Jackson's willingness to cut his ties with McNairy, one of his oldest friends, speaks to his confidence in Blount's social network.[12]

Jackson's loyalty to the Tennessee senator was tested in 1797, however, when Blount was expelled from office for conspiring with John Chisholm, a friend and Indian agent living in Knoxville, to conquer Florida and Louisiana. Blount's motivation was to protect his land interests by ensuring that the Mississippi River and the port city of New Orleans were open to American trade. He communicated his plan too openly, though, and one of his letters found its way to newly elected President John Adams, who forwarded it to Congress. The House charged Blount with conspiracy to produce "a military hostile expedition" and passed articles of impeachment against him. In response, on 8 July 1797, the Senate voted overwhelmingly to expel the Tennessee conspirator. For several months the body deliberated over whether it could place an expelled senator on trial for conspiracy. The Senate eventually brought Blount to trial in late 1798 but concluded the following January that its jurisdiction did not extend to these circumstances. In the meantime Blount had been elected to the Tennessee senate, where he continued to exert influence over state politics.[13]

One of the votes in favor of Blount's 1797 expulsion was cast by William Cocke, a longtime resident of East Tennessee and a former state attorney. He and Jackson possessed a good enough relationship that Cocke had acted as mediator during the controversial 1796 militia election; the two were also fellow Masons. Now Cocke's perceived betrayal of Blount forced Jackson to choose between his patron and his friend. He chose to challenge Cocke for election to the Senate. With Blount's influence Jackson defeated Cocke by a twenty-to-thirteen vote in the state legislature. Weeks later the former friends, now rivals, were at odds in a more dangerous contest. Cocke publicized one of Jackson's letters without permission. Jackson wrote a testy missive accusing Cocke of using the letter to harm his reputation "in an ungentlemanlike manner." Six months passed, then Jackson renewed his attack. In addition to the letter faux pas, Cocke had called Jackson a liar. "I call upon you as a gentleman," Jackson angrily wrote, "to meet and give me such satisfaction as is due from one Gentleman to another." Masonic brothers, probably including Anthony Foster, Robert Hays, William Maclin, and James Robertson, attempted to head off a duel, but Jackson rebuffed their involvement. Cocke was more amenable to a peaceful solution. Despite Jackson's declaration that "the Gods of fate must decide between you & me" on the dueling grounds, cooler heads finally prevailed, averting a bloody confrontation.[14]

Jackson's behavior during this period was exacerbated by his financial situation, which had become dire as a result of an old colleague, David Allison. In May 1795 Jackson was in Philadelphia looking to acquire products for the store that he and Samuel Donelson had opened. To help his liquidity, he agreed to sell 68,750 acres of land at 20¢ an acre to Allison. Instead of cash, Allison paid the $13,750 with three promissory notes, which Jackson then used to purchase store goods to be shipped to Nashville. Shortly after returning to Tennessee, Jackson received a letter from the merchant from whom he had purchased some of his goods. "*We* have little or no expectations of getting paid" from Allison's notes, it read, so "we shall have to get our money from you." Jackson had not realized that even as they were conducting business in May, Allison was already in dire financial straits. Early in 1796 other creditors stepped forward demanding that Jackson pay off the defaulted Allison notes that he had used to purchase store inventory. Blount's agreement to cosign the notes provided some relief, but years later the two men were still attempting to get Allison's heirs to pay the debts. (Allison died in debtor's prison in September 1798.)[15]

The Allison debacle threatened Jackson's financial security and his political future. "I can assure you," he wrote Overton in February 1798, "there are no hopes of Payment." Therefore, like Allison, he potentially faced debtor's prison. His record as senator during these months was uninspiring; he rarely participated in the chamber's debates. A bruising fall on the ice that same February hardly helped his mood. In April Jackson went home to Nashville and resigned his Senate seat. His appointment as a judge on the Tennessee superior court made the decision easier. The six hundred–dollar annual salary, second highest only to the governor in state government, promised to alleviate some of his financial concerns, while his position on the court would also make it more difficult for creditors to pursue payment.[16]

Jackson's interim appointment to the state superior court was made by Governor Sevier. The two men had set aside their previous disagreement, but within just a few years they would have a violent confrontation that threatened to undo all of Jackson's hard work in becoming part of the Nashville gentry.

V

"You Cannot Mistake Me, or My Meaning"

Up to this point Jackson's efforts to establish himself as a member of the southern gentry had been largely successful. He had married into an influential kinship network and become relatively wealthy via land speculation. He had established a prominent law practice, which had enabled him to receive appointments to Congress and the Tennessee superior court. Optimism over those accomplishments, however, had been tempered by personal conflicts, first over his marriage to Rachel, then over perceived insults and real misunderstandings with former political allies, and finally by the Allison debts. The next few years would be some of the most difficult of Jackson's life, as episodes of violence seemingly stalled his advancement in Nashville society.

According to James Parton, an early biographer, Jackson's decisions as superior court judge were "short, untechnical, unlearned, sometimes ungrammatical, and generally right." He also did not suffer fools lightly. One account spoke of his confrontation with Russell Bean, a Jonesborough rifle manufacturer. Bean returned from a long trip to find that his wife had given birth to a child, an impossible occurrence if he were the father. Devastated by her infidelity, Bean drank himself into a violent fit, during which he cut off the ears of the child. He was convicted of the assault, then pardoned for helping put out a fire that threatened to destroy the town. Still, he sought revenge against the man who had seduced his wife. Word of Bean's plan to avenge his honor reached the sheriff, who attempted, unsuccessfully, to arrest him. Jackson intervened at this point and personally convinced Bean to surrender himself to the court. According to one version, Bean purportedly acquiesced to the judge's will because "I looked him in the eye, and I saw shoot, and there wasn't shoot in nary other eye in the crowd; and so I says to myself, says I, hoss, it's about time to sing small, and so I did." Whether apocryphal or true, the story captured the impression that most of Jackson's contemporaries saw him as someone with whom not to trifle.[1]

Jackson was not entirely happy as judge, however. In 1801 he wrote relative Robert Hays that his finances were still shaky: "I am in possession of a verry independent office, but I Sink money—the Salary is too low." Partly for that reason, and under pressure from unnamed friends, he thought about another run for Congress, though doing so would mean giving up his influential judicial seat. An up-and-coming lawyer, Hugh Lawson White, was being considered for appointment to the superior court, but he had indicated that he would only accept the post if Jackson served with him. Jackson thus decided to stay on the bench, telling Hays, "If my remaining on my present Seat will be conducive to the object, it is a duty I owe my country to do so."[2]

By 1802, however, Jackson had decided to move on to something that would advance his career in new directions. He stood for election as major general of the Tennessee militia, the highest military post in the state. His opponent was John Sevier, who was no doubt surprised at facing a contested election. Having just finished three consecutive terms (the constitutional limit) as governor, he expected to make a smooth transition into the major generalship. Since William Blount's death in 1800, Sevier, also known as "Nolichucky Jack," the hero of the Battle of Kings Mountain, had become the preeminent political figure in Tennessee. Sevier was undoubtedly chagrined when thirty-four of the thirty-seven brigadier generals and field officers of the militia split their votes evenly between him and Jackson. (The remainder went to James Winchester.) In the event of a tie, the governor cast the deciding vote, and Archibald Roane, Jackson's old friend and another Blount protégé, chose Jackson to head the militia.[3]

Then matters between Jackson and Sevier worsened. In 1797 Jackson had become aware of a conspiracy that stretched from the Tennessee frontier to the North Carolina capital. Speculators sold fraudulent land warrants with the complicity of James Glasgow, the North Carolina secretary of state. The names of two of the speculators drew Jackson's attention. One was Stockley Donelson, his brother-in-law, who also happened to be married to Glasgow's daughter Elizabeth. The other was Governor John Sevier. In the report to the North Carolina governor exposing the conspiracy, Jackson mentioned Stockley but not Sevier. Jackson was not close to his brother-in-law, who lived in East Tennessee and was prone to financial trouble, so naming him risked little. With Blount weakened nationally by his expulsion from the Senate, and with his own finances in trouble, however, Jackson had to be careful not to alienate Sevier, as he had almost done in early 1797. He probably also calculated that the information would prove useful at a later time.[4]

That time came in 1802. Jackson may have given Roane the evidence against Sevier in exchange for his tie-breaking vote in the militia election. If not, he made the revelation soon after. The following summer Roane used the information in his contest against Sevier for the state's governorship. Jackson went public with his evidence, conveniently neglecting to give his reasoning for publicly exposing Nolichucky Jack some six years after the fact. No matter—his efforts failed to help Roane, who convincingly lost the election to Sevier.[5]

A little over a week after Sevier's inauguration, on October 1, the new governor confronted Jackson in Knoxville. According to Isaac T. Avery, son of Jackson's former dueling opponent, Waightstill Avery, Sevier insulted Jackson by mentioning the inappropriateness of his relationship with Rachel prior to her divorce. They exchanged shots without bloodshed, but the following day Jackson issued a public challenge to a duel: "The ungentlemany Expressions, and gasgonading conduct, of yours relative to me on yesterday was in true character of your self, and unmask you to the world, and plainly shews that they were the ebulutions of a base mind goaded with stubborn proofs of fraud, and flowing from a source devoid of every refined sentiment, or delicate sensation . . . I request an interview, and my friend who will hand you this will point out the time and place, when and where I shall Expect to see you with your friend and no other person. my friend and myself will be armed with pistols. you cannot mistake me, or my meaning." Over the next several days the two men tried to decide the particulars of the duel. Jackson was prepared to meet anywhere, but Sevier did not want the confrontation to take place within Tennessee, where dueling was illegal. Frustrated by what he saw as Sevier's multiple excuses to avoid him, Jackson ended the affair by placing an announcement in a Knoxville newspaper that declared Sevier "a base coward and paltroon" who was willing to "basely insult, but has not the courage to repair the wound."[6]

But it was not over. Jackson's public denouncement of Sevier spurred the former governor into action. He agreed to meet Jackson's challenge on Cherokee land southwest of Knoxville. Jackson and his second, Dr.

Thomas J. Vandyke, waited for Sevier for a couple of days, but when he did not appear, they began the return journey to Knoxville on Sunday morning, October 16. Just outside Kingston the two men met Sevier's party, which consisted of the former governor; his son James; Andrew Greer; and John Hunter. The resulting confrontation was dangerously comedic. The two protagonists, pistols drawn, yelled insults at one another. They then put their pistols away, but Jackson was not finished. He threatened to cane Sevier, who drew his sword, which, according to Greer, "frightened his horse, and he ran away with the Governors Pistols, and Judge Jackson immidiately Drew his Pistol and advanced again, on which the Governor when behind a tree and damned Jackson Did he want to fire on a naked man." The seconds drew their pistols, but "after some parley" the immediate tension eased. Sevier recovered his horse, and both sides rode back to Knoxville as a group, with Jackson and Sevier continuing to trade verbal jabs. Aside from a physical confrontation between Jackson and Tennessee's secretary of state, William Maclin, over a related anti-Jackson letter to a Knoxville newspaper, the feud between the two Tennessee titans ended.[7]

The results of the public dispute with Sevier exposed Jackson's weakness as Blount's political protégé and successor. The land fraud accusations failed to keep Sevier from defeating the incumbent Roane in the gubernatorial election. Under Sevier's governorship the legislature had divided the state into two militia districts, diminishing Jackson's power over the militia. Middle Tennessee remained under Jackson's leadership, while William Cocke took over the East Tennessee district. One historian has speculated that Jackson sought to kill Sevier as "an *unconscious* attempt at political assassination" because he knew that he could not defeat him in the political arena. Jackson may have calculated his options and decided that Tennesseans still possessed enough of a frontier mind-set that it was worth the risk. More likely, however, Sevier's taking of "the Sacred name of a lady in your poluted lips" made Jackson angry enough to challenge the most popular politician in the state to an affair of honor.[8]

Jackson further harmed himself by fighting yet another duel in 1806. Long a lover of horses, Jackson had partnered with John Coffee and John Hutchings to build a racetrack and stables at their Clover Bottom business. Jackson's early forays into horseracing had

failed to produce victories, so in 1805 he purchased from John Verrell a bay named Truxton, which had gained notoriety in Virginia as a winner. Truxton proved his worth in his first race under
Jackson's care, leading him to expand his stable to sixteen horses.[9]

This growth placed Jackson in competition with Joseph Erwin, a local
horse owner and breeder. A race between Jackson's horse, Greyhound, and
Erwin's horse, Tanner, resulted in Greyhound's victory. Chagrined, Erwin
issued another challenge. This time he wanted to put his horse, Ploughboy, up against Truxton for the sum of two thousand dollars, with an eight
hundred–dollar forfeit fee if one of the horses could not race. The financial agreement between the two men also specified that certain promissory
notes, some long-term, some payable immediately, would be used to meet
either the stakes or the forfeit. When Erwin withdrew Ploughboy from the
November 28 race, he and Charles Dickinson, his partner and son-in-law,
agreed to pay the forfeit, but there was a misunderstanding about which
promissory notes would be used. The matter was quickly cleared up, however, and Jackson received his payment.[10]

That should have ended the affair, but rumors began to fly in Nashville
that Jackson was unhappy with Erwin's attempt to switch the notes promised as payment. At a meeting with Erwin and Dickinson in late December Jackson denied his discontent with Erwin's payment and stated that
whoever was spreading the rumors was "a damn'd Lyar!" ("Giving the
lie," as this accusation was called in southern society, was an "unmasking"
of a man as false and dishonorable and often led to an affair of honor.)
The man who had been gossiping was Thomas Swann, a Virginia lawyer
recently arrived in Middle Tennessee; exactly why he interjected himself
into the Jackson-Erwin affair is unclear. Whatever his motivation, Swann
found Jackson's depiction of him as a liar insulting and told him so. Jackson's reply ignored Swann's hint at a duel, to which the young Virginian,
through Nathaniel A. McNairy, brother of John McNairy, demanded satisfaction "in the field of honor." Jackson responded through John Coffee
that he would cane Swann instead, which he did at a local tavern shortly
thereafter. He made it clear that he did not consider Swann a gentleman,
which would have required a duel between equals; instead, Jackson chose
a form of punishment reserved for a social inferior.[11]

Jackson thus violently dismissed Swann's challenge, but he also focused most of his first letter to the lawyer on Dickinson, whom he called a "cowardly assassin tale bearer." "As he wishes to blow the coal," he wrote about Dickinson, "I am ready to light the blaze that it may be consumed at once, and finally extinguished." The origin of the dispute between Jackson and Dickinson remains uncertain. Jackson's first biographer, James Parton, noted that sometime between November 1805 and January 1806 Dickinson, who was prone to drunken bravado, besmirched Rachel's name in public. Nowhere in the private correspondence or public exchanges that took place during these months, however, does Rachel's name appear as a pretext for the enmity between the two men.[12]

For whatever reason Jackson directed his ire at Dickinson, who was all too happy to engage him in an exchange of insults. After recounting his conversations with Swann, Dickinson stood his ground: "As [to] the word *Coward, I think it is as* [appli]cable to yourself as to any one I [know]." He then left for New Orleans on a trip without waiting for Jackson's reply. During Dickinson's absence tempers flared. Jackson and Nathaniel McNairy sniped at one another via letters in a Nashville newspaper, with McNairy snidely calling out Jackson: "Risk yourself for once on equal terms, at least at ten yards. The risk is not great when you consider that your opponent will be under the impression that he has come in contact with *the brave, magnanimous, invincible and honorable Major General Andrew Jackson,* of Tennessee." One individual reported that the two met on the dueling grounds and negotiated a nonviolent compromise. (McNairy also dragged Coffee's name into his attack, which resulted in a comedic duel between the two.)[13]

When Dickinson returned to Nashville in May, he responded to Jackson's account of events published in the Nashville newspaper, the *Impartial Review*. Dickinson accused him of altering his memory of events to correspond with his witnesses, and then he threw down the gauntlet. Jackson had stated in his 10 February 1806 letter to Thomas Eastin, editor of the *Impartial Review,* "Mr. Swann . . . has acted the puppet and lying valet for a worthless, drunken, blackguard scounderal." Dickinson's response was, "Should Andrew Jackson have intended these epithets for me, I declare him . . . to be a worthless scoundrel 'a paltroon and a coward.'" He received the reaction that he wanted. Jackson dashed off a letter to Eastin that accused Dickinson of using Swann as a pawn to incite him then making the cowardly decision to write a public letter of insult as he knew he was leaving town. "I hope sir your courage will be an ample security to me, that I will obtain speedily that satisfaction due me for the insults offered," Jackson concluded. His friend Thomas Overton delivered the letter to Dickinson and was authorized to make arrangements for settling the dispute in an honorable manner. Overton and Dr. Hanson Catlet, Dickinson's second, agreed that the duel would take place in one week in Logan County, Kentucky. Pistols were the weapon of choice, with the protagonists set to stand twenty-four feet (roughly eight paces) apart, facing one another with pistols pointed at the ground until they were given the order to fire.[14]

Jackson and Dickinson met as agreed on Friday, May 30. Gamblers in Nashville placed most of their money on Dickinson, who was widely regarded as an excellent marksman. (He also had an ego, making a three hundred–dollar bet with Thomas E. Waggaman that he would kill his opponent.) Acknowledging Dickinson's superior skill with a firearm, Jackson determined to take his chances by waiting for him to fire first. He anticipated taking his time and calmly returning the shot without the pressure of firing quickly. Jackson also wore a large coat, which he hoped would mask his figure. When Overton called "Fire!" things went exactly as Jackson planned. Dickinson shot first and hit Jackson in the chest, but Jackson failed to fall. Dickinson began stepping away from his mark, a violation of the dueling protocol. Forced to return to his position, he avoided looking at his opponent. Jackson pulled the trigger, but the gun did not discharge. He reset the trigger and fired again. This time the bullet crashed through Dickinson's body, between his ribs and his hip. He bled to death later that night.[15]

Jackson was hurt more than he let on while on the dueling grounds. Dickinson's bullet had broken at least one rib and was not able to be removed because of its proximity to his heart. He was bedridden for several days, during which time one would have expected him to rest. Not so. He was furious that Nashville newspapers, in response to a petition of seventy-three individuals, had placed a black mourning border on their pages, along with a public letter of condolence to Dickinson's young widow. Jackson demanded the names of those who had signed the petition. (The signatures included those of Catlet, Swann, Waggaman, Felix Robertson,

Thomas G. Watkins, John, Nathaniel, and Boyd McNairy.) He was particularly incensed at the involvement of Watkins, whom he considered "the chief promoter" of the petition. Jackson accused him of using the excuse that he was honoring Dickinson's widow "to give my reputation a stab." He wanted satisfaction from Watkins but was unable to follow up on his threat. There were also questions about whether Jackson had violated the dueling guidelines by re-cocking his pistol after it misfired.[16]

Jackson learned nothing from the Dickinson duel. The following March, having recovered from his wounds, he tussled on a Nashville street with Samuel Dorsey Jackson, a former business partner. The cause of the fight was a disagreement over some financial notes. Bad blood built up between the two; what happened next depended on whom one believed. Samuel Jackson argued that, without provocation, Andrew hit him, then, as Samuel tried to find a rock with which to defend himself, Andrew ran him through with a cane sword. Andrew Jackson's account differed significantly. His story blamed Samuel for throwing "a large ro[ck at th]e head of the General, which, if it had struck him, as intended; from its size and form, must have put an end to his existance." When Samuel started to throw another rock, Andrew "thrust" his cane sword at him, "pierc[ing] a loose-coat that Sam Jackson had on, but not his flesh." The resulting fistfight "was soon put an end to by the bystanders." A jury acquitted Andrew Jackson of assault and battery later that year.[17]

In all of these violent encounters Jackson laid claim to his position as a southern gentleman. Dueling allowed him the opportunity to defend his honor by addressing his social equal in ritualistic fashion, thus validating his place among Tennessee's gentry. Whipping or caning was the accepted form of confrontation for a member of the upper class to address his social inferior violently. Jackson understood what was required of southern society and reacted accordingly. By agreeing to face him in affairs of honor, Sevier and Dickinson acknowledged his place among the gentry.[18]

Physical confrontations with perceived enemies were not Jackson's only crises during this period, however. He also became enmeshed in an alleged conspiracy that threatened to separate the old Southwest Territory, including Tennessee, from the United States. Jackson's complicity in the matter was never conclusively settled and became a political millstone around his neck.

Aaron Burr, the former vice president of the United States, fomented the conspiracy. In 1804, while still in the vice presidential seat, Burr had killed former Secretary of the Treasury Alexander Hamilton in a duel. Forced to leave New York, his home state, Burr took up residence in Georgia. From there he began planning something, although exactly what remains unclear. Most historians believe that Burr wanted to create a separate nation, with himself at the head, or that he sought a chance to redeem his national reputation by seizing territory from the Spanish. He alternately approached Spain and Britain with requests for financial support to stymie American expansion westward while warning Americans on the frontier of Spain's plots to reclaim its former North American territory.[19]

When Jackson and his wife hosted the former vice president in May 1805, he had no idea of Burr's actual intentions, but he became involved anyway. Understanding why is not hard. Jackson had resigned his position on the state superior court in July 1804 for reasons of poor health, legal conflicts of interest and business demands, as well as the loss of status after the Sevier feud. He also expected President Thomas Jefferson to appoint him governor of the new Territory of Orleans (modern-day Louisiana), part of the recent Louisiana Purchase. Jefferson instead gave the post to W.C.C. Claiborne, governor of the Mississippi Territory and the man who had succeeded Jackson in the U.S. House of Representatives. With this rejection and the numerous other difficulties of the past few years fresh in his mind, Jackson looked for redemption in Burr's plan. Burr had been a friend to Tennessee when it was seeking statehood in 1796, and he represented the defiant attitude of those, like Jackson, who opposed the national government's increasing power.[20]

Burr spent several days with the Jacksons then traveled to New Orleans to confer with General James Wilkinson, a United States military officer who had been appointed governor of the Territory of Louisiana (minus the Territory of Orleans). Wilkinson had been a Spanish secret agent since the 1780s, and he appeared more than willing to help Burr in his plotting. To carry out their cryptic plan, they wanted prominent leaders in the Old Southwest to support them. They identified Jackson as crucial to the endeavor, but he had to be handled carefully. The best way to secure his support, they concluded, was to emphasize the Spanish threat to Americans living on the frontier.[21]

Jackson hosted Burr again in September 1806, at which time the former vice president convinced him that war with Spain was imminent. Jackson leapt into action, warning friends of the danger that Spain posed to the United States and issuing orders to the brigadier generals under his command to prepare for military action. He also agreed to furnish boats and provisions. Jackson had no inkling of what Burr intended, evident in the transparency with which he issued the general order to the Tennessee militia and discussed its organization with President Jefferson. No doubt part of Jackson's motivation was his desire to use Burr's name in restoring his own reputation following the Dickinson duel a few months earlier.[22]

Jackson learned of Burr's conspiracy about a week after contacting Jefferson. Captain John Fort, a relative of one of Burr's conspirators, visited the Hermitage on his way to New Orleans and mentioned in passing Burr's plot against the United States. Shocked, Jackson dashed off letters to Governor Claiborne and Tennessee senator and Donelson relative Daniel Smith. He told Claiborne, "I fear there is something rotten in the State of Denmark," and warned him, without offering details, "you have enemies within your city own City, that may try to subvert your Government, and try to separate it from the Union." To Smith he wrote a lengthier and more detailed explanation of the conspiracy but did not name names. Jackson also wrote Burr a strongly worded letter, informing him that until he explained his suspicious activities, "no further intimacy was to exist between us." He did deliver the boats and provisions to Burr, however, perhaps because he had already paid for them and needed the money, perhaps because rumors had not quite convinced him that treason was afoot. Undoubtedly, Jackson hedged his bets that he had received inaccurate intelligence. If not, then he himself was likely to be accused of treason, and his public career, already teetering on the edge of collapse, would be over.[23]

Jackson's heart must have dropped when, on 1 January 1807, he received a letter from Secretary of War Henry Dearborn requesting his service in opposing the alleged conspiracy. In the Jefferson administration's eyes Burr's complicity was apparently unquestioned; now Jackson had to scramble to put himself in the best light. Despite thinking little of Dearborn ("not fit for a Grany" is how he described him to one acquaintance), he immediately raised twelve militia companies and promised another thirty in the coming weeks. By this time General Wilkinson had determined to arrest his former coconspirator in order to save himself. Burr got wind of his change of heart and tried to escape but was captured and taken to Richmond, Virginia, for trial on charges of treason.[24]

Jackson's emotions got the better of him during the months leading up to Burr's trial. He wrote a letter to Dearborn excoriating him for implying that he had conspired to dismember the Union. He accused Dearborn of being in league with Wilkinson, his "intimate friend and supporter," and determined that his actions were borne out of a grudge held against Jackson from a prior dispute. Thankfully, he had the good sense not to send the letter, but his suspicion that Wilkinson, not Burr, was behind the conspiracy continued long after the trial. Subpoenaed to testify, Jackson made a short trip to Richmond, where he defended Burr publicly, although his presence on the witness stand was never requested. In the end Burr was found not guilty, but Jackson's association with the scandal was one more sign that a once-promising political career seemed in trouble.[25]

Jackson's propensity toward violence was a lifelong characteristic. Borne partly out of his cultural ancestry, partly out of his personality, and partly out of his childhood in the Waxhaws, the expectations of the southern gentry accentuated this tendency. Jackson used violence during these years to establish his reputation as an honorable gentleman. These affairs of honor ignited not from the flamboyant chest pounding of a wild frontiersman but from the deliberate calculation of an aspiring southern planter determined to force recognition of his place among the elite. While moderately successful in that endeavor, his actions undoubtedly left many Tennesseans wondering exactly how long he would live.[26]

VI

"Ten Dollars Extra, for Every Hundred Lashes"

While violence and controversy marked Jackson's public career during the late 1790s and early 1800s, his private life was less volatile, although not always free from conflict. He spent a great deal of his time trying his hand at the mercantile business. He also pursued the life of a gentleman-planter, which required increasing the number of slaves he owned. This growing slave community posed its own problems, as the enslaved challenged Jackson's patriarchal authority. Concomitant with these financial interests, he extended his kinship network, giving himself the opportunity to identify potential heirs to whatever success he might attain.

In 1796 the Jacksons moved to Hunter's Hill, a tract of 640 acres on the Cumberland River originally owned by Lewis Robards. Eight years later Jackson sold the land to Virginian Edward Ward for ten thousand dollars and purchased from Nathaniel Hays 425 acres to the south that formed the basis of his future home and plantation, the Hermitage. Unlike the modern mansion that one associates with the Hermitage, the original house on the land was a simple two-story log building, with other smaller cabins nearby for visitors and slaves.[1]

Jackson sold Hunter's Hill in part to pay off creditors in Philadelphia for the lingering debts from the Allison fiasco, as well as the dissolved partnership with John Hutchings and Thomas Watson the previous year. A new partnership with Hutchings and John Coffee, formed in April 1804, was more financially successful. Stores at Clover Bottom, Gallatin, and Lebanon, as well as Muscle Shoals, Alabama, offered dry goods, foodstuffs, gunpowder, and boats in exchange for cash crops (especially cotton), meat, and furs.[2]

While mercantile activity took up some of Jackson's time, farming remained central to his financial existence. He continued to buy and sell slaves, purchasing at least fifteen and selling at least seven. Some of these slaves left a more substantial record than others, although their escape from historical anonymity depended solely upon their importance in either benefiting or exasperating Jackson.[3]

Dinwiddie (sometimes spelled Dunwoody) was one such example. He was in his early thirties when his owner, John Verrell, sold him to Jackson for eight hundred dollars. Dinwiddie was a noted horse trainer and caretaker to whom Jackson entrusted his stables for the next four decades. In 1810 Dr. William Purnell, one of the original white settlers of the Cumberland region, accused Dinwiddie of poisoning one of his horses. Jackson wanted to know in exact detail how the horse had acted before it died, what it ate, and the conclusions of the doctor who examined its corpse. "If the horse was poisoned," he wrote, "the villain that did it ought to & must be punished." If Dinwiddie had been falsely blamed, however, the accuser "deserves punishment." Purnell denied accusing Dinwiddie of the act, even enclosing an affidavit from an alleged witness to his statements that supported his claim. Jackson let the matter drop. His defense of Dinwiddie was notable for its plea for "innocence[,] that even on [of] a slave."[4]

While Jackson valued Dinwiddie because of his experience with horses, other slaves gave him nothing but headaches, such as Tom Gid, who ran away in June 1804. In a September newspaper advertisement announcing a fifty-dollar reward for returning him, Jackson described Tom as a "mulatto . . . about thirty years old." Just over six feet tall, "stout made and active," he had a stooped walk and "a remarkable large foot." Jackson also noted that he "talks sensible" and probably portrayed himself as a free man, as he had procured papers showing himself as such. He believed that Tom was headed for Detroit. In addition to the reward, Jackson offered "ten dollars extra, for every hundred lashes any person will give him, to the amount of three hundred" if Tom was caught outside of Tennessee. A resident of the Indiana Territory believed that he had found Tom the following winter, but whether it actually was him is unclear.[5]

George and Osten, two other runaway slaves, also cost Jackson time and effort. George and his wife, Moll, had been bequeathed to Rachel in her father's estate. George had previously run away and had been able to pass as a free black. In 1804 the thirty-five-year-old man "enticed away" Osten, who was "a little darker" than his fellow fugitive. They passed through Hartford, Kentucky, before making it to western Ohio. Osten apparently was captured and returned to Jackson, but George made his way to New Orleans, where he disappeared.[6]

Why Tom, George, and Osten ran away is unknown, but by offering rewards for their return and sending friends to track them in distant cities, Jackson obviously considered them valuable property. The state of Tennessee would not establish slave patrols until 1806, so slave owners and their friends were responsible for controlling slave property. The financial inducement for someone to give Tom extra lashes upon capture, perfectly allowable under Tennessee law, suggests Jackson was aware of the value of maintaining harsh discipline among his slaves, who numbered in the teens and probably higher by 1804. Keeping them working was essential, especially at this time in his life, as he began to move out of public service into agricultural production at the Hermitage and the mercantile business across the Middle Tennessee region. Tom's punishment, in particular, sent a message to other malcontents within the Hermitage slave community that Jackson would not tolerate running away, and he would use coercion as a tool to keep them obedient and compliant.[7]

Jackson's participation in slave trading increased too. In 1810 he formed a business partnership with former Nashville mayor Joseph Coleman and Natchez merchant Horace Green. The three men agreed to have Green accompany products, such as cotton and tobacco, from Nashville to New Orleans, where the merchandise would be sold and the profits shared. One shipment was made in the spring of 1811; a second shipment, composed of slaves, was made later that summer. Green failed to dispose of the slaves, however, and decided to leave them in New Orleans and walk away from his business partners. John Hutchings kept them at his Port Gibson plantation until Jackson traveled there in December to try his hand at selling them. Finding as little success as Green, he set out for the Hermitage with twenty-six slaves.[8]

Traveling through Indian territory along the Natchez Trace, Jackson encountered Silas Dinsmoor, the United States agent assigned to the Choctaw, several miles north of present-day Jackson, Mississippi. Appointed in 1802, Dinsmoor had been reprimanded for taking too many vacations and for speculating in Choctaw land that was protected by the very treaty provisions that he was supposed to be enforcing. In response a petulant

Dinsmoor began strictly enforcing the federal requirement that travelers had to show a passport to travel along the Natchez Trace. Additionally, because of the practice of runaway slaves escaping through Indian territory, he served notice that he would "arrest and detain every negro found traveling in the Choctaw country whose master has not a passport as the law requires, and also evidence of property in such negro." Despite being ordered not to impede the journey of "any person traveling through the country in a peaceable manner on the public road or highway," Dinsmoor continued his disruptive practice.[9]

Jackson's recollections of what transpired on the trip were inconsistent, but the basic outline is ascertainable. On his way to the Natchez area Jackson witnessed several families and their slaves detained at the Choctaw agency for lack of passports and proof of ownership. He complained to the deputy agent, a man named Smith, about the practice of prohibiting the use of "a road which was by law free for every American citizen." He also observed that Dinsmoor detained white travelers and slaves to work for him and billed slaves' owners for lodging. While in Natchez, Jackson heard rumors that "his high mightiness" Dinsmoor was preparing a small army of whites and Choctaw to stop him on his way back to Nashville. Jackson armed himself and the slaves for a confrontation, but Dinsmoor was characteristically absent when he passed through, and Deputy Agent Smith made no effort to stop him.[10]

For Jackson the incident was important because it demonstrated the overarching power of the federal government and the corruption of one of its agents. He complained to Tennessee governor Willie Blount that Dinsmoor was responsible for "hundreds of cases of equal despotism." Surely the Madison administration understood that Dinsmoor was a "barbarian" who used "savages" to "[infringe] on our territorial rights" and a coward who "delights in alarming women." These were insults no self-respecting southern gentleman could allow to continue. Part of Jackson's fury also stemmed from Dinsmoor's attempt to utilize travelers' slaves for his own use. "This is making money in true Yankee stile," Jackson declared, and it only added to his condemnation of Dinsmoor's conduct.[11]

In later years political opponents emphasized Jackson's involvement in the slave trade, a charge that he always denied. In fact, during the Dickinson dispute he criticized the young lawyer for "making a fortune of speculating on human flesh" by purchasing slaves in Maryland then selling them in Natchez and New Orleans. Ironically, this practice was almost identical to what Jackson had done with his business partners: the slaves were bought from a Virginia tavern owner and sent to New Orleans to be sold. His inability to see himself in the same light as Dickinson, someone whom he would have considered a slave trader, indicates the emerging negative stereotype of slave traders. As one historian of the domestic slave trade has noted, "Southerners wanted to believe that there was a small group of itinerant and underhanded traders who . . . sold most of the bondspeople." They "destroyed slave families, escorted coffles, sold diseased slaves, concealed the flaws of bondservants, and corrupted whites through speculation. All others who bought or sold slaves, even if they did so on a full-time basis, were innocent." Jackson would undoubtedly have placed himself in the latter category.[12]

Jackson acted as patriarch not only of his slave community but also of his own kin. He learned from his early experience in North Carolina and his later move to Nashville that having a kinship network was important to success. His marriage into the Donelson family gave him access to an established circle, but he also wanted to create his own sphere of influence. Because he and Rachel were unable to have children naturally, Jackson adapted by serving as guardian for at least twenty-four individuals, some related by blood, some not. Many male members of this kinship network later played an important role in advancing his public career.[13]

The Jacksons first assumed responsibility for Edward and Isabella Butler's children: Anthony Wayne, Caroline, Edward George Washington, and Eliza Eleanor. The family lived in Robertson County, but their exact relationship to the Jacksons is unknown. They were close enough, however, that when Edward died in 1803, his widow indicated a desire to have Jackson serve as the minors' guardian. The integration of the families was not without controversy. Caroline married Robert Bell, a local planter who shared Jackson's love of racehorses. In 1810 she became embroiled in "a little feamale controversy." The exact cause of the controversy was not recorded, but it involved seven women, some of them Donelson relatives, and touched in some way on Rachel Jackson's character. Andrew Jackson was concerned enough that he wrote Caroline's mother, Isabella (who had married William B. Vinson the previous year), asking for information about the alleged besmirching of his wife. Isabella assured him that it was a simple misunderstanding among family members.[14]

Another set of Butlers also came under the Jacksons' guardianship. Colonel Thomas Butler, Edward Butler's brother, moved to Tennessee in 1797 to help negotiate honest treaties between the state and the Cherokee. Jackson encountered him in 1798, when Thomas Butler arrested Judge David Campbell for trespassing on Cherokee land. Jackson considered Butler's action "an Outrage against the Dignity of the State, and the rights of Civil liberty." By 1804 he had forgiven Butler and defended him in a spat with his commanding officer, General James Wilkinson. Wilkinson had issued an order in 1801 that officers could not wear their hair in a queue. Butler refused to comply, whereupon Wilkinson had him arrested for disobedience, as well as for delaying the taking up of his post at Fort Adams on the Mississippi River. Jackson was furious at Wilkinson's "despotism" and believed that he brought the charges against Butler "to drive the Colo. out of the service." Despite efforts by Jackson and others to prevent his court-martial, in July 1805 Butler was found guilty on two different occasions and sentenced to a year's suspension. He died of yellow fever before suffering his punishment. Jackson never forgave Wilkinson for persecuting Butler, "a man of Worth, of honest principle & incorruptible hart."[15]

Jackson's language in defending Thomas Butler reflected his belief that Wilkinson's conduct was unrepublican. A letter that he drafted to send to President Jefferson was suffused with references to the "oppression" and "tyranny" that Butler would suffer if Wilkinson was allowed to continue to "tyranise" the junior officer. Yet Jackson also acknowledged that two fundamental southern ideas—hierarchical order and honor—were at stake. If Wilkinson insisted on arresting him, Jackson told Butler, then surely Jefferson's "republican charector" would intervene. If not, then Congress was certain to do so in order to expose Wilkinson's "wanton act of Despotism." Jackson encouraged Butler to persevere in defending himself, reminding him that his health and wealth were secondary to his "honor." At a later date he again alluded to Jefferson's honor. If the president allowed this order to stand, Jackson wrote, "it appears like a prostitution thereof, which should not be passed unnoticed" and required "just indignation."[16]

Thomas Butler's wife, Sarah, preceded him in death, which meant that their four children—Thomas Jr., Robert, Lydia, and William Edward—

became orphans. Andrew and Rachel assumed care for the two young-est; Thomas Jr. and Robert were already on their own. Thomas Jr. would eventually become a lawyer and judge in Louisiana. Robert married Rachel Jackson's niece, Rachel Hays, and acted as Jackson's adjutant during the War of 1812 and the First Seminole War. William Edward, who became a doctor, also served with Jackson during the War of 1812. He married Martha Thompson (Patsy) Hays in 1811, on the same day that his sister, Lydia, married Patsy Hays's brother Stockley.[17]

The Jacksons also brought into their home the three sons of Samuel and Mary Michie Smith (Polly) Donelson: John Samuel, Andrew Jackson, and Daniel Smith. Samuel Donelson was one of Rachel Jackson's brothers; Polly was the daughter of Daniel Smith, a prominent land surveyor and politician in the Southwest Territory. Jackson met Smith shortly after his move to Middle Tennessee, and Smith became a longtime friend, business associate, and political ally. Jackson and Samuel operated a store together in the mid-1790s, until the Allison debts forced its closure. Jackson also assisted his former business partner in eloping with Polly in 1796. Her father was very protective of his fifteen-year-old daughter, but that did not prevent the plot carried out by Jackson, Samuel Donelson, and John Caffery, a brother-in-law of both men. The three men went to Rock Castle, the Smith residence, and helped Polly escape from her second-story room by placing a ladder under her window. Samuel and Polly then married at Jackson's home, Hunter's Hill, much to the chagrin of Daniel Smith. He angrily ordered Jackson to convey his displeasure to his daughter. "Tell her to forget that she has a father and a mother," he exclaimed, "and we shall forget that we ever had a daughter." He also warned Samuel and Jackson himself to steer clear of his presence. Eventually, however, he forgave the two conspirators.[18]

The shared danger and excitement of the elopement and marriage undoubtedly fortified the bond between Jackson and Samuel Donelson. When Samuel died of pneumonia in 1804, Jackson acted as his estate's executor. Samuel and Polly's three sons eventually came under the Jacksons' care when their mother married James Sanders in 1806. Once friends, Jackson and Sanders split in 1807, when Jackson received word that Sanders had accused him of being "'engaged in the treason of Colo. Burr.'" He demanded that Sanders produce proof of his treason or apologize publicly. "I have but one life to loose, that I have risqued in behalf of my reputation, I will again," Jackson wrote. "By the gods I never will permit such an attempt to assassinate my reputation go unpunished." Sanders quickly replied that he had never spread such rumors and that there had simply been a miscommunication.[19]

This episode undoubtedly influenced Jackson's attitude toward Sanders. When young John Samuel Donelson appealed to his guardian a couple of years later, Jackson took his side against his stepfather. Polly had ordered John to stay at her house, which he refused to do, allegedly saying that Jackson had told him to ignore her. Sanders "scholded" John, told him that Jackson "had no wright to give Such Orders," and threatened to discipline the boy with "cowskin." Jackson took umbrage at John's treatment, having undoubtedly been told by his brother Andrew about an incident when Sanders had beaten him for pulling a prank. Jackson threatened to use his own "cow hide" on Sanders, leading the stepfather to warn him, "Be a ware how you youse yo[r] cow hide, or it may fall never to rise." Nothing came of this incident, but enduring animosity between the two men remained.[20]

Jackson oversaw the Donelson boys' education throughout their childhood and early adulthood. While they were young, he provided them with private tutoring at the Hermitage. Andrew studied at Cumberland College (formerly Davidson Academy, in the future called the University of Nashville), West Point, and Transylvania University; Daniel also attended West Point, Jackson underwriting their education the entire time. John accompanied Jackson for a short time during his 1814 military campaign and died in 1817 while surveying land in Middle Tennessee.[21]

The most significant of the wards taken in by the Jacksons was the boy whom they named Andrew Jackson Jr. In December 1808 Elizabeth Rucker Donelson, the wife of Rachel Jackson's brother Severn, gave birth to two sons: Thomas Jefferson and Andrew Jackson. Shortly thereafter, perhaps even within a few days, the boy named for his uncle went to live at the Hermitage and came to be considered Andrew and Rachel's adopted son. It does not appear that Andrew Jackson Jr. (or simply Junior) was ever legally adopted, and the reason Severn and Elizabeth were willing to give a twin boy to the Jacksons to raise as their own is also unknown. Biographers have speculated that they were showing compassion to a despondent woman who could not bear her own children; others have cited Elizabeth's poor health.[22]

Whatever the reason for this literal or symbolic adoption, Junior filled a void in the Jacksons' lives. When Junior was still a toddler, Jackson wrote his wife, "The sensibility of our beloved son, has charmed me, I have no doubt, from the sweetness of his disposition, from his good sense as evidenced, for his age, that he will take care of us both in our declining years." While he was away from home, Jackson's letters to Rachel often closed with the acknowledgment that he had sent Junior a gift or with the request that she "kiss our little son for me."[23]

Caring for these wards served a number of purposes. For Rachel the children filled the void caused by the Jacksons' inability to conceive and provided companionship during her husband's many absences. For Andrew they expanded his kinship network and strengthened his claim to be a patriarch, especially within the Donelson family. His ability to help young relatives obtain an education and build a network of their own was another measure of his importance in Nashville society. Many of these male wards played an important role in Jackson's future public career, which revived when the United States declared war on Great Britain in 1812.[24]

VII

"We *Will Destroy Our Enemies*"

In 1809 Jackson warned Nashvillians that the United States's enemies would take advantage of the nation's divisions if Americans were not vigilant. He alluded to the "attempts" at separating the Union that had taken place in recent years. Despite "the peculiar situation" that the South played in these plots, he confidently asserted that "we are deeply impressed with the truth & importance of the maxim–United we stand–divided we perish." The European powers, particularly France and Great Britain, would find that the United States was "united in sentiment & undismayed by the storm that's approaching." Jackson's prediction of war proved prescient, and as a result, by early 1815 his transformation from Tennessee planter and militia officer to national hero was complete.[1]

During the decade between 1803 and 1812 the United States and Great Britain frequently clashed over a number of issues, including neutrality rights, shipping embargoes, and the impressment, or forced service, of United States sailors into the Royal Navy. Many Jeffersonian Republicans also suspected that the British were responsible for the increased Indian hostility toward Americans along the southern frontier. Stopping the violence was imperative for whites who wanted to settle on Native Americans' land. The frontier's volatility also encouraged slaves to run away and join Native Americans in the fight against white southerners. By 1812 it appeared that war between Great Britain and its former colonies was inevitable.[2]

His reputation marred by the perception that he had been disloyal during the Burr affair, Jackson worked assiduously to demonstrate his national devotion in the years prior to 1812. During the 1808 presidential campaign Jackson, "at considerable trouble and expence," supported James Monroe, whom he apparently believed would take a stronger stance against Great Britain and France than the outgoing president, Thomas Jefferson, or Monroe's major intraparty competition and the eventual winner, James Madison. The federal government's unwillingness to respond aggressively to Jackson's accusations that the British were inciting the Creek continued during Madison's administration. Jackson spoke openly both to the militia under his authority and to the people of Tennessee about his belief that the British in particular were seeking to reclaim the United States and the need for Americans to stand at the ready to defend themselves from "the beligerent powers of Europe." Jackson's patriotic proclamations undoubtedly arose from his genuine commitment to the nation, but they also proved important in preparing him for the prominent role that he was about to play on the battlefield.[3]

By April 1812 Jackson was convinced that unless politicians in Washington lost their nerve, war "appears unavoidable." His certainty followed in part a Creek attack on white residents near the Duck River in Humphreys County. Seven members of two families, the Manleys and the Crawleys, were killed in the assault, and Martha Crawley, the family's matron, was taken captive. Jackson interpreted the action as part of a larger Native American conspiracy fomented by Tecumseh, the Shawnee leader, and his brother, Lalawethika, known as the Prophet. The two men had been attempting to unite Indian tribes into a confederacy that would oppose white expansion. Jackson blamed Tecumseh for the bloodshed: "That incendiary, the emissary of the *Prophet,* who is himself the tool of England, has caused our frontier to be stained with blood, and our peacefull citizens to fly in terror from their once happy homes." The Manley-Crawley attack offered not only an opportunity for revenge, Jackson argued, but also a chance to weaken the Indian presence on the southern frontier. "The sooner we strike," he wrote Governor Willie Blount, the half-brother of Jackson's late patron, "the less resistance we shall have to overcome; and a terrible vengeance inflicted at once upon one tribe may have its effect upon all others."[4]

Jackson would not get his wish immediately, as the Madison administration determined to negotiate with the Creek for Martha Crawley's release. Jackson asked Governor Blount to intervene. "When we judge to ourselves our beloved wives and little prattling infants, butchered, mangled, murdered, and torn to pieces, by savage bloodhounds, and wallowing in their gore," he protested, "you can Judge of our feelings." Blount deferred to President Madison. None of them knew, however, that Martha Crawley had escaped in late June and was already safe. By that time Congress, spurred on by War Hawks in the West and South, had voted along sectional and partisan lines to declare war against Great Britain for its numerous provocative actions against the United States.[5]

Some writers have argued that Jackson's hatred of the British, stemming from the loss of his family during the Revolution, motivated his actions during the War of 1812. His speeches to the Tennessee militia and volunteers in June mention the British and their tyranny, but his primary focus was on defeating the Native American tribes and conquering territory in the South. "Turn your eyes to the South!" he told volunteers in July. "Behold in the province of West Florida, a territory whose rivers and harbors, are indispensable to the prosperity of the Western, and still more so, to the eastern Division of our State." Rumors of an armistice between the warring nations, he warned, were only intended to weaken the United States: "While the American army shall sheathe its sword, the tomahawk and the scalping knife will redouble their activity, and mingle together the blood of grayheaded age, of the tender mother, and the infant babe."[6]

Despite Jackson's urgent pleas, the Madison administration did not ask Governor Blount to muster Tennessee troops into action until October. Under the leadership of Jackson, commissioned as a major general of United States volunteers, they were ordered to New Orleans to support General James Wilkinson in defending the port city from a likely British invasion. Jackson considered it "a bitter pill" to assist a man whom he blamed for the Burr conspiracy, but "for my countries good," he wrote George W. Campbell, "I will swallow [it]." In early January 1813 Jackson and just over two thousand Tennessee troops set out for the mouth of the Mississippi River. On his staff were William B. Lewis, assistant deputy quartermaster; William Carroll, brigade inspector; Thomas Hart Benton, first aide-de-camp; John Reid, second aide-de-camp and Jackson's private secretary; and John Coffee, cavalry commander.[7]

This campaign was a disaster for Jackson and his men. Provisions for the unexpectedly cold weather proved inadequate. When Wilkinson ordered Jackson to stop his advance at Natchez and to stay there until he received further instructions, the two men exchanged letters in which they danced around their dislike of one another while maintaining the propriety required of military officers in official communications. The final blow came in mid-March, when Jackson received an order from the new secretary of war, John Armstrong, that "the causes for embodying & marching to New Orleans the Corps under your command having ceased to exist," he and his troops were "dismissed from public service." Jackson was furious. He responded to Armstrong's letter with dramatic descriptions of how, by ordering his troops back to Nashville, the Madison administration was consigning them to "a barbarous clime" in which they would "fall a sacrafice to the Tomhawk and scalping knife of the wilderness."[8]

Before marching his men back to Tennessee, Jackson addressed them in a rousing speech intended to honor their service and to bolster them for the grueling journey ahead. He recognized their "patriotism," lauded their "alacrity," and trumpeted their "attention to duty." He cautioned them to remember their military discipline on the trek home. "We have to pass a savage country," he acknowledged, one inhabited by native inhabitants who were committing "unheard of brutality and murder of our brethern." "Still," Jackson said, "it becomes us untill we are ordered by government[,] to withhold our hands from vengeance least we strike the innocent and bring disgrace and guilt upon our heads." Echoing language that he had used in a letter to Rachel the day before, Jackson pledged as the soldiers' "father" not to leave anyone—sick, wounded, or otherwise—behind to die. On the trip back to Nashville the forty-six-year-old commander gave up his horse and walked so that sick soldiers could ride. Jackson also encouraged his men when their will faltered. Incredibly, although burdened by 150 sick soldiers and possessing only eleven wagons, the troops managed to march an average of eighteen miles a day. Jackson's paternal commitment to his men on the journey earned him the sobriquet that would stick with him beyond the grave: Old Hickory.[9]

Upon returning to Nashville, Jackson became embroiled in a controversy that led to a shootout on the city's streets. For unknown reasons Littleton Johnston, an officer in the Twenty-fourth U.S. Infantry, challenged Jackson's brigade inspector, William Carroll, to a duel. Carroll refused. Jesse Benton, a friend of Johnston's and no stranger to duels, interjected himself into the dispute. He offered to stand in his friend's place if Carroll's hesitation was due to his belief that Johnston was not his social equal. Carroll then approached Jackson for advice. In his speech to the troops before departing Natchez several months earlier, the general had made a point to praise Carroll's "attention, industry, and knowledge of tactics." He also considered him "a mem[ber of my] family." Bearing in mind his friendship with both men, Jackson offered to mediate the dispute "honourably." He suggested that Benton discuss the propriety of his course of action with Robert Purdy, an older, experienced military man. Benton refused and immediately challenged Carroll to a duel. In the agreement worked out between Jackson, who agreed to serve as Carroll's second, and John M. Armstrong, Benton's second, the two men were set to meet with pistols at a distance of ten feet. The two would stand back to back, take the specified paces, then "wheel erect" and fire. Carroll chose the weapon and distance, Benton the time and place. On Monday, 14 June 1813, the duel took place. Benton breached the rules by stooping as he wheeled to fire. His shot hit Carroll's thumb; Carroll's aim directed his bullet into Benton's buttocks.[10]

While this dispute came to a boil, Jesse's brother and Jackson's aide, Thomas Hart Benton, was in Washington seeking reimbursement for the failed military campaign. The relationship between Thomas Benton and Jackson was already tense because Benton had publicly criticized William B. Lewis's capacity as quartermaster. Livid about Old Hickory's participation in his brother's duel, Benton wrote a pointed letter to his commanding officer. He told Jackson that he was too old to take an active part in a duel "between young men who had no harm against each [other]." Even worse, he had "conducted it in a savage, unequal, unfair, and base manner" by changing the rules to favor Carroll and by not informing Jesse Benton of the changes until the last minute. He also said that Jackson had accused Thomas Benton, implicitly, of "mutiny." In a lengthy reply Jackson outlined the evolution of the duel from his perspective but skimmed over Thomas Benton's reference to disloyalty. Yet he made his position clear. "It is the charector of the man of *honor* and particularly of the *soldier* not to quarrel & brawl and [back bite] like the fish-woman," he wrote. As a soldier, Benton should do him the honor "if in Error to say or promptly to demand of me satisfaction for any injury you may think I have done you."[11]

Passions remained high on both sides until early September, when Jackson and the Benton brothers met in downtown Nashville. The Bentons stayed at the City Hotel, while Jackson and several kinsmen and friends took up residence at the Nashville Inn. According to Thomas Benton's account, the Jackson party went to the City Hotel looking to kill him. Seeing Thomas unarmed, Jackson allegedly said, "Now defend yourself, you damned rascal!" and pointed a pistol at him. Jesse responded by firing at his brother's intended assassin. At that point all hell broke loose. Both sides fired their pistols then drew knives and went at each other in hand-to-hand combat. Jesse, still recovering from the wound to his buttocks, was nearly killed by Jackson's relative, Stockley D. Hays. Several of the other participants walked away with wounds. Jackson was shot in the left shoulder and the arm and, in the most dramatic accounts, either had his arm almost amputated or nearly bled to death.[12]

This confrontation reveals the depth of emotions contained in southern male society. Jackson did not have to brawl with the Bentons, but avoiding the confrontation became impossible once it became public. Honor required Jackson to challenge his former aide, a man who had supported him during the recently aborted military campaign. Masculinity was also at stake, as Jackson indicated by his invocation of language insulting Thomas Benton as a gossiping, petulant woman. Following years of public disappointment in Tennessee and smarting from the recall of his military forces, Jackson was unwilling to back down from the confrontation with the Bentons. His reputation as a southern gentleman demanded it.[13]

Less than a month later Jackson had recovered sufficiently from his wound to lead troops on a new military campaign. Their enemy was the Red Sticks, a Creek faction composed mostly of younger male residents of the Upper Creek towns located on the Alabama, Coosa, and Tallapoosa Rivers. The Red Sticks vehemently opposed American expansion onto Native American lands in the South. Infuriated by an American attack on Creek Indians who had been trading with the Spanish in Pensacola, a group of Red Stick Creek attacked Fort Mims, an American stronghold located near the Gulf Coast and in close proximity to Spanish Florida. Total American casualties in the 30 August 1813 battle were close to 250, although reports at the time had them as high as 600. Many of the dead were white civilians who had been encouraged to seek refuge from the unrest at the fort. Reports of individuals being burned alive, pregnant women being cut open, and children's heads being smashed against the fort's walls understandably caused hysteria among white settlers living nearby, as did rumors, which were true, that runaway slaves and free blacks had assisted in the massacre. Because the Red Sticks resided mostly in towns located in what is now northern Alabama, Tennesseans especially feared that they would soon come under attack. Governor Blount and the Tennessee General Assembly responded to the Madison administration's call for troops by agreeing to raise 5,000 men, 3,500 more than the requested number.[14]

In early October 1813 Jackson took command of the 2,500 men who initially gathered at Fayetteville, Tennessee, just a few miles north of modern-day Huntsville, Alabama. Joined by friendly Creek (called White Sticks), they moved quickly, attacking Creek settlements at Tallushatchee (November 3) and Talladega (November 9). "We have retaliated for the destruction of Fort Mims," Jackson proudly announced after the former battle. John Coffee, who commanded the Tennessee forces, reported 186 Creek killed and 84 taken prisoner, while losses for the Tennesseans totaled 5 dead and 41 wounded. At Talladega 15 Tennesseans lost their lives, with 87 wounded; Creek fatalities numbered 299. One of Jackson's men, David Crockett of later Alamo fame, reported that the Creek were shot "like dogs," while another, Richard K. Call, later the governor of Florida, described bodies burned by fire and eaten by dogs.[15]

Jackson's march of vengeance and conquest now stalled. A lack of supplies, especially food and winter clothing, and confusion about when their terms of service ended led many of Jackson's soldiers to begin returning to Tennessee. Governor Blount and Madison's secretary of war, John Armstrong, initially declined to support Jackson. A frustrated Old Hickory pleaded with Blount to keep a force in the field to protect white settlers and preserve the nation's honor: "Save yr frontier from becoming drenched in blood—and yourself from being damned for it . . . You have only to act with a little energy . . . Withhold it, and all is lost and the reputation of the state and yrs with it."[16]

Fortunately for Jackson, his letter resonated with the governor. Blount sent him newly enlisted troops, which Jackson used to complete his objective of crushing Indian resistance in the Southeast. In late January 1814 engagements at Emuckfaw and Enotachopco forced the Red Sticks to retreat to their stronghold at Tohopeka (Horseshoe Bend) on the Tallapoosa River, leaving them susceptible to annihilation if Jackson massed his forces. This he did on March 27. His army of nearly 5,000 soldiers overwhelmed the estimated Red Stick force of 1,000 male warriors. "The fighting continued with some severity for five hours," he reported. To Rachel he wrote: "The *carnage* was *dreadfull* . . . it was dark before we finished killing them." Most of the approximately 350 Creek women and children survived, but an estimated 850 Creek warriors were cut down. The dead and wounded among Jackson's combined forces of Tennesseans and Creek Indian allies numbered only 45 dead and 146 wounded.[17]

This defeat at Horseshoe Bend broke the Red Sticks's resistance in Alabama. Approximately 1,000 of them moved to Pensacola in Spanish Florida seeking refuge with the Seminole, a part of the Creek confederation. As for Jackson, the battle earned him a promotion to major general in the United States Army and appointment as commander of the Seventh Military District, which included Tennessee and the Mississippi Territory, comprising the modern states of Alabama and Mississippi. Already angry with the Red Sticks, Jackson became incensed when the British began supplying and training them and their black and Seminole allies in western Florida. In August 1814 Jackson demanded that Creek representatives meet him at Fort Jackson, located at the confluence of the Coosa and Tallapoosa Rivers in central Alabama. He wanted to punish the Creek—all of them—and take their land. He succeeded. As he told the Creek: "You have followed the counsel of bad men, and made war on a part of your own nation and the United States. This war has cost the United States a large sum. You must yield as much of your land as will pay this sum. But it must be taken from your whole nation, in such a manner as to destroy the communication with our enemies every where." Ignoring the protests of Creek chiefs, Jackson stated forcefully: "We *will* run a line between our friends and our enemies . . . We *will destroy our enemies* because we *love our friends & ourselves.* The safety of the United States and your nation requires, that enemies must be seperated from Friends." The Indian representatives finally conceded the inevitable; thirty-five friendly chiefs and one Red Stick chief signed the Treaty of Fort Jackson on 9 August 1814. It ceded almost twenty-two million acres of land to the United States, covering nearly half of Alabama and a significant portion of southwest Georgia. The Native Americans also gave Jackson, Creek agent Benjamin Hawkins, and two interpreters land in the cession "as a token of gratitude." It is unclear whether these land grants were true gifts, desperate bribes, or sarcastic gestures; regardless, Congress refused to allow them.[18]

Jackson's trouble with the Creek Indians was not over, however. Colonel Edward Nicolls, a British officer with abolitionist sentiments, organized the Creek—as well as the Seminole, free blacks, and runaway slaves in the Pensacola area—into a fighting force. Fearing a pending military offensive, Jackson sought authorization to seize the Spanish town. Secretary of War Armstrong's reply was inexplicably delayed until January 1815 and was vague in its wording: "The case you put is a very strong one & if all the circumstances stated by you unite, the conclusion is inevitable. It becomes our duty to carry our arms where we find our enemies." On September 11 the feared British offensive began. A British-led force attacked the American stronghold at Fort Bowyer, located at the opening of Mobile Bay. Not yet having received Jackson's report on the Fort Bowyer attack and more concerned with an anticipated British move against New Orleans, the new secretary of war, James Monroe, ordered Jackson to "take no measures" that would engage the United States in any war with Spain. Jackson, however, failed to receive Monroe's orders in time to stop his intended invasion. Without authorization his men surrounded Pensacola on November 7, forcing its surrender. Receiving news that the British were indeed preparing soldiers and sailors for an attack on New Orleans, Jackson retreated toward Mobile, then moved to the Crescent City.[19]

At New Orleans, Jackson scored the victory that would win him national notoriety. Arriving on December 1, he assessed the city's defenses. Earlier he had agreed with the suggestion of the territorial governor, William C. C. Claiborne, that free black men be given the right to defend New Orleans. "They must be either for, or against us," he wrote Claiborne, "distrust them, and you make them your enemies, place confidence in them, and you engage them by Every dear and honorable tie to the interest of the country who extends to them equal rights and priviledges with white men." To the free blacks of New Orleans he announced: "As Americans, your Country looks with confidence to her adopted Children, for a valorous support, as a partial return for the advantages enjoyed, under her mild and equitable government." If they fought, Jackson continued, they would also receive "the same bounty in Money and lands" as the white soldiers. This statement hardly eased the fears of some prominent white citizens, who "anticipate[d] much evil" from the city's "mix'd population." Jackson stood firm, no doubt trying to counter British efforts to recruit (and encourage) runaway slaves. After some hesitation Jackson also agreed to allow pirates, led by Jean Lafitte, to join his forces. A brief but costly skirmish with British troops two days before Christmas demonstrated the need for every man, white and black, to help defend the city. Both sides lost approximately 10 percent of their engaged forces: the British counted 46 dead, 167 wounded, and 64 captured, while the United States reported 24 dead, 115 wounded, and 74 taken prisoner. Jackson's chief engineer, the Frenchman Arsène Lacarrière Latour, recalled that during the battle "no man could possibly have shown more personal valour, more firmness and composure," than the general.[20]

Having now tested one another, the opposing forces prepared for the climactic battle. On January 8 a British force of approximately 8,000 troops attacked Jackson's nearly 4,000 men along the Rodriguez Canal separating the Chalmette and Macarty plantations. The Americans had fortified the canal by digging it deeper and using the dirt to build up defenses. Several circumstances, including British troops forgetting to bring ladders needed for climbing the American ramparts, contributed to an overwhelming and unexpected victory for the United States that day. Jackson numbered the British casualties at 1,800 (400 dead and 1,400 wounded), with another 500 taken prisoner. The British count was lower but still astonishing: 291 dead, 1,262 wounded, and 484 prisoners. Jackson initially reported 6 dead and 7 wounded, but those numbers were later revised to a still miniscule 13 dead, 39 wounded, and 19 missing.[21]

Yet controversy accompanied the victory celebration. Jackson had placed New Orleans under martial law on 16 December 1814, and after January 8 he continued to impose military rule, not realizing that the Treaty of Ghent, signed on 24 December 1814, signaled that the war with Britain was near an end. Not until 13 March 1815 did official word of the treaty reach New Orleans, and only then did Jackson remove martial law; in the meantime he placed several prominent public officials, including Judge Dominick A. Hall, in prison for defying his authority. This determination to maintain order in New Orleans prompted a trial for contempt of court that resulted in Jackson being fined a thousand dollars. The execution of six militiamen also created problems. Prior to the invasion of Pensacola the previous fall, a number of Tennessee militia had abandoned their posts, claiming their enrollment was up. Jackson court-martialed six of the men thought to be the leaders of the munity and ordered their execution: John Harris, David Hunt, Henry Lewis, Edward Linsey, David Morrow, and Jacob Webb. This order was carried out in Mobile on 21 February 1815. (These executions were not the first under Jackson's command: Private John Wood had been court-martialed and shot in March 1814 for disobeying orders, disrespecting his commanding officer, and mutiny.)[22]

Jackson also faced pressure from white Americans who wanted to ensure that their slaves, some of whom the British had confiscated or recruited to serve in their army, were returned. Within a month of the battle at New Orleans, Louisiana governor William C. C. Claiborne sent an official request to Jackson, indicating that he was willing to form a commission to undertake the recovery of slave property. Jackson responded that he had already contacted the British commander, Major General John Lambert, who "assured" him that "the negroes who flocked to his Army will be delivered upon application." To private individuals who wrote him about their missing slaves, Jackson promised, "I have taken and will take every step which my official duty will allow, to procure a restoration of their property." His efforts came to naught. Lambert's successor, Major General Manley Powers, informed Jackson that his superior officer "did every thing in his power, to induce" the former slaves to return to their masters, "but he did not feel himself authorized, to resort to compulsion, to obtain that end, as they had served with the British army voluntarily, and threw themselves upon his protection." With that in mind, Powers reported, Lambert had sent them to Bermuda. Stymied by this British recalcitrance, Jackson dropped the matter.[23]

These controversies failed to temper the American people's celebration of the gray-haired Jackson. Despite the reality that the United States and Great Britain had already signed a peace treaty (not ratified until mid-February 1815) by the time the battle had been fought, news of Jackson's triumph led many Americans to perceive the war as a victory over the British. The general, "haggard" and skeletal from gunshot wounds and dysentery, who had faced down mutinous troops, overcome equivocating support from superiors, and defeated the mighty British army, entered the national consciousness. Until the end of his life Andrew Jackson was called the "Hero of New Orleans."[24]

VIII

"An End to All Indian Wars"

As a reward for Jackson's success during the war, in May 1815 President Madison appointed him commander of the Southern Division, encompassing four military departments composed of the District of Columbia, the Carolinas, Georgia, Kentucky, Louisiana, Tennessee, Virginia, and the territories of Illinois, Mississippi, and Missouri. For the next several years, in what one historian has called "an epilogue to the War of 1812," Jackson used his position to combat foreign and domestic enemies, in the process opening the door for the territorial expansion of the United States and the growth of the cotton South.[1]

Jackson's official duties included solidifying the United States's control over the Gulf region. The Negro Fort, a British enclave at Prospect Bluff on the Apalachicola River in West Florida used as a base of operations during the recent war, posed an immediate obstacle. The British and their Native American allies abandoned the fort in the summer of 1815, leaving behind a maroon community of approximately five hundred free blacks and runaway slaves. Many of the men had been trained by the British as part of the Royal Colonial Marines, and members of the community, who came from Africa, the Caribbean, and the United States, had been exposed to ideas of liberty, freedom, and collective resistance. Jackson understood that the Negro Fort threatened not just "the peace of the nation" but also the plantation economy of the South. "If the fort harbours the Negroes of our citizens . . . or hold out Inducements to the Slaves of our Citizens to desert from their owner's service, this fort must be destroyed," he wrote General Edmund P. Gaines, who was responsible for the campaign against the maroon community. In late July 1816 the combined forces of the United States Army and Navy leveled the fort with a lucky shot that hit the enclosure's powder magazine, killing 270 of the 334 who remained behind to defend it.[2]

After the Negro Fort's destruction, Jackson, as he had done following the Battle of New Orleans, attempted to help southern slave owners recover their runaway slaves. Gaines had previously informed Jackson that several Native American allies had agreed to assist in the recovery effort, asking for a fifty-dollar bounty for each runaway returned to his or her master. Following the battle Jackson corresponded with his subordinates and with private citizens about the recovery of other slaves who had been stolen or captured in Indian territory. The War Department also instructed him to ensure that the Spanish government in Florida "prevent[ed] the illicit introduction of slaves into the U. States."[3]

In addition to defending the Gulf Coast, Jackson was charged with "civilizing the Indians." He interpreted this authority as permission to seize even more Native American land. In the process he ignored Article 9 of the War of 1812's Treaty of Ghent, which specified that Indian groups who had allied with the British would have their lands restored to them. Jackson refused to acknowledge Creek claims to the land ceded in the Treaty of Fort Jackson and worked assiduously to acquire more land from the Cherokee, Chickasaw, and Choctaw. He was helped in that regard by his longtime friend General John Coffee. Coffee, who had served with Jackson in the war, was appointed as an alternate to a three-person commission authorized to survey the boundaries between United States and Indian land affected by the Treaty of Fort Jackson. With Creek agent Benjamin Hawkins too ill to participate, Coffee took charge of the survey; the other two commissioners, Gaines and Captain William Barnet, ceded control to him, probably in deference to Jackson's desire to have his kinsman take the lead.[4]

Native American leaders protested the land grab, arguing that some of the land claimed under the Treaty of Fort Jackson did not belong to the Creek. They consequently refused to accompany the American commissioners as they ran the boundary line. Jackson responded to their recalcitrance with a warning: "I now tell you that line must and will be run, and the least opposition brings down instant destruction on the heads of the opposers . . . Friends & Brothers—Justice will be done by the President of the, u. states to all his red children, he will protect his friends and punish his enemies." Repeated warnings continued for the next few years as Jackson oversaw treaty negotiations with the Cherokee, Chickasaw, and Choctaw. Oftentimes Jackson used "small presents" as "the sole remedy" to overcoming Indian resistance to negotiation. These bribes helped him complete four treaties that resulted in additional millions of acres being added to the United States in the present-day states of Alabama, Georgia, Kentucky, Mississippi, Missouri, and Tennessee. In a continuation of the policy instituted during the presidential administration of Thomas Jefferson, part of the negotiations with the Cherokee centered on their removal to land west of the Mississippi River. White southerners celebrated this land grab by "the IMMORTAL JACKSON." "People are already flocking to" the treaty land in Alabama "by hundreds," one observer reported. "I never saw such a migration in my life; there is not a day, but what the streets of Huntsville are crowded, with men, women, children, Cattle and Dogs, all for the new purchase."[5]

Everything did not go exactly as Jackson wished, however. Secretary of War William H. Crawford halted Coffee's survey of the Creek lands, rupturing relations between the secretary and the general. In the spring of 1816 Crawford overrode Jackson's objections to the transfer of an officer, Eleazar Wheelock Ripley, who had transformed a personal quarrel with another officer into a court-martial proceeding. Jackson was concerned that Ripley's transfer would disrupt "the most perfect Harmony" of the officers under his command. Shortly thereafter, Crawford reacted coolly to Jackson's proposal to build a road between Nashville and New Orleans to facilitate the movement of military supplies and troops. He also lectured him on Jackson's responsibility as commander to remove white settlers on Native American lands. "It is expected, that you will use your influence to arrest" the settlers' "momentary delusion" that the land belonged to them without the government's approval. By the end of the year Jackson told Coffee that Crawford opposed American expansion because "he does not like us, wishes at the hazard of the safety of the union to cramp our growing greatness . . . and because I have recommended it." Two years later Jackson continued to believe that Crawford held an "implacable hostility" toward him and warned President James Monroe that Crawford, newly appointed as secretary of the Treasury, and House Speaker Henry Clay were already laying the foundation for the Virginian's defeat in the 1820 election.[6]

Significantly, too, these treaties did not bring an end to conflict along the United States–Florida border. Blacks fleeing the destruction of the Negro Fort settled on the Suwannee River in East Florida and announced

their intention to gain revenge against the Americans. They allied themselves with Bowlegs, a Seminole chief, who gave military command to his
most prominent slave, Nero. Both the blacks and the Seminole also found
allies in four foreigners, three of whom were British. George Woodbine,
an agent to Native American groups in Florida during the War of 1812,
incited the Indians and blacks by telling them that Britain was preparing
to renew its war with the United States. Josiah Francis, also known as Hid-
lis Hadjo, one of the surviving leaders of the Red Stick Creek, had sought
British intervention in the conflict with the United States but was told during a visit to London that a peace treaty was the best course for the Creek.
Alexander Arbuthnot, a Scots merchant, openly expressed his sympathy
for the Indians and appointed himself an unofficial spokesman for them.
Finally, Robert C. Ambrister, a lieutenant in the Royal Marines, served
with Edward Nicolls and Woodbine during the War of 1812. Of the four
Woodbine, and perhaps Ambrister as well, encouraged blacks and Seminole to conduct scavenging forays across the border into Georgia. On the
other hand, Arbuthnot and Francis, while supportive of Indian claims to
land, did not actively encourage resistance.[7]

The Seminole-black raids into the United States prompted General
Gaines to demand that Neamathla, Seminole chief at Fowltown, turn over
those Indians who had killed several white Georgians. He also notified
Neamathla, "You harbor a great many of my black people among you at
Sahwahnee." The Seminole chief replied, "It is I that have cause to com-
plain." White Americans had killed his men while they were hunting. As
for the stolen slaves, "I harbor no negroes," he told Gaines. Over the years
slaves had settled with the Seminole, but "it is for you white people to settle those things among yourselves, and not trouble us with what we know
nothing about." The Seminole's recalcitrance was enough to cause Gaines
to take action. On 21 November 1817 United States troops burned Fowltown to the ground. In retaliation Indians and blacks attacked an American boat, killing most on board, including women and children. Similar
assaults continued for several days.[8]

In the meantime two significant changes resulted in Jackson returning to Florida. In Washington, President Monroe appointed John C. Calhoun, a former U.S. representative from South Carolina and one of the

most ardent supporters of the War of 1812, as his new secretary of war. Two of Calhoun's first decisions were to move Gaines to another part of Florida and to order Jackson to Fort Scott in Georgia, the staging ground for the attack on Fowltown. He told Jackson to "adopt any necessary measures to terminate a conflict which it has ever been the desire of the President, from considerations of humanity, to avoid." Calhoun also sent Jackson copies of his orders to Gaines, which specified that Gaines should only go after the Seminole, leaving Spanish posts and settlements alone. In early January 1818 Jackson advised President Monroe that such a limitation was a sure plan for defeat: "The arms of the United States must be carried to any point within the limits of East Florida, where an Enemy is permitted & protected or disgrace attends." Further, he wrote, "the whole of East Florida [should be] seized & held as an indemnity for the outrages of Spain upon the property of our citizens." This action would also eliminate further Native American and black opposition on the Gulf Coast as well as keep Spain from uniting with another European power, such as Great Britain, against the United States. "This can be done without implicating the Government," he concluded. If Monroe agreed with these sentiments, Jackson requested that he send word through Tennessee congressman John Rhea. Whether Jackson ever received that unofficial authorization is a question that remains controversial today.[9]

Once in command of Fort Scott, Jackson invaded Spanish Florida. He marched first to the remains of the Negro Fort (rebuilding it and renaming it Fort Gadsden) then proceeded to burn down the towns of the Mikasuki tribe and any black settlements that he encountered. The discovery of fifty white scalps from the Fowltown retaliation only incensed Jackson more. The Spanish commander at nearby Fort St. Marks emphasized the threat that he felt from the Indian "barbarians & negroes" but also expressed his reluctance about allowing the Americans to take over the fort without authorization from his government. Jackson had no such compunctions. He marched into the fort, capturing Arbuthnot and discovering that members of the U.S. Navy had already seized Josiah Francis. On April 8 he ordered Francis hanged. The following day he moved his army to attack Bowlegs' Town, located on the Suwannee River. In the process Jackson's forces encountered blacks fighting a rearguard action. The Americans quickly took the field but found Bowlegs' Town deserted. A few days later, without realizing that the town was occupied by the United States, Ambrister arrived and found himself immediately arrested.[10]

Returning to St. Marks, Jackson ordered Arbuthnot and Ambrister court-martialed based on their assistance to the Seminole and black forces aligned against the United States. As evidence against Arbuthnot, the military court considered a number of factors. One was a letter that he had sent to his son, in which he warned Chief Bowlegs to evacuate his town in advance of American forces and explained that Jackson's objective was "to destroy the black population of Suwany." The case against Ambrister was easily proved, both from his correspondence and his leadership of a group of black soldiers who accompanied him when he stumbled onto Jackson's men. The courts-martial sentenced Arbuthnot to be hanged and Ambrister to be shot; the executions took place on 29 April 1818.[11]

Jackson shed no tears mourning these men, whom he considered British spies. After returning to Fort Gadsden on May 2, he received word (incorrectly, it turned out) that approximately five hundred "Indian Warriors" were residing at Pensacola, where the governor, José Masot, allegedly provided them protection. Masot's denials failed to deter Jackson, who marched into Pensacola on May 24. He declared that he had been forced to seize Pensacola, not "from a wish to extend the Territorial limits of the United States" but in order to protect the United States and its citizens from "all the horrors of savage massacre" perpetrated by the Seminole and their black allies. Because Governor Marot had fled to nearby Fort Carlos de Barrancas, Jackson attacked that fortification as well, forcing its capitulation. Believing that his conquests over the past two months had "put an end to all Indian wars," in late May Jackson headed back to Nashville.[12]

Rumors of Jackson's forays reached the newspapers in mid-June 1818, while official confirmation of his actions, written in Jackson's own hand, arrived in Washington on July 7. President Monroe called together his cabinet to discuss the administration's strategy in addressing the issue. Secretary of State John Quincy Adams defended Jackson, realizing that the general had made acquiring the Floridas from Spain that much easier. Secretary of War Calhoun, on the other hand, denounced the Tennessean for breaching the Constitution by making war without congressional authorization. He wanted Jackson censured. The rest of the cabinet, including

Crawford, joined Calhoun in this disapproval. After much debate Monroe sent Jackson a letter in which he offered to edit Jackson's correspondence to temper some of the aggressive language that he had used prior to invading Florida. Jackson declined the president's offer. He had only followed orders given to him, he argued, and he accepted the sole responsibility for what had transpired.[13]

A movement was already afoot in Congress to assign blame to Jackson. Politicians such as Representatives Thomas W. Cobb and Henry Clay, the House Speaker, and Senators John Forsyth and Abner Lacock were unflagging in their criticism of Jackson and their demands for his censure and removal. Jackson had taken unconstitutional action that threatened not only war with Great Britain and Spain but also the very future of the United States, they said. In a 20 January 1819 speech given on the House floor, Clay articulated what many of Jackson's critics believed, "Remember that Greece had her Alexander, Rome had her Caesar, England her Cromwell, France her Bonaparte, and, that, if we would escape the rock on which they split, we must avoid their errors."[14]

Throughout the congressional debate over the invasion of Florida, Jackson fumed. John Henry Eaton, a U.S. senator who had served as one of Jackson's military aides following the War of 1812, cautioned his former commander to stay in Nashville to avoid the "little finesses and cunning practiced . . . by the little glow worms" in Washington. Jackson ignored Eaton's advice, however, and traveled to the nation's capital to observe "one of the basest combinations ever formed." The alleged conspiracy included Clay, Crawford, and General Winfield Scott. Rumors had Jackson threatening to cut off his opponents' ears and challenging Clay to a duel. In the end the House voted against condemning the hotheaded Old Hickory for his actions in Florida. A bloc of approximately one hundred representatives (roughly 60 percent of the House membership) voted down several censure resolutions; there were simply too many Jackson supporters to carry the day. In anticipation of the Adams-Onís Treaty of 1819, ceding Florida to the United States for the payment of five million dollars in residents' claims, the Senate tabled its report condemning Jackson. The document implied, however, that his actions in Florida had been prompted partly by interest in land speculation for financial gain. The reality was that Jackson had helped the United States take an important step in territorial expansion, and the Senate was unwilling to chastise him for the result.[15]

Significantly, at the same time the Senate was discussing what to do about Jackson's actions in Florida, Congress was also debating the matter of slavery in the Louisiana Territory. Bills to consider statehood for the Missouri portion of the Louisiana Territory had been introduced in 1818, its residents assuming that slavery, which had been allowed in the territory since it had been acquired as part of the Louisiana Purchase in 1803, would continue to exist. That expectation was challenged, however, when House member James Tallmadge Jr. of New York introduced an amendment to the Missouri statehood application that coupled a limit on slave importation into Missouri with gradual emancipation for those already living there. A lively debate ensued, with one southern congressman "prophetically accusing Tallmadge of having 'kindled a flame which all the waters of the ocean cannot put out, which seas of blood can only extinguish.'"[16]

John Eaton kept Jackson updated on the "unpleasant question" concerning the Missouri debates. With the Senate having decided in early February 1820 not to restrict slavery, Jackson told John Coffee, "Congress may now begin to do something for the National benefit, as yet they have done nothing, but spend the public money in useless debate." To Andrew Donelson he revealed a prescient trepidation. Jackson feared that the discussion of Missouri was "the entering wedge to separate the union," as "the Eastern interest" competed with the "southern & western states" for "political asscendency, and power." "I hope I may not live to see the evills that must grow out of this wicked design of Demagogues," he confided to his nephew in April, "who talk about humanity, but whose sole object is self aggrandisement regardless of the happiness of the nation." When the U.S. House refused in late 1820 to admit Missouri unless it removed a clause in its proposed constitution barring free blacks and mulattoes, Jackson told President Monroe, "I shudder for the consequences" if the lower chamber did not "see the evil of this rash despotic act."[17]

The Missouri Compromise settled for the short term the sectional divisiveness over slavery in the Louisiana Purchase. Congress granted Missouri statehood with the provision that it would not enforce its constitutional exclusion of free blacks and mulattoes from entering the state. Congress also prohibited slavery north of the 36°30' line in the Louisiana Territory, excepting Missouri. This congressional compromise ultimately did not distract the United States from its goal of acquiring Spanish Florida. After nearly two years of delay on the part of Spain, the ratification of the Adams-Onís Treaty drew near in early 1821. With the pending transfer of land, President Monroe offered Jackson appointment as the territorial governor of Florida in recognition of his military service. He accepted the post, in part because Secretary of War Calhoun was in the process of recommending reductions in the size of the military, and Jackson's military post was targeted for elimination. According to his nephew Andrew Donelson, Jackson was also looking forward to "the promotion and assistance of his friends." Although insisting that he wanted to retire, Jackson agreed to accept the appointment. He noted, however, that because of his finances, he planned to "resign as soon as the Government is organized and in full operation."[18]

Assuming the governorship took longer than Jackson expected. He received his commission on 10 March 1821. In mid-April he, along with Rachel, Junior, and several other relatives and friends, traveled to New Orleans, where the hero of January 8 was feted. Joined by Andrew J. Donelson, the party then traveled to Blakely, Alabama, "a sickly town" that they were "anxious" to leave. They moved quickly to nearby Montpelier, where Jackson remained from May 9 to June 16 because diplomatic obstacles postponed the official transfer of Florida to the United States. Jackson believed that the delay was actually the result of the Spanish desire to import "a number of Africans into Florida before the change of Government," which he called "a dreaded evil." Congress had already noted its concern about the illegal slave trading taking place in Florida, particularly in the vicinity of Amelia Island in East Florida, and wanted it stopped, presumably to protect the value of slaves owned in the states bordering the Spanish territory. Jackson ordered three of his companions—his aide-de-camp, Richard K. Call; his physician, Dr. James C. Bronaugh; and a Pennsylvania lawyer, Henry M. Brackenridge—to travel to Pensacola as his representatives to Governor José Maria Callava. The Spanish governor refused to cede Florida until he received official orders from authorities in Havana, Cuba. His intransigence exasperated Jackson, who chastised the Spanish governor for his tardiness. Cooler heads eventually prevailed, and on July 17 Jackson took control of Florida.[19]

Jackson's administration lasted less than four months and was disappointing in all respects. President Monroe appointed none of the men whom Jackson had recommended for prominent government posts in Florida. Former Spanish governor Callava refused to turn over documents related to the settlement of a deceased Spaniard's estate, leading Jackson to arrest Callava and seize the papers by force. Rachel was miserable, and Jackson's creation of laws to reduce swearing and gambling failed to make his pious wife happy in the "heathen land." His recommendation that the United States remove the Creek from Florida was met with Secretary of War Calhoun's note that President Monroe believed it "improper" at the moment. Already determined to make his stay in Florida as short as possible, Jackson used these events to leave Pensacola in early October. Back at the Hermitage, he tendered his resignation to Monroe on November 13.[20]

Jackson bluntly gave the reasons for his resignation. "I am truly wearied of public life," he wrote the president. "I am happy at so seasonable a time to be able to embrace that relaxation which my enfeebled constitution requires." He also said he needed to "resusitate my declining fortune to inable it to support me in my declining years." Jackson clearly intended his resignation from the governorship to signify his retirement from public life to pursue his plantation interests. Yet William H. Crawford identified him as a potential threat in the 1824 presidential election. His congressional allies initiated an investigation into Jackson's tenure as Florida's governor in 1821, and there was even talk of impeaching the general. These developments caused Jackson to reconsider his decision, but he was too late: Monroe had already accepted his resignation, convinced that separating from Jackson was a prudent political maneuver. This awkward end to Jackson's governorship confirmed to him that the Washington establishment was not his friend.[21]

IX

"I Feel an Unusual Sympathy for Him"

Jackson's commitment to his public career kept him away from home for long periods of time during the 1810s and 1820s. These frequent and lengthy absences, while not unusual for male members of the southern gentry, challenged his mastery of those closest to him. Nevertheless, he remained the patriarch of his family as he exhibited the paternalistic attention common to many southern planters. He also used kinship ties to construct networks of men who helped maintain his gentry status and expand his public influence.[1]

Rachel was frequently on Jackson's mind during his years away in the military and on the national stage. He thanked his wife for her "determined resolution, to bear out our separation with fortitude." On another occasion he assured her that although he had to tend to his responsibilities as a military commander, "my heart is with you." Rachel's responses were often maudlin and filled with pious reminders. "Do not My beloved Husband let the love of Country fame and honour make you forgit you have me," she wrote shortly after Jackson left in early 1813. "How many pangs how many heart rending Sighs has your absence cost me." Upon learning of the death of her nephew Alexander Donelson, Rachel was inconsolable about her separation from her husband: "My prayers is unceaseing how long o Lord will I remain so unhappy no rest no Ease I Cannot sleepe all can come home but you I never wanted to see you so mutch in my life."[2]

Junior's well-being and education also concerned Jackson in his absence. "Tell Andrew I fear he will think I am runaway from him," he wrote Rachel in 1814. In another letter Jackson conveyed the message, "Tell him his sweet papa labours hard to get money to educate him, but when he learns & becomes a great man, his sweet papa will be amply rewarded for all his care, expence, & pains." In partial fulfillment of his promise, Jackson sent Junior to study with Joseph Priestley in Nashville.[3]

To ease Rachel and Junior's loneliness, Jackson sent captured Indian infant boys to the Hermitage. The first was Theodore, who died in early 1814. His replacement was Lyncoya, a Creek infant left orphaned by the carnage at Tallushatchee. "A little Indian boy," Jackson told Rachel, had been found in his dead mother's arms and needed someone to care for him; his own people "would have nothing to do with him but wanted him to be killed." "He is a Savage [but one] that fortune has thrown in my h[ands]," Jackson wrote. "He may have been given to me for some Valuable purpose." Lyncoya seemed to have a difficult time adjusting to his new life. "I have been much hurt to see him there with the negroes, like a lost sheep without a shepherd," Jackson observed. Charley, a third Indian boy, arrived at the Hermitage in March 1814. He was given to Jackson by a White Stick Creek with the English name of James Fife. Jackson intended Charley for his nephew and ward Andrew Donelson, but Rachel told her husband that their son was jealous of his cousin's gift. "I told him we Could not keepe so maney" was her explanation to Junior. Perhaps to indulge her son, Rachel allowed him to keep the young Indian boy until Lyncoya's arrival. Rachel reported that Junior was "much pleased with his Charley," but her son disagreed: "I like Charly but he will not mind me."[4]

Jackson's actions toward Native Americans during this period were by any definition contradictory. On the one hand, he endorsed the slaughter of Indians during and after the War of 1812 in the name of national security; on the other hand, Jackson rescued infant Indian boys and sent them to the Hermitage to be raised alongside his other wards. There is no question that, like many white southerners, Jackson was furious at what he perceived as Native American unrest threatening the stability of Tennessee, the South, and the nation. He had grown up in an area permeated with distrust of Native Americans, and his early experiences in Middle Tennessee had provided no reason for him to change his attitude. While scholars have speculated widely about his motivation in keeping young Indian boys, Jackson's comment about Lyncoya gives the only substantial insight into his reasoning. "When I reflect that he as to his relations is so much like myself," he wrote Rachel in December 1813, "I feel an unusual sympathy for him."[5]

In addition to Rachel and Junior, Jackson also considered the men around him kin. The term that best describes his relationship with them is *patron,* an older, wealthier male who entered into "a non-contractual arrangement" with younger, less well-off men (called "clients") in which both sides "agree[d] on the basis of mutual interest and cordiality to do favors for each other." In other words, Jackson took male relatives and friends under his wing, serving as a public and private role model and mentor. He gained their loyalty and service; they in turn received access to power and the promise of future social, economic, and political advancement. The patron-client relationship was "supposed to be voluntary, with merit and affection, not material gain, the basis." Realistically, money was often a factor in these relationships, but emotions and political calculation played prominent roles as well.[6]

The patron-client relationship was not unique to southern society, but the hierarchical structure and honor culture of the South made it particularly important in Jackson's life. "[Imagining] himself an infallible judge of others," as one historian observed, Old Hickory placed great value in these relationships, so much so that failure to please him usually resulted in a permanent severing of ties. Although these relationships were mutually beneficial, Jackson's patriarchal authority required subordinates to demonstrate unquestioned loyalty to gain the advantages of his leadership. Jackson's replacement of his absent natural family ties with the construction of a kinship network accentuated his prickliness about fidelity. It also explains why he craved these relationships: they were exactly what had allowed him to escape his social position in the Waxhaws, become a lawyer in North Carolina, and establish himself as a member of the Middle Tennessee gentry. Now his role was to play the patron for the next generation of leaders.[7]

Between his arrival in Tennessee in 1788 and the eve of the War of 1812, Jackson advanced socially to the point that he built a client network on which he could depend. Prominent among his early contacts were John Overton and John Coffee. A year older than Jackson, Overton for years played an important role in supporting his friend's social advancement. That support continued during the controversy over Jackson's Florida invasion between 1818 and 1820. Overton allegedly saw President Monroe's letter authorizing Jackson to move into Spanish territory, and he defended the invasion in a pseudonymous publication that argued for the pragmatic reality of United States territorial expansion. Not politically ambitious himself, Coffee, Jackson's nephew-in-law, was nevertheless an important factor in Jackson's success in the 1810s. He led Tennessee volunteers during the Creek campaign of 1813–1814 and was present at the climactic Battle of New Orleans, earning him the rank of brigadier general. After the war not only did Coffee act as alternate commissioner in surveying the territory taken from the Creek, but President Monroe also appointed him surveyor of the northern district of the Mississippi Territory. Coffee used this post to speculate extensively in land for himself and his friends, including Jackson.[8]

Three other early clients who continued to support Jackson in the 1810s and beyond were George Washington Campbell, Felix Grundy, and Hugh Lawson White. Campbell served as U.S. representative, senator, and judge during the early 1800s; James Madison appointed him secretary of the Treasury in 1814, during his second presidential term. As a U.S. House member in 1804, Campbell recommended that President Jefferson appoint Jackson governor of the Orleans Territory, which in 1812 became the state of Louisiana. In the U.S. Senate he was one of the most strident War Hawks advocating war with Britain and supporting territorial expansion, which Jackson undoubtedly appreciated. Campbell also looked out for Jackson's private interests. As a state judge in the early 1810s, he warned Jackson that his title to the Allison lands was not clear and free. Campbell also helped Jackson's nephew Andrew Donelson secure his appointment to West Point in 1817. Grundy was a well-regarded lawyer who had moved to Nashville from Kentucky; he served in the U.S. House during the War of 1812. Shortly after moving to Tennessee, he defended Jackson during his indictment for assaulting Samuel D. Jackson in 1807. He also sold him two slaves in 1810. Like Campbell, Grundy was a staunch War Hawk and supported the Hero of New Orleans during the Florida invasion. Close to William Blount, Jackson's own patron, White was a state superior court justice who served with Jackson for a number of years on the bench. During the War of 1812 he mediated a dispute between Jackson and another Tennessee general, John Cocke, over Cocke's inability to provide adequate supplies for his troops. When his brother-in-law, John Williams, criticized Jackson's invasion of Florida, White made a public defense that Jackson called "the best penned thing I ever saw . . . [it] shews his independence, friendship, & his Justice." Jackson's relationships with these three men were not as deep as with others, but they were extremely important in building a potential political machine.[9]

During the War of 1812 other young men also came under Jackson's patronage. Prior to their falling out in 1813, Thomas Hart Benton engendered Jackson's trust by prosecuting the man who had killed Patton Anderson, one of Jackson's Tennessee business acquaintances. No doubt that gesture helped Jackson decide to appoint Benton as one of his aides in 1812. Several other men attached to Jackson were involved in writing his postwar biography. Edward Livingston, a former New York City mayor, moved to New Orleans in 1804. There he opened a law practice and speculated in land. Already acquainted with Jackson, Livingston began research on a biography shortly after the Battle of New Orleans, but he apparently never progressed beyond that point. John Reid, a Williamson County lawyer who had served as Jackson's aide-de-camp and secretary during the war, then took up the project. Reid completed only four chapters before he died from pneumonia in January 1816. The task of finishing the biography fell to John Eaton, who had also served with Jackson during the war. The volume was published in 1817, and subsequent revised editions appeared in the 1820s, when Jackson ran for the presidency. Eaton's service proved his loyalty and allowed him to become one of Jackson's closest friends in the coming years as they engaged in land speculation and political maneuvering.[10]

Additional protégés emerged during the conflict with Britain. William Carroll, whose duel with Jesse Benton precipitated the 1813 brawl in downtown Nashville, was a member of Jackson's militia when the war began. He served with distinction under him during the Creek and New Orleans campaigns and later was elected Tennessee's governor six times. A Virginia transplant to East Tennessee, Sam Houston lived with the Cherokee and took a turn as a schoolteacher while still a teenager. At age twenty, at the beginning of the War of 1812, Houston joined the army. Attached to Jackson's forces, Lieutenant Houston fought at the Battle of Horseshoe Bend, where he was shot in the arm with a musket ball and in the groin with an arrow. Jackson personally asked him to remain out of the fight as he recovered, but Houston ignored the request. He made an impression by his courage, which Jackson remembered when Houston was himself looking to enter the Nashville gentry. William B. Lewis was yet another loyal client. Lewis married Margaret Lewis, one of several daughters of the prominent early Tennessean William Terrell Lewis (no relation). Jackson and the elder Lewis had occasionally gambled together, and that friendship carried over to the new son-in-law. Margaret's death early in their marriage left William B. Lewis with sizable property holdings, which proved helpful to Jackson during the War of 1812. Lewis's appointment as assistant deputy quartermaster in 1812 was partly due to his financial connections, which allowed Lewis to draw on credit when the state government failed to provision Jackson's troops properly.[11]

Jackson's friendship with these men, only some of whom were related but all of whom he considered family, was instrumental to his political success as he moved onto the national stage. Three kinship networks were especially important. The first was Jackson's personal network, the Donelson family. Many members of this group, such as John Coffee, had already played prominent roles in his public success; others would make important contributions in the future. A second, smaller kinship network was that of Hugh Lawson White, whose brother-in-law was John Overton. The final network belonged to William B. Lewis. He was not the only Jackson client to marry a daughter of William Terrell Lewis: John H. Eaton married Myra Lewis, and a later Jackson client, Alfred Balch, married Mary Lewis. Eaton and Lewis would form the core of Jackson's campaign team as he ran for the presidency in the 1820s. Even those clients not attached to Jackson via kinship networks were often part of important families. Edward Livingston's brother, Roger, for example, was a member of the committee that drafted the Declaration of Independence; Felix Grundy's sister-in-law and eldest daughter married into the prominent Nashville family, the McGavocks; William Carroll married Cecilia M. Bradford, Dolley Madison's cousin; and George W. Campbell married Harriet Stoddert, the daughter of the first secretary of the navy, Josiah Stoddert. Livingston excepted, Jackson's protégés were all Tennesseans when they entered his world. While his immediate client network was still confined to his home state at this point, its members and their connections proved crucial to Jackson's national political career.[12]

Anticipating his retirement in the late 1810s, Jackson decided to build a new house on his Hermitage land. According to William B. Lewis, Rachel chose the site. The two-story house was simple in design, with each floor containing four rooms separated by a central hallway. A garden for Rachel was created on the east side of the house, with slave cabins located in the rear, away from the front entrance. Intended as a retreat for an aging southerner to supervise his plantation, the Hermitage instead served as the locus of family and politics.[13]

During the initial years of Jackson's return to Nashville, the Hermitage buzzed with activity. Several of his many wards still lived there, while others were away at college. Of foremost concern was Junior, to whom Jackson freely dispensed advice. First and foremost, he wanted his son to take care of Rachel. "You owe her a debt of felial gratitude that you can never pay," Jackson reminded him. Junior was also "never to promise to do any thing without due reflection & when you make a promise never fail to execute it." The dictates continued to flow: "Never on any occasion whatever depart from the truth, be Just to all, learn your Book, become well informed." The result would be that he would "be esteemed by all." Along with such a torrent of advice, Jackson also sent his son updates on the management of the Hermitage and on neighborhood gossip.[14]

Junior's education remained a major concern as the boy entered adolescence. After placing his son with private tutors, Jackson strove to ensure his continued education by enrolling him at nearby Cumberland College. Already schooled in French and Spanish, Junior took dancing lessons and attended lectures by Robert Goodacre, a leading astronomer then touring the United States. He already exhibited some of the traits, however, that would cause his father many headaches later in life. Junior was never good with money, and in 1825 he charged $309 to his father's account with a local merchant. An unseemly amount, one scholar estimated it was sufficient to provision "the average Tennessee family for a year." At the very least the size of this expenditure flew in the face of everything Jackson was trying to teach his wards about being economical.[15]

Andrew Jackson Hutchings, the son of Jackson's late nephew-in-law and former business partner, John Hutchings, also began living at the Hermitage in the late 1810s. Shortly before his death in 1817, the elder Hutchings appointed Jackson as his son's guardian and placed under his control the family's Alabama lands and slaves. Because Jackson was away so much, direct oversight of Hutchings's Alabama plantation fell to John

Coffee, who resided nearby. Young Hutchings lived at the Hermitage, and the advice that Jackson sent to Junior he intended also for Hutchings. Even more than Junior, Hutchings caused his guardian problems. While in Washington in early 1825, Jackson wrote William B. Lewis that he wanted Hutchings "under the charge of some good man who will controll him." Jackson's choice was Philip Lindsley, the newly appointed president of Cumberland College. Hutchings's tutelage under Lindsley did not last, however; he was expelled in 1828 "for bad conduct." Jackson engaged a local tutor for his ward but confessed his inability to manage him: "I fear when out of my sight he will not be controlled, his conduct has given me much pain."[16]

A third young man residing at the Hermitage during these years was Lyncoya, the Creek infant whom Jackson had sent to Junior as a "pett," a name Jackson often used to refer to children. Jackson provided Lyncoya with the same educational opportunities as Junior and Hutchings, sending him to private tutors and Cumberland College. Jackson even wanted to secure his appointment to West Point and asked Rachel to have him write a response. Several weeks later Lyncoya sent a letter that parroted Jackson's advice given so often about what it meant to be part of his family, "Since he is not told that [when?] a big man, he must have the white mans [sk]in, but to be just, to [avoid] only evil actions, to do good, is to be the *bigerest* of men, he hopes to have this stature of the ma[n.]" When the cadet appointment was not forthcoming, Lyncoya worked as a saddler's apprentice in Nashville. He died on 1 June 1828 of unknown causes; Jackson's extant correspondence does not mention his passing, although an obituary appeared in several newspapers.[17]

Like Hutchings, other Jackson wards faced difficulty in pursuing their educations. Anthony W. Butler, the son of Edward and Isabella Butler, initially enrolled at Yale College but decided to transfer to Princeton in the spring of 1819. Butler's "breach of promise" and requests for additional money to purchase watches caused Jackson "to lose all confidence in him." "When a youth becomes so far lost to propriety, as to forfeight his word to his friend," he wrote Andrew Donelson, "he is on the road to ruin." Much to his patron's chagrin, Butler did not reform his ways. In 1823 he applied to Jackson for money to pay courts costs and fines associated with whipping another man. While Jackson might have applauded Butler for meeting the man's insult with violence, he was disturbed by his lack of financial acuity. "If you cannot live upon seven hundred & fifty dollars a year," which was Butler's annual allowance from a deceased relative, Jackson asked, "how is it possible for me, to support my family & four students when my farm last year did not produce me that sum?" Butler's education was costing twice that of Jackson's other wards, yet "still you have been pressed for funds." This contentious relationship ended tragically in 1824, when Butler died while traveling back to Yale from New Orleans.[18]

Holding out hope that a military education would help his nephew Daniel S. Donelson, Jackson appealed to Secretary of War Calhoun for a West Point appointment. Daniel "is an orphan and without means of his own to finish his education . . . He is a fine material for a military man–large, portly, and a good constitution." Daniel entered West Point in the summer of 1821. By the end of the next year, however, he informed his uncle that he intended to resign his commission and enter Yale College. Before advising his nephew, Jackson consulted with Daniel's brother, Andrew; his grandmother, Sarah Michie Smith; and his stepfather, James Sanders. All three opposed Daniel's transfer to Yale. In the end Daniel heeded their advice and stayed at West Point, from which he graduated in 1825.[19]

Jackson's difficulties with Junior, Hutchings, Anthony Butler, and Daniel Donelson were softened somewhat by the course taken by two other wards: Edward G. W. Butler and Andrew Jackson Donelson. Anthony Butler had disappointed Jackson, but his brother, Edward, chose a different path. Having entered West Point in 1816, Edward committed himself to his studies and graduated in 1820. Like all of Jackson's male wards, he spent too much money, but unlike his brother, he was apologetic for his lack of economy and promised to repay Jackson when his land inheritance was settled. When Congress cut funding for the U.S. Army, Edward informed his patron that he was considering joining the Russian army. Jackson admonished him to stay in his present position and wait out the financial tightening; "things will not always be as they are," he reminded Edward. Despite losing three children within a year, Edward assisted Jackson during the 1828 presidential campaign with reports from his residence in Cincinnati.[20]

After graduating from West Point and accompanying his uncle to Florida, Andrew Donelson entered Transylvania University in Lexington,

Kentucky, to study law. There he evaluated potential slaves for Jackson's purchase and updated him on the political debates over economic reform taking place in the state. An infrequent writer while at West Point, Andrew finally embraced his uncle's advice about writing often, but, like Junior, financial frugality escaped him. Nevertheless, Jackson had high hopes for him. He sent him missive after missive outlining what constituted honorable and virtuous conduct and explained that he had placed Andrew at West Point and Transylvania to help him build his own political and social networks. "I look forward," Jackson informed his nephew, "to the time when you will be selected to preside over the destinies of america." To help Andrew after his September 1824 wedding to his first cousin, Emily, Jackson presented him with the deed to just over 348 acres of land adjoining the Hermitage property and a male slave, John Fulton, whom Jackson had purchased in Alabama.[21]

Jackson also supported Andrew and Daniel Donelson in a dispute with their stepfather, James Sanders. During Daniel's vacillation in 1822–1823 over whether to stay at West Point or go to Yale, the question of how to continue funding his education arose. Andrew Donelson suggested selling part of the land left to the brothers by their maternal grandfather, Daniel Smith, but Jackson opposed the sale. He promised to continue paying for Daniel Donelson's schooling, wherever he chose to attend. After Daniel graduated in 1825, his brother asked their stepfather to satisfy a financial obligation undertaken during his course of study. Sanders refused, and a legal suit ensued over the disputed land. An arbitration committee ruled in favor of the Donelson brothers. Notable in the family infighting was Jackson's silence. Given Jackson's previous problems with Sanders and his support of his nephews, there is no question that he would have intervened if he deemed it necessary. One can only surmise that he was letting Andrew and Daniel exercise their masculinity in the fight with their stepfather, and he was no doubt satisfied with their moxie.[22]

Jackson's relationship with these young men often followed the expectations of southern genteel society. Social custom dictated that family patriarchs use college attendance to test their young male relatives' ability to demonstrate independent thinking and practice leadership. They often employed guilt and pleading letters to push the young men in the right direction. They also tried to teach their male dependents how to manage money, both for their own sake and for that of their future families. All of these efforts were meant to help Jackson, as patriarch, shape his wards' masculinity to make them successful members of the southern gentry, which would in turn reflect well on him. Wards, like clients, had to show potential; men such as Jackson "did not feel obliged to move any numb-skull ahead."[23]

Jackson's attempts, however, were frequently met with passive resis-tance, exposing the tension between the abstract social expectations of southern patriarchs and the reality of their wards' expressions of mascu-linity and independence. Younger men recognized that southern honor culture required them to display "manly autonomy." They could not be-come "obvious sycophant[s]" in a society that expected genteel men to act independently. Yet the irony of southern honor was apparent in "the dis-crepancy between honor as obedience to superior rank and the contrary duty to achieve place for oneself and family." Because openly defying their patriarch and benefactor was a difficult proposition, they frequently acted out or ignored his admonitions. Jackson failed to realize the impetus for his wards' actions, perhaps because his own consuming ambition to climb to the top required hard work, something that was largely missing from the life he gave his wards.[24]

X

"A Great Field Is Now Open"

Jackson was not just a concerned husband and father, a paternal protector of infant Indians, and a patron to his clients. He was also a planter. Although not strictly an absentee owner, Jackson faced challenges managing his plantations and slaves that were common to public men who frequently traveled away from home for months on end. He relied on friends and family to manage his crops and slaves, all the while speculating in more land to expand his property. The financial downturn of 1819 exposed the fragility of southern plantation life and demonstrated Jackson's dependence on his network.[1]

Being away from the Hermitage for months at a time required Jackson to write Rachel about the management of his plantation, often sending instructions through her to his overseer. "I would be glad to hear how my overseer [Mr. Nollyboy] conducts," he told Rachel in 1813, "whether he has come up to his contract & whether he has complied with his promise in his attention to you." When reports reached Jackson that one of his male slaves, Sandy, was causing trouble, he expressed his hope that Nollyboy "has done his duty, and amply punished him." Jackson's hope was not realized, so he dismissed the overseer. "You will no longer be pestered with his neglect or impertinence," he assured Rachel. He asked her to tell John Fields, Nollyboy's replacement, "to have as much land cleared as he can, to take care of my stock, and see that you are comfortable." He was not, however, "to abuse [C]lum," one of the slaves. Rachel was also authorized to negotiate with an associate in nearby Gallatin for the leasing out of Dinwiddie, Jackson's enslaved horse trainer, and Truxton, his prized bay. Rachel reported on the slaves' health and informed her husband, "If I live we will own fewer of them for theay vex me often and in my situation it is hurteful."[2]

Male relatives and associates periodically checked on Rachel and the plantation. In late 1814 James Jackson, a longtime business associate, updated Andrew Jackson on his horses and the progress of the search for a new overseer. James Jackson and Robert Hays also informed him that one of his slaves, Aaron, had been shot by a neighbor after allegedly trespassing on his property and attacking him with a knife. In late 1815 and early 1816 Robert Butler reported on a bout of illness that claimed the life of one of Jackson's female slaves and left "several others sick but none dangerous." While Jackson served as Florida's governor in 1821, Richard Ivy Easter "made particular Enquiry how your Black family were" while visiting the Hermitage.[3]

Expanding his slaveholdings became an important goal for Jackson during these years. By 1812 he owned around twenty slaves at the Hermitage, and he continued to acquire more. In September 1814 he purchased five slaves who had been owned by one of the victims in the attack on Fort Mims and three more from a Pensacola resident. Jackson bought another slave three months later. When he and John Hutchings bought land at Melton's Bluff, Alabama, in November 1816, a male slave, Jame, was included in the sale; a female slave, Jenny, was also sold to the two partners in a separate transaction. An additional eight slaves were added to Jackson's slaveholdings between 1818 and 1822. All told, Jackson invested at least $5,599 (approximately $79,000 in 2010 U.S. dollars) in slave property during these years. While Jackson did not appear to have the extra thirty slaves to sell that Edward Livingston thought he did in 1816, he certainly had enough to work his plantations.[4]

Owning slaves and controlling them were two different matters. Runaway slaves posed significant problems for Jackson during these years. One male slave, Jesse, ran away in early 1812, leading Jackson to pay a $20 reward and $22.50 for sixty-eight days of confinement for the man after his capture. Another male slave, Ned (b. c. 1784), ran away in August 1815; Jackson offered a twenty-five-dollar reward for his return. In 1820 Jackson's agent, James Jackson Hanna, purchased five slaves for him in Portsmouth, Virginia. Hanna told Jackson that he "was rather taken with" one of the slaves, Tom, who, despite a limp, "will Make as good a field Negroe as any I have purchased. He has got about Sense enough to do What he is told, & Strength to do any thing." Within the year Tom had run away from the Hermitage back to Virginia, as had Ned (b. c. 1798), one of the other slaves whom Hanna purchased. Jackson apparently considered purchasing Ned's wife, living in Virginia, to keep him from running away, but that acquisition seems not to have occurred. It appears, however, that Tom and Ned were returned to the Hermitage to continue their forced servitude.[5]

Other slaves defied Jackson's mastery less openly but not without the threat of punishment. Female slaves were particularly rebellious. Robert Hays wrote in December 1814 that the Hermitage overseer, John Fields, "canot command the negro women," who were working too slowly in harvesting oats. Fields was still having trouble the following fall. "Your wenches as usual commenced open war," Robert Butler reported, "and they have been brought to order by *Hickory oil*," a reference to whipping. In 1821, while the Jacksons were living in Florida, Rachel told her husband that her slave, Betty, "has been putting on some airs, and been guilty of a great deal of impudence." Jackson had purchased Betty and her mother, Hannah, in 1794; thus, she had been in the Jackson household for almost thirty years. Betty must have previously defied her owner, as Jackson told his doctor, James C. Bronaugh, that she was "capable of being a good & valluable servant, but to have her so, she must be ruled with the cowhide." He instructed Bronaugh, his nephew Andrew Donelson, and his steward, Ephraim A. Blain, that if she stepped out of line, then they were to punish her with fifty lashes at "the public whipping post." The sin that precipitated this harsh response was Betty's washing clothes for individuals outside of the Jackson household "without the express permission of her Mistress."[6]

At times, however, Jackson's treatment of slaves seemed as contradictory as his actions toward Native Americans. He expressed concern about Nollybrook's treatment of Sandy, for example, and on another occasion he grew upset over an overseer's abuse of a slave who appears either to have been elderly or in some way disabled. He also considered reuniting slave families, as he tried to do with Ned. Yet Jackson forced Ned to leave his wife behind in Virginia, the man eventually marrying the defiant slave Betty. Another example of Jackson's concern occurred in 1819. James Houston, Sam Houston's cousin, wrote Jackson that he had "in Possession two negroes a son & daughter of old Peter that I am informed you own." A mutual acquaintance had told him that Jackson "wanted the family all together & had authorized him to purchase mine." Upon receiving an estimated sale price of eighteen hundred dollars for the five slaves, Jackson replied that "if funds could be raised I would take them." The family does not appear to have been reunited, however, probably because the money needed to purchase them was dependent on Jackson's failing business prospects in Alabama.[7]

At this time in his life Jackson's mind-set reflected the attitudes of many slave owners living in the Lower South. Where a benevolent form of paternalism, with its reluctance to use violence against slaves except when necessary, was emerging in the Upper South, slave owners in the Lower South saw things differently, at least in the early 1800s. The rapid influx of slaves via the domestic slave trade caused consternation among planters living in Alabama, Florida, Georgia, Louisiana, Mississippi, and South Carolina. They sought to maintain control over their society, and that often meant using violence against slaves. Jackson epitomized these sentiments. Benevolent expressions toward his slaves were rare; much more frequent was the episodic violence that he authorized or endorsed. It was a risk, of course, but like other southern slave owners, Jackson strove to find a balance that demonstrated his power while not inciting active, organized slave resistance.[8]

During these years Jackson's involvement in a lawsuit caused him to consider selling the Hermitage. To satisfy David Allison's mortgage of eighty-five thousand acres to a Philadelphia creditor, Norton Pryor, in 1802, Jackson, acting as Pryor's agent, purchased the land. He received ten thousand acres as payment, which he subdivided and sold at a substantial profit. Jackson guaranteed buyers that he possessed clear title to the land, promising to buy back the land at its current value if he were wrong. In 1808 Pryor gave Andrew Erwin, a Bedford County land speculator and trader, and his partner, James Patton, title to forty thousand acres of the Allison land. The other thirty-five thousand acres went to Joseph Anderson, who had succeeded Jackson in the Senate in 1798. Sometime in 1811 Jackson was warned that the men who sold the land to Allison were claiming that the court had not been authorized to grant him its clear title. If true, then Jackson was financially responsible for any disputed claims for the entire eighty-five thousand acres. He set out for Georgia to meet with Allison's brothers and settle the issue. The Allison brothers agreed to sell their claim on the land to Jackson for five hundred dollars and the release of Allison's heirs from future financial entanglement; this land included the acreage purchased by Erwin. Efforts to resolve the competing claims held by Jackson and Erwin led to a decade-long legal proceeding and an even longer-lasting political quarrel.[9]

Jackson's uncertainty about the result of the lawsuit prompted him to entertain offers for the Hermitage. He estimated that his land, livestock, furniture, tools, and forty slaves he was willing to part with were worth nearly seventy thousand dollars. "The interest of this sale would suffi-ciently support me when I retire to private life," he wrote his business as-sociate, James Jackson, who advised him to hold off on the widespread sale of most of his property. The exception was his slaves. "You have much too great a quantity of Negroe property," James argued. If he sold off his ex-cess slaves, the general would find that "the remaining Negroes & stock would produce more profit from your farm." Jackson reconsidered and kept his Hermitage property, but he did not heed his friend's advice about relinquishing his slaves.[10]

Additionally, Andrew Jackson used his knowledge of the lands that he seized from the southeastern Indians to benefit himself and his friends. He agreed to finance or serve as security for Daniel Parker, a fellow military officer, in purchasing land in Alabama. Jackson assured another interested party, Francis Smith, that John Coffee, recently appointed surveyor of the northern Mississippi Territory, would work quickly to bring the land in his district to market. "Should you be inclined to invest funds in those lands," Jackson said, "it will afford me pleasure to give you any aid in my power." Jackson concluded by telling Smith, "This section of country present[s] to the capitalist greater prospects of advantage—than any other[.] what little I can command will be invested in land in that quarter." Jackson also part-nered with James C. Bronaugh, John Coffee, James Gadsden, and James Jackson in their ventures to purchase land in Alabama via the Yahoo/Mammoth and Cypress land companies. In November 1816 he and John Hutchings bought land on Melton's Bluff, located in Lawrence County in the northwestern part of the state. Jackson purchased another plantation at Evans Spring, in Lauderdale County, in March 1818. At the same time he acquired property nearby for his ward Andrew J. Hutchings. Later that year Jackson bought a section near Big Spring in Franklin (present-day Col-bert) County at two dollars an acre; his purchase was "hailed by the unani-mous shout of a numerous & mixed multitude" in attendance, he bragged.[11]

Jackson used his land in Tennessee and Alabama in the fashion typical of a southern planter. At the Hermitage his slaves grew cotton, corn, hemp, and tobacco, and they raised livestock. How much cotton was produced during these years is difficult to ascertain. In 1814 Rachel sold ten thousand pounds of seed cotton to two neighbors who owned a local spinning factory, netting a price of $4 per one hundred pounds. In 1821 the Hermitage's cotton brought in $551. Hemp, a labor-intensive crop, was produced on site to provide cloth and rope for baling cotton. As Jackson instructed Robert Butler in 1815, "Have as much hemp broke as will make a sufficient quanty of Bailing to Bale my cotton & set the wenches to spin it." He also tried tobacco in 1817, but it appears to have been a short-lived experiment. He had a similar failure in attempting to breed cows. Additionally, Jackson maintained a cotton gin and grain mill at the Hermitage.[12]

Jackson continued his lifelong love of horses, committing considerable resources to maintaining stables at the Hermitage. Numerous accounts exist of Jackson racing and betting on his horses, including Greyhound, Pacolet, and Truxton. In 1814, for instance, James Jackson informed the general that his seven-year-old, Pacolet, had defeated Doublehead four times in one-mile heats, with the stakes for each heat at four thousand dollars. Jackson's winnings helped offset the three thousand dollar–investment he had made in the horse. He also ensured that his horses' bloodlines were passed on by hiring them out for breeding. Jackson's interest in horses enabled him to cultivate business partnerships that benefited him in other ways as well. The Clover Bottom racetrack that Jackson co-owned in the early 1800s was one example of using horses to expand influence in the business world. Another was his business partnership with James Jackson, a noted horse breeder in his own right.[13]

Jackson faced considerable challenges in managing his Alabama plantations. John Hutchings supervised the Melton's Bluff farm with some initial success, Jackson predicting in June 1817 that it would produce up to ninety bales of cotton. By September his optimism had waned as sickness affected the slaves he had transferred there from the Hermitage. A change in overseers and the construction of a cotton gin on the property failed to make it profitable, and Jackson gave up on the enterprise the following year so he could concentrate on his Evans Spring plantation. Prospects there were not good either. By August 1819 he told James Gadsden that he hoped to rid himself of the farm. Runaway slaves and poor weather finally caused Jackson to sell this property to Richard C. Cross, one of Andrew Donelson's West Point classmates, for seventy-five hundred dollars. A similar experience at the Big Spring farm, worsened by corrupt and incompetent overseers, led to the sale of that property to Anthony Winston Jr. in late 1822.[14]

Questions about his motives in seizing land from Native Americans and Spaniards haunted Jackson throughout the late 1810s and early 1820s. His critics, including Andrew Erwin and John Williams, discovered that William B. Lewis was profiting from a salt lick located on ceded Chickasaw territory along the Big Sandy River in West Tennessee. They accused Jackson of negotiating the treaty merely to serve his friend's interest. Lewis vehemently denounced this charge under oath, and others supported his version, which disavowed Jackson's complicity in the alleged scheme. Jackson also denied accusations that he had invaded Florida to serve the interest of his and his friends' land speculation, but these public denials were disingenuous. Privately, he encouraged comrades and relatives to jump on the opportunity to turn a profit. "If our Mutual friends James Jackson & Capt [John] Donelson has not set out for Pensacola," he wrote Coffee, "say to them that real property has risen in Pensacola, and if they wish to sell, now is the time." To John Donelson, Jackson predicted that around Pensacola "a great field is now open to the real capitalist, and real property well situated in a few years must become very valluable."[15]

The Panic of 1819 exacerbated Jackson's financial challenges. Following the Napoleonic Wars, prices fell in Europe, but in the United States territorial expansion and the accompanying cotton boom, each fostered by Jackson's implementation of government policy to open up millions of acres of southern land for white settlement and cultivation, ameliorated the economic crisis. Then the speculative bubble collapsed in 1819. Cotton prices bottomed out, and foreign banks began pressing U.S. banks for payment of loans. To meet these obligations, domestic banks looked to their investors, such as land speculators (Jackson included) as well as aspiring yeoman farmers. Without the ability to pay their debts, farmers lost their property, including land, crops, and slaves. Even Jackson faced difficulty. He told Andrew Donelson, then a cadet at West Point, that Thomas Kirkman, a Philadelphia merchant and brother-in-law of James Jackson, was unable to provide him with the requested funds. "My dear young friend there never was such a pressure," he observed, "houses breaking—banks suspending payment—& all confidence between man & man destroyed."[16]

The panic reshaped Tennessee politics and revealed cracks in Jackson's client network. Several of Jackson's friends—namely, John H. Eaton, William B. Lewis, Pleasant M. Miller, John Overton, and Hugh Lawson White—controlled the banking movement in the state after the War of 1812 and spearheaded efforts to obtain a branch of the Second Bank of the United States for Nashville. When the depression hit, Tennesseans demanded financial relief and banking reform. Felix Grundy, representing Davidson County in the General Assembly, proposed a state-level loan office (essentially a state bank) to help those mired in debt satisfy their creditors. Most of Jackson's friends opposed this legislation, not wanting to cede their economic power. Jackson agreed with them, calling the bill unconstitutional. In the 1821 gubernatorial election William Carroll, who supported Grundy's proposed bank, defeated Jackson's neighbor and friend Edward Ward, who opposed it. Two years later Grundy defeated Jackson's lawyer Patrick H. Darby in election for a seat in the General Assembly. Caught between friends and politics, Jackson chose ideological opposition to the new state bank and backed the two losing candidates, Ward and Darby, at great cost to his friendships with Carroll and Grundy.[17]

Tennessee's political landscape also shifted in response to the festering quarrel between Jackson and Andrew Erwin. Convinced that William H. Crawford had been behind the U.S. Senate's criticism of his Florida invasion, Jackson looked for allies to help him undermine the Treasury secretary. He found help from John Clark, an anti-Crawfordite in Georgia who was investigating rumors that Crawford's friend and former Georgia governor David B. Mitchell had smuggled slaves into the United States through Amelia Island, located on the Florida-Georgia coastal border. Jackson approved of this investigation, as it also implicated Erwin in the scandal. Jackson wrote President Monroe in opposition to Erwin's appointment as a federal marshal in West Tennessee, criticizing his rival's smuggling activities in "inhuman & illegal traffic." The accusations against Erwin nearly prompted a duel with Eaton, who took offense at some published comments about himself, James Jackson, and Jenkin Whiteside, Andrew Jackson's lead lawyer in the suit against Erwin. Jackson and Erwin finally settled their legal dispute over the Allison lands in 1823, but its consequences reverberated in state and national politics for years.[18]

Meanwhile, Jackson lost the friendship of James Jackson, his business partner, and Patrick H. Darby, a member of Jackson's legal team, both men feeling financially injured by the Erwin settlement. Darby believed that Andrew Jackson had agreed to the settlement in order to secure Grundy's support for his election to the U.S. Senate. James Jackson openly broke with his former friend during the 1824 presidential campaign, citing his tariff votes as U.S. senator. More likely, however, it was the Erwin settlement that led to the separation.[19]

The enmity between Jackson and Erwin proved particularly important to Jackson's political future. Erwin and his kinship network were persistent and strident critics of Jackson. Senator John Williams, who married one of Hugh Lawson White's sisters, Melinda, was also the brother-in-law of Andrew Erwin's son, John Patton Erwin, a Nashville newspaper editor. Another of Andrew Erwin's sons, James, married Anne Clay, the daughter of Speaker of the House Henry Clay. With the connection to Clay, the Erwin kinship network extended its influence in opposition to Jackson beyond Tennessee to the national level.[20]

Historian Charles Sellers once argued that after 1804 "never again was Jackson to engage in any considerable speculative venture." The facts do not bear out this claim. Jackson speculated widely in land during the 1810s in an effort to benefit himself. Given his direct involvement in land seizures during the 1810s and his subsequent correspondence about prospects in Alabama, Florida, and the Mississippi Territory, it stretches credulity to imagine that he did not calculate these moves to help his land-speculating associates turn a profit as well.[21]

Sellers also suggested that the 1823 state legislative election between Darby and Grundy led to "Jackson's recognition that personal friendship was no longer an adequate basis for political alliance." In fact, nothing could be farther from the truth. Subscribing to the belief that "all politics is local," Jackson knew that his political success depended upon surrounding himself with a network of men, composed of kin and clients, on whom he could depend. He trusted unquestioningly the men who directed (Eaton and Lewis) and formed the core of his presidential campaigns, including relatives John Coffee and Andrew Donelson. Jackson's reliance on this southern network benefited him as he moved onto the national political stage, just as it proved a detriment once he achieved the presidency.[22]

XI

"Pure & Uncontaminated by Bargain & Sale"

Despite Jackson's determination in 1821 to live out his life as a planter at the Hermitage, he had already been mentioned as a possible successor to President Monroe. In late June 1822 Felix Grundy asked Jackson if he would be open to having his name submitted to the Tennessee General Assembly as a presidential candidate. Jackson's reacted tepidly. "I never have been a candidate for office, I never will," he wrote to Richard K. Call, but "the people have a right to call for any mans services in a republican government—and when they do, it is the duty of the individual to yield his services to the call." The resolution nominating Jackson was introduced by Knox County legislator Pleasant M. Miller the next month. It commenced a months-long process by which the Willie Blount–John Overton faction, of which Jackson was a supporter, sought some way to diminish the control of Tennessee politics held by Governor William Carroll and his allies.[1]

While some Tennesseans greeted the news of Jackson's nomination with incredulity and disbelief, supporters across the nation, without the aid of a national committee, quickly took up his cause. In Tennessee the so-called Nashville Junto trumpeted Jackson's suitability for the presidency. They worked through public meetings and newspapers to spread the word that if voters wanted to root out corruption and end the dominance of the political caucus, then Jackson was their man.[2]

Historians have used the term *Nashville Junto* interchangeably with *Nashville Central Committee,* the official campaign committee that was announced in 1827; whether a Nashville Junto actually existed as an organized body pre-1827 is unlikely. Unquestionably, though, Jackson benefited from having a group of men, connected both to him and to one another, working on his behalf: the three Johns (Coffee, Eaton, and Overton), Andrew Donelson, Felix Grundy, William B. Lewis, and Hugh Lawson White. Although Overton was a longtime friend and political ally, Jackson justifiably possessed doubts about his commitment and that of his brother-in-law, Hugh Lawson White. The two men appeared to have precipitated Jackson's nomination simply to help Pleasant M. Miller advance his own political ambitions in the state. Coffee lived on his North Alabama plantation, but he helped finance, as well as gave advice on, some of the campaign material produced by Eaton. Grundy, who usually maintained his independence from the state's factional politics, threw his support to Jackson because the potential benefits for his own career outweighed any possible backlash that might result. Donelson, young and fresh from studying law at Transylvania University, was entrusted by his uncle with minor secretarial tasks, such as finding and copying correspondence that Eaton could use to defend him against charges related to his conduct during the Monroe administration.[3]

Although they could not have accomplished Jackson's nomination by themselves, the unquestionable campaign managers were the brothers-in-law Eaton and Lewis. By 1824 both men were widowers, but Lewis had remarried. His second wife, Adelaide Stokes Chambers, provided Jackson with an important political connection. Adelaide Lewis was the daughter of Montfort Stokes, the brother of lawyer John Stokes, Jackson's friend from North Carolina. William B. Lewis traveled there in 1822 to secure Montfort Stokes's support of Jackson's candidacy. Stokes had already committed to Calhoun, but he agreed that the Tennessean was his second choice. Lewis also visited William Polk, another prominent North Carolina politician and a cousin to Tennessee's James K. Polk, who was just beginning to enter Jackson's orbit. After conversing with Lewis, William Polk agreed to switch his allegiance from Crawford to Jackson. Eaton, who represented Tennessee in the U.S. Senate, functioned as the campaign's national coordinator. He wrote letters for Jackson, settling disputes with former enemies and addressing questions about policy stances. Like Lewis, Eaton also made trips throughout the South to solicit support. Additionally, he sent campaign material to sympathetic newspaper editors for publication.[4]

Jackson's supporters emphasized several consistent themes throughout the campaign. Their candidate was above partisanship and opposed corruption, particularly as it was manifested in the congressional caucus system. By this process a small group of congressmen chose their party's presidential nominee, a selection that resulted from the constant jostling for the executive office by sitting cabinet members. Seeking to break the grip of larger states such as New York and Virginia and seeing the possibility of a House election in 1824, small-state politicians were especially supportive of this campaign rhetoric. In a series of articles that he wrote under the pseudonym "Wyoming," Eaton postulated that Jackson was a second Washington, poised to return the nation to its classical republican principles if the voters chose him for the presidency.[5]

Jackson faced several challengers in his attempt to win the presidency. Secretary of State John Quincy Adams, Secretary of War John C. Calhoun, Speaker of the U.S. House Henry Clay, and Secretary of the Treasury William H. Crawford all emerged as candidates, although Calhoun decided to withdraw and wait for a less-crowded field. Despite suffering what was likely a stroke, which left him debilitated for months, Crawford eventually won the endorsement of the congressional caucus in 1824. That decision fueled the Jacksonians' desire to overthrow the political system. Crawford was not only the caucus choice, but he was also the southern candidate, considered safe on the major questions that concerned his region: the tariff, internal improvements, and slavery.[6]

As expected of presidential candidates at the time, Jackson remained in the background as his supporters argued the case for his election. In October 1823, however, he was thrust into the political fray. When it became clear that none of the potential challengers to Senator John Williams, a member of the Carroll faction in Tennessee, were going to defeat him for reelection, Jackson's allies convinced the general that he was their only hope. Jackson balked at the proposal but eventually agreed to allow his name to be submitted as a candidate for Williams's seat. Jackson successfully won the legislative balloting, thirty-five to twenty-five, and by December was in the nation's capital representing Tennessee in the Senate. Before leaving, Jackson wrote John Coffee that his election was "a circumstance which I regret not more than any other of my life."[7]

It would be easy, given his eventual determination to win the presidency, his service as chief executive for two terms, and his statesmanship within the Democratic party, to dismiss Jackson's lack of enthusiasm in 1822–1823 as false modesty. His reticence, however, appears to have been genuine. He turned fifty-six years old in 1823 and suffered from various physical infirmities, including dysentery, a chronic cough, and a "palpitation of heart" episode that left him with "occasional bli[n]dness" during one trip home from Murfreesboro. Additionally, two bullets—one from the 1806 duel with Charles Dickinson and the second from the 1813 fight with the Bentons—remained embedded in his body. Not only was Jackson tired of the politics that he had endured over the past several years, but Rachel was also less than enthusiastic about the idea of her husband returning to public service. Additionally, he had expressed his interest in simply being a planter. Jackson believed in classical republican ideals sufficiently to set aside all of these compunctions, however, and surrendered himself to the pressure placed upon him by his political friends. Nevertheless, one observer probably summed up many voters' thoughts about Jackson: "I don't think he stands much chance."[8]

Jackson's time in the Senate was unremarkable in its scope and influence, but it gave voters a chance to observe his political principles in action. As chair of the Committee on Military Appropriations, Jackson predictably supported appropriations that he deemed necessary to the military's strength. He voted for internal improvements that made it easier for the military to transport men and equipment and for a tariff that protected burgeoning industry. He wanted to ensure, he wrote William B. Lewis, that "our own manufacturers shall stand on a footing of fair competition with the labourers of Europe." In a letter to one of the supporters of his presidential nomination, Jackson explained himself further. He saw the tariff as a means to pay off the national debt, which he considered "a curse to the republic" because it was "calculated to raise around the administration a monied aristocracy, dangerous to the liberties of the country." Finally, Jackson endorsed an agreement with Great Britain to end the African slave trade, but this legislation failed to pass the Senate. Since the Panic of 1819 and the Missouri Crisis of 1819–1821, southerners had become increasingly more conservative in their views on federal power, especially as they concerned internal improvements, the tariff, and slavery. Many looked to Crawford as their savior from these threats, but if Crawford's support of southern principles faltered or if health made him unable to continue the campaign, Jackson provided an alternative.[9]

To strengthen his appeal among southerners, Jackson took advantage of the commemoration of the nation's past triumphs. A series of ceremonies honoring his military service was set in Washington for early 1824.

While not breaching political protocol by openly campaigning, his public comments reminded observers that his actions during the War of 1812, in subsequent treaty negotiations with Indian tribes, and during the Seminole campaign clearly demonstrated his commitment to protecting southern society from the threat posed by Native Americans and slaves. At a March ceremony at which Jackson received a congressional medal for his service during the War of 1812, for example, he reminisced about the "patriotic ardor" that had led men like himself "to protect our frontier from the ruthless savage & the inroads of a British foe." The Marquis de Lafayette did not endorse a candidate during his 1824–1825 tour of the United States. Yet his presence no doubt reinforced the Jackson campaign's claim that its candidate provided the best opportunity to continue the legacy for which Lafayette had fought alongside Washington.[10]

As the election approached, Jackson appeared positioned to win the presidency. Crawford's health remained questionable, while Clay's candidacy had sputtered to a standstill, with anemic strength in the Upper South and Old Northwest. Adams ran strong in New England, but the Mid-Atlantic states were divided between the secretary of state and Jackson. When the election returns were tabulated, Jackson had won ninety-nine electoral votes, a plurality but not the required majority. Adams placed second, with eighty-four electoral votes. Despite his ill health, Crawford won forty-one electoral votes, outpacing Clay, who secured thirty-seven. Lacking a majority, under the Twelfth Amendment to the U.S. Constitution, the names of the top three electoral vote-getters were submitted to the House of Representatives, where each state delegation would cast one vote and elect the next president.[11]

Jackson's reaction to the election uncertainty was characteristic. "If party or intrigue should prevail, and exclude me, I shall retire to my comfortable farm with great pleasure," he wrote John Overton. Other friends received the same assurance, even as rumors circulated in January 1825 that Clay, whose fourth-place finish had left him out of the House election, was using his influence as speaker to ensure Adams's election. When the rumors were confirmed, Jackson maintained his composure. If conspiracies came to light to deprive him of the presidency, he would still "return to my Hermitage, carrying with me, my independence & my poli[ti]cal principles, pure & uncontaminated by bargain & sale, or combinations of any kind."[12]

This equanimity disappeared when the House voted to make Adams president. Clay convinced several congressional delegations to ignore the decisions rendered by their voters the previous fall and instead cast their states' votes for Adams over Jackson. Despite his earlier vow to retire even if the election were stolen from him, Old Hickory grew angry. The president-elect's nomination of Clay as his secretary of state shortly after the House election, however, enraged Jackson. "The *Judas* of the West has closed the contract and will receive the thirty pieces of silver," he fumed to William B. Lewis. After taking a few days to digest the news, Jackson was more circumspect about his own political fate but remained pessimistic about the nation's future. "If it had not been for the means used," he told Lewis in a repetition of earlier comments, "I would be happy at the result." Yet the "corrupt bargain" between Adams and Clay made him "shudder for the liberty of my country." Casting a vote against Clay's nomination to the State Department was of small consolation to the Tennessean, especially when the Senate confirmed him anyway.[13]

Jackson returned to Nashville in April 1825 to great acclamation at the city's crowded courthouse. He reiterated his commitment not to seek political office once his Senate term ended, but friends continued to write him of his ongoing political support in Kentucky, New York, and Pennsylvania while emphasizing Clay's unpopularity everywhere. Jackson took note, and throughout the summer of 1825 he renewed his criticism of the Kentuckian. When in October the Tennessee General Assembly once again nominated Jackson for president, he resigned his Senate seat to avoid accusations of using it for his "own aggrandisement" and began preparing for the 1828 campaign. Once he had been nominated, he wrote John Coffee, "Political consistancy at once pointed to the course I must adopt."[14]

XII

"The Old Hero Stands Heedless of the Pelting Storm"

Jackson made his decision to pursue the presidency for a second time because of the "corrupt bargain," the conspiracy that he believed had stolen the 1824 election from him and "the people." The 1828 election was a personal crusade for Old Hickory. As the campaign developed, several key questions arose about Jackson's southern identity. With Adams possessing a strong grip on electoral votes in New England and with Clay wielding his influence over the West, winning the election depended in large part on convincing southerners that Jackson best represented their interests.

The corrupt bargain charge played a prominent role in the 1828 campaign from the moment "the old cod-fish" Adams, as one Jackson man described the president, appointed Clay secretary of state. The Kentuckian continued to deny the charges that he had conspired to win his cabinet position by approaching both Jackson and Adams with the offer of his influence on the House election. While Jackson preferred not to discuss the matter publicly, when it became necessary to do so, he provided what he considered to be definitive proof of the plot. He named Pennsylvania congressman James Buchanan as the liaison who brought him Clay's proposal. Clay denied the charge, while Buchanan equivocated. It made no difference to Jackson. "The people now understand their wicked course," he wrote Coffee.[1]

Convinced that he was fighting for the people, Jackson aligned himself with savvy politicians in a national coalition capable of victory in 1828. In June 1826 Vice President Calhoun offered to join Jackson "on the side of liberty" in the fight against the "corrupt patronage" that Adams and Clay surely would use to consolidate their power. Jackson accepted Calhoun's offer with the statement "We shall march hand in hand . . . on the side of the people." Having secured a strong southern ally, Jackson also benefited from New York senator Martin Van Buren's decision to throw his support behind Old Hickory. Van Buren had worked assiduously for Crawford's nomination in 1824, believing that the Georgian was the safest candidate to protect states' rights against encroaching national power. Calculating that Crawford possessed little chance of winning the presidency in 1828, Van Buren switched to Jackson as the best political alternative. Adams and Clay had shown their true Federalist colors, and Calhoun was a possible obstacle to Van Buren's own presidential aspirations. Jackson's age and his desire to serve only one term undoubtedly encouraged Van Buren that if he made himself invaluable to Jackson, then Old Hickory might later support him for the presidency. Tennessean Alfred Balch, a Van Buren ally, used his influence to pave the way for the New Yorker's acceptance by Jackson's southern supporters. Sam Houston also assured the General of Van Buren's fidelity: he "will support you in all good faith . . . your friends who know him best are satisfied as to his course."[2]

During the 1824 election the Jackson campaign found it unnecessary to publicly declare its commitment to protecting southern rights. The circumstances leading up to the 1828 election were different, however. Supporters of Calhoun and Crawford wanted assurances that Jackson would protect slavery and continue the removal of Native Americans from fertile southern soil. Van Buren acknowledged these regional interests in a January 1827 missive to Thomas Ritchie, editor of the *Richmond Enquirer:* "Political combinations between the inhabitants of the different states are unavoidable & the most natural & beneficial to the country is that between the planters of the South and the plain Republicans of the north." Van Buren believed that the proposed alliance would create loyal partisan supporters, unmask the corruptness of the Adams-Clay cabal, and ensure Jackson's victory as the virtuous candidate.[3]

It was not that simple, though. On the one hand, Jackson had eliminated threats to regional security posed by Native Americans and runaway slaves, had seized territory on which southern planters could grow cash crops, and by virtue of his own identity as a slave owner, would almost certainly ensure slavery's continued protection from the growing antislavery clamor. On the other hand, his appeal to "the people" threatened to destroy the South's republican institutions and undermine its racial order. If the lower classes began using Jacksonian rhetoric, then the southern gentry potentially would lose control over the men and women who had heretofore shown them deference. If white solidarity and supremacy faltered, then the long-standing racial division in the region might also begin to crumble as slaves and free blacks demanded their physical and economic freedom. Southern elites wanted to make certain that Van Buren's conception of Jackson as the virtuous republican matched their own.[4]

Other issues also concerned southerners. In 1825 the American Colonization Society (ACS) began an aggressive campaign to secure state and national funding for the colonization of free blacks to Africa. Taken in conjunction with Adams's support of internal improvements and his tendency to interpret the Constitution loosely, some southerners predicted that the future of slavery was dire and at the very least more government involvement in colonization would precipitate unrest among the slave and free black populations residing in the South. The ACS named Jackson one of its vice presidents, a ceremonial title given to many prominent men. Some of them, such as Henry Clay, supported its goals, while others, such as Jackson, were not even consulted before being awarded the position. Uncertainty also surrounded Indian removal. Specifically, southerners were upset with the decision of the Adams administration to interfere with treaties negotiated with native groups. In 1825, for example, the state of Georgia indicated its intent to implement the provisions of the Treaty of Indian Springs, which had been fraudulently negotiated. President Adams stepped in and ordered Governor George M. Troup to stand down. Troup responded by linking the administration's assertion of its right to set aside the treaty with its intention to interfere with slavery. Given his past actions, Jackson certainly seemed like a safer choice on both of these issues.[5]

The formation of the Nashville Central Committee proved crucial to Jackson's attempt to solidify his support among southern voters. The committee was composed of nineteen men who were politically well connected, both locally and nationally. Many knew Jackson through business transactions and legal proceedings. Edward Ward, for example, had purchased Jackson's Hunter's Hill home from him. Others, including George Washington Campbell and John McNairy, had been political allies (and in McNairy's case, for a time, an enemy) for decades. Some, such as John Catron, Thomas H. Claiborne, and Dr. John Shelby, were fellow Masons, while others, including Claiborne and Shelby, had served with him during the War of 1812. Jesse Wharton worked alongside Jackson as a trustee of Cumberland College.[6]

Additionally, the men who had guided the 1824 campaign—Coffee, Donelson, Eaton, Grundy, Lewis, Overton, and Hugh Lawson White—continued to contribute their leadership and support. Clearly, the Nashville Central Committee did the bidding of this smaller inner circle that rightfully could be called the Nashville Junto during the 1828 campaign. Overton was the only member of both groups and almost certainly served as a liaison between them. While he was not "Jackson's alter ego," as one historian has claimed, Eaton continued his previous role as de facto campaign manager, even as he remained behind the scenes. Eaton was instrumental, for example, in getting Calhoun's Missouri ally Duff Green to become editor of the *United States' Telegraph*. This publication soon became the leading Jacksonian newspaper in Washington and the nation. To help Green purchase the paper in 1826, Jackson loaned him $3,000; Eaton was part of a group of twelve, including James K. Polk, who endorsed Green's note. Eaton, along with Coffee, Donelson, Ephraim H. Foster, Lewis, and Donelson relative John C. McLemore, also made another loan of $1,412 to Green later that year.[7]

Two other Tennesseans who began to grow in prominence during these years also assisted the Jackson campaign. Following his service in the War of 1812, Sam Houston remained in the military until his resignation in 1818. He practiced law in Lebanon and Nashville, was appointed major general of the state militia, and in 1823 won election to the U.S. House from Tennessee's Ninth District. He served two terms, until 1827, when he resigned to run for the governorship of Tennessee, a position that he won later that summer. Likewise, James K. Polk, from Maury County, who had studied law under Felix Grundy, was persuaded by the Overton faction to seek election in 1825 as U.S. representative from Tennessee's Sixth District. Polk successfully defeated Clay supporter and Jackson nemesis Andrew Erwin and won reelection in 1827 as well.[8]

Observers rightly predicted a "warm election" in 1828, and they were not disappointed. As the presidential campaign began, Jackson's opponents quickly identified several aspects of his southern identity that they considered vulnerable. His violent past was a frequent point of attack. Philadelphia editor John Binns's "Coffin Handbill" contained some of the most inflammatory accusations against Jackson. It placed the execution of the six militiamen during the War of 1812 within the broader context of Jackson's violent behavior. Binns presented readers with what he considered numerous examples of Jackson's temper, outbursts, and bloodlust, supporting them with excerpts from Jackson's own correspondence. He concluded by asking the public to "mark the perfect indifference with which Gen. Jackson shoots, hangs or stabs his fellow beings, with or without trial, and the more than callous, aye, even exulting composure, with which he details his horrid and bloody deeds!"[9]

Opponents also questioned Jackson's military record. Pennsylvania state representative Jonathan Roberts argued in a public letter that Jackson had hesitated to defend New Orleans in 1814 and only did so at the Madison administration's urgent behest. At a private dinner attended by former secretary of state and President James Monroe, Secretary of the Navy Samuel L. Southard allegedly commented that "Mr. Monroe and not Genl Jackson was entitled to the credit for the victory at Neworleans." Jackson had given up on the city's defense, Southard supposedly stated, and was only compelled to return by the "energetic measures" of Monroe. More seriously, one of Monroe's letters came to light suggesting that Calhoun had not supported Jackson's invasion of Florida in 1818, forcing the vice president, a crucial member of the Jacksonian coalition, to formulate a plausible explanation for his previous criticism. These attacks disparaged Jackson's martial spirit and called into question his honor as a military leader.[10]

Adams' supporters also pandered to prurient interests. They accused Jackson's mother of being "a prostitute who intermarried with a negro" and intimated that Jackson and his oldest brother, Hugh, were the products of that relationship. More luridly, the Jackson marriage became a campaign topic as well. In the fall of 1826 Charles Hammond, an Ohio journalist, began gathering information about the questionable circumstances surrounding the Jacksons' marriage. He subsequently published an exposé the following March. The marriage had briefly been mentioned during the 1824 election, but now it became an obsession for pro-Adams publications. They accused Rachel Jackson of breaching the law by committing bigamy and castigated Andrew Jackson for shaming her by running for public office. Ultimately, however, these critics questioned the morality of allowing Rachel to become the nation's First Lady. "THERE IS POLLUTION IN THE TOUCH, THERE IS PERDITION IN THE EXAMPLE OF A PROFLIGATE WOMAN—'HER WAYS LEAD DOWN TO THE CHAMBERS OF

DEATH AND HER STEPS TAKE HOLD ON HELL,'" one Massachusetts paper warned its readers.[11]

In Tennessee, William G. Hunt, the editor of the *National Banner and Nashville Whig*, spent considerable ink addressing controversial episodes in Jackson's past. His violent tendencies garnered little public attention, attempts by William P. Anderson and Jesse Benton to revive the controversy over the Dickinson duel falling flat. A similar fate awaited criticism of Jackson's execution of the six militiamen during the War of 1812. Jackson's land dealings, however, came under frequent scrutiny. "A TENNESSEAN" accused him of swindling David Allison's heirs, while others charged him with using his authority as Indian commissioner to profit his friends from the Chickasaw land cessions after the War of 1812. Another topic of great debate was Jackson's role in the Burr conspiracy. Boyd McNairy claimed that the evidence "*most clearly and incontrovertibly established*–that Jackson was intimately associated with Aaron Burr" during his 1806 conspiracy. He also accused Jackson and his friends of producing a conveniently undated letter to prove Old Hickory's innocence.[12]

Other explosive allegations centered on Jackson's involvement in the slave trade and his treatment of slaves. Andrew Erwin produced several editions of a pamphlet that excoriated Jackson for being a slave trader and for mistreating his slaves. The main allegation accused Jackson of "*trafficking in human flesh.*" "*If there were not a hundred other good reasons why he ought not to* be president," Erwin wrote, then Jackson's practice of "*buying, selling and transferring slaves as merchandize*" should demonstrate his "*total disqualification and unfitness* for office." Erwin also alluded to the killing of Jackson's slave Gilbert by his overseer, Ira Walton, in August 1827. Walton attempted to whip Gilbert, a frequent runaway, when the slave attacked the overseer. In the ensuing fight Walton stabbed Gilbert, who died shortly thereafter. Erwin accused Jackson of trying to protect Walton and implied that he had caused Gilbert's death by ordering "an unmerciful sentence" of one thousand lashes for the runaway slave.[13]

And the attacks kept coming. Boyd McNairy told voters in Tennessee's Seventh District that all Jackson had ever accomplished was related to his military duties; in every other public endeavor he had prematurely resigned. Jesse Benton self-righteously proclaimed, "I often told my brother, in 1813, that God was angry with Jackson for his crimes and permitted his attempt to assassinate us on the very spot where I now sit, in order to make us the instrument of his punishment." Although he later retracted some of his statements, William P. Anderson's hatred was palpable in an open letter addressed directly to Jackson:

1st. Your besetting sins are, ambition, and the love of money. To acquire the latter you will act *miserly* and oppress your best friends; and when in pursuit of either, you are not what you profess to be.

2d. You are naturally and constitutionally irritable, overbearing and tyrannical.

3d. You are incapable of extending any charity towards those who happen to differ with you in opinion.

4th. You cannot investigate dispassionately any interesting or important subject—and if you could, your knowledge and abilities are not equal to the task.

5th. When you become the enemy of any man you will put him down if you can, no matter by what means, fair or foul, honorable or dishonorable; and if it be consistent with your views of popularity and interest, you will turn about and support the very men you have before attempted to destroy and pull down . . .

6th. You are miserably deficient in principle and have seldom or never had power without abusing it.[14]

Amos Kendall, editor of the pro-Jackson *Argus of Western America* in Frankfort, Kentucky, summarized the attacks on Old Hickory with his usual wit. "Mutineers and deserters, infamous rogues and savage murderers justly executed for their crimes, have been transformed into martyrs," he wrote. "Glorious victories bought with American blood, have been pronounced cold-blooded massacres . . . an unspotted life cannot shield even female virtue." A letter circulated among Kentucky supporters reinforced Kendall's identification of injustice. "Deserters, thieves, traitors and Indian murderers, have been held up to the country's sympathy, while bravery patriotism and self devotion, are covered with obloquy and made the subject of reproach," it argued. Jackson "bared his bosom to the bayonets of a foreign invader; let us protect him from the tongues of domestic slanderers."[15]

Despite Eaton's wish that the general "keep clear of all excitement, and let the storm rage," Jackson worked closely with the Nashville Committee in responding to the Adams campaign's many attacks. He asked John Overton to address charges that his brother, Thomas, who had served as Jackson's second during the Dickinson duel, had intimidated Dickinson's second into favorably describing Jackson's conduct that day. To counter the charge that he had unfairly executed the six militiamen, Jackson coordinated a public response with James K. Polk and Hugh Lawson White, who submitted to a Nashville newspaper a letter from General Edmund P. Gaines proclaiming it "an act of mercy to shoot cowardly deserters." Sam Houston helped defend Jackson's military career. He questioned Virginian Chapman Johnson's criticism of Jackson's "cold blooded massacre" at the Battle of Horseshoe Bend, which called into question not only Jackson's honor but also that of the soldiers who had fought with him. Houston also served as a courier between Jackson and Southard as the two men argued over Jackson's role as the protector of New Orleans during the War of 1812. Defending his mother's reputation was also important to Jackson, so, with the assistance of Polk, he secured affidavits from several men who had lived in the Waxhaws region contemporaneously with his own family. These affidavits all attested to Elizabeth Jackson's character and that of her family and expressed disbelief that anyone who knew her "would state any thing the least disrespectful to the family and mother of Genral Jackson, unless they were totally abandoned in character and principle."[16]

The attacks on the Jackson marriage understandably merited considerable attention. After receiving notice that Hammond was conducting research on Rachel's marital fidelity, Jackson solicited statements from three women who were acquainted with his wife during her marriage to Lewis Robards and the subsequent divorce. The women attested to Rachel being "chaste and virtuous" and agreed that her first husband possessed a "jealous disposition and vicious habits." Jackson identified "the Coalition," headed by Clay and including Adams, Andrew Erwin, Hammond, and Southard, as being behind the attacks. To Duff Green, Jackson lamented these accusations: "I never war against females, & it is only the base & cowardly that do." Convinced by his campaign managers not to involve himself directly in Rachel's defense, Jackson nevertheless penned a letter to Clay that is insightful. "Surely as your enmity is against me it would have been better to have pointed it at the proper object," he wrote, "rather than to have sought by stirring up the record of more than thirty years' standing to harrow up the feelings of an aged lady whom you and every one else acquainted with her has esteemed for her piety, virtue and benevolence." Jackson concluded his missive, "I have only to add that Mrs. J. and myself hurl at you our defiance. A virtuous and well-spent life has secured to her a skirt which such men as you and your worthy associate, Charles Hammond, cannot sully." The letter, written in late 1826, was not sent, probably at the behest of Eaton. Even one Adams newspaper editor reportedly denounced the publication of "'all the filth that can be hunted up'" against Jackson.[17]

Jackson took the lead in refuting the charges that he had knowingly supported Burr's conspiracy against the United States in 1806 and that he had used his position as Indian commissioner in the 1810s to profit his friends. In early 1828 he challenged Tennessee judge Nathaniel W. Williams's public assertion that he had recruited him for the Burr scheme. When Williams referenced letters that allegedly proved his charge, Jackson sent his nephew Andrew Donelson to Nashville to verify their authenticity. Upon ascertaining that the letters were either forgeries or misconstrued for political purposes, Jackson urged Lewis to have the Nashville Central Committee respond publicly, which Eaton did in September: "During all of this war of words & slander, the old Hero stands heedless of the pelting storm—cool & self possessed." Jackson also coordinated a response to the charge that he had used the 1818 treaty negotiations with the Chickasaw to secure land near present-day Huntsville for friends such as Lewis. Despite Eaton's claim that his friend "is found to bear patiently the severest assaults of slander," this issue agitated Jackson. He sent Donelson to Alabama to determine what role his former business partner James Jackson had played in the attack. If James Jackson did not give a satisfactory answer, Donelson was ordered "instantly to make it a personal affair." Donelson agreed, writing Coffee in advance of his visit, "I suspect the cudgil will be the most fitting argument" to persuade James Jackson. Eaton learned of the general's directive to his nephew and pleaded in large, scrawling script with Coffee to intervene and stop the altercation. Donelson's "feelings are perfectly alive," he wrote, but "he only needs to be informed as to the right course, & when properly to act, & how to act." Coffee succeeded in sending Donelson home without having stepped on the dueling grounds, while Eaton did his part in convincing Jackson that this point of honor was too minor to pursue further.[18]

Jackson also worked assiduously to defend himself against the charge that he was not a "humane slave holder." With the assistance of Donelson, he compiled testimony that showed that he had provided security for his business partners Coleman and Green in 1811 but that he had not personally engaged in slave trading. "I wish you to state how long you have lived near me," Jackson told his neighbor Robert Weakley, "& whether since your first acquaintance, you ever knew me to buy a negro with a view of selling him again for profit, or ever knew me engaged in any speculations in negroes to the lower country or to any other place." As for Gilbert's death, Jackson wanted his friends to expose Erwin "as the vilest lier on earth." He forwarded to Lewis documents from his overseer, Ira Walton, and district attorney Andrew Hays demonstrating that he had taken appropriate legal action in the death. Letters from other acquaintances and friends defending Jackson on this issue also appeared in the press.[19]

Facing such intense scrutiny nationally and locally, Jackson had to trust his political alliance to look out for his best interests. This trust was put to the test in late 1827, however, when New York congressman Silas Wright Jr., in conjunction with Martin Van Buren, his political mentor, authored tariff legislation intended to sway the Mid-Atlantic and Western states of Kentucky, Illinois, Indiana, Missouri, New York, Ohio, and Pennsylvania to vote for Jackson. Van Buren calculated that the southern states were already safely in Jackson's column and that failing to pass a moderate tariff now would only allow the possibility of higher tariff later. Some southerners, however, particularly in South Carolina, were incensed at the bill, particularly after it passed Congress over their objections in May 1828. To them the federal government's ability to impose higher duties that penalized the South was but the first step in an abolitionist conspiracy to encroach on its slaveholdings. A committee of pro-Adams Kentuckians pointed out the paradox of Jackson and his supporters "stak[ing] the contest in the South" by informing southerners that Old Hickory opposed internal improvements and the tariff while telling Pennsylvania and Kentucky just the opposite.[20]

Political supporters in the South expressed to Jackson their dissatisfaction with the "Tariff of Abominations," as some southerners quickly came to call it. "The new tariff," Senator John Branch of North Carolina informed Jackson shortly after its passage, "has depressed the spirits of our southern friends no little." Branch predicted that by supporting the tariff, congressional Jacksonians such as Van Buren threatened the "harmony and union" of the nation. South Carolina representative James Hamilton Jr. blamed "this infamous Administration" for passing "this most iniquitous Tariff against the South with I believe the express hope of driving us into Rebellion." Other South Carolinians believed that Jackson was on their side. At a January 1829 celebration of the victory at New Orleans, Arthur P. Hayne, who had served with Jackson's army throughout the 1810s, lauded him for sharing his state's views on "the all important subject of *State-rights*." The president-elect was a slave owner and "derives his *revenue* and *subsistence* from the same *agricultural production upon which we depend*." "Is this nothing?" Hayne asked the celebrants.[21]

Jackson sidestepped the issue in his response to Branch, preferring to focus on the personal attacks that Adams's supporters were making against him. To Hamilton, however, he was more forthright: "To regulate a Judicious tariff, is a subject of great difficulty at all times, & ought to be discussed, with great calmness & due deliberation, with an eye to the prosperity of the whole Union." Hamilton's allusion to disunion also elicited a response. "There is nothing that I shudder at more than the idea of a seperation of the Union," he told the South Carolinian. If disunion were to occur, then liberty would disappear with the nation's unity. Recognizing the importance of keeping a check on the federal consolidation of power in the executive branch, Jackson nonetheless expressed "great confidence in the virtue of a great majority of the people." The Republic would remain safe, and "the designing demagogues" would be defeated by "a majority of the people." "It is the durability of the confederation upon which the general government is built, that must prolong our liberty," Jackson wrote. "The moment it seperates, it is gone." Letters from South Carolinians Vice President Calhoun and Senator Robert Y. Hayne, two of the leading critics of the tariff in coming years, went unanswered.[22]

Throughout the summer and fall of 1828 pro-Adams newspapers across the nation, led by the *Daily National Journal*, argued that Jackson's election would lead to disunion. "What better agent could be found to dissolve the

Union," the paper asked, than the presidential candidate "disposed and accustomed to arbitrary rule?" By associating with Burr's conspiracy two decades earlier, Jackson had already proven his willingness to tear asunder the Union, and now, Adamsites argued, he was linked to the disunionist rumblings in South Carolina. Had not James Hamilton Jr., one of the prime agitators, stated publicly that he supported Jackson because he was "'a Southern man, with Southern interests and Southern feelings?'" Even his supporters wondered whether Jackson's election would "be apt to create a Civil War," though not one of his creation. Francis W. Pickens, editor of the pro-nullification *Charleston Mercury*, denied that there was a southern movement afoot to dismember the Union or that Jackson was central to this nonexistent plot. Pickens was wrong about disunion, of course; even then, secession was on the mind of some southerners. Jackson, however, was not one of them.[23]

The Jackson campaign did not sit idly by as Adams's supporters hurled their many invectives. They emphasized the "corrupt bargain" charge, helped by the defection of Kentucky newspaper editor Amos Kendall, once a friend of the Clay family. Jacksonians also emphasized Adams's elitism. His purchase of a billiard table, even though it was paid for with his own money, was a sign of a president out of touch with the average American. Another example of Adams's snobbery was his public toast at a War of 1812 commemoration in Baltimore in October 1827. He quoted a passage from Voltaire: "Ebony and Topaz, General Ross's posthumous coat of arms, and the republican militia men who gave it." Sensing that the toast's meaning was lost on his audience, Adams was forced to explain its meaning, further exemplifying for his opponents his inability to relate to the people. The final, and most scurrilous, accusation made against the president was that while serving as minister to Russia, he had pimped for the czar. The charge was baseless, but like some of the stories about Jackson, it provided enough titillation to keep tongues wagging.[24]

Despite the political assaults that came his way during the presidential campaign, Jackson won a resounding victory. His electoral vote total of 178 swamped Adams's 83; the 56 percent of voters who supported Jackson with their ballot also spoke to his undeniable triumph. The South gave Jackson a clean electoral sweep. After having secured only 42.2 percent of the southern popular vote in 1824, his percentage increased to 70.6 percent in 1828. In three of the five Lower South states (Alabama, Georgia, and Mississippi), Jackson won no less than 81.1 percent of the popular vote. (The South Carolina legislature gave its electoral votes to the Jackson-Calhoun ticket, while the unique nature of Louisiana's politics garnered Jackson only 53 percent of the popular vote.) In the Upper South, Jackson performed least well in Maryland (49.8 percent) and Kentucky (55.5 percent) but scored significant victories in Virginia (69 percent), Missouri (70.6 percent), North Carolina (73.1 percent), and Tennessee (95.2 percent).[25]

During the summer of 1828 John Breathitt, running for the lieutenant governorship of Kentucky, lamented the attacks on Jackson. "After having contributed so much, yea more, than any other man now living, to the service and glory of his country, to be told that he is *unfit for office, a tyrant, a military chieftain,* and *dangerous to the liberties of his country*" was distressing, he wrote the people of his state. As Breathitt noted, many political issues played a role in the 1828 election, but Jackson's victory undeniably depended in part on his ability to convince white southerners that he was their best, and only, choice, even if some had to ignore their apprehension about his tariff views. In this effort he succeeded, giving white southerners every reason to expect that the president-elect, the owner of nearly one hundred slaves at his Hermitage plantation and the man who had opened up the Deep South to the expansion of cotton and slavery, would support their interests.[26]

XIII

"Et Tu Brute"

Rachel Jackson's death late in the evening of 22 December 1828 understandably affected her husband's first term as president. She had been apprehensive about going to Washington as first lady but had resigned herself to her fate. "I owe to myself & my husband to try to forget, at least for a time all the endearments of home & prepare to live where it has pleased heaven to fix our destiny," she wrote a friend. To boost her determination, John Eaton reminded Rachel of what was at stake. Her husband's inner circle had solicited the presence of sympathetic women to socialize with her in Washington. "If you shall be absent," he told her, "how great will be the dissapointment. Your persecutors then may chuckle, & say that they have driven you from the field of your husbands honors." Yet Rachel's resolve was no match for her health. After a trip into Nashville to select clothing for the upcoming transition, Rachel was "taken suddenly ill, with excruciating pain in the left shoulder, arm, & breast"; almost certainly, she had suffered a heart attack. Venesection (bleeding) failed to help her condition. Despite her age, weight, and history of health problems, Rachel's death shocked Jackson.[1]

Jackson prepared to leave the Hermitage for Washington in early 1829 with Rachel's death haunting his thoughts. During the recent presidential campaign he and his wife had weathered the trouble caused by their ill-timed romance while she had been married to Lewis Robards and the questions about whether Rachel was a bigamist and Andrew an adulterer. Political opponents had lobbed "arrows [of] wormwood & gall" at Rachel's character, a fact of which she was well aware. The loss of "the dear companion of my bosom," as he frequently called his late wife, placed Jackson in a distressed emotional state that explains in part his vigorous defense of John Eaton's marriage to the recently widowed Margaret O'Neale Timberlake. Jackson's sense of southern honor also influenced his interpretation of attacks on the Eaton marriage during the first two-and-a-half years of his presidency. The contradictory southern expectations of both patriarchal obedience and independent masculinity tested the steadfast loyalty that Jackson demanded from his clients and wards. Ultimately, his determination to force acceptance of the Eatons threatened to split not only his political coalition but also his family, some of whom stood at the vanguard of criticism.[2]

Jackson arrived in Washington in mid-February 1829. While waiting to take office, he assembled his cabinet, choosing friends, like-minded allies, and politicians who would provide regional balance. William T. Barry, who once taught Andrew Donelson at Transylvania, received the postmaster-general post. Samuel D. Ingham, a moderate on the tariff and a supporter of Vice President elect John C. Calhoun, became the head of the Treasury. The navy post went to John Branch of North Carolina, and John M. Berrien of Georgia was appointed attorney general. Branch and Berrien were strong on southern issues, such as supporting slavery and advocating low tariffs. Branch's time in the Senate had allowed him to befriend Jackson and Eaton, while Berrien, a supporter of Indian removal, was well known to William B. Lewis, second only to Eaton in terms of influencing Jackson.[3]

For the secretary of war post Jackson considered both Eaton and Hugh Lawson White. When White declined consideration, Jackson turned to his close friend. The choice of Eaton was logical for many reasons: the senator was as close to the president-elect as any man; he had headed Jackson's two presidential campaigns; and his views on southern issues, particularly the future of Native Americans, corresponded with Jackson's own. Jackson rewarded other important supporters with cabinet appointments—Martin Van Buren with the State Department, for example—but Eaton remained a key member of Jackson's inner circle.[4]

Both friends and foes criticized Jackson's choices. Friends denounced Jackson's failure to consult any other Tennesseans besides Eaton and Lewis about his cabinet appointments. Enemies called the cabinet "a compound of embicility, tyranny and hypocrisy" as well as a "numerous host of sycophantic parasites." Unwilling to believe that its members were competent and convinced that Jackson certainly was not, they eventually accused the president of being under the influence of a group of unofficial advisors, dubbed the "Kitchen Cabinet." Its alleged members included, among others, Lewis and Kentucky newspaper editors Amos Kendall, who arrived in Washington in December 1828, and Francis P. Blair, who established the *Washington Globe* as Jackson's mouthpiece in late 1830.[5]

His cabinet choices made, Jackson proceeded to take office. Held on the Capitol's east portico, the swearing-in on 4 March was witnessed by approximately twenty thousand people. After taking the oath of office, the sixty-one-year-old Tennessean, "pale and thin" and dressed in a black suit out of respect for Rachel, read his 1,126-word inaugural address. Jackson promised to perform the duties of the executive office "without transcending its authority" and pledged to "cultivate friendship on fair and honorable terms" with other nations. When it came to "the rights of the separate States," he emphasized his commitment "not to confound the powers they have reserved for themselves." Extinguishing the national debt and supporting all parts of the nation's economy, even internal improvements if necessary, were also his goals. Not surprisingly, Jackson assured Americans that he would sustain the military and encourage reform. Indian tribes would be treated with "a just and liberal policy," buoyed by "humane and considerate attention to their rights and their wants which is consistent with the habits of our Government and the feelings of our people." Finally, Jackson said he would appoint men to office "whose diligence and talents will insure in their respective stations able and faithful cooperation." A year later Jackson summarized his presidential agenda for Martin Van Buren: "The Federal Constitution must be obeyed, State-rights preserved, our national debt *must be paid, direct taxes and loans avoided* and the Federal union preserved."[6]

After his speech Jackson rode to the White House, where democracy was on full display. Alcohol consumption loosened restraints as "the noisy and disorderly rabble in the President's House" caused havoc on furnishings. "The Majesty of the People had disappeared," replaced by "a rabble, a mob, of boys, negroes, women, children, scrambling, fighting, romping," throughout the executive mansion. The crowd to see, speak to, and touch Jackson grew so great that he fled out a window to avoid being crushed. Emily Donelson believed that most of the people who attended the inauguration, which she described as "by far the largest crowd that ever was seen in Washington," visited the White House that night.[7]

Throughout the inauguration day into the nighttime festivities, prominent women ignored Margaret Eaton, wife of the new secretary of war. The recently married John and Margaret began their life together under a dark cloud of gossip. Margaret was the daughter of the owner of a Washington boardinghouse at which congressmen frequently stayed. Beautiful, vivacious, and outspoken, she had gained a reputation as a flirt prior to her first marriage, at age sixteen, to naval purser John Timberlake. Timberlake's frequent absences at sea left her alone, and John Eaton, a widower and close family friend, became her escort to social functions. Washington rumormongers suspected more than platonic companionship, however. Timberlake's apparent suicide in April 1828 confirmed their notions that he had discovered his wife and friend's adulterous treachery. Whether John and Margaret were engaged in an affair is unclear, but their choice to marry on 1 January 1829 was imprudent. It validated the gossip that had been circulating about their relationship, gossip that was already being used to attack the incoming president.[8]

From the beginning Jackson fully supported the Eaton marriage. He had known the O'Neale family for years, having resided in their boardinghouse with Rachel while in Congress during the winter of 1824–1825. When John Eaton approached him with the idea of marrying Margaret, Jackson endorsed the idea. Eaton's description of the trials that he and Margaret faced, written in early December 1828, must have sounded familiar to Jackson: "She who had in association with me, been censured by a gossiping world had been placed in a situation by the hand of Providence where it was in my power by interposing myself, to snatch her from that injustice which had been done her."[9]

At the head of the Eatons' critics was the president's niece, Emily Donelson. Upon Rachel's death, Emily assumed the mantle of hostess at the President's Mansion. She thought very little of Margaret, telling her sister, "I have been so much disgusted with what I have seen of her that I shall not visit her again." Margaret was not the only target of Emily's acerbic pen; Lewis she deemed a "sycophant" who "pretended to come along out of friendship to the Genl" in order to secure "a fat office and . . . save himself all expense" while Jackson was president. If her uncle had wanted to reward his close friends, Emily wrote, "there were others that had done more for him and deserved more at his hands than either Eaton or Lewis."[10]

The wives of other Jackson supporters agreed with Emily's opinion of the Eatons, especially of Margaret. Their actions sent an unmistakable message. In the spring Floride Calhoun, the vice president's wife, refused to return a call to Margaret because she did not want to associate with someone of such disreputable character. Subsequently, the Calhouns spent most of 1829 in South Carolina. At the president's first official dinner, held in November, Mrs. Calhoun was still in South Carolina, but the tension among the women was palpable; guests left as quickly as they could. When Van Buren hosted a dinner shortly thereafter, none of the cabinet wives attended.[11]

The obvious female social opposition to Margaret Eaton could not help but affect Jackson's relationship with his advisors. In one of the most extraordinary moments of any presidency, on 10 September 1829 he convened his official cabinet (minus Eaton), along with Andrew Donelson and Lewis, in order to confront two religious ministers, John N. Campbell and Ezra Stiles Ely, who had accused the Eatons of sexual transgressions prior to their marriage. Nineteenth-century Jackson biographer James Parton offers the most detailed account of this surreal meeting, at which cabinet officers and presidential advisors observed the chief executive lambasting clergy for questioning a woman's morality. Jackson dismissed any suggestion that his late wife had disliked Margaret, picked apart one story that had Margaret miscarrying John's child, and judged as insufficient hearsay testimony that had John and Margaret sleeping in the same bed in New York before they were married. When Reverend Ely admitted that the case against John Eaton was collapsing, Jackson pressed him to say the same about Margaret. "On that point," Ely reportedly said, "I would rather not give an opinion." Jackson's explosive response undoubtedly shocked the meeting's attendees: "She is as chaste as a virgin!"[12]

Andrew and Emily Donelson did not agree with Jackson's assessment. Having come to Washington to assist their bereaved uncle, they chose not to socialize with the Eatons. In April 1829 John Eaton chastised Emily for allowing herself to be swayed by a "little nest of inquisitors," a remark that drew a sharp response from both Donelsons. A misunderstanding between Emily and Margaret on a trip later that summer led Margaret to threaten the Donelsons with exile to Tennessee. Andrew Donelson told his uncle later that "it was impossible that I could submit to the degradation of having a tribune of that character constituted for the purpose of determining within what limits my good behaviour might secure the station which I held." The relationship between relatives continued to deteriorate in June 1830. When Margaret refused to visit the President's Mansion because of the Donelsons' "unkind treatment" and "injustice," Jackson blamed his niece and nephew, not Margaret. Ironically, Jackson intervened in the dispute between Andrew Donelson and John Eaton in order to keep his secretary of war "from making it a serious matter."[13]

Things worsened throughout 1830. A trip to Tennessee that summer revealed the affair's toll on Jackson. At a stop in Bowling Green, Kentucky, one observer heard a rumor that the president was about to resign, "for he says he cannot perform the duties that his office requires." One look at the president, who was "quite grey," confirmed this man's certainty about the tale. Once Jackson arrived in Nashville, the Donelsons' decision not to stay at the Hermitage in order to avoid the Eatons piqued Jackson, who saw his niece and nephew as "the instruments, and tools" of "the combination and conspiracy to injure and prostrate Major Eaton, and injure me." When Jackson returned to the nation's capital in September, his nephew accompanied him, but Emily was left behind. She would remain in exile, Jackson ordered, until she was ready to give "the same comity and attention to all the heads of Departments, and their families." The pent-up frustration between uncle and nephew finally exploded in late October. After a face-to-face argument over Emily's exile, the two men stopped speaking, choosing instead to exchange letters while living under the same roof. Their correspondence centered on the same themes as their conversations: Jackson wanted his family to treat the Eatons fairly, out of respect for his paternal authority, while Donelson wanted his uncle to accord him the same consideration. The two continued sniping at one another for the next several months. In June 1831, certain that Calhoun was using Donelson, Jackson proclaimed that "a House divided cannot stand" and sent his nephew home to Emily.[14]

Jackson reacted as one would expect from a southern patriarch. He demanded that his nephew, who bore his name and from whom he expected great things, bend to his will as president and head of household. In his effort to exercise control over his own family, Donelson chose to challenge his uncle's authority. Given Jackson's past interactions, the end result was

predictable. Defiance of his will, especially by family members, was disloyalty, which Jackson did not accept. The psychological projection that
Jackson must have unconsciously employed because of the similarities between his late wife and Margaret only exacerbated the estrangement from
his family.[15]

Yet Jackson's problems were not just with his family. Despite William T.
Barry's claim that "politically speaking, there is no division" within Jackson's administration because of the Eaton affair, he could not have been
more wrong. During the early months of his presidency Jackson identified
his nemesis, Henry Clay, and "his minions" as being behind the Eaton opposition. By November 1829, however, he was convinced that Calhoun
was the real culprit. The "persecution" of the Eatons "was founded in
political views, looking to the future," he wrote to his relative John C.
McLemore. "Jelousy arose that Eaton might not be a willing instrument
to those particular views, that his popularity was growing and it was necessary to put him out of the Cabinet & destroy him." The implied future
that Jackson mentioned was Calhoun's presidential aspirations. The vice
president certainly held them, and by isolating himself in South Carolina
for much of 1829, he allowed those opposing his ambitions to encourage
Jackson's suspicions about him. In December Jackson wrote a private letter to John Overton endorsing Van Buren as his successor. He deemed the
New Yorker "well qualified" to assume leadership of the nation and protect
the "rights and liberty" of the people. "I wish I could say as much for Mr.
Calhoun and some of his friends," he wrote. "You know the confidence I
once had in that gentleman . . . but I have a right to believe that most of
the troubles, vexations, and difficulties I have had to encounter, since my
arrival in this City, have been occasioned by his friends."[16]

Understanding why Jackson latched on to John C. Calhoun as the primary conspirator behind the Eaton affair is not difficult. Despite their
shared southern identity, the two men held different perspectives about
how best to benefit their region. Jackson was interested in establishing
white equality at the expense of nonwhites, including African Americans
and Native Americans. The distinction between whites was based on character, actions, honor, and, ultimately, whether one agreed with him. Calhoun was a classical aristocrat who held to the notion that the white elite
should govern over not only slaves and Native Americans but also lower-

class whites. Jackson supported the tariff; Calhoun did not. They also found themselves on opposing sides when it came to the Second Bank of the United States and the distribution of the federal surplus. The political expediency that brought Jackson and Calhoun together was unable to keep them together.[17]

Besides the Eaton affair, nullification served as a significant ideological division between Jackson and Calhoun. After the passage of the Tariff of 1828, the South Carolina state legislature had asked Calhoun to write a challenge to the measure. He responded with "Exposition and Protest," in which he criticized the tariff as an unconstitutional attempt to tax the minority interests of southerners for the benefit of the rest of the nation. To counter this move, and any unconstitutional laws, he argued, states should elect delegates to conventions, where national legislation could be vetoed if it infringed on a state's sovereignty. Specifically for southern states, this veto mechanism, called "interposition" or "nullification," would serve to protect plantation agriculture and the slave labor needed to grow cash crops such as cotton and sugar.[18]

In addition to Calhoun's anonymous views on nullification, which became public despite his attempts to conceal them, there was also the Seminole controversy. By the time he was elected, Jackson was fully aware of Calhoun's criticism of his 1818 invasion of Florida. His friend Henry Lee had sent Old Hickory evidence through Sam Houston during the 1828 campaign. Eaton and Lewis advised ignoring Calhoun's duplicity for the sake of the election. Jackson agreed to go along with their counsel, but his suspicion of Calhoun's trustworthiness festered. Calhoun's reluctance to support the Eatons in 1829 and his wife's refusal to accord Margaret the respect due her position only cemented Jackson's view of his vice president. In May 1830 the president received a letter from his former political opponent William H. Crawford outlining Calhoun's criticism of him during the late 1810s. Jackson now determined to expose his vice president.[19]

In a letter to Calhoun later that month, Jackson expressed his "great surprise" at Crawford's accusation. He wanted to know if Calhoun had supported an attempt in Monroe's cabinet to have him censured or removed from his command. Calhoun replied with a lengthy recounting of the timeline and circumstances related to the Seminole affair. He criticized Crawford extensively for reigniting the controversy and for causing the president to question his loyalty. Despite his verbose explanation of his actions in the Monroe administration, Calhoun wanted Jackson to realize that he was not apologizing or making excuses for performing his official duties as Monroe's advisor. The vice president's reply failed to satisfy Jackson. "I had too exalted an opinion of your honor and frankness, to believe for one moment that you could be capable of such deception," the president wrote. "I had a right to believe that you were my sincere friend, and, until now, never expected to have the occasion to say to you, in the language of Caesar, *Et tu Brute*."[20]

The two men's relationship continued to deteriorate. By the end of 1830 Calhoun had decided to take his case to the public in the pages of the *U.S. Telegraph*. (By this point the *Globe*, edited by Kentuckians Blair and Kendall, had replaced Green's publication as the official administration organ.) In mid-February 1831 the *U.S. Telegraph* published a fifty-two-page overview and defense of Calhoun's actions regarding the Seminole controversy. Jackson, who anticipated this broadside from the Calhoun camp, announced that his vice president and his editorial friend "have cut their own throats, and destroyed themselves in a shorter space of time than any two men I ever knew."[21]

Calhoun's public self-immolation allowed Jackson and his allies to bring the Eaton affair to a favorable conclusion. First, Eaton and Van Buren resigned on 7 April 1831. What seemed counterintuitive was actually brilliant. Van Buren's idea allowed Jackson to request the resignations of his other cabinet members (excepting Barry, who managed to stay above the fray). Jackson thus freed himself from the divisiveness among his official advisors, allowing him to form a new, more malleable cabinet. Van Buren calculated that he could prove his loyalty to Jackson by offering himself as a sacrifice. To make the plan work, however, the secretary of war had to leave as well. Eaton had considered such a move less than two months into Jackson's administration; now here was another opportunity to divest himself of the burden that accompanied his public appointment. After what was likely a tense discussion with his wife, Eaton agreed to join Van Buren in leaving the cabinet. To cover his departure, in his letter of resignation Eaton wrote that he had never wanted to be part of the cabinet and had been looking for an opportunity to leave at "the first favorable moment." Berrien, Branch, and Ingham saw through the thinly veiled ploy to force their resignations and protested publicly but to no avail. As he often did, Jackson got his wish, but not before Eaton and Ingham almost fought a duel over the former Treasury secretary's alleged besmirching of Margaret's name.[22]

Later that year Jackson's family also reconciled. Andrew and Emily Donelson, along with relatives Mary Eastin and Mary McLemore, returned to Washington on September 5. Friends and relatives in Tennessee had paved the way for the reunion by emphasizing Jackson's need to have family by his side. The president was still angry, telling Van Buren, "They know my *course,* and my wishes, and I hope, they come to comply with them." Assuming his former position as private secretary, Andrew Donelson asked John Coffee to burn his letters on the Eaton affair to save Jackson and himself embarrassment. To mollify their uncle, he and Emily avoided socializing with those who had opposed the Eatons. Jackson the patriarch had implemented his will, for that moment restoring order to his family.[23]

Historians have offered many interpretations of the Eaton affair, beginning with James Parton's titillating claim in 1861 that "the political history of the United States, for the last thirty years, dates from the moment when the soft hand of Mr. Van Buren touched Mrs. Eaton's knocker." For decades historians simply ignored the affair, and when they mentioned it, they offered it as an example of the competition between Calhoun and Van Buren for the presidency. Recent scholars have looked at the affair through the prism of women's history, examining what it says about gender expectations in the early republic.[24]

The controversy over the Eaton marriage also speaks, however, to tensions within southern society. Honor and patriarchal authority were at stake, as Jackson attempted to control not only his political allies but also his clients and kin, specifically Andrew and Emily Donelson. Andrew Donelson's reluctance to follow his uncle's instructions regarding the Eatons in particular displayed a level of disloyalty that threatened their relationship as patron and client, as well as guardian and ward. Jackson's belief that his nephew and niece were allowing Calhoun, the "great Magician," to manipulate them also demonstrated their lack of fidelity to him as their patriarch. As Jackson told John Coffee, "The nation expects me to controle my household."[25]

The Eaton imbroglio also exposed southern dissatisfaction with Jackson over the tariff. "For certain participants," one historian of the Eaton affair wrote, the so-called Petticoat War "was more an expression of anti–Van Buren and anti-tariff sentiment than of support for Calhoun's presidential aspirations." Although Jackson strove to avoid pitting Calhoun and Van Buren, two of his major allies, against one another with his cabinet selections, that is exactly what happened as the Eaton affair developed. Disloyalty to the Eatons became conflated with disloyalty to Van Buren; opposing either man put one at odds with Jackson. Within the administration Berrien, Branch, and Calhoun criticized Eaton and Van Buren not only for their social influence over Old Hickory but also because the two advisors had allegedly orchestrated passage of the 1828 Tariff of Abominations. Thus, Eaton and Van Buren, not the president, controlled the Jackson administration's approach to the tariff issue. Outside of Washington, especially in South Carolina, the Eaton affair alerted some southerners that Jackson could not be trusted to do his duty as a slave-owning planter. Associating the Eaton affair with the tariff thus threatened not only to divide Old Hickory's political supporters but also to tear the nation apart.[26]

Rachel Jackson portrait, by Louisa Catherine Strobel (after Ralph E. W. Earl), c. 1831.
Courtesy The Hermitage: Home of President Andrew Jackson, Nashville, Tenn.

Andrew Jackson Jr. portrait, Ralph E. W. Earl, c. 1835.
Courtesy The Hermitage: Home of President Andrew Jackson, Nashville, Tenn.

Andrew J. Donelson portrait, Francis Alexander, c. 1831.
Courtesy The Hermitage: Home of President Andrew Jackson, Nashville, Tenn.

Andrew J. Hutchings portrait, unknown artist, c. 1835.
Courtesy The Hermitage: Home of President Andrew Jackson, Nashville, Tenn.

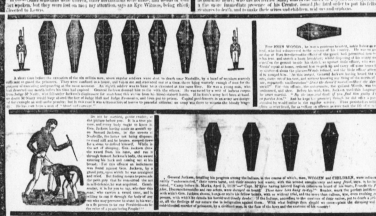

"Some Account of Some of the Bloody Deeds of General Jackson" ("Coffin Handbill").
Courtesy Prints and Photographs Division, Library of Congress, LC-USZ62-43901.

"King Andrew the First."
Courtesy Prints and Photographs Division, Library of Congress, LC-USZ62-1562.

Aunt Hannah, W. G. and A. J. Thuss of Nashville, c. 1880.
Courtesy The Hermitage: Home of President Andrew Jackson, Nashville, Tenn.

XIV

"To the Brink of Insurrection and Treason"

The Eaton affair and its question of presidential authority posed serious problems for Jackson early in his administration. A congressional debate over public lands, however, set the stage for the most dangerous political crisis of his first presidential term. The situation forced Jackson to navigate treacherous political waters between his southern identity as a slave owner and his presidential responsibilities. Central to the choice was the tension between states' rights and the Union.

In January 1830 a proposal by Senator Samuel A. Foot of Connecticut to limit federal land sales attracted the ire of Jackson's former enemy Senator Thomas Hart Benton of Missouri and Senator Robert Y. Hayne of South Carolina. The debate quickly took on more momentous consequence as Benton argued that Foot had introduced the legislation to limit western emigration in order to provide workers for eastern factories. Hayne expected that northerners intended the bill, like the 1828 Tariff of Abominations, as a blow to states' rights. In a series of speeches he defended the doctrine of nullification and the institution of slavery as bedrock southern principles. Daniel Webster of Massachusetts, the "Demosthenes of America," responded by extolling the viability of national sovereignty, concluding one of his speeches with an emotional appeal to "Liberty and Union, now and forever, one and inseparable!"[1]

Jackson was fully aware of this congressional debate and Calhoun's authorship of "Exposition and Protest." The president made his first public acknowledgment of the ideological divide separating him from his vice president at the annual Jefferson Day banquet held on 13 April 1830. Among those present at the event was the featured speaker, Robert Y. Hayne. With assistance from Van Buren and Andrew Donelson, Jackson composed a toast to respond to Hayne's expected support of nullification. Hayne avoided addressing the topic directly in his speech, but his toast after dinner made clear his views: "The *Union* of the States, and the

Sovereignty of the States." Heads turned to watch Jackson when it was his turn. Standing at his seat, Jackson raised his glass and proclaimed, "Our Union: *It must be preserved.*" An electrified crowd looked to Calhoun for his response. "The Union. Next to our liberty most dear," he asserted but then weakened the effectiveness of his concise retort by providing a short lecture. The printed modification of Jackson's toast to "Our federal Union," which he had intended to say, failed to lessen the significance of the line drawn between Jackson and the South Carolinians.[2]

Despite William T. Barry's belief that "no public evil is likely to result from their personal difference," relations between Jackson and Calhoun continued to deteriorate as the Eaton affair and the Seminole controversy dragged into 1831 and the nullification question loomed larger. Everywhere Jackson looked, he saw Calhoun conspiring to encourage nullification throughout the South. He criticized his vice president for convincing Hayne, Governor James Hamilton Jr., and the people of South Carolina to support this "nulifying doctrine" that "threatens to desolve our happy union." Calhoun, "the ambitious Demagogue . . . would sacrafice friends and country, and move heaven and earth, if he had the power, to gratify his unholy ambition." Jackson also believed that the possible election of Governor Gabriel Moore of Alabama to a U.S. Senate seat was "the secret intrigue of the great *nullifyer.*" When two South Carolinians refused to pay the tariff because they deemed it unconstitutional, an associate informed Jackson that "Mr. Calhoun is at the bottom of this thing." Jackson agreed and stated forcefully, "*The union shall be preserved.*" While some observers believed that Van Buren was "the efficient agent" using nullification to drive a wedge between the president and vice president, in truth it was Jackson who chose to distance himself from Calhoun.[3]

Calhoun's "capacity for self-delusion," as one biographer described it, led him to come out publicly in 1831 with his support of nullification. Throughout the year South Carolina radicals, such as Hayne, Hamilton, James Henry Hammond, and George McDuffie, amplified their rhetorical attacks on the 1828 tariff and the Jackson administration's support of it. Calhoun, seeking to maintain his position in the state and to lessen the radicals' fury, issued a statement on the tariff and nullification in July. Commonly known as the Fort Hill Address, this message clearly indicated Calhoun's support of a strident states' rights doctrine. In addition to outlining his defense of a state's right to veto unconstitutional national legislation, Calhoun also indicated his fear of the tyranny of the majority. *"Let it never be forgotten,"* he wrote, *"that, where the majority rules without restriction, the minority is the subject."*[4]

Jackson totally rejected Calhoun's ideas. They struck at his belief in majority rule and his unquestioned support of the Union. "For the rights of the states, no one has a higher regard and respect than myself, none would go farther to maintain them," he wrote Hayne early in 1831. "But how I ask, is this to be effected?" If the executive or legislative branches overstepped their constitutional authority, Jackson believed that "the remedy is with the people." The solution was not open revolt or violence but through "their free suffrage at the polls." Calhoun's address also confirmed Jackson's conviction that his vice president was plotting his demise. Calhoun and editor Duff Green had sought "some plan to destroy me," he told Van Buren, but "they have fell into the Pitt they had dug for me." "Mr. Calhouns nullification expose has destroyed his prospects forever, in reaching the Presidential chair," Jackson proclaimed.[5]

The future that Jackson predicted for his vice president came true. In January 1832 Calhoun, in his role as president of the Senate, sealed his fate within the Jackson administration by casting the tie-breaking vote against the president's nomination of Van Buren as minister to Great Britain. "I have no hesitation in saying that Calhoun is one of the most base hypocritical and unprincipled villains in the United States," Jackson wrote John Coffee. His "vote in the case of Mr. Van Buren, has displayed a want of every sense of honor, justice or magnanimity." Calhoun's actions "dam'd him by all honest men in the senate" and would "not only dam him and his associates, but astonish the american people." The vote benefited Van Buren and solidified his place on the Democratic ticket in the upcoming election, a decision ratified by the first Democratic party national nominating convention, held in Baltimore in May 1832.[6]

As the Democrats adjourned their convention, a resolution to the tariff issue seemed imminent. Congress passed a new tariff in June that possessed bipartisan, bisectional support. Average rates dropped to about 25 percent overall. Rates were cut on certain products important to the South, such as coffee, cotton bagging, and the cheap woolen cloth, called "negro cloth," used to make slave clothing, while protectionist rates on certain goods, such as iron, cotton, and woolens, remained near 50 percent. A majority of both northern and southern congressmen supported the new tariff; in the U.S. House, 60 percent of the congressional representatives from slaveholding states voted for it. Recognizing that the national debt was nearly paid off and that tariff revenue would shortly produce a substantial surplus, Jackson signed the tariff into law. The sectional crisis that some predicted seemingly had been averted.[7]

Not so for South Carolina nullifiers. They believed George McDuffie's erroneous claim that the tariff was costing cotton planters the equivalent of forty out of every one hundred bales. Yet more than the economic cost of paying tariffs was at stake during the 1832 nullification debate. Nullifiers also believed that ceding constitutional ground on the tariff would jeopardize slavery's future. They were persuaded of this certainty for several reasons. First, Henry Clay proposed that the tariff revenue and projected surplus should be distributed to the states in order to assist in colonizing emancipated slaves. Nullifiers were also appalled by the publication on 1 January 1831 of the *Liberator's* inaugural issue, edited by William Lloyd Garrison. The Boston abolitionist explained his purpose in founding the newspaper: "I determined, at every hazard, to lift up the standard of emancipation in the eyes of the nation, within sight of Bunker Hill and in the birthplace of liberty. That standard is now unfurled; and long may it float, unhurt by the spoliations of time or the missiles of a desperate foe—yea, till every chain be broken, and every bondman set free! Let Southern oppressors tremble—let their secret abettors tremble—let their Northern apologists tremble—let all the enemies of the persecuted blacks tremble." Southern slave owners could not fail to notice Garrison's determination and potential influence. Another shock was the slave rebellion led by Nat Turner in Southampton County, Virginia, in August 1831. Although lasting only seventy-two hours, Turner and his supporters killed approximately fifty-eight whites. South Carolinians, especially those living in and around Charleston, were aware of the population disparity that left them vulnerable to potential slave uprisings, such as the one formulated by former slave Denmark Vesey in Charleston in 1822. All of these events signaled a growing discomfort with slavery's existence.[8]

Throughout 1832 prominent South Carolinians thus warned of a disastrous future if a stand against the tariff was not soon taken. At a Fourth of

July gathering Robert J. Turnbull, a longtime and prominent supporter of nullification, appealed to the example of the American Revolution in urging his listeners not to compromise on the tariff issue. Only "an unflinching, uncompromising firmness" would help keep them from their "present degraded condition of slaves and colonists." James Henry Hammond, a Columbia, South Carolina, lawyer and newspaper editor, urged his fellow citizens to nullify the tariff quickly. They should not wait for a united southern movement to act against the national government's encroachment. Otherwise, the moment might be lost. In another speech given that Independence Day, state legislator Robert Barnwell Smith (later Rhett) referred to the threat to slavery posed by northerners emboldened by a victory over nullifiers. Governor James Hamilton Jr. conducted a tour of the state's militia units, during which he attempted to rally white men against the forces of tyranny that he feared would incite slaves to revolt.[9]

On October 22 Governor Hamilton convened a special legislative session and requested that the legislators call for a nullification convention as soon as possible. The South Carolina legislature voted in support of his proposal; delegates were elected, and the convention met in Charleston on November 19. The only notable absence was Calhoun, who was finishing out his term as vice president. A committee of twenty-one delegates produced an ordinance of nullification and several addresses expounding their reasoning. The documents nullified the tariffs of 1828 and 1832, demanded a tariff rate of 12 percent, and warned that any attempt to forcibly collect the tariff under existing rates would lead to violence. The ordinance was scheduled to go into effect on 1 February 1833. On November 24, by a vote of 136 to 26, delegates approved the ordinance. Hamilton then asked the legislature to authorize the creation of a twelve thousand–man army in case President Jackson attempted to enforce the tariff collection. In a series of moves that indicated that Calhoun, while not present at the nullification convention, approved of its course, Hayne resigned his Senate seat in order to assume the governorship from Hamilton. This move allowed the legislature to elect Calhoun as Hayne's replacement; Calhoun resigned the vice presidency on December 28.[10]

Jackson was furious. During a meeting with several South Carolina representatives in Lexington, Kentucky, on his return to Washington early in the fall, the president reportedly promised to "hang them as high as high Olympus" if South Carolina did not collect the mandated tariffs. Yet Jackson kept his temper in check in composing his fourth annual message. He mentioned the tariff controversy without naming South Carolina and sent a firm but gentle warning that if the nullifiers refused to allow "moderation and good sense" to prevail, then "the laws themselves are fully adequate to the suppression of such attempts as may be immediately made." Less than a week later, however, Jackson issued a stronger and less generous proclamation to the people of South Carolina indicating his resolve to maintain the Union. Drafted by Francis Blair, Secretary of War Lewis Cass, Amos Kendall, Secretary of State Edward Livingston, and Jackson himself, the Nullification Proclamation articulated a strong nationalist stand against the actions taken by the South Carolina dissidents. "An attempt, by force of arms, to destroy a government is an offense," he argued, "and such government has the right by the law of self-defense to pass acts for punishing the offender." Jackson also employed the language of paternalism that had been a hallmark of his communications with Native Americans during the 1810s: "Fellow-citizens of my native State, let me not only admonish you, as the First Magistrate of our common country, not to incur the penalty of its laws, but use the influence that a father would over his children whom he saw rushing to certain ruin." Men such as Calhoun had led the state "to the brink of insurrection and treason," which Jackson said he would stop. "The laws of the United States must be executed. I have no discretionary power on the subject; my duty is emphatically pronounced in the Constitution," he warned. "Those who told you that you might peaceably prevent their execution deceived you . . . They know that a forcible opposition could alone prevent the execution of the laws, and they know that such opposition must be repelled." Their goal, Jackson cautioned, was disunion, and "disunion by armed force is treason." "Are you really ready to incur its guilt?" he asked. "If you are, on the heads of the instigators of the act be the dreadful consequences; on their heads be the dishonor, but on yours may fall the punishment."[11]

Jackson had been readying himself for the "dreadful consequences" for months. "I am prepared to act with promptness and energy; and, should the laws be resisted, to enforce them with energy and promptness," he wrote William B. Lewis in late August. After boasting that he could enlist ten thousand Tennesseans to help him, Jackson assured his friend, "Fear not; the Union shall be preserved." Throughout the months leading up to the presidential election, Jackson ordered military officials in Charleston to prepare for possible action. In the fall he dispatched George Breathitt, the brother of Kentucky governor John Breathitt, clandestinely to Charleston, under the guise of inspecting the city's post office; his real mission was to spy on the nullifiers and assess defense preparations should conflict ensue. Regular reports from Joel R. Poinsett, a former minister to Mexico and a staunch South Carolina Unionist, assisted Jackson in assessing the threat to peace in Charleston as 1832 drew to a close. "With respect to the officers of government who are aiding and abetting the nullifying party," Poinsett observed, "there are many. The post Office is entirely filled with them. The Post Master, His Deputy, his son, and all the clerks are active Agents of that party and clamourous Nullifiers."[12]

With confrontation in Charleston seeming more likely every day, on 16 January 1833 Jackson asked Congress to approve his actions already taken and allow him the latitude to make military decisions without warning the nullifiers. Jackson's Tennessee ally Senator Felix Grundy moved that Jackson's message be taken up by the judiciary committee, which was weighted in the president's favor. Several days later the committee produced legislation, often referred to as the "Force Bill," that gave Jackson what he wanted: power to collect tariffs in a secure location, legal protection for federal officers collecting those tariffs, and authorization to use the national army and navy to enforce their collection. A spirited debate in the full chamber ensued, with Calhoun, now seated in the Senate, and Webster, seemingly moving into Jackson's camp, wielding their rhetorical swords. Jackson's message faced stiffer opposition in the House, where Tennessean John Bell was unable to win an affirmative vote on similar legislation coming out of that chamber's judiciary committee. Incensed at Jackson's actions but treading carefully as congressional consideration continued, South Carolina's nullifiers agreed to delay nullification, originally scheduled to go into effect on February 1, until after the congressional session ended in March. "There is nothing certain," Henry Clay remarked, "but that the will of Andrew Jackson is to govern."[13]

Behind the scenes two men, Calhoun and Clay, quite unexpectedly were formulating a compromise that would end the standoff between Jackson and South Carolina. Seeing that efforts by some of Jackson's congressional supporters, including James K. Polk, to pass a compromise tariff were foundering in the U.S. House, Clay approached Calhoun with a proposal. Calhoun agreed to support Clay's legislation, which the Kentuckian introduced to the Senate floor on February 12. His plan called for a gradual reduction of tariff rates listed over 20 percent in the 1832 tariff. Once all tariff rates were down to 20 percent or lower in 1840, a two-year moratorium would take effect. The plan gave manufacturers time to adjust to the changing rates, which had been one of the major obstacles to the compromise tariff proposed by Polk and other Jacksonians in early January. Calhoun pronounced his endorsement of Clay's proposal, signaling a possible end to the nation's crisis.[14]

The deal between his two enemies displeased Jackson. So, too, did the decision by his Tennessee ally Hugh Lawson White, president pro tempore of the Senate, to make Clay the chair and Calhoun a member of the committee charged with hammering out the details of a compromise. The president tried to influence White's selection of the committee, but his protests fell on deaf ears. White selected a committee of diverse opinions in order to ensure passage of whatever legislation emerged. Jackson declared himself "mortified" that White had ignored his request; the two men, already drifting apart, were headed toward a public separation.[15]

With Jacksonian Democrats wanting to avoid both violent confrontation and a potential alliance between the president and the untrustworthy Webster, the Clay-Calhoun alliance gave Jackson a significant victory. After much parliamentary maneuvering and partisan posturing, on February 20 the Senate passed the Force Bill; six days later the House passed the compromise tariff. On March 1 the House passed the Force Bill, and just a few hours later the Senate passed the tariff bill. The next day Jackson signed both bills, starting with the Force Bill. When the South Carolina nullifiers met on March 11, they voted to abandon their earlier nullification ordinance, thus ending the crisis. Intent on demonstrating their defiance of Jackson's executive authority, however, they voted to nullify the Force Bill. The president had not clung to his "Southern principles," one observer noted, but he had respected the Constitution, "throw[ing] himself in the breach . . . disregarding his maternal feelings" for his native state.[16]

Jackson believed that he had defeated Calhoun and the nullifiers. "Nullification is dead," he wrote Reverend Andrew J. Crawford, "its actors and exciters will only be remembered by the people to be execrated for their wicked designs to sever and destroy the only good government on the globe." He was not fooled, however, by South Carolina's efforts. "The tariff is only the pretext and disunion and a southern confederacy the real object. The next pretext," he warned, "will be the negro, or slavery question."[17]

XV

"A Man Indebted Is a Slave"

While serving the public was Jackson's primary responsibility, his family and Hermitage plantation were never far from his mind during his years as president. Several relatives—principally Andrew and Emily Donelson and their children as well as Junior, his wife, Sarah Yorke, and their children—resided at the White House for extended periods. Jackson made four trips back to Tennessee during the summer months of 1830, 1832, 1834, and 1836. These journeys sometimes included political events, such as meetings with Native American representatives, but they were primarily to help him observe the progress of his plantation and spend time away from the pressures of the nation's capital.[1]

When not in Nashville, Jackson relied on a number of kin and friends to ensure that his farming affairs were in order. Charles J. Love, one of Jackson's longtime Tennessee friends and business associates, was a frequent visitor to the Hermitage, his Mansfield plantation being nearby. He reported on the conditions of Jackson's crops, the aptitude of his overseers, and the treatment of his slaves. Old Hickory also trusted the reports of his former military aide Robert Armstrong, whom he appointed as Nashville's postmaster in 1829. Junior, Andrew Donelson, and William B. Lewis also corresponded frequently with Jackson.[2]

Jackson retained several overseers during his presidency. The first, Graves W. Steele, was hired before Jackson left for Washington in 1829. He signed a four-year contract to manage the Hermitage as well as Andrew Donelson's adjoining plantation. Jackson paid him five hundred dollars annually and agreed to allow Steele's brother Nathaniel to assist him. Trouble surrounded Steele's tenure as overseer from the start. Jackson's relative James G. Martin reported that Steele had problems controlling Donelson's slaves. Within six months three of Jackson's male slaves died. The president ordered Junior to determine whether Steele's "cruelty" was responsible for the death of one slave, Jim, and to discharge the overseer if so. Love reassured Jackson that Jim's death was not Steele's fault, a report that Junior corroborated. The president still possessed reservations, however, telling his son that he wanted to keep Steele "if he will only treat my slaves with hummanity."[3]

Jackson's uncertainty about Steele grew that fall, when the Hermitage suffered a "great loss of horses & oxen." Jackson demanded that the overseer account for the losses, threatened to dock his pay, and warned him that he was expendable. John Coffee indicated his dislike of Steele to Andrew Donelson, who also had a vested interest in the overseer's success. William Donelson, who held a positive view of Steele from the beginning, interceded on his behalf, attributing some of the losses to the overseer's "ignorance and the want of proper experiance." Steele failed to endear himself to Jackson by writing him "a very insolent letter" announcing his determination to leave by mid-1830. Steele's threat never materialized.[4]

Steele learned from his mistakes, at least for a while. Jackson's New Orleans factor, Maunsel White, reported in January 1831 that the overseer had "done his duty so far" in providing good bales of cotton for the market. A few months later Coffee wrote that Steele had the Hermitage "in good order" and had been an amiable host to members of the family. Ultimately, however, Steele's lack of financial acuity, misuse of Jackson's horses, and general insubordination cost him his job at the end of 1832. Jackson warned Junior not to let Steele know about the intended change. "This must be kept secrete from him or he will neglect all business and leave everything, crop & all, in as bad a state as he can," Jackson predicted.[5]

Given Steele's incompetence, Jackson could have moved on to another overseer much earlier. That he did not is puzzling, although several factors may have prevented a change. Upper South planters tended to employ overseers for several years, a social norm with which Jackson would have been familiar. He probably preferred a multiyear contract, especially given the frequent turnover in the overseer position; prior to Steele's hiring, Jackson's Hermitage overseers often lasted only one to three years. Stability at the position, especially for an absentee planter, was prized. Jackson also had the security of friends and relatives nearby to keep an eye on his affairs and intervene if necessary.[6]

Jackson's next two overseers proved just as disappointing as Steele. Burnard W. Holtzclaw assumed the overseer duties in 1833. His first extant letter to Jackson conveyed news of the death of a colt and a male slave, Samson. "I Git alongue With you Negrows Verer will indeede," he reassured his employer. Holtzclaw's indifference to the illness of a slave child resulted in the boy's death, leading to questions about the overseer's character. Reassuring letters convinced Jackson to keep Holtzclaw on, especially because he reportedly could manage the slaves without too much discipline. Yet Holtzclaw's demise came after just one year. He only raised eighty-six hogs to kill in the fall; Jackson believed that close to four hundred should have been ready to slaughter. The president left the decision up to Junior, but he instructed his son not to change the terms of service. "Better to abandon farming than to keep it up for the benefit of an overseer bringing me in debt," Jackson complained, "as it has for two years past."[7]

Jackson originally considered hiring Holtzclaw's successor, Edward Hobbs, in 1832 but delayed retaining him until 1834. The president instructed Junior to articulate fully in writing Hobbs's responsibilities. The overseer's specific duties "should be all enumerated in your agreement, or he may say hereafter that nothing but what was enumerated was he bound to take the superintendence off," Jackson advised his son. "The old adage, 'deal with all men as tho they were rogues,'" was his recommendation. By the spring of 1835 Jackson pronounced himself "delighted" with Hobbs's "course and proceedings." But like Steele and Holtzclaw, Hobbs began to disappoint. That fall he demanded higher wages, despite the poor prospects for cotton's profitability. By March 1836 Jackson complained that Hobbs was derelict in his duties, especially regarding his livestock and horses. "They are overfed some days and starved the next," he told Junior. Hobbs's job was either to take care of the animals himself or discipline the responsible slave until he worked more consistently. Neglecting to provide adequately for the Hermitage slaves and failing to update Jackson on Emily Donelson's illness sealed his fate as Jackson's overseer beyond 1836.[8]

Jackson's interaction with his overseers underscored his desire for efficient and profitable farming. He fired Steele, Holtzclaw, and Hobbs primarily for not meeting his expectations regarding the Hermitage's crops and livestock. Jackson's annual presidential salary of twenty-five thousand dollars was substantial, but his expenditures in Nashville were also significant. His dealings with the overseers also demonstrated the value that he placed on his slaves. Jackson expected his overseers to manage the enslaved labor without compromising the plantation's operations. An over-seer had to correct actions that led to a decline in slave productivity, or he might find himself looking for a new position.[9]

While Jackson's overseers were important agricultural managers, pri-mary responsibility for the plantation's oversight fell to Junior, who often failed to reward the confidence placed in him by his father. "You are young, and now for the first time distant from me," he reminded Junior shortly after taking office, "but I have confidence that you will steer clear of evil company, & all disapation." Two years later the refrain was simi-lar: "It is now time to settle yourself and your mind to business." Jackson sent his son specific instructions about what needed to be done with the cotton, the livestock, and his mother's tomb. Jackson also regularly sent directions about whether to buy or sell land and horses. Additionally, the president expected Junior to make sure the overseers treated slaves appro-priately and managed the farm's resources wisely. A further responsibil-ity was passing on the neighborhood and family gossip. "I have heard that Mr. J[ames Glasgow] Martin has become deranged," Jackson wrote in Au-gust 1829, "please advise me, correctly, on this unpleasant subject." Jack-son's missives were often met with silence. "I was growing uneasy to hear from you, lest some accident might have befallen you," he wrote Junior in July 1831. "Be sure to write your cousin Andrew J. Donelson," Jackson rec-ommended the following year. "He says he has wrote you several times and has not recd. one letter in return." When his coaxing failed to pro-duce more letters, Jackson told his daughter-in-law that he was not going to "write him [Junior] again until I hear from him."[10]

Jackson was especially frustrated with Junior over the rebuilding of the main house at the Hermitage. In mid-October 1834 the roof of the house caught fire, causing considerable damage to the second story. Robert Arm-strong estimated that Jackson could rebuild the house, using the undam-aged main walls, for no more than twenty-five hundred dollars. Jackson ordered Junior to begin the rebuilding process, cautioning him to "act with oeco[no]my" regarding the cotton crop, which was the only means of "re-pairing" their home. Junior supervised the reconstruction of the house, which lasted well into 1836. As the work was completed, Robert Arm-strong informed the president that he owed the laborers eight hundred dol-lars beyond the eighteen hundred dollars that Jackson had budgeted. Jackson wrote Junior a pleading letter asking him to examine the remaining accounts to ensure that no more surprises arose. He wanted to put an end to being "constantly harassed with calls for money when I have none." Junior failed to receive his father's advice in time and incurred another debt that prompted Jackson to order his son, "Draw no more on me until I can get funds." A rebuilding project that had been estimated at no more than twenty-five hundred dollars ballooned to nearly four thousand dollars and eventually cost Jackson over five thousand dollars.[11]

Jackson tried to deal with such matters by freely dispensing financial advice to his son, whether he wanted it or not. He warned Junior "never to go in debt–a man indebted is a slave, & placed under circumstances with his creditors, that may subject his feelings to injury & insult." Jackson had been "ruined" two times by becoming security for someone else; the lesson for him was never to loan money unless he was able to live without seeing the debt repaid. When Jackson asked his son to look into making a land purchase near the Hermitage, he reminded him to be "guarded." "Conclude no contract . . . without furnishing me with the propositions and have all the propositions reduced to writing before you accede to any" was Jackson's order. After Junior purchased tools that were "not fit for coarse work," his father admonished him to live frugally: "Never buy any thing that is useless, or that you have not immediate want of–and particularly when you do not pay for it."[12]

In addressing Junior's financial troubles, Jackson found himself in a position familiar to that of other southern patriarchs. He had trained Junior to be dependent on him, never trusting him with total autonomy while serving as president. Therefore, Junior never stood alone or learned from his own mistakes. His inability to become a successful "planter-patriarch" highlighted one of the ironies of southern society noted by historian Michael Johnson: "The nature of their fathers' estates and ideals caused sons to be constantly tempted by idleness, a state combining subordination and autonomy in near paralysis." Ever the protective patriarch, Jackson seemed unwilling to allow Junior to suffer the effects of his bad choices, thereby undermining his desire to see his son become independent.[13]

There was one area in which Jackson had special reason to keep close watch over his son. In early 1835 he cautioned Junior about his excessive drinking. Jackson held up examples of two young men who had lost standing in the community because of their "intoxication" and reminded Junior that people watched the president's son to ensure that he followed "the rules of strict decorum and propriety." Jackson's political enemies would use Junior's intemperance against the president, but, Jackson warned, Junior also needed to consider the effect on his wife and children. Additionally, Jackson was concerned about how his son's conduct would reflect on his own legacy. He proclaimed himself pleased with Junior's decision not to drink from the "poisonous c[h]alice" because "in your reputation, my future fame depends." The early-nineteenth-century United States was an alcoholic republic, but in Jackson's house, where bourbon flowed freely, intemperance was verboten.[14]

As if worrying about Junior's financial mismanagement and alcohol abuse were not enough, Jackson also had to ensure that his son's courtship manners did not entangle him in dishonorable conduct. In 1829 Junior had set his sights on Mary Florida Dickson. Flora, as she was called, was the ward of Jackson's friend Edward Ward. Junior's attempts to woo her fell flat, leading Jackson to observe that "she has give herself up to coquettry." Junior was better-off, "as I seldom ever saw a coquett, make a good wife." He reminded his son that "my happiness depends much on the prudence of your choice" of a wife. The following year Junior failed to win the heart of Mary Frances Trigg Smith, daughter of a Virginia saltworks operator. Jackson was forced to write her father, Frances Smith, when Junior neglected to indicate to Mary's parents "his honorable intentions." Jackson asked Smith to forgive his son's "error" and "ascribe it to his youth, diffidence and inexperience." Jackson noted later that fall that Junior's "dulcinea is coquetting him."[15]

As late as September 1831, Jackson hinted that Junior should consider pursuing Mary Ann Lewis, daughter of William B. Lewis. "You know she is a great favorite of mine, and that she was also your dear deceased mother," he told his son. "I have no doubt that she would make a sweet and affectionate companion." Junior, however, had already met his future wife, Sarah Yorke of Philadelphia, who, along with her two sisters, had been orphaned and raised by two aunts. Junior and Sarah married in Philadelphia on 24 November 1831. Pressed with completing his annual message, Jackson did not attend, sending the artist and family friend Ralph E. W. Earl in his stead.[16]

Junior and Sarah had two children while Jackson was president. The first, Rachel, was born on 1 November 1832 at the Hermitage. Jackson despaired of Sarah's health throughout the pregnancy and chastised Junior frequently for not updating him on her condition. Once Rachel was delivered safely, Jackson became the doting grandfather. "Nothing could give me equal pleasure to that of seeing you all, and taking little Rachel in my arms, kissing & kissing it," he wrote. Indeed, Jackson's nickname for her, Little Rachel, stuck; he often referred to her as his "little pet." Little Rachel "is spritely, but as wild as a little pa[r]tridge, & a little petted and spoiled," he told Mary Eastin Polk. On 4 April 1834 Sarah delivered a son, Andrew Jackson III. Jackson was thrilled once again, telling Junior that he hoped "providence" would allow the infant to "be a blessing and comfort to his parents in their declining years, an ornament to that society in which he may be placed." Within just a few months Jackson proclaimed him "a fine stout fellow."[17]

Another of Jackson's continued concerns was the conduct of Andrew J. Hutchings, who was suspended from the University of Nashville in early 1829 for assaulting a professor. He returned to the Hermitage, where Charles Love reported that he was "very much in the way." Jackson's brother-in-law John Donelson told him that relatives were at their wits' end with Hutchings. "He was asked some time ago what he intended," Donelson relayed, "his answer was a D[amn] rich old farmer like the rest of his kin Folks." An exasperated Jackson wrote Coffee that he had "lost all hope of making Hutchings a classic scholar," but he still would try to get him a place at Nashville's Harpeth Academy. To Hutchings, Jackson wrote, "I must again i[m]press upon your mind the great [value] of an education," reminding him that he had spent too much of his "time in idleness & folly." When Hutchings refused to attend a school in nearby Franklin, Tennessee, Jackson considered sending him to a Washington, D.C., Catholic school, where he would "be able to controle him & convince him of the impropriety of his ways."[18]

By late 1829 Hutchings had enrolled at Georgetown College. Within a few months, however, Jackson sent him back to Tennessee to study at a school in Columbia. Jackson admitted to Coffee that his presidential duties in Washington made it impossible for him to keep track of Hutchings. The young man soon ran into trouble with Jackson's overseer at the time, Graves Steele, who objected to Hutchings's "misuse" of the Hermitage slaves. The two men fought, prompting Jackson to order Hutchings to leave the slaves' management and discipline to Steele. The pattern of trouble continued in 1832, when Hutchings was dismissed from the University of Virginia for not attending classes. The following year Hutchings finally reached his majority and took control of the Alabama estate that Jackson and Coffee had superintended. He married Coffee's daughter Mary in October 1833. Mary proved to be the "good affectionate wife" that Jackson had recommended to his former ward, one whose "amiable temper, good sense and economy" tamed the wild youth who had successfully challenged Old Hickory's paternal authority.[19]

The disagreement between Hutchings and Steele over the slaves' management highlighted a persistent problem for Jackson (and other slave owners): how best to keep slaves healthy and productive. There were those who died under Steele and Holtzclaw, and there were others who suffered from disease. In those cases Jackson's attitude reflected his religious sentiments: "It is our duty to see that they are comfortable & well attended, this being done, our duty is performed to them, and when the summons comes, we must with patience submit to its call." When several other slaves also died from neglect or mistreatment, their demise drew Jackson's immediate attention. Andrew Donelson reported in 1833 that two Hermitage slaves had died and a number seemed "as tho they were entirely abandoned by their owners, and in a state of despair." Jackson immediately instructed Junior to visit the slaves and "encourage [and] convince them that we are constantly watching over them, and their good treatment, and will not permit them to be ill-treated or misused."[20]

Such problems failed to dissuade Jackson from continuing to acquire slaves, who numbered ninety-five at the Hermitage. Prior to leaving for Washington in January 1829, he purchased Candis and Betsy, the wife and daughter of his slave Titus. After assuming office, Jackson engaged in additional transactions involving at least twenty slaves. He purchased fourteen slaves, placing some at the Hermitage and giving several as gifts to relatives. Jackson also underwrote the purchase of two slaves, a boy and a girl, by Andrew Donelson. Sometimes these purchases stretched Jackson financially. Junior purchased a female slave, Rachel, and her child in late 1833, for example, but failed to pay the full amount, leading the seller,

George Hibb, to press the president for the funds. Jackson sent his son a harsh letter, asking why the eight hundred dollars that the sale of a horse had generated was not "sufficient to pay for the wench and child." Junior excused his behavior because he needed extra money to cover the cost of travel and illness. Jackson's response was typical: he paid his son's debt but not without several lectures on practicing frugality and punctuality.[21]

Jackson handled his personal affairs and conducted his presidential duties while suffering from continual physical pain. At various times during his administration, doctors bled him to provide relief from internal hemorrhaging and bloody expectorations from coughing. In 1832 Dr. Thomas Harris removed the bullet embedded in Jackson's left shoulder from his 1813 street brawl with the Bentons. This surgery provided some relief, but headaches, internal abscesses, and the common ills of a man in his sixties frequently left the president in discomfort and short of temper. It also led him to ask too much of his kin. In the fall of 1836 Jackson suffered a near-fatal hemorrhage that led family physician Dr. Henry Huntt to take "upwards of 60 ozs. [of] blood" from him. Andrew Donelson, who had been preparing to return to Nashville to tend to his ailing wife, delayed the trip to help his uncle finish his annual message. By the time Donelson made it home in mid-December, Emily was dead.[22]

Family and business responsibilities took up a considerable amount of Jackson's time while president. Of particular concern were Junior's prospects for becoming a successful planter. Ensuring that Junior kept a close eye on plantation affairs was not easy, given his record of irresponsibility. Even Junior's marriage failed to alleviate Jackson's concern that his son was maturing and could sufficiently supervise the overseers, slaves, and relatives who lived at the Hermitage. Preserving his father's wealth, and thereby his own inheritance, was his responsibility. It was a role for which Jackson had been preparing Junior for years.

Jackson's admonitions to Junior in his teenage and early adulthood years make this point clear. Jackson focused his advice to Junior primarily on finances, even after his son was an adult husband and father. Early in their lives Jackson had sought, and usually won, West Point appointments for many of his other male wards, including the Butler and Donelson brothers, Hutchings, and even Lyncoya. Junior, however, was different. It appears that by the time his son approached adulthood, Jackson had determined that while Andrew Donelson was his political heir, Junior was his best hope for securing economic security. Jackson's final will, written in 1843, attests to this interpretation: Junior received Jackson's wealth, while Donelson received only a sword symbolic of Old Hickory's devotion to the Union. Fighting political battles was masculine theater writ large, but in Jackson's eyes providing financial security for one's family was also a sign of southern genteel manhood.[23]

XVI

"That My White and Red Children May Live in Peace"

While dealing with pressing family matters in his first presidential term, Jackson struggled to maintain the loyalty of his advisors during the Eaton affair. At the same time he began to move on a major legislative agenda item: Indian removal. He was not the first president to endorse removal, but given his background as an expansionist and Indian fighter, white southerners could not have asked for a better chief executive.

Jackson entered the presidency already convinced that removal was the only option. During the 1828 campaign he demonstrated that his thinking when he was an Indian commissioner following the War of 1812 had not changed. In 1826 Jackson wrote an Indian commissioner negotiating with the Chickasaw that removing the southern tribes to land west of the Mississippi River would "[strengthen] our Southern border with the white population." The best strategy to accomplish that objective, he said, was to remind the Indians that if they remained, "they will always be exposed to encroachment from the white people" who want their land. As inducement, U.S. commissioners needed to promise them money and suitable other land. Reassurance that the land would be permanently theirs and that "they will never be asked to surrender an acre more" would go a long way toward convincing Native Americans that removal was their best option. To Georgia representative Wilson Lumpkin, Jackson explained his paternalistic justification for supporting removal. Indian tribes "can only be perpetuated as tribes, or nations, by concentrating them west of the Mississippi upon lands secured to them, forever, by the united States, where its homanity, & liberal protecting care, can be extended to them; and where they can be shielded from the encroachments of the whites."[1]

Shortly after taking office, Jackson sent the chiefs of the Creek nation a letter detailing these expectations. The impetus for the communication was the murder of a white settler, Elijah Wells. Jackson called himself the Creek's "father and friend" and reminded them that he did not speak "with a forked tongue" but always "in the language of truth." Wells's murder, he said, required them to give up the killers in order "to prevent the spilling of more blood." The Creek also needed to understand that they and Jackson's "white children are too near each other to live in harmony and peace." Too few animals existed for the Creek to sustain themselves via hunting, and they were unwilling to pursue agriculture as an alternative. The only solution, then, was for the Creek to move to land "beyond the great river Mississippi" where their father (Jackson) promised them land that "will be yours for ever . . . in order that my white and red children may live in peace."[2]

Implementing a successful Indian policy was among the reasons that Jackson appointed John H. Eaton as secretary of war and John M. Berrien as attorney general. When, in March 1829, Jackson sent his letter to the Creek, Eaton encouraged Creek agent John Crowell to convince the Creek of the necessity of moving westward. Less than a month later, in a missive to a Cherokee delegation headed by Principal Chief John Ross, Eaton wrote that the national government could not protect the Cherokee while they remained in Georgia. Berrien, a Georgian, had long been an outspoken advocate of removal. Jackson believed that he could count on both men's assistance in executing his vision.[3]

The Indian Removal Bill of 1830 was Jackson's major legislative initiative to push Native Americans out of the South. Two Tennessee allies, Hugh Lawson White in the Senate and John Bell in the House, chaired the congressional committees with oversight of Indian affairs. On the Senate committee also sat Thomas Hart Benton, Jackson's onetime enemy, now a political ally, and George M. Troup, the former Georgia governor who had advocated removal during the John Quincy Adams administration. In addition to Bell, the House committee had six Jacksonians among its seven members, including four supporters from the South. In a coordinated strategy the two congressional committees issued similar reports within two days of one another in February 1830. At their core they both called for the voluntary removal of Indians from their native lands in the East to new land in the West.[4]

The Senate took up the question first in early April. Theodore Frelinghuysen of New York led the charge against the bill, citing legal and constitutional precedents and invoking religion. The Cherokee, he contended, had become "rational, educated, Christian men" as well as "respectful, devout, and . . . sincere worshipers." God considered Cherokee converts "the 'apple of his eye.'" Other anti-removal senators echoed Frelinghuysen's sentiments, as did some voters. In Vicksburg, Mississippi, lawyer William S. Bodley called the bill "wholesale robbery." "When a President manifests such readiness to set at nought the claims of an injured race of men founded on the most solemn pledges repeatedly given by the Govt," he cautioned, "it is time for the people to look out." "The peculiar attitude of protection of parental guardianship" taken by the Jackson administration was ironic, given that the only reason the United States possessed its "very *power* of protection & guardianship" was the Native Americans' "kindness to our ancestors when the Indians were strong & we were comparatively powerless & absolutely defenceless," Bodley concluded.[5]

Removal supporters, including John Forsyth of Georgia, criticized northerners for their hypocrisy regarding removal, noting that other parts of the Union had removed Native American groups without much debate. Forsyth also argued that the move west was beneficial for Native Americans. He contended, for example, that a small group of Cherokee who had moved west in the late 1810s had "advanced more rapidly . . . in the arts of civilized life" than those who remained in the South. Despite the opposition of Frelinghuysen and others, the Senate bill passed by a vote of 28 to 19. Sixty-eight percent of the affirmative votes came from southern senators; 79 percent of the opposition hailed from outside of the South. Members of the House began debating the Senate bill in mid-May, with discussion continuing along similar lines as in the Senate. After significant parliamentary maneuvering to keep the bill alive, the legislation passed 102 to 97, with southern representatives voting 79 percent in favor of the bill and non-southerners voting 67 percent against it. The measure called for the exchange of land, with Native American groups receiving their new territory in the West in perpetuity. Indians who had improved their land had the option of receiving an allotment of property on or near their tribal land. A total of a half-million dollars in federal funds was also set aside for completing removal. Jackson signed the Indian Removal Bill into law on May 28.[6]

Jackson was confident that the process would occur quickly and smoothly. To carry out his policy, he relied on Eaton, John Coffee, and, to a lesser degree, Tennessee governor William Carroll to communicate his will to the various southern Native American groups. At the same time, Jackson also never hesitated to intervene directly in the negotiations, assuming the role of "Great Father" to remind Native Americans of his past record in treaty making. He returned to the Hermitage in the summer of 1830, for example, in order to meet with Chickasaw chiefs from Mississippi. Jackson, Eaton, and Coffee sat down with the Chickasaw representatives and outlined a preliminary treaty. Two years later the treaty was finalized, but not until 1837 did the emigration of the nearly five thousand Chickasaw and their nearly twelve hundred slaves occur.[7]

The Choctaw in Mississippi presented, as one historian has argued, the "test case" of Jackson's removal policy. Upon concluding talks with the Chickasaw in Franklin, Tennessee, in late August 1830, Jackson sent Eaton and Coffee to Noxubee County, Mississippi, to meet with Choctaw representatives there. One Choctaw leader, Greenwood LeFlore, had attempted to negotiate a treaty with Jackson earlier in the year, so expectations for a successful meeting were high. The terms of the Treaty of Dancing Rabbit Creek were settled by late September. They called for emigration to take place in three annual moves, beginning in 1831 and ending in 1833, with the Choctaw traveling to present-day Oklahoma. The plan was beset with obstacles from the start. Full-blooded and mixed-heritage Choctaw disagreed over whether emigration was the best plan. Before the first group departed in 1831, Eaton resigned, leaving the new secretary of war, Lewis Cass, scrambling to implement removal in an orderly fashion. The expense of the Choctaw removal ballooned beyond estimates, leading to cost-cutting measures, such as the deliberate distribution of old meat, in order to keep expenditures reasonable. Nevertheless, the United States spent over five million dollars on the relocation of the 12,500 Choctaw alone, after estimating that the total cost of removing all of the Native Americans east of the Mississippi would only reach three million dollars.[8]

By the time Jackson took office, the Creek, whom he had targeted in the 1810s, resided on five million acres in Alabama. As with the Cherokee in Georgia, Alabama's state legislature insisted on extending its laws over the Creek and refused to interfere with white intrusion on Creek land. Jackson met the Creek appeals for honoring past treaties with his standard response: removal was the only answer. In 1831 a smallpox epidemic and famine conditions combined to weaken Creek resistance. The following year Creek leaders signed a treaty ceding control of part of their land in return for private allotments and the promise of federal protection. This agreement allowed whites to purchase or defraud land from individual Creek; the Jackson administration did little to uphold its end of the treaty. Some Creek moved west, but most remained in Alabama. By 1836 their situation was so desperate and the violence between Creek and white settlers so intense that the Jackson administration initiated removal, which ended with approximately fifteen thousand Creek relocated to land promised them in the West. As Georgia governor Wilson Lumpkin asked Jackson, "Ought not these Indians to be considered and treated as the helpless wards of the Federal Government?"[9]

The Cherokee presented the highest-profile case of removal. Residing primarily in northern Georgia, western North Carolina, and southeastern Tennessee, the Cherokee were the most assimilated of the southern tribes. By 1828 they had adopted a republican government with a written constitution, and many had converted to Christianity. The wealthy elite, including Principal Chief John Ross and Joseph Vann, also built plantation homes, from which they could watch their slaves working in the cotton fields.[10]

The pressure on the state government of Georgia to remove the Cherokee increased in the summer of 1829, when gold was discovered in Indian territory. White settlers urged the Georgia legislature to seize the land and, not waiting for politicians to take action, began to move in themselves. In December of that year Georgia declared that the Cherokee Nation no longer existed within the state, effective June 1830. Jackson had foreseen the growing conflict between the Cherokee and Georgia in June 1829 and sent Carroll as a special agent to convince the Cherokee to be moved. This effort failed.[11]

When 1 June 1830 arrived, the Cherokee Nation lost its power to enforce its laws. The Cherokee had already hired former attorney general William Wirt to plead its case for sovereignty in the American judicial system. Jackson was displeased with Wirt's decision to represent the Cherokee, calling it "wicked." Fighting removal in court, he opined, "will lead to the distruction of the poor ignorant Indians." In their suit, *The Cherokee Nation v. The State of Georgia,* filed in late December 1830, Wirt and his legal team argued that the United States had recognized the Cherokee nation's sovereignty in fourteen separate treaties. They also pointed out that the federal government had already taken away the western land in Arkansas promised to a small group of Cherokee who had been removed earlier. On 18 March 1831 Chief Justice John Marshall gave the Supreme Court's ruling in the case. Challenging Wirt's assertion that the United States had long recognized the sovereignty of Indian nations, the Court pronounced the Cherokee a "domestic, dependent nation," an independent people located geographically within the boundaries of the United States yet dependent on its government for protection. The Cherokee, Marshall concluded, had no standing to bring suit against Georgia in this case.[12]

Georgia responded to the *Cherokee Nation v. Georgia* ruling by denying white men access to the Cherokee if they had not been granted a state license. The legislature aimed to keep missionaries from encouraging the Cherokee in their cause, as had been the case to this point. Two missionaries, Elizur Butler and Samuel A. Worcester, broke the law and sued the state of Georgia when they were imprisoned. Their case, *Worcester v. Georgia,* reached the Supreme Court. On 3 March 1832 Marshall and his court ruled that Georgia had usurped the missionaries' right to travel to an independent Cherokee nation. The state of Georgia could not require licenses to visit the Cherokee, and the state's superior court had been wrong in supporting the law.[13]

Jackson allegedly reacted to the *Worcester* ruling by saying, "Well: John Marshall has made his decision: *now let him enforce it!*" This outburst, heard secondhand and reported some thirty years after the fact by Horace Greeley, almost certainly did not occur. The process of enforcement was complicated and did not necessarily fall on the executive branch. The Supreme Court decision necessitated a written response from the Georgia court. A refusal to comply at that point required the Supreme Court to issue a contempt order to the state of Georgia. If Georgia failed to abide by the ruling, then the Cherokee legal team could ask Governor Wilson Lumpkin for the missionaries' release. An appeal to the president for enforcement was the next step if the governor refused to obey. At any point Jackson could have requested that Lumpkin free the missionaries; if he declined, then the president could shift the responsibility of military enforcement to Congress. Jackson, however, chose not to pursue this course. While he probably did not challenge Marshall to enforce his decision, Jackson did tell Coffee that the Court's decision "has fell still born" and that any armed conflict between the Cherokee and Georgia would result in the "destruction" of the Cherokee Nation.[14]

Several factors converged in the summer and fall of 1832 to influence Jackson's reaction to the *Worcester* decision. The presidential election pitted Jackson and Van Buren against the National Republican ticket of Clay and John Sergeant of Pennsylvania and Anti-Masonic third-party candidates William Wirt and Amos Ellmaker of Pennsylvania. Jackson's reelection would ensure that his removal policy continued to be carried out. The looming nullification fight with South Carolina also played a prominent role. Jackson had to tread carefully if he wanted to keep South Carolina isolated from Georgia, its neighboring state. He faced a conundrum: how could he move forcefully in opposing South Carolina's claims of state sovereignty regarding a political principle that he considered dangerous to the nation yet support Georgia in its exercise of state sovereignty over an issue with which he was in total agreement? A concerted campaign by Van Buren and his supporters led to the release of the imprisoned missionaries in January 1833, just days before Jackson asked Congress to endorse the use of force against South Carolina nullifiers; this action solved the president's dilemma of facing down southern states united against executive power.[15]

Following the *Worcester* decision, several Cherokee leaders, including Elias Boudinot, John Ridge, and Major Ridge, formed a faction that sought to negotiate with the Jackson administration. This Treaty party represented a minority of the Cherokee; most chose to trust John Ross's ability to stave off removal. Seeing an opportunity to exploit the tribal division, Jackson sent Indian commissioner John F. Schermerhorn to negotiate an agreement with the Treaty party. The resulting Treaty of New Echota, signed by fewer than eighty Cherokee on 28 December 1835, surrendered their land in the Southeast for five million dollars. This "Christmas trick" led Ross to plead with the Jackson administration for reconsideration of the treaty, given his absence and the small number of attendees at the negotiations. A memorial and protest sent to the U.S. Senate failed to stop ratification of the treaty on 18 May 1836 by a narrow one-vote margin. After Jackson left office, his successor, Martin Van Buren, oversaw the removal of the Cherokee. Approximately one-quarter of the eighteen thousand Cherokee died during this 1838 removal process, many on what came to be known as the Trail of Tears.[16]

The Cherokee may have been the most recognized victims of Andrew Jackson's removal policy in the South, but only the Seminole in Florida fought a war of opposition. The Second Seminole War (1835–1842) recalled Jackson's efforts to subjugate the South's Native American tribes in the 1810s and shared with those battles white southerners' fears of slave insurrection. In 1832 the Jackson administration pressured Seminole leaders into signing a treaty that would force their tribe's "voluntary" transference west within five years. Complaints about the coercive nature of the negotiations were ignored. Unlike many Cherokee, most Seminole had not assimilated, and like the Cherokee, some Seminole chose to move rather than face a certain deadly fate. Fearful that southern whites would force removal upon them and take away their slaves, the remaining Seminole attacked and killed over one hundred American soldiers near present-day Tampa in December 1835. This attack precipitated the start of the war, for which the Jackson administration and Congress were ill prepared. For seven years the United States government waged a war that cost twenty million dollars and the lives of nearly fifteen hundred soldiers. It finally ended in the death of Chief Osceola (in 1838), the removal of most of the surviving Seminole, and the confinement of those who remained to a reservation in southern Florida. White southerners breathed easy when the slave revolution that they feared would accompany the war failed to materialize. Although Jackson did not take to the field himself, several of his former military comrades—namely, Richard K. Call, Edmund P. Gaines, and Winfield Scott—led soldiers against the Seminole, along with a number of notable future military officers, including Braxton Bragg, George G. Meade, William Tecumseh Sherman, and Zachary Taylor.[17]

Jackson's presidency was a disastrous period for Native Americans. According to one estimate, approximately ninety thousand Native Americans were displaced between 1830 and 1843. For Jackson it was all satisfactory. Certainly, it offered him the opportunity to reward his friends and relatives, such as appointing Eaton secretary of war and Coffee Indian commissioner. Jackson promised his nephew-in-law Robert J. Chester "some profitable employment" once the Chickasaw and Choctaw were removed from Mississippi. Most important, Indian removal opened up land for cotton and slavery and removed multiple national security threats to white southern society. This goal was not only one with which Jackson wholeheartedly sympathized; it was also one that he had pursued for decades.[18]

XVII

"I Have Been Opposed Always to the Bank"

As a result of his actions during the Eaton affair and his stance in favor of Indian removal and against nullification, Jackson made many enemies during his first presidential term. During his second four years Jackson's opponents united to form a new political party, the Whigs, as a result of his conflict with the Second Bank of the United States (BUS). More than any other issue, the so-called Bank War displayed the fissures in Jackson's support, as charges of executive dictation and concerns about the nation's economic future led the president's southern allies and even his kin to flee to the Whig party.

Jackson had not always opposed financial institutions such as the one on Philadelphia's Chestnut Street, even after losing thousands of dollars because of bad financial decisions. But he had long distrusted them. He told Thomas Hart Benton in 1832 that a "secrete and combined movement of the aristocracy" had tried to establish a BUS branch in Nashville several years earlier, and he had opposed its charter. He believed that it "would drain the state of its specie to the amount of its profits for the support and prosperity of other places, and the Lords, Dukes and Ladies of foreign countries who held the greater part of its stock." "I have been opposed always to the Bank of the u.s. as well as all state Banks" that issued paper money, he explained to the Missouri senator.[1]

Jackson held suspicions about the BUS and its corrupting influences during the 1824 and 1828 campaigns, and they persisted into his presidency. Although Jackson initially indicated to the Bank's president, Nicholas Biddle, that he bore no particular ill will toward the institution, his mind changed as reports came from Kentucky early in his presidency that the Lexington and Louisville branches of the BUS had deliberately supported Adams and refused loans to Jackson's allies. After an investigation Biddle reported that no illegalities had taken place. The accusations in Kentucky were followed by more allegations of wrongdoing in New

Hampshire. Once again, Biddle concluded that it was a misunderstanding and dismissed any further talk of improper influence.[2]

Jackson did not immediately act against the Bank. In his first annual message, delivered in December 1829, he gave only two paragraphs to the subject. While not rancorous, the message gave Biddle fair warning that Jackson was on watch. The president recognized the effect that his comments would have on Bank supporters, "who prised self interest more than the perpetuity of our liberty, & the blessings of a free republican government." Over the next two years Jackson continued to hint at his suspicions about the Bank. His second annual message suggested that the BUS should "be shorn of the influence" that allowed it to "[operate] on the hopes, fears, or interests of large masses of the community." Its continuation would only lead to "occasional collisions with the local authorities and perpetual apprehension and discontent on the part of the States and the people." Distracted by the breakup of his cabinet over the Eaton affair, the president seems to have given little real thought to the future of the BUS. His third annual message agreed to let Congress decide the issue.[3]

Biddle failed to grasp the conciliatory branch that Jackson had extended to him. He continued to authorize the publication of newspaper articles defending the Bank against what he viewed as unwarranted attacks by the administration. When warned that his actions simply reinforced Jacksonian charges that the Bank was inappropriately involved in politics, Biddle refused to heed such counsel. Henry Clay, who early on in Jackson's first term began positioning himself as the president's major challenger in 1832, encouraged his stubbornness. The Kentuckian was looking for an issue to galvanize voters behind his campaign, and he believed the Bank was just what he needed. He was convinced that any attempt to veto a recharter bill would likely prove the death knell to Jackson's election chances. Clay advised Biddle to request a recharter from Congress, even though the existing contract was not due to expire until 1836. Clay believed that Jackson and his followers would either have to support the recharter and undermine their public opposition or reject it and risk alienating voters who were concerned about their financial future.[4]

At Clay's prompting pro-Bank supporters introduced a memorial for its recharter in January 1832. Anti-Bank Jacksonians leapt into action and, in the words of their Senate leader, Thomas Hart Benton, sought "to attack incessantly, assail at all points, display the evil of the institution, rouse the people—and prepare them to sustain the veto." They submitted a House resolution requesting an investigation into the Bank's dealings. Even though the committee, controlled by Biddle's backers, returned a vote of confidence in the Bank's innocence, Jacksonians remained steadfast in their opposition.[5]

Jackson, of course, ran for reelection under the Democratic banner—several state legislatures had already nominated him by 1832. To ensure that the process went smoothly at the Democratic National Convention, held in Baltimore in May 1832, John Eaton and John Overton attended as delegates. Although Overton became ill and was unable to serve a president pro tempore as planned, the remaining 334 delegates made two significant decisions. Nominations would require a two-thirds majority, and state delegations, whatever their size, would have to vote as a unit. The second decision was the overwhelming selection of Van Buren as the vice presidential nominee, defeating Philip P. Barbour of Virginia and Richard M. Johnson of Kentucky. The Jacksonians, as they had in 1828, ran a populist campaign, using pomp and circumstance to rouse the party faithful. Innuendo once again played a part in the Democratic strategy, as they accused Clay of being a gambler and frequent visitor to houses of ill repute.[6]

The Jacksonians' election-year confidence was challenged when the recharter bill passed in the Senate (28–20) and the House (106–84) during the summer months. The votes reflected both partisan and regional divisions. Seventy-five percent of the senators and 70 percent of representatives who voted for recharter identified themselves as either pro-Adams or anti-Jackson, while 74 percent of pro-Jackson/anti-Adams representatives and all of the like-minded senators voted against it. Sixty-three percent of both southern senators and representatives opposed the recharter; 80 percent of northern senators and 68 percent of northern representatives voted for the Bank's renewal. While Jackson counted on his political allies to support him if he chose to fight against the Bank, he had every reason to believe that he could rely on southern congressmen as well.[7]

And choose to fight he did. "Providence has had a hand in bringing forward the subject at this time to preserve the republic from [the Bank's] thraldome and corrupting influence," he confided to his advisor Amos Kendall. Jackson decided to use the executive veto to stop the Bank's momentum. His veto message, authored primarily by Kendall, clearly indicated that this battle would not end easily or amicably. In his message to Congress and the American people, Jackson emphasized the danger posed by the Bank to "the purity of our elections in peace and for the independence of our country in war." He also pointed to the class and regional consequences if the Bank's defenders allowed its corrupt practices to continue. "By attempting to gratify their desires we have in the results of our legislation arrayed section against section, interest against interest, and man against man, in a fearful commotion which threatens to shake the foundations of our Union." Acknowledging that Jackson was the government official best suited to interpret the Constitution would prevent the "prostitution of our Government to the advancement of the few at the expense of the many."[8]

The usual suspects led the charge against Jackson's veto message. Senator Daniel Webster accused the president of trying to stifle the prosperity of the country by undermining the Constitution and attempting to seize sole interpretive authority for himself. "There never before was a moment in which any President would have tolerated in asserting such a claim to despotic power," the godlike Webster roared. Henry Clay found similar reasons to object. Jackson's use of the veto, he argued, indicated that he was unacquainted with the intent of the founders or simply defied it. Biddle also entered the fray, suggesting that what Jackson delivered was "really a manifesto of anarchy, such as Marat or Robespierre might have issued to the mob" during the French Revolution.[9]

The stage was thus set for the fall presidential campaign, and the Bank emerged as the main issue. A vote for Clay was a vote for the Bank's continuation, while a vote for Jackson was a vote against it. Both sides exchanged barbs over who posed the greatest threat to the future course of the country. *Globe* editor Francis Blair, Jackson's attack dog in Washington, wrote, "When the company of British Lords and gentlemen asked the government to make them a present of some ten million of dollars, General Jackson said VETO!—*and our liberties and institutions are still safe.*" Jacksonians pointed out Biddle's financial contributions to the political campaign being waged against their candidate as proof of the Bank's corruption. Biddle spent an estimated ninety-five thousand dollars in 1831 and 1832 defending his financial institution in newspapers. Democrats viewed this action as direct interference in the political process. "If the Bank, a mere monied corporation, can influence and change the results of our election at pleasure, nothing remains of our boasted freedom except *the skin of the immolated victim*," Blair screamed. "Let the cry be heard across the land. Down with bribery–down with corruption–down with the Bank."[10]

Such attacks did not impress Bank supporters. "The will of a DICTATOR is the Supreme Law!" cried the Washington *National Intelligencer*. A *Boston Daily Atlas* editorial attributed the veto message to "the whole kitchen cabinet–of hypocrisy and arrogance; of imbecility and talent; of cunning, falsehood, and corruption," informing Americans that "if the doctrines avowed in this document do not arouse the Nation, we shall despair that any thing will, until the iron hand of despotism has swept our fair land, and this glorious Republic, if not wholly annihilated, shall have been fiercely shaken to its very foundations." The editor ended with a warning: "Let it be remembered that every military chieftain, Sylla, Caesar, Cromwell, all have obtained unlimited and despotic power by pretending to be the sole friends of the People and often by denouncing the rich, and by cajoling the poor with prospects, which they never intended to be realized, or only realized with chains and slavery, and dungeons, or enrollment in the legions assembled to add to the power of the tyrant." Kentuckian E. A. Dudley's language was more lowbrow: "We are chanting a funeral anthem . . . to the power of Granny Jackson and the kitchen cabinet."[11]

While the Bank remained the primary issue in the 1832 election, other issues were also important. Southern congressmen, even those "disgusted" with the alleged machinations of the Kitchen Cabinet, reportedly campaigned for Jackson because of Clay's "tariff principle." Others believed that Van Buren's place on the ticket would cost Jackson southern votes. Indian removal loomed large, and while it was not yet at a crisis point, the nullification movement also played a role.[12]

Despite Clay's certainty that Jackson's "incompetency," cabinet turmoil, and Bank position would doom Old Hickory, the results of the 1832 election were similar to those of 1828. Jackson won the popular vote convincingly, with 688,242 votes (55 percent) to Clay's 473,462 (37 percent) and just over 100,000 to the Anti-Masonic party's Wirt. The Electoral College gave Jackson 219 electoral votes from sixteen states, including all-important New York and Pennsylvania; Clay garnered 49 from Kentucky and five other states on the East Coast; and Wirt received 7 from Vermont. The other 11 votes went to Virginia governor John Floyd, whom South Carolina endorsed as a protest against Jackson's opposition to the growing nullification movement. As the president had hoped, Van Buren defeated his competitors to obtain the vice presidency.[13]

Astute political observers had expected Old Hickory to do well in the South. They were right. William T. Barry told his daughter that while the Bank veto would cost Jackson some states, it would "make the entire South, Virginia, etc., firm in his cause." Indian removal helped as well. Excluding South Carolina, the other eleven southern states gave Jackson 67.8 percent of their popular votes. He narrowly lost Delaware and Maryland, while Kentucky went for its native son, Clay, with 54.5 percent of the vote. Comfortably in the Jackson column were Louisiana (61.6 percent), Virginia (74.6 percent), and North Carolina (84.5 percent). Jackson faced little opposition in his home state of Tennessee (95.2 percent). The remaining three states—Georgia, Mississippi, and Missouri—gave him their unanimous endorsement. Based on their votes, the majority of southern voters were overwhelmingly satisfied with Jackson's first presidential term, but there were dissenters. Kentuckian William H. Hurst, for example, lamented that "the destiny of so great and glorious a nation could [be] influenced by such a mute liveried parisite as Kendall, or such a hireling dog as Blair."[14]

Clay wanted this election to be a referendum on the Bank issue, and he got his wish. Jackson used his victory to declare that he had a mandate from the people to destroy Biddle's hydra-headed monster. As the Eaton affair had consumed Jackson's attention during his first term, the Bank War became his obsession during his second administration and, in doing so, tested southerners' loyalty to Old Hickory.

Following the election Jackson asked Blair, Kendall, and Attorney General Roger B. Taney to help him formulate a strategy to kill the Bank. They recommended removing the government's deposits from the BUS, forcing it to die a slow death from lack of funds. Jackson let this plan be known in his fourth annual message, delivered in December 1832. He announced that Secretary of the Treasury Louis McLane would take steps to ensure that the deposits "may be regarded as entirely safe." Jackson notified James K. Polk shortly after the message that "the hydra of corruption is only *scotched, not dead*." He asked Polk to organize an investigative committee in the House to look into the Bank's practices during the recent presidential campaign, which Polk readily agreed to do.[15]

In early 1833 Jackson discussed his plan with Blair, who took an informal survey of the other advisors and discovered that many of them opposed removing the deposits. Jackson would not be dissuaded. After the House of Representatives returned a vote of confidence in the safety of the government deposits, the president brought his cabinet together and outlined his reasons for wanting the deposits removed. McLane, who opposed removal, displayed the most reasoned defense of the Bank. "It has been urged against the national bank that it would be an instrument of power in the hands of government, to be used for political purposes," he noted, but "in adjusting the charter of the present bank it was endeavored to guard against such abuses." The real danger, McLane pointed out, came from the local banks. Jackson agreed with some of McLane's points but decided that the secretary of the Treasury would have to go in order to accomplish the Bank's demise.[16]

Pennsylvanian William J. Duane replaced McLane as Treasury secretary in June 1833. Duane, whose editor father had famously been prosecuted under the Sedition Act of 1798, proved intractable when pressed to prepare for the removal of deposits. At one point he informed Jackson that if asked to do so, he would resign. Duane resented the president telling him how to run the Treasury, but his reluctance did not dampen Jackson's fervor. Jackson proceeded to ask Kendall to find state banks in which to place the funds taken from the BUS. After Kendall compiled a preliminary list, Jackson convened his cabinet in September and asked its members' advice. Most advisors continued to be less than enthusiastic. The president asked them to reconsider and come back the next day. At that meeting Jackson determined to press his argument. He requested Taney read a document that the two of them had composed during the summer months. The formal paper contained language sanitized by Taney in a rewrite. The original draft, made by Andrew Donelson at the Rip Raps, Jackson's vacation retreat near Hampton Roads, Virginia, dripped with hatred for the Bank. The president, it read, "entertains . . . serious doubts whether it be possible to preserve that high degree of purity and simplicity which constitute the only sure foundations of Republican institutions from the corrupting influence of" the Bank.[17]

The response from the cabinet members was subdued except for Duane, who defied the president. After some wrangling between Jackson and Duane over whether the president had the authority to order the secretary of the Treasury to remove the deposits, Jackson fired Duane and replaced him with Taney. This decision prompted some of Jackson's opponents to add yet another charge to their list of his so-called tyrannical acts. They argued that Senate confirmation was necessary to appoint a cabinet member; thus, the president had overstepped his executive powers. Jackson had ostensibly done the same thing during the Eaton affair, so Duane's firing simply confirmed suspicions about Jackson's dictatorial tendencies.[18]

With Taney in charge, the secretary began depositing government revenue into selected state banks while using the remaining money left in the BUS to pay off government expenditures. By December the government was almost free from the Bank's financial grasp. The country, however, was not. Angry and seeking revenge, Biddle met with the Bank's board and began restricting the BUS's loans. State banks, in turn, were forced to call in their own loans to maintain financial solvency. All of a sudden a strong American economy found itself in a recession.[19]

Biddle's retraction of BUS money had its intended effect. Americans clamored for the president to do something. While other parts of the nation, particularly New England and the Northwest, had given the Bank its strongest support, the retraction also struck fear in the minds of many southerners. Some who had supported Jackson's 1832 recharter veto changed their minds and stood at the forefront of demands for relief. Planters speculating in the recently opened Lower South lands were especially interested in seeing Jackson's Bank policy reversed. Their agricultural prospects depended on credit, and anything that threatened the increasing demand and stable prices for cotton required opposition. The ripple effects were felt even in southern urban areas such as Baltimore and New Orleans. A committee of Baltimore citizens met with Jackson and asked him to seek a compromise with Biddle. The president reminded the committee members that the Bank had exploited the South and West to "oppress the State banks in your city." The time for compromise had passed, and Jackson intended "to put his foot upon the head of the monster, and crush him to the dust."[20]

With these concerns in mind, some southerners suddenly agreed with previous accusations that Jackson was acting the role of a tyrant. Even some of Jackson's congressional supporters urged him to relent and redeposit the government funds into the Bank. Jackson adamantly refused. The Bank's action in his opinion demonstrated conclusively the level of corruption of Biddle and his cronies. They would bring down the nation's economy and possibly the government itself to maintain their control over its financial dealings. Kendall added his support. He tried to rally a faltering House member by reminding him that "this is a struggle to maintain a government of the people against the most heartless of all aristocracies, that of money." The argument worked, according to Kendall's memoirs, but other Jacksonians wanted a more concrete resolution to the problem. Several suggested establishing a new bank. Jackson accepted only the idea of restricting the availability of paper money in favor of specie.[21]

When Congress met in December 1833, the Democrats, the minority party in the Senate, were in chaos. Their leaders were unable to maintain party discipline, thus allowing opposition senators to open a debate over the removal of the deposits and the firing of Duane. When Clay demanded that Jackson turn over the original draft of the cabinet paper read in September, the president refused. Clay then introduced a resolution censuring Jackson for removing the government's deposits from the BUS. "Whether it will be practicable to rescue the Government and Public Liberty from the impending dangers, which Jacksonism has created," he wrote Virginian Francis T. Brooke, "depends, in my opinion, mainly on the South."[22]

The ensuing debate over the censure resolution added to the acrimony already present between Democrats and the emerging opposition coalition. Calhoun and Clay led the attack, Clay bluntly castigating the president for a variety of reasons, economic and political. "We are in the midst of a revolution," he cautioned, "hitherto bloodless, but rapidly tending towards a total change of the pure republican character of the Government, and the concentration of all power in the hands of one man." Clay warned that if Jackson continued unrestrained, Americans would "die—ignobly die— base, mean, and abject slaves; the scorn and contempt of mankind; unpitied, unwept, unmourned!" Calhoun added his diatribes against Jackson in January 1834. He compared the president to Julius Caesar, who "forc[ed] himself, sword in hand, into the treasury of the Roman Commonwealth."

From New York, Philip Kearny remarked that Jackson "can't live without quarreling, his removal of the deposits & the distress and Ruin that his violence is producing is nuts for him . . . Did not Nero burn Rome to see the conflagration[?]"[23]

In late March 1834 Clay's censure resolution passed the Senate by a vote of twenty-six to twenty. Southern senators split their vote fourteen to nine against the resolution, revealing the discomfort that the region felt over the issue and the lingering resentment of southern politicians who believed that the president had not proven true to his southern roots. Jackson responded to the censure by sending the Senate a "Protest" message on April 15. The president defended himself on constitutional and legal grounds. The language with which he upheld his removal of Duane, however, was most telling. "The Bank of the United States, a great moneyed monopoly had attempted to obtain a renewal of its charter by controlling the elections of the people and the action of the Government," Jackson began. Congress had investigated and discovered "the use of its corporate funds and power in that attempt," and it was obvious, to Jackson at least, that the Bank continued to use the same tactics.[24]

The simultaneous contest for the U.S. House speakership also demonstrated the growing split between pro- and anti-Bank southerners. The departure of Virginian Andrew Stevenson in 1833 led to a months-long competition between Tennesseans John Bell and James Polk to succeed him. Bell had been publicly silent during the Bank debates but privately critical of Jackson's course regarding the institution. Polk, meanwhile, had acted as Jackson's alter ego in the House. He had every reason to believe that the president supported his campaign in return. Complex and smart maneuvering by anti-Jackson, anti-Bank representatives allowed Bell to win the speakership in June 1834, disappointing Jackson and bringing into sharp relief the divisions among Jacksonians, southerners, Tennesseans, and even the president's inner circle.[25]

The end of the attack on the Bank came later in 1834. House Democrats, finally in control of their own ranks, passed a series of resolutions against the BUS in April. The first resolution recommended that the Bank not receive a new charter in 1836. The second confirmed Jackson's removal of the deposits. The third suggested that the state pet banks remain in place as government depositories. The last resolution established a committee to inquire into the Bank's actions during the recent recession. Biddle defiantly refused to cooperate with committee members, lessening his waning popularity even more. He did convince the Senate to conduct its own investigation of the Bank's affairs, but by the time the Senate committee presented its report, in December 1834, Democrats had already won the fall elections, and Jackson had established a new banking system.[26]

One of the consequences of the Bank War was the consolidation of the anti-Jackson forces into a nascent political party. The Whigs, as they called themselves, primarily feared "King Andrew" and his tyrannical power. Their name recalled the eighteenth-century English opposition political party battling an English despotic monarch. This time, however, the fight was in the United States against an American president. Whigs tended to be those who supported the Bank, opposed Indian removal, and believed that evangelical Christianity could reform society's ills. Prominent members of the Whig opposition included Jackson's usual enemies—Adams, Calhoun, Clay, and Webster—as well as emerging politicians, such as Louisianan Judah P. Benjamin, New Yorker William H. Seward, and Virginian John Tyler. While southern Democrats did not flee en masse to the Whigs, Jackson alienated a number of his supporters in the region.[27]

Old Hickory's presidency had resulted in the development of the national Whig party; thus, to no one's surprise, it affected Tennessee's politics as well. Some politicians whose loyalty had been questioned remained Jackson allies. Tennessee governor William Carroll, for example, whom Jackson relative John C. McLemore had once accused of conspiring to form an anti-Jackson party, supported Van Buren's nomination at some cost to his own popularity. Others, such as David Crockett, broke with Jackson because of his overbearing, dictatorial personality. Two of the most important defections were Bell and Hugh Lawson White. Early in Jackson's presidency Bell competed with Polk for Old Hickory's approval. Although Bell had opposed the Bank's recharter in 1832, by 1834 Jackson came to believe that his friend was actually part of the Bank conspiracy. Indeed, Bell understood which way the political winds were blowing and explored ways to defeat Van Buren, the presumptive Democratic nominee in 1836. White's decision to oppose his former friend proceeded in part from Jackson's decision in early 1829 to allow him and Eaton to decide who would serve in his cabinet. Eaton outmaneuvered White to stay in the president's inner circle, and this development created a breach in his relationship with Jackson. That division widened as Van Buren gained prominence. White harbored aspirations for the presidency himself, and his jealousy got the better of him. Undoubtedly, Bell and White's connection to the Erwin kinship network also played a role in their break with Jackson. In 1833 Bell married Jane Erwin Yeatman, widow of Nashville banker Thomas Yeatman and sister of John Patton Erwin. He thus became, like White, part of the clan that had consistently opposed Jackson since the 1810s. While not the essential force in pulling Bell away from Jackson, the Erwin network supported him in his move and gave him a home once the decision had been made.[28]

Questions also arose about the loyalty of Jackson's two closest political operatives, William Lewis and Jackson's "favorite son," John Eaton. Lewis's influence began waning following the Eaton affair, and his support of Bell instead of Polk during the 1834 House speakership contest marked him as out of step with Jackson's political agenda. Although Lewis later pleaded innocent to betraying Jackson, his shadiness elicited significant criticism from Donelson and Polk, both of whom had the president's ear. Although Eaton became Florida's territorial governor in 1834 and thus was distant from the locus of political conflict, he was often accused of disloyalty because of his association with Lewis and support of Bell during the 1833 speakership election. Eaton's critics offered Jackson's refusal to unequivocally support him in his 1833 bid for a Senate seat as the motivation for his alleged untrustworthiness. While Jackson did not publicly break with either man, his relationship with both noticeably cooled.[29]

As Jackson entered the midway point of his second term, he faced considerable resistance from southerners. The Bank War emphasized the partisan divisions that already existed and exposed the discomfort that some southerners felt about Jackson's leadership style. They welcomed his heavy-handed use of executive authority when it benefited their interests, but when it worked against them, some, including members of the president's inner circle, sought refuge in the Whig party. The upcoming presidential election promised to strain the bonds of southerners' identification with Jackson even more.[30]

XVIII

"Firebrands of Anarchy and Bloodshed"

Adhering to Jackson's wishes, in 1835 the Democrats nominated Martin Van Buren to be Old Hickory's successor in the White House. Jackson worked assiduously to convince Americans, particularly southerners, that the New Yorker was a safe choice. Issues that threatened southern interests, however, made the task difficult. While Jackson saw Van Buren elected, those issues, especially abolitionism and Texas annexation, continued to pose problems for the South and the nation.

The United States witnessed significant violence during Jackson's presidency. Between 1828 and 1835 seventy-three disturbances broke out, with the majority coming in the summer and fall of 1835. Americans rioted for a number of reasons during these years, with tension over slavery and anger at banks the leading precipitators of the public chaos.[1]

In August 1835 racial tension caused a violent outbreak in the nation's capital. The "Snow Riot," as the Washington mobbing was termed, proceeded from a confluence of events that emphasized the growing importance of slavery as a volatile issue for the nation and Jackson's administration. An alleged attack on Anna Maria Thornton, widow of William Thornton, the Capitol's architect, provided the initial spark. In the early morning of 5 August 1835 one of Thornton's slaves, John Arthur Bowen, entered her bedroom, ax in hand, "with the intention we suppose of murder," she reported. District authorities charged Bowen with attempted murder. Rumor held that abolitionists had encouraged the attack. Shortly after Bowen was jailed, a Georgetown man reported that local physician Dr. Reuben Crandall possessed a number of abolitionist pamphlets. District residents rather quickly made a connection between Bowen and Crandall and took to the streets looking for black victims on which to vent their frustration. For nearly a week rioters threatened to lynch Crandall, but they eventually settled for burning African American schools and homes and the restaurant of a free black man, Beverly Snow, whose name became attached to the riot.[2]

Jackson was vacationing at the Rip Raps when the Snow Riot began, and he returned to the nation's capital immediately. During a walk around the city the following year, Jackson pointed out to his companion, Nicholas P. Trist, some houses in the Kalorama neighborhood that had been burned by the rioters. Trist recalled that the mob had been looking for Augustus, "a remarkably fine looking mulatto" who served Jackson in the White House. A "deputation" visited the president and demanded that he remove Augustus from his position, but Jackson refused. His servants were "amenable to me alone, and to no one else," he insisted.[3]

While Jackson claimed authority over the slaves in his household, the court system meted out justice to Bowen. A jury convicted the slave of attempted murder in December 1835 and sentenced him to be hanged on 26 February 1836. Mrs. Thornton attempted to intercede for Bowen, claiming that he had been intoxicated at the time of his failed attack, but Bowen's own words called her testimony into question. He allegedly told the arresting officers that "'he had a right to be free, and until they [slaves] were free, there would be so much confusion and bloodshed as would astonish the whole earth.'" In her petition for a presidential pardon Thornton argued that Bowen, while susceptible to alcohol, had been a loyal family slave. She acknowledged that he spent time with "free negroes . . . most actively engaged in propagating notions of general abolition, and disseminating inflammatory pamphlets from the north on the subject," but she blamed "the recent alarms and agitations" regarding slave insurrections and "the firebrands of anarchy and bloodshed" for his conviction.[4]

After this personal plea to Jackson, Thornton organized a coordinated campaign to save Bowen. She enlisted influential men in the city to sign a memorial to the president, including Van Buren, Andrew Donelson, and Jackson's personal physician, Dr. Henry Huntt. The president considered Thornton's request, and under advisement from Attorney General Benjamin Franklin Butler, he granted Bowen two reprieves, in February and early June. Jackson finally issued a pardon on June 27, effective on July 4. Exactly why Jackson finally made this decision is unclear. He may have been convinced by the legal arguments, the influence of friends, or the pleas of the widow Thornton. One intriguing explanation is that he knew that John Eaton, serving as territorial governor of Florida, wanted to purchase Bowen, which he did on July 8. Thornton mentioned in her February petition that immediately after the alleged attack in August 1835, she "resolved to sell him" and "had made a bargain with a slaveholder which would have been immediately carried into effect if the subject of it had not been taken out of her hands by the mandate of the law." While purely speculative, it would not have been out of character for Jackson to use his presidential pardoning power to help Eaton, his former campaign manager and the man for whom Jackson had fought so dearly early in his presidency, acquire a slave.[5]

Intertwined with the Snow Riot and the Bowen case was a much larger, potentially more explosive national discussion of slavery and abolition. While the president was vacationing in July 1835, a ship carrying bags of abolitionist pamphlets docked in Charleston, South Carolina. The pamphlets' arrival, part of a coordinated abolitionist mailing effort to flood the South with roughly 175,000 items denouncing slavery, prompted widespread public protest and attention throughout the South. Postmaster General Amos Kendall, a slave owner himself, relayed his instructions to southern postmasters, vague enough to be subject to interpretation, that the pamphlets be withheld unless requested by their subscribers. He asked the president for his advice on the appropriateness of this decision.[6]

Jackson assured Kendall that he had made the right choice. He denounced the "monsters" who were using the antislavery pamphlets "to stir up amongst the South the horrors of a servile war . . . they ought to be made to atone for this wicked attempt, with their lives." He also criticized the "spirit of mob-law" demonstrated by the Charlestonians who had stolen the mail. Jackson recommended that southern postmasters make a list of those citizens who wanted the pamphlets so that they could be "exposed thro the publik journals as subscribers to this wicked plan of exciting the negroes to insurrection and to massacre." Fellow southerners would force those sympathetic to the abolitionist cause to "desist" in their support of slave freedom "or move from the country."[7]

Jackson's awareness that slavery was already influencing the pending presidential election framed his response to the abolitionist tracts. In May 1835 more than six hundred Democratic delegates met in Baltimore and unanimously nominated Van Buren for president. The vice presidential contest stirred up some controversy because of division over whether the delegates would support Richard M. Johnson of Kentucky or William C. Rives of Virginia. Opposition to Johnson's nomination centered on his well-known relationships with two of his female slaves, one of whom, Julie Chinn, had borne him two daughters. On the other hand, he was regarded as a hero of the War of 1812. Van Buren calculated that Virginia would support him regardless of the vice presidential nomination, so in order to win Kentucky's votes, his supporters chose Johnson for second place on the ticket.[8]

Van Buren's loyalty secured Jackson's, and the party's, endorsement, but Democrats did not universally trust the New Yorker. Despite Van Buren's work as secretary of state to recover fugitive slaves fleeing to Canada, southerners in particular were concerned that he really supported the suddenly vocal abolitionist movement. Most of the opposition came from Calhounites, who not only wanted to see slavery protected but also had not forgotten Van Buren's role in the Tariff of 1828 and the Eaton affair. They used the issue of antislavery petitions presented to Congress to try to derail Van Buren's candidacy and even talked, unsuccessfully it turned out, about forming a southern party. Sensing a chance to embarrass Van Buren, in December 1835 Senator Calhoun and Representative James Henry Hammond put forward a proposal not to allow any antislavery petitions to be presented to Congress. While the House considered Hammond's recommendation, Van Buren wrote a letter that firmly and clearly declared his intention not to interfere with slavery's existence. In May 1836 representatives overwhelmingly agreed to pass what they called the "gag rule," the House's refusal to consider antislavery petitions. This decision lessened the pressure on Van Buren to continue addressing the slavery issue, but it did not remove it as a potential political stumbling block. Even Tennessee Democrats found it difficult to throw their complete support behind Van Buren. The division within the state ran so deep that they had not even sent a delegation to the national nominating convention. Instead, they found Edmund Rucker, a Tennessean visiting Baltimore, and convinced him to enter Fourth Presbyterian Church, where the delegates were meeting, and cast his state's votes for the Van Buren–Johnson ticket.[9]

Despite the lack of Democratic enthusiasm for Van Buren, the Whigs failed to find enough cohesion to name a single challenger. To avoid intraparty discord, Whigs allowed state legislators and newspapers to select candidates. The three men who emerged–Daniel Webster of Massachusetts, William Henry Harrison of Ohio, and Tennessee's Hugh Lawson White–represented the different regional constituencies. Webster appealed to New Englanders, who remembered his fights against Jacksonian authoritarianism. Virginia-born Harrison drew attention from Whigs in the Upper South and Midwest as the hero of the Battle of Tippecanoe during the War of 1812. Southern Whigs constituted White's political base and threw down the gauntlet to Tennessee voters, who were forced to choose between loyalty to Jackson and his handpicked northern successor or their native son from East Tennessee, whose only obvious sin was opposing Van Buren.[10]

White's candidacy left Jackson incensed. He labeled his former friend an "apostate," joining the ranks of John Bell and David Crockett. White would be disappointed, Jackson wrote James K. Polk, when he discovered that the Whigs were simply using him to divide southern and western voters and actually planned to make Clay their candidate. Thomas Hart Benton's continued call for debating a resolution to expunge the president's 1834 Bank veto censure gave Jackson hope that his former Tennessee allies, especially White, would be forced to display their disloyalty. The debate would "kill him and Bell politically," he wrote Polk. To Felix Grundy, Jackson disclosed how deeply White's defection had offended him: "Let the Tennessee Brutus come."[11]

Another issue that concerned Jackson because of its potential to derail Van Buren's election was Texas annexation. As early as 1820, Jackson had identified Texas as a potential place for American defense against Native American attacks. Texas's importance to the United States grew throughout the 1820s, as the northern Mexican frontier became more Americanized with the growing emigration of white southerners and their slaves. Missouri empresario Stephen F. Austin, for example, founded a colony in Texas that in 1825 included 1,800 settlers, 443 of whom were slaves. By 1830 nearly three-quarters of the 20,000 residents were Americans; by 1835 the number of Americans residing in Texas was close to 30,000, outnumbering Tejanos by a ten-to-one margin.[12]

Throughout his presidency Jackson watched developments in the West. One supporter warned him in 1831 that "British traders and colonists" dominated the western fur trade and were "gathering strength every day in our territory & preparing the minds of the Indians to oppose" American settlement in the West. Jackson's obvious interest in Texas led some critics to accuse him of conspiring to bring about its revolution and secession from Mexico. Rumors swirled in 1829 that Jackson's Tennessee friend and supporter Sam Houston had left his wife and gubernatorial seat in order to lead the alleged revolution. Based on "frequent conversations" with Houston, Daniel S. Donelson outlined the disgraced governor's supposed "grand scheme" to his brother, Andrew, and pronounced him a "scoundrel." Anti-Jacksonians picked up this allegation and embellished it into an immense conspiracy that implicated the president. Jackson reacted to the news of Houston's resignation by questioning whether his friend was "deranged, or what is worse bewitched." Jackson denied involvement with Houston and indicated that he had instructed the governor of the Arkansas territory, William S. Fulton, to report any "illegal enterprise" and take action to "put it down."[13]

While not involved in an unlawful conspiracy to overthrow Mexican control of Texas, Jackson certainly hoped to bring about its peaceful separation during his presidency. In this endeavor he was disappointed. Early in his administration Jackson had to recall South Carolinian Joel R. Poinsett as chargé d'affaires to Mexico when the American diplomat found himself in a "very unpleasant & mortifying" position with the Mexican government due to his intemperate interference with internal politics. His replacement, Anthony Wayne Butler, was a longtime Tennessee state legislator who had served with Jackson during the War of 1812 and possessed extensive business contacts with Texas. In August 1829 Butler met with Van Buren to discuss Texas. The secretary of state showed Butler's arguments for U.S. involvement in Texas to Jackson, who concluded that the time was right to replace Poinsett with a man whom he had trusted in battle. He adopted many of Butler's justifications for pressuring Mexico to sell Texas to the United States. Such a development, Jackson and Butler believed, would protect New Orleans, secure land for settling displaced Native Americans, and establish "a natural boundary" between the two nations. He authorized the new minister to offer the Mexican government up to five million dollars to procure Texas.[14]

Unfortunately, Butler's mission proved a failure. The chargé pursued a slow course that frustrated Jackson. "I hope to see you soon with the Treaty," the president wrote in early 1833, and later that year he urged Butler to "close this negotiation soon—four years has nearly elapsed since it commenced." These promptings produced nothing positive and may have induced Butler to act irresponsibly. He proposed provoking the Mexican government into war by occupying disputed territory, an idea that Jackson rejected. Butler also reported that Mexican officials had asked for bribes and requested specific instructions on how he should proceed. Jackson answered with a stern rebuke, telling Butler that the chargé had implied that "my private letters authorised you to apply to corruption, when nothing could be farther from my intention." The chargé defended his interpretation of Jackson's orders, but the damage was done: U.S. negotiations for Texas came to an end. The president replaced Butler with Mississippian Powhatan Ellis in early 1836.[15]

Butler's recall was prudent. The Texas Revolution, which began in October 1835, demanded that the Jackson administration take a more cautious approach to its relations with Mexico. American sentiment, particularly in the South, favored the revolution. One Jackson friend, Nashville lawyer John Catron, compared the "butchery" at the siege of the Alamo and the execution of nearly four hundred men following the Battle of Coleto Creek in early 1836 to the 1813 massacre of white settlers at Fort Mims. Nevertheless, Jackson temporized. The success of the revolution in 1836, which led to Mexico's recognition of Texas independence in May, altered the question from one of American support for independence to whether the United States would annex the new Lone Star Republic. Mexican officials wondered if Jackson had been planning this result since taking office. Domestically, prominent abolitionists, including Benjamin Lundy and Reverend William E. Channing, pronounced the revolution a bold attempt "to spread the infection" of slavery.[16]

Jackson chose to tread carefully because he did not want to jeopardize Van Buren's chances to succeed him as chief executive. With three Whigs in the 1836 presidential race, the vice president faced a potential House election if he could not maintain Democratic unity. Jackson early on saw the danger of sectionalism to Van Buren's chances. He told Gallatin lawyer Joseph C. Guild that Hugh Lawson White was the tool of those intent on constructing "a colossal monied power to corrupt and over shadow the government." Chief among the conspirators was John Bell, who sought to "[build] up a southern party in conjunction with Mr. Calhoun, founded exclusively on sectional feeling and prejudice." As the fall elections of 1835 drew near, Jackson tried to keep Texas from becoming Van Buren's downfall. "Our nutrality must be faithfully maintained," he scribbled on a plea from Stephen F. Austin for the United States to declare war on Mexico. When General Edmund P. Gaines, stationed along the Louisiana-Texas border, requisitioned troops from southern states on the pretext of preventing Native American attacks, Jackson "vetoed" the order to prevent accusations that "it was done to aid Texas, and not from a desire to prevent an infringement of our territorial or national rights."[17]

Jackson helped his vice president successfully pass the test with voters. Van Buren won the 1836 presidential election with 170 electoral votes to the combined 113 electoral votes of the Whig candidates. Van Buren secured just under 51 percent of the popular vote, however, demonstrating that the election was much closer than it appeared in the Electoral College. His showing among southern states was disappointing, narrowly losing the majority of popular votes, 212,693 to 212,936. Out of the twelve southern states in which voters chose electors, Van Buren obtained popular majorities in only seven. His most substantial victory occurred in Arkansas, where he gained 64.1 percent of the vote; his worst loss, ironically, was in Tennessee, where he only mustered 42.1 percent. White, Van Buren's main rival in the South, ran extremely well, winning his home state and Georgia and losing narrow elections in most of the other southern states. Historians have postulated that slave owners, frightened by questions about Van Buren's fidelity to southern principles, turned out in force and nearly cost Democrats the presidency. Jackson, who was recovering from a "sever hemorrage from the lungs," offered his typical assessment: Whigs had made White "a stool pidgeon," and his former ally was no better off than Burr had been after his treasonous conspiracy.[18]

Following Van Buren's victory Jackson continued to exercise caution regarding Texas. His last annual message in December 1836 deferred discussing Texas until later that month. Jackson asked Congress to delay recognition of Texas's independence "until Mexico itself or one of the great foreign powers" had taken the first step. He concluded with the assurance that he would follow Congress's direction. By March 1837 the Senate voted to recognize Texas; Jackson responded on his final day in office by appointing a chargé and receiving Texas diplomats in return.[19]

With the election over, Jackson prepared for retirement. One last triumph came his way during his final weeks in office. In mid-January the Senate expunged its censure of him. Thomas Hart Benton led the Democrats in passing the resolution. After a moment that witnessed "a storm of hisses, groans, and vociferations" from observers in the gallery, the censure was crossed out of the Senate journal. A physically weak president invited his Senate supporters to a dinner, where they celebrated the victory that saw Jackson's political opponents "vanquished" and forced to "exhale their griefs in unavailing reproaches, and impotent deprecations."[20]

As Jackson prepared to retire from the presidency, the events of the past eight years weighed heavily on his mind as well as on his body. His concern for the future of the nation was clear in his farewell address of March 1837. Men were "sow[ing] the seeds of discord between different parts of the United States and to place party divisions directly upon geographical distinctions." This sectional animosity had even stretched to the recent presidential election, making "the possible dissolution of the Union . . . an ordinary and familiar subject of discussion." The retiring president called on Americans to remember the warnings of George Washington in his own farewell address in 1797. "What have you to gain by division and dissension?" Jackson asked. "Delude not yourselves with the belief that a breach once made may be afterwards repaired. If the Union is once severed, the line of separation will grow wider and wider, and the controversies which are now debated and settled in the halls of legislation will then be tried in fields of battle and determined by the sword." He predicted that the rift would not only become permanent but would also result in further separation. "New fragments would be torn off, new leaders would spring up, and this great and glorious Republic would soon be broken into a multitude of petty States, without commerce, without credit, jealous of one another, armed for mutual aggression, loaded with taxes to pay armies and leaders, seeking aid against each other from foreign powers." European nations would soon threaten to move in to conquer the former United States, forcing Americans "to submit to the absolute dominion of any military adventurer and to surrender their liberty for the sake of repose."[21]

Jackson's identity as a southern president was significant. His adherence to the region's code of honor during the Eaton affair had split his advisors, leading to the ostracizing of an important southern ally, John C. Calhoun, and the elevation of Martin Van Buren as Old Hickory's chosen successor. Jackson's determination to move southeastern Indians west of the Mississippi River continued the policies that he had prosecuted during the 1810s. Removal won him nearly universal acclaim among white southerners, but it permanently altered Indian life, with tragic consequences that stretched well beyond the Trail of Tears. He had also acted decisively in limiting the influence of abolitionist literature, an example that future presidents would follow as they attempted to stem the voices raised against slavery.

Other events that took place during Jackson's administrations illustrated, however, that white southerners did not fully agree that Old Hickory was their president. Nullifiers in South Carolina and other Deep South states had warned that the Tennessean was consolidating power unconstitutionally, thereby threatening individual citizen and states' rights. Many of the same arguments appeared during the Bank War: Jackson was a Caesar who threatened the American Republic. Southerners also questioned why he had caved to Whig pressure when the question of Texas annexation arose during his second term.[22]

While all of these issues were notable, Jackson's legal legacy was just as important for the South and the nation. He appointed four Supreme Court justices while president: John McLean of Ohio (appt. 1829), James M. Wayne of Georgia (appt. 1835), Roger B. Taney of Maryland (appt. 1836), and John Catron of Tennessee (appt. 1837). Three of the four justices repeatedly reinforced southern interpretations of states' rights and defended the institution of slavery. McLean held antislavery views, but Catron and Wayne owned slaves, and they, along with Taney, a former slave owner, consistently supported the right of white southerners to their slave property. In 1857 they formed a core group that rendered the majority opinion in *Dred Scott v. Sandford,* a decision pronouncing that African Americans could not be citizens and destroying the Missouri Compromise. While most of Jackson's own legal activities were nondescript, his Supreme Court appointees sent the nation further down the road to civil war.[23]

XIX

"There Would Be Great Risk"

Jackson departed Washington on March 7, intent on finally retiring to live the life of a "farmer." He would get his wish, though not quite in the way that he expected. While he had opportunity to spend time with family, visit with friends, and opine on politics, Jackson was also forced to commit much of the remaining eight years of his life trying to keep his son from bankrupting their farming ventures.[1]

Jackson arrived home to familiar surroundings on March 25. While he had been in Washington for the past eight years, the Hermitage had increased in size due to Junior's purchase of neighboring land. His family had also grown, with two grandchildren, Rachel and Andrew III, now living at the Hermitage. Sarah's sister, Marion, and her three sons, John, Andrew, and William Adams, moved in after the death of her husband, William, in 1837. Ralph E. W. Earl, an artist who had been Jackson's "constant companion" in Washington, returned to live at the Hermitage as well. Earl's death in September 1838, Jackson wrote, deprived him of "an invaluable friend." Although Emily Donelson died in December 1836, her husband, Andrew, and their four children were still in residence less than a mile away. Andrew Donelson's presence, along with the network of neighbors who welcomed Jackson back to Nashville, helped the retired president return to his former life.[2]

Jackson faced an immediate concern with Junior's debts. Despite receiving a salary of $376.53 for three months' work in the General Land Office in 1836, Junior looked to sell a recently ordered carriage to ease his financial burden. He asked Major William Noland, Washington's commissioner of public buildings, to look after the matter for him, which he did without success. Junior also directed Noland to tell his creditors that they should not be "uneasy, as they shall certainly soon be paid with interest." Junior's neglect was such that William B. Lewis speculated that he would "not be surprised" if one creditor appealed directly to Jackson for the money owed.[3]

Despite Junior's debts, Jackson eventually supported his son's purchase of a plantation in Coahoma County, Mississippi. Junior had been exploring the possibility of establishing a farm in the state since the fall of 1835, when Mississippi resident and physician William McKendree Gwinn offered to find land for Junior and Andrew Donelson. Jackson expressed initial reservations about the prospect, warning Junior that "there would be great risk in buying on the river." He identified flooding as an almost certain problem and foresaw disease as potentially hazardous to the slaves who would work the land. Jackson urged his son to wait until unsurveyed Chickasaw land became available. Junior initially heeded his father's advice, but in November 1838 he decided to buy nearly twelve hundred acres on the Mississippi River at twenty dollars per acre.[4]

Their new plantation, named Halcyon, was a problem from the start. They purchased it just as the Panic of 1837 gripped the country in economic depression. Tennesseans suffered significantly from the strain, with land and slave values declining severely and cotton prices falling as low as three cents per pound. Circumstances in Mississippi were not much better, with a depreciated currency and defaulted loans leading to widespread bankruptcy among the planter class. Another impediment to their success in Mississippi was the weather. As Jackson predicted, torrential rains flooded the cotton fields, sometimes leaving them under several feet of water. As a result, the overseer reported in 1844, the slaves had "sore feet from gowing in the water." The "freshetts" also washed away cut wood and drowned livestock.[5]

Jackson and Junior also encountered many difficulties with their Halcyon overseers. They first hired James Howerton, a religious-minded Virginian who had moved to Coahoma County in 1838. Howerton initially held Junior in high regard, calling him "one of the best men I have ever met with in my life." This cordiality quickly faltered. By August 1840 Jackson was convinced that Howerton was "worth nothing" and needed to be replaced. He ticked off the overseer's shortcomings: his family of nine was too large, he communicated too infrequently, and he moved too slowly. Howerton, who suffered from ill health prior to moving to Mississippi, agreed that the change would be good for his and his family's health. When he failed to receive full payment of his wages, however, he sued Junior, accusing him of misleading Jackson about the overseer's effective-

ness and of swindling him out of his "just earnings." "Sir God is above the
deavil. I am sure he will not suffer the rich to grind the faces of the poor,"
Howerton scolded Jackson. "If he (A.J. jr) surposed to scare me into his un-
just proposition by his bosting of the millions he had to spend at Law, he
barked up the wrong tree." The two sides finally agreed to an out-of-court
settlement of less than three hundred dollars.[6]

The tenure of the next overseer, James M. Parker, was troubled from
the beginning. Jackson asked Andrew J. Hutchings, who shortly thereafter
left Alabama for Cuba in an attempt to restore his health, to hire Parker
as Howerton's replacement. During what must have been an awkward
few weeks, the two overseers resided at Halcyon while management of
the plantation was transferred to Parker. The new overseer encountered
the same obstacles as his predecessor: frequent flooding, sick slaves, and
Jackson's unrealistic expectations of success. He also seemed incapable of
completing the simplest tasks, such as sending important papers to the
Hermitage when needed. In December 1844 Jackson informed his longtime advisor and *Washington Globe* editor, Francis P. Blair, that Junior was
traveling to Mississippi to replace Parker, who had "been behaving badly."[7]

Jackson and Junior should have been able to control other problems on
the Mississippi plantation, but they often failed at these too. Jackson had
originally envisioned Halcyon as a place not only to farm cotton but also
to take advantage of the state's burgeoning lumber industry to provide
steamboat firewood. In January 1840 he confidently predicted to Sarah
that "ten hands will cut twenty cords of wood in the day," generating
thirty dollars daily in cash, with the potential of reaching six thousand dollars per year. Five years later Jackson still looked for the woodcutting business to turn a profit. "If Andrew had obayed my advice, and attended to
the wood instead of pushing the cotton," Jackson complained to Blair, then
his son's debts could have been reduced. Junior had ignored him, however. Worse, the overseer Parker duped the young man by buying land
near Halcyon, putting Junior's slaves to work cutting his wood, and then
selling it for his own profit; all the while Junior's wood sat cut but unsold.[8]

Halcyon's failures became only one of Jackson's problems with his son.
Junior continued to accumulate debts, which opened him up to lawsuit
after lawsuit. Between 1838 and 1845 he was sued at least thirteen times,

for a total of nearly six thousand dollars. The bulk of the court proceedings took place between 1839 and 1842; Junior lost at least half of the suits. In September 1840 Jackson calculated that he had paid twelve thousand dollars of his son's debts over the past two months, and still more remained. Sensing a political conspiracy, Jackson blamed "every Whigg" to whom Junior owed money for causing his son to become ill from the stress.[9]

In an effort to help his former commander out of debt, Jean-Baptiste Plauché, a prominent New Orleans resident and War of 1812 veteran, offered Jackson financial assistance in 1841. Hearing rumors about his friend's "pecuniary circumstances," Plauché asked Jackson to corroborate news of his financial bankruptcy. Old Hickory responded by blaming the rumors on political enemies and attributed Junior's debts to his being "too confident in the honesty of men whom he believed to be his friends." Whether Jackson asked for a loan is unclear, but even if he did not, Plauché still ascertained the need. He initially offered a loan of six thousand dollars, increased later to seven thousand dollars after Jackson reported poor crops and low prices. Two years later, when Old Hickory expressed discomfort about his indebtedness to Plauché, the Louisianan and his business partners assured him that it was their pleasure "to prevent the sacrilegious hands of the whigs to grasp your property."[10]

Plauché's loan proved insufficient to help Jackson keep Junior financially solvent. Cognizant of Jackson's struggles, Blair also offered him a loan, which he accepted. Jackson told his friend that while he himself owed less than five hundred dollars, Junior had been victimized by "a combination of sharpers, [and] swindlers." The loan's eventual terms were 6 percent interest on ten thousand dollars offered by Blair and his partner, John C. Rives. Annual payments were required, with the loan scheduled to be paid off in March 1846. Jackson used the Halcyon plantation and thirty slaves as security for the loan. Jackson made the first annual payment of six hundred dollars on time, but the lack of success at Halcyon in 1843 led him to request a deferment of the next year's payment, which Blair and Rives granted. The former president assured his friend that doing so enabled him and Junior to pay off all debts except the ten thousand–dollar loan. The ongoing inability to make Halcyon profitable led Jackson to make a similar request for deferment in late 1844, to which Blair replied favorably once again. Just three months later Blair and Rives offered Jackson the opportunity of taking out a loan of up to one hundred thousand dollars; he settled for seven thousand dollars.[11]

Jackson even used politics to gain financial relief. In March 1842 Missouri senator Lewis Field Linn asked Congress to refund Jackson's one thousand–dollar contempt of court fine, plus the interest accumulated for twenty-seven years, levied by Judge Dominick Hall following the Battle of New Orleans. A political battle ensued, with national political consequences. Democrats and Whigs used the issue to explore the present condition and future course of the nation's political system. Jackson understood the implications of the debate. While he certainly cared about gaining a measure of vindication and removing the stain on his reputation that the fine occasioned, the money at stake was not a small sum for a man struggling to stop the financial bleeding. He sent frequent missives to Washington friends, encouraging them to keep pressing for the reimbursement. When the bill was passed by Congress and signed by President John Tyler in early 1844, Jackson welcomed the $2,732.90 refund.[12]

Junior's finances and the Panic of 1837 ultimately cost Jackson one of his passions. A lifelong lover of horses, he was forced to divest himself of part of his stable. "Sell the fillies if you can," he ordered Junior in the fall of 1840, and use the proceeds to "pay Mr. Crutcher and Capt. Dodson what you owe him." Within a few months Jackson sold more horses to help Junior buy additional land in Mississippi. Even his gifting of a horse was tied to Junior's debts. In gratitude for Blair's financial generosity in making the ten thousand–dollar loan, Jackson sent his friend's daughter a four-year-old filly named Emuckfau.[13]

Jackson's indebtedness prevented him from purchasing many slaves during his retirement years. He bought only 5 slaves between 1837 and 1845, selling 4 of them back to their original owner in order to pay one of Junior's debts. Despite the financial crunch, Jackson remained one of Tennessee's largest slave owners. Kentucky-born sculptor Joel Tanner Hart, on an 1839 visit to present Jackson with a bust, remarked that 140 slaves lived at the Hermitage. The 1840 census counted 111 slaves there. Overseer James M. Parker listed 51 slaves at Halcyon in 1841, while in February 1842 Jackson estimated that a combined 150 slaves worked on the Hermitage and Halcyon plantations.[14]

Jackson's relationship with his slaves continued to be complex. At times he exhibited compassion. He helped a deceased relative's slave, for example, send a letter to her family in Liberia, where they had settled upon emancipation. He also expressed concern about his slaves' health. When Andrew Hutchings's slave John faced the loss of his eyesight, Jackson sent him to a local doctor whom he trusted, "as John was so valuable and humanity required that every thing might be done for him." The doctor saved one of John's eyes, Jackson reported weeks later, allowing the slave to "thread a needle, and see the second hand of a watch."[15]

Jackson also contributed significant time and financial resources to defending four of his slaves who had been accused of murder. In December 1838 a group of between forty and one hundred slaves, including some of Jackson's, had gathered at a neighborhood holiday party. As a result of the drunken revelry, a fight broke out, leading to the death of a male slave, Frank, owned by Jackson's nephew Stockley Donelson. Stockley had not even waited to hear the testimony of the slave witnesses before swearing out the warrant against four of Jackson's slaves: Alfred, George, Jack (or Jacob), and Squire. Adding to Jackson's irritation was the complicity of William Donelson, another nephew, in encouraging Stockley's decision. An incensed Jackson pointed out that there "were many in the riot," not just his four men. He also argued that "it was a constitutional right, that all men by law presumed to be innocent until guilt was proven."[16]

Jackson hired three prominent Nashville lawyers as his slaves' advocates. A jury acquitted Alfred, Jack, and Squire "in two minutes," according to Jackson. (The charges against George were dismissed by the grand jury.) "The ransaked, the drunken hords of Negroes, worthless Whig Scamps, & worthless fishermen" had "swore too much—contradicted each other, and their credit was blown sky high," he reported to James K. Polk. Defending his slaves cost Jackson a considerable amount of money. Already struggling with debt accrued by his son, he contemplated selling several slaves to pay for the trial; he chose instead to sell some of his land in Florence, Alabama.[17]

While Jackson's primary concern in this conflict was protecting his slave property, he also wanted to settle a family quarrel that had been brewing for nearly a decade. Early in his presidential administration Jackson suspected that Stockley Donelson had been speaking ill of the Eatons.

During this period Jackson also heard that Stockley was allowing Charlotte, one of the Hermitage slaves, to slander her owner, a charge that his nephew denied. When the Whig party organized during Jackson's second term, relative John C. McLemore warned Andrew Donelson that Stockley and William were wavering about supporting Martin Van Buren in the 1836 election. McLemore's admonition proved prescient: after Jackson retired to the Hermitage in 1837, William Donelson came out publicly as a Whig. The former president was astounded that his nephew would allow himself to be used by "secrete combinations." Many Whigs were "sniggering already how they have duped" William, he observed. When the 1838 fight and murder took place, the three relatives were in a disagreement over a road that Stockley and William wanted cut through their uncle's land. Because the two Donelson relatives were unsuccessful in prosecuting his slaves, Jackson fumed, "they have thro the means of some of their subalterns since raised a whirlwind about roads." The three men eventually went to court over the dispute, with Stockley dropping the suit after Jackson's death.[18]

Jackson also may have defended his four male slaves for two other reasons. Southern planters came to view their enslaved as "quasi-kin," or members of the family. While not equal to white family members, slaves were considered part of the plantation community. Undoubtedly, Jackson wanted to protect Alfred, George, Jack, and Squire, as he had Dinwiddie decades earlier, because it reflected well on his paternal authority. He also may have recognized in their actions an attempt to protect their honor. While Jackson never matched Alfred's braggadocio in proclaiming that "he was the best man in the House," he certainly would have identified with his slave's assertion of masculinity, even if he could not countenance freedom for Alfred.[19]

Jackson's retirement failed to provide him with the respite that he had sought for nearly two decades. Debt and family quarrels dominated his thoughts during these years, as he sought ways to secure a stable financial future for his son and his family. At every turn it seemed that some obstacle stood in the way or some individual thwarted the peace that he coveted. Old Hickory was determined to remove or overcome each one, even if it killed him.

XX

"Texas Must, & Will Be Ours"

Even in retirement, Jackson paid close attention to the political world. He dispensed advice freely to prominent Democrats, including Francis P. Blair, James K. Polk, and Martin Van Buren, while longtime enemies, such as John Quincy Adams, John C. Calhoun, and Henry Clay failed to escape his written invective. Some of the major political issues that he faced as president, such as abolitionism and Texas annexation, grew in importance during his retirement years, and Jackson was not shy in stating his views, which correlated with those held by many white southerners.

One of Jackson's disappointments was his successor's inability to sustain the momentum that he had built as president. The Panic of 1837, a severe economic crisis that surpassed that of 1819, paralyzed Van Buren, the masterful, behind-the-scenes strategist. Some southerners blamed Jackson for having created the policies that in their estimation were "primary cause of the evils which we are suffering." Henry Clay, ever critical of his Tennessee nemesis, called Jackson "the author of all our present calamities." "Not satisfied with the desolation which he prepared for us while at Washington," he continued, Old Hickory was "now, from his Hermitage, urging his successor upon new & fatal experiments, destined, if not arrested, to plunge the Country into still deeper distress and embarrassment."[1]

Understanding that Old Kinderhook was vulnerable, the Whigs ran William Henry Harrison during the 1840 presidential election. They used Harrison's status as a military hero of the War of 1812 to out-Jackson the Democrats. Despite the Whigs bragging that they could carry southern states, Jackson predicted that "the Federalists hard cider drinkers and Coon worshipers" would only win Clay's home state of Kentucky. He was wrong. The "Tippecanoe and Tyler Too" ticket won in an electoral landslide, 234–60; the popular vote favored Harrison and John Tyler, his vice presidential running mate, 52.9 percent to 46.8 percent. Tellingly, Van Buren lost the majority of the South, winning only Arkansas, Georgia,

Missouri, South Carolina, and Virginia. The region that had voted solidly for its native son Jackson turned its back on another four years of his successor. Jackson blamed "corruption, bribery and fraud" for Van Buren's downfall, especially in Tennessee. Nevertheless, he retained his faith in the people, certain that they would "rally and check at once this combined corrupt coalition and on their native dunghills set them down." Harrison's death a month into office elevated Tyler to the chief executive seat, but the new president's support of nullification hardly comforted Jackson.[2]

At the head of this "corrupt coalition," in Jackson's estimation, was former president Adams. Never one to allow grudges to die easily, Jackson repeatedly criticized the New Englander, who had been elected to the U.S. House in 1830. He denied Adams's claim that the general had approved the boundary line in the Adams-Onís Treaty prompted by his 1818 invasion of Florida. In contemplating the possibility of Texas joining the Union, Jackson recommended to William B. Lewis that any annexation treaty be kept quiet. Otherwise, "that wicked & reckless old man, John Q. Adams, will write hundreds of memorials & send them over the whole country to get signers." Worse, he cautioned, "all the abolitionists & many more will sign them."[3]

Jackson was well aware that the abolitionist movement was gaining members and political traction during the late 1830s and early 1840s. Like most southern slave owners, he viewed it with trepidation. He commented favorably on Catherine Beecher's *Essay on Slavery and Abolitionism, with Reference to the Duty of American Females* (1837), a publication that included Beecher's private letters to abolitionist Angelina Grimké, who advocated female activism in opposition to slavery. Beecher contended that northern abolitionists were interfering with a southern domestic institution, and the southern response, as expected, was the same as if outsiders were indicting a "community" for "the practice of a great sin." She also argued that women should not be directly involved in direct political activism outside of their domestic influence. Jackson indicated that he had read the essay "with attention" and declared "there is much good sense in this little work."[4]

On another occasion, in 1844, Jackson took note of Frances Wright's abolitionist lecture in the nation's capital. In the mid-1820s the Scottish-born Wright had attempted to combine Robert Owen's ideas about a utopian community with her abolitionist sentiments. The Nashoba settlement, located near Memphis, failed, and Wright took to the lecture circuit, where she encountered crowds hostile to her support of emancipation and racial equality. Jackson recalled that "she once settled in Tennessee, western District, to liberate all the Southern Slaves. I told her the plan never could succeed, and after a trial she found it so." Solicited by former newspaper editor Moses Dawson for his views on the noted feminist's political stance on slavery, Jackson was unequivocal. "If the free States never had attempted to interfere with the rights of the South about Slavery," he wrote, "I have no doubt but Slave holding States would have taken measures to have introduced an amelioration of their Slaves." Instead, he continued, "these firebrands of abolition who wish a Servile War regardless of the consequences, have forced the South to restrict their Slaves more than their inclinations or feelings desired." What if the abolitionists succeeded and "all the slaves were liberated[?] Where are they to live; are they to amalgamate with the Whites[?] Of these Eastern abolitionists some are for amalgamation even *female*. and some are for prohibiting them going & living amongst them." Citing physical exhaustion as a reason to close his letter, Jackson concluded with an observation about Wright's political influence on the nation's politics: "There have been great exertions to split & divide the Democracy on the subject of the presidency and throw firebrands in our midsts, and I am sure Miss Wrights lectures will not be a means to allay them at present . . . *She may do harm there, but can do no good.*"[5]

Jackson's comment referred to the 1844 presidential election between Clay and Polk. Central to that election was the discussion about the annexation of Texas, an issue that drew much of Jackson's attention during his retirement years. Faced with a variety of challenges as president, Van Buren had distanced himself from calls for Texas's annexation. Jackson found, however, that he could not do the same. In 1837 Adams revived the charge that Old Hickory had conspired with Sam Houston earlier in the decade to incite revolution in Mexico's northern province. Jackson marshaled evidence refuting the "demented" congressman's accusations. When critical letters were missing, he claimed that Adams and his supporters had "purloined" them. Blair talked him out of publishing a pointed and inflammatory public letter to Adams, in which Jackson accused him of possessing "the stolen property" and lectured him on "criminal law" regarding theft. In late 1838 Jackson also addressed claims that he was associated with the questionable land speculation in Texas undertaken by Samuel Swartwout, the collector of customs at the port of New York. Jackson denied that he was in any way associated with Swartwout's efforts "to aid the Texians in their contest with Mexico." A political appointee whom Jackson regarded favorably for "his honesty, honor and integrity," Swartwout's close ties to the Texas Revolution and his apparent attempt to profit from acquiring large parcels of Texas land caused Jackson a great deal of trouble. Swartwout further strained their relationship when he fled the country; he was later found responsible for embezzling some two million dollars from the federal government.[6]

The Texas annexation issue took on renewed importance in 1843 when Texas's president Houston began pressuring the Tyler administration for a decision while at the same time informally discussing annexation to the United States with Mexico and Great Britain. Tyler seized on the news of Britain's interest in acquiring Texas and abolishing slavery there to push Congress to accept an annexation treaty. Proslavery southerners needed little convincing that a foreign threat existed to their chattel labor. Arguments that acquiring Texas would actually hasten slavery's demise, encapsulated in a pamphlet written by Mississippi senator Robert J. Walker, were intended to soothe northerners who felt queasy about supporting a treaty.[7]

At the Hermitage Jackson observed these events with intense interest. Behind the scenes he insisted to Walker and other prominent pro-annexationist Democrats that Texas was "ready to act promptly on the subject." He offered his public views on annexation in a letter to Tennessee congressman Aaron V. Brown, written in February 1843 but not published (in the *Washington Globe*) until 20 March 1844. He blamed the Monroe administration, and especially Adams, for inexplicably ceding Texas to Spain during treaty negotiations in the late 1810s. He offered as a possible explanation that "it was the jealousy of the rising greatness of the south and west, and the fear of loosing the political asscendency in the north." He also recounted efforts to purchase the territory during his own presidency in order to keep the United States and New Orleans safe. Then Jackson identified the real threat that existed if the annexation effort failed. Great Britain could make an "alience" with Texas that would allow it to march an army into the southern states, allowing it to "excite the negroes to insurrection" and incite "a servile war." Combined with a military strike out of Canada, this invasion held the potential to bring the United States to its knees.[8]

Clearly, Great Britain loomed large in Jackson's demand for Texas's annexation, and many Americans agreed. Anglophobia was deeply ingrained in the antebellum American consciousness. In the North, New Englanders and members of the upper class tended to idealize British society and custom, but the working class, influenced by Irish immigrants, resented Britain's cheap goods. Some southern planters possessed an Anglophilia that made them "more unendurable than the nobility of Britain," according to one Kentuckian. But not many southerners did, and certainly not Jackson. He held no great love for the imperial head of the former colonies and was suspicious about its attempts to undermine the American economy. Many white southerners shared his fear that Britain was conspiring to encourage "a servile war" in order to force Texas's submission. Jackson also predicted the incitement of Native Americans if Britain succeeded in taking charge of Texas. Controlling the southern slave population and avoiding bloodshed like that which had precipitated the War of 1812 were thus paramount in Jackson's mind.[9]

Events in early 1844 significantly altered the annexation debate. On February 28 President Tyler, members of his cabinet, and an array of notable guests visited the USS *Princeton,* the United States Navy's newly constructed warship. During a demonstration of the Peacemaker, one of two guns on board the ship capable of firing heavy projectiles over three miles, the cannon's breech exploded. The president and many of the guests were below deck when the accident occurred, but eight people lost their lives, including Secretary of State Abel P. Upshur. Jackson lamented the secretary of state's death and questioned whether his successor, John C. Calhoun, would "be able to do the subjects as much justice."[10]

Despite Jackson's lack of confidence in Calhoun, the South Carolinian completed a preliminary treaty that was signed by diplomatic representatives from both sides on 12 April 1844. As the Senate debated the treaty over the next few weeks, however, Calhoun threw fuel on the fire of opposition. In a move calculated to undermine British abolitionist influence and encourage southern support for annexation, he sent a letter to Richard Pakenham, British minister to the United States, arguing that slavery was essential to the peace of the nation and the health of the enslaved. The letter helped defeat the annexation treaty in the Senate in early June 1844.

Jackson criticized the "craven hearted Senators" who had voted against the treaty as "traitors to the best interests of our country, and to our Glorious Union." Ironically, Jackson also berated Calhoun for having "displayed a great weakness and folly to introduce" the connection between annexation and slavery. "The power of the states over slavery was not necessary by him then to have been brought into view," he commented, ignoring his own alarms about Britain's influence on southern slavery. He undoubtedly shared Blair's belief that Calhoun and other nullifiers used Texas "only as a bone of contention" to further their sectional divisiveness.[11]

The 1844 presidential election thus assumed great importance for deciding the nation's future political relationship with Texas. Clay, the presumed Whig candidate, opposed immediate annexation because of its potential to divide the Union along sectional lines, preferring to focus on the benefits of his American System. He went public with his views on Texas in a April 17 letter written from Raleigh, North Carolina, prior to receiving his party's nomination. Although Van Buren had lost the 1840 presidential election, he still appeared the obvious choice for the Democrats. The New Yorker met with his advisors, including Benjamin F. Butler and Silas Wright Jr., and decided that the annexation issue was too dangerous to leave open for debate during the upcoming campaign. Van Buren made the decision even though he knew that his views conflicted with Jackson's wishes. In response to a letter from Mississippi congressman William H. Hammet requesting his opinion on the topic, Van Buren wrote a lengthy justification for opposing immediate annexation. It was published in the evening edition of the *Globe* on April 28, coincidentally the same day that Clay's similar letter appeared in the *National Intelligencer*.[12]

Van Buren had made a fatal miscalculation. What had been an almost certain party nomination and, Jackson predicted, an election in which the New Yorker would win every "south and western state" instead became a total failure. Despite an alliance and friendship with his former vice president that stretched almost two decades, Jackson withdrew his support. Annexation was just too important to the future of the party and the nation. Privately, Jackson predicted that Van Buren's "illfated letter" would cost him southern and western votes and would only encourage Great Britain to continue its plans of "destroying the vallue" of slave property and "opening a way for our slaves to run away to Texas." Publicly, he warned that Texas was "the Key to our safety in the south and the West" from "the numerous hords of savages within the limit and on her borders." These "hords" only awaited the agitation that Great Britain was sure to bring before they acted. Jackson was not willing to support President Tyler, whom he did not trust, so he decided to call on Polk, the former speaker of the House, to run, despite his friend's two failed gubernatorial campaigns in 1841 and 1843. Jackson wrote Blair that the delegates to the Democratic convention in Baltimore needed to select Polk as the vice presidential candidate if Van Buren had any chance to win. In the background, however, he summoned Polk to the Hermitage and told him that he, with his pro-annexationist views, was the only prospect that the Democrats had for victory.[13]

The Baltimore convention produced the result that Jackson wanted. Polk had supporters among the Tennessee delegates—William G. Childress, Andrew Donelson, Cave Johnson, Samuel H. Laughlin, and Gideon J. Pillow—who worked to keep Van Buren and the other leading candidate, Lewis Cass of Michigan, from achieving the two-thirds votes necessary for the nomination. They planned to offer Polk as a compromise candidate. The strategy worked. After two days of balloting, northern delegates approached members of the Tennessee delegation with the idea of placing Polk at the head of the ticket. Seeing their opportunity, the Tennesseans agreed, and by the afternoon of the next day Democrats had chosen Polk, with George M. Dallas of Pennsylvania eventually receiving the vice presidential nod. Jackson lauded Van Buren's "purity and noble disinterestedness" in accepting his fate and hailed Polk and Dallas as "pure, tried, competent, & honest."[14]

Jackson kept a close watch on the presidential campaign, which centered on Texas. "Texas must, & will be ours," he told one Arkansan. He proclaimed Polk the best choice for southerners and westerners because of his support for annexation. "It would be almost as easy to turn the current of the Mississippi, as to turn the current of popular opinion in the south and west from speedy annexation," Jackson observed to Blair. It would "put to rest the vexing question of abolitionism, the dangerous rock to our Union." Reports that Thomas Hart Benton had allied with Adams on the annexation question led Jackson to call the Missouri senator "deranged" and blame him for leading Van Buren "into his unfortunate Texas position." He was also concerned that Calhoun's advocacy of annexation in order to expand slavery would reawaken the nullification movement. "Every democrat must put his face against any meeting of *Disunion*, or nullification," he told Polk. In sending Blair an invitation to attend a Democratic rally in Nashville, Jackson wanted his friend to know that he "will find no nullification or disunion here." Tyler's reluctance to withdraw his name from the campaign exasperated Jackson. The president claimed that he remained in the race to force the Texas issue to a head, hopefully in favor of annexation. Jackson saw things differently. Tyler's stubbornness threatened the Democrats' chances for the White House, and Jackson advised him to withdraw, believing that "he would do nothing to promote Clay or injure Democracy." When Tyler capitulated, Jackson's tone changed. He told the president that he "fully approve[d] of his just and energetic course he has adopted with regard to Mexico & Texas."[15]

Voters in the fall election endorsed the Democrats' annexationist platform but only barely. Polk and Dallas won 170 votes, while the ticket of Clay and Theodore Frelinghuysen of New Jersey won 105. In the popular vote, however, the Democrats secured only a plurality. Polk even lost a close election in Tennessee, "by the vilest frauds that have ever been practised," according to Jackson. The presence of a third party, the Liberty party, and its presidential nominee, James G. Birney, did not help Whig efforts in several northern states, especially New York. Nevertheless, Jackson felt vindicated by the electoral victory. Comparing himself to Simeon in the New Testament, the "just and devout" man who had been promised that he would not die "before he had seen the Lord's Christ," Jackson pronounced himself ready to "'depart in peace,' for I now see our beloved country's glorious union safe & placed on a basis that will long endure."[16]

Bolstering his confidence in a successful resolution to the annexation issue was his nephew's appointment as chargé d'affaires to Texas in September 1844. Since his uncle's retirement in 1837, Andrew Donelson had assisted him in strengthening the Democratic party at the local, state, and national levels. He had also worked assiduously for Polk's nomination at the Democratic national convention, proving his effectiveness as Jackson's representative. Tyler recognized the advantage of support from someone who possessed a close relationship with both Jackson and Houston. He hoped that Donelson's appointment would "have a controuling influence with Genl. Houston and incline him, if he entertains any feelings antagonistical to the U. States and favourable to England, to pause ere he declares against annexation."[17]

Donelson left for the Texas capital of Washington-on-the-Brazos in October, spending the next nine months spearheading the annexation effort. Meanwhile, Jackson used his nephew to keep Sam Houston apprised of the political winds in the United States. He cautioned that Texas would fall prey to Great Britain's colonial expansion if it did not accept annexation to the United States. Foreigners would overrun the Lone Star Republic, and abolitionism would take hold. He gave Donelson permission to convey his opinions to Houston, who surely could see "how much more honorable, Honorable, to be a senator representing a free and enlightened people, than the president of a people, a mere colony of England, and fightting against the United States that gave them birth, to rivet the chains of despotism upon the only free people on earth." Donelson explained that Houston had not written Jackson for the past few months because he "despaired of the success of the Democratic party" and wanted to maintain flexibility if Texas decided to remain independent. Polk's election, however, had apparently convinced him that "reannexation" was the best option for his government. Houston wanted Jackson to understand that he still held him in high regard, Donelson reported.[18]

Jackson could proudly point to his nephew's efforts as chargé when President Tyler, as he departed the White House, signed a joint congressional resolution of annexation. In January 1845 Donelson's dispatches convinced House Democrats to consider every option available to accomplish annexation. The ensuing resolution, proposed by a Tennessee Whig, brought Texas into the Union as a state. The resolution also incorporated the Missouri Compromise by allowing for the possibility of four new states created out of Texas, with the 36°30' line marking the allowance or prohibition of slavery. In the Senate debate the following month Benton retreated from his opposition to immediate annexation and offered a measure including many of the treaty provisions that the Senate had rejected the previous year. Robert J. Walker then offered a compromise resolution, which allowed the president the option of choosing annexation under either the House or the Senate resolution. Tyler chose the House plan, leaving the details to Polk, the incoming president. Jackson rejoiced upon receiving the news. "The Federal Union must be preserved, and Massa-chusetts blue light federalist, her abolishinists, and her whole [coonery] and whiggery combined may foam and threaten," he told Blair, "but all will vanish like smoke."[19]

Jackson's interest in Texas blended politics and personal finances. In March 1839 Thomas J. Alsbury, a longtime Texas resident, visited the Hermitage, and Jackson convinced him to buy one of his horses on credit for a thousand dollars, plus interest. Alsbury was unable to pay the debt, so he gave Jackson the deed to a tract of land along the San Bernard River, concluding the transaction in March 1844. That fall, as Andrew Donelson set out for Texas, Jackson asked him to check on the tract and ensure that the taxes had been paid. The following spring Jackson noted to his nephew that "if the land is good the title secure, and its localety favorable, I might get something for it that would aid me out of my pecuniary liabili-tys,–now pressing hard." Even with this momentous political issue, Jackson could not escape the financial cloud that seemed always to be hanging over him.[20]

During the final months of his life Jackson was drawn into a debate about the future editorship of the *Washington Globe,* which tested key bonds of kinship. Blair, the newspaper's founding editor, had used its columns to criticize Calhoun's efforts to produce an annexation treaty in 1844. But he also expressed support for Benton and Van Buren, both of whom were temperate in their approach to annexation. These public stances left him exposed when Polk, whose campaign had hinged on immediate annexa-tion, organized his administration. Aware that his old friend was vulner-able, Jackson advised the president-elect to keep him as the *Globe's* editor. Along with Lewis, Jackson said, Blair would help him "ferret out & make known to you, all the plotts & intrigues Hatching against your administra-tion." Polk, however, began casting about for someone either to take over the *Globe* or to start a competing newspaper. He did not trust Blair and his partner, John C. Rives, to look out for his or the party's best interests. "Blair and his paper are so identified with certain men of the party, and has increased the hostility of certain other of the party," he wrote Jackson shortly after taking office, "that it is impossible, for him to command the support of the whole party." Jackson finally and reluctantly agreed that Polk should make the change, although he warned him, "Your course with regard to the Globe & Blair will sour the minds of many firm democrats." After considering several potential editors, including Andrew Donelson, Polk settled on *Richmond Enquirer* editor Thomas Ritchie as Blair's replacement for the new *Washington Union*. Jackson sent Blair his regrets for Polk's decision to remove him. He lauded Blair for "set[ting] an example for all real patriots to follow" in selling the *Globe* without committing "an act inju[ri]ous to the great democratic cause, in which you had so long and faithfully labored."[21]

Jackson abruptly concluded his letter to Blair with a catalog of the physical ailments tormenting him. "I have wrote thus much in great pain, with a shortness of breath that almost suffocates me in being carried ten feet," he complained. "I am I may say a perfect Jelly from the toes to the upper part of my abdome[n], in any part of which a finger can be pressed half an Inch and the print will remain for minutes—added to this I have a bowell complaint, several passages with gripping daily, with a severe attack of piles." "This is my situation," he pronounced, "and in what it may result God only knows." Andrew Jackson had less than two weeks to live.[22]

Conclusion

Jackson had lived longer than he and many others expected. The bullet embedded in his body from the 1806 duel with Dickinson, which was never extracted, frequently became infected. Added to this wound was the dysentery and malaria from which Jackson suffered during the War of 1812 and thereafter. Well-intentioned medical treatment only worsened his condition. He frequently underwent bloodletting, via cupping or venesection, and ingested sugar of lead and calomel. Both medications were recommended courses of treatment in that era, but their side effects slowly poisoned him. Jackson's health was so bad that nearly every letter that he wrote in his retirement years included some mention of his debilities.[1]

Junior optimistically reported his father's health as "a little better," although "still very feeble," in the spring of 1845. Yet by late May, Jackson was essentially infirm. On Friday, June 6, Old Hickory's death march began. A severe discharge of diarrhea left him weakened. He was strong enough, however, to discuss farm affairs with Junior. Jackson also commented on "the certainty" that the Texas government would accept annexation to the United States. That night he wrote President Polk about alleged corruption within the Treasury. On Saturday his constitution declined considerably, leaving him unable to attend church on Sunday. Following the morning service the minister, members of the Jackson family, several slaves, and Jackson's doctor, John Esselman, gathered in the dying patriarch's room. After taking communion, Jackson told his grandchildren and other young relatives that "they must all be obedient children." After speaking briefly to Junior, Jackson pronounced, "I want to meet you all in heaven, both black and white . . . be good children & we will all meet in heaven." "He then dozed away calmly & resignedly expired. at 6 Oclock in the evening 8th of June 1845," Junior reported. Elizabeth Donelson, Andrew Donelson's second wife, noted that Junior "seemed bewildered" by his father's death, while Sarah went into "spasms" after his passing.[2]

Elizabeth recorded other details of Jackson's deathbed scene for her husband, who remained in Texas. After telling everyone that they would meet in heaven, she recalled, the Old Hero "addressed himself particularly to his servants and exhorted them to their duty and to look to Christ as their only Savior, and that as much was expected of them according to their opportunities as from the whites." "Oh my husband I wished you were there," Elizabeth lamented.[3]

In 1880 Jackson's slave Hannah also recounted her memories of Jackson's final hours. When the doctor instructed Junior "to order the servants out" of his father's room, they refused. "The darkees would not be driven out," she observed. "They looked on him as if they had as much right to him as Massa Andrew." Thus, Hannah and George were in the room when Jackson spoke his final words, which she recalled as being "I want all to prepare to meet me in Heaven; I have a right to the Tree of Life. My conversation is for you all. Christ has no respect to color. I am in God and Gods in me. He dwelleth in me and I dwell in him." After Jackson drew his last breath, Hannah and the other slaves took care of Sarah after she fainted. A grief-stricken Hannah wailed, "Our master, our father is gone."[4]

On Tuesday, June 10, Nashville "had all the appearance of a Sabbath" as prominent citizens and friends made their way to the Hermitage for Jackson's funeral. The Old Hero's body "was laid out in the parlor with the face uncovered" for visitors to pay their last respects. Many of Jackson's former soldiers wept as they took a last look at the man who had led them into battle. At 11:00 a.m. the minister preached a sermon from the Book of Revelation 7:13–14. The passage speaks of a future day when the heavenly saints will have their robes washed "white in the blood of the lamb." Doubtless, some people who had prayed for the salvation of Jackson's soul were pleased to hear that he had become "an humble follower of the lamb" in 1838. Then pallbearers carried Jackson's coffin to the Hermitage garden, where he was placed in the ground next to Rachel. An eyewitness pronounced himself "struck . . . very forcibly" by the "sorrow universal" expressed by Jackson's slaves. The general "has always been charged with being tyrannical," yet approximately eighty of his slaves reportedly stood "in silent grief, the tears rolling down their dark faces."[5]

Reaction to Jackson's death varied around the South. Locally, the *Nashville Republican Banner* noted the passing of the man who possessed "an intellect of extraordinary vigor—a will of iron." The *Nashville Whig* observed that because of the strong feelings that he elicited, "of General Jackson's political acts and opinions it is not now fit to speak; nor of his character as a politician and statesman." What could be said, the editorial observed, was that "as husband, father, friend or master, were the conditions of the relationships fulfilled in the most exemplary manner on his part." Beyond Tennessee's borders Kentuckian James Pearce wrote his sister: "We have just heard of Genl Jackson's death. I wonder who now will be the dictator and head of the democratic party. Now that he is dead I find that I was very proud of him. He was a great man and though he and Mr. Clay are so opposite—in some respects, in many others they are strikingly alike. The same indomitable will & strength of purpose. And the 8th January—Ah! that was a great day, and I suppose that others than planters will admit that there are glorious recollections of [that day]." A funeral procession honoring Jackson was held in Louisville at the same time he was laid to rest at the Hermitage.[6]

Jackson's death left a void in his family. His indomitable will had governed minute and major details in their lives. Sometimes it was unwelcome, but he always demanded their attention. Despite his frequent missives to his son about finances and responsibility, Junior continued to invest in speculative ventures. He kept the Halcyon plantation until 1849, experiencing no more success than before. He also bought land in Kentucky, on which he hoped to establish a profitable ironworks and lead mine; neither proved viable. By 1855 Junior had turned his inheritance of $100,000 into $150,000 of debt. He was so financially desperate that in 1856 he sold the Hermitage to the state of Tennessee. This decision contributed to Junior's estrangement from his cousin Andrew Donelson, fracturing the kinship network that Jackson had cultivated.[7]

Despite the split between the two Andrews, Jackson's influence on their lives was unmistakable as he furthered the geographic movement of Old South ideals from the Carolinas into the Deep South. Jackson was not a Lockean blank slate when he moved to Middle Tennessee in the late 1780s. His early life had been shaped by kin, peers, and mentors who owned slaves and passed on their assumptions and expectations about what constituted notions of genteel status and masculinity. Jackson brought those ideas to the Upper South and passed them on to his male wards, including Donelson and Junior. His legacy continued, as these two wards in particular passed on to their sons the same advice, sometimes verbatim, that Old Hickory gave them about vice and virtue, money and marriage. Interestingly, several of his wards—including Donelson and Junior as well as Edward Butler and Andrew Hutchings—eventually moved into the Lower South, transferring Jackson's planter ideals to the cotton frontier.[8]

Junior's financial ineptness altered the lives of Jackson's enslaved. In 1850 there were still 137 slaves living at the Hermitage. In 1853, however, Junior sold 33 individuals in a transaction along with his Kentucky ironworks. Two years later approximately 60 slaves were included in an announced auction of Hermitage property, which did not take place. Many of the remaining slaves eventually were moved to plantations in Delhi, Louisiana, and Hancock County, Mississippi. Some of those remaining at the Hermitage shared their thoughts of Jackson in later years. In 1882 one reporter visited the Hermitage and found "Aunt Gracie" and "Uncle Alfred" still in residence. The two showed him around the grounds, winding up at the general's tomb in the garden. "'He didn't have a servant but would 'a' died for him,' said Aunt Gracie softly," the reporter noted. When the Tennessee legislature debated a bill that would help pay off the state's debt on the Hermitage, "old Alfred got all the negroes within his influence to vote for it 'for the sake of Gen. Jackson's home and honor,'" the article concluded. Thirteen years later Alfred, "an old negro who never tires of telling you that he was born in 1803, and is the only one of the servants left there," still gave tours of the Hermitage.[9]

The testimony of Alfred, Grace, and Hannah exposes the complexity of slaves' relations with their owners and the memory of those relationships. Filtered through white reporters, their memories reflected the Lost Cause nostalgia that predominated during the post-emancipation years. Ignored in their recollections was the violence visited upon the Hermitage slave community, including Alfred's mother, Betty, in 1821, when Jackson ordered her whipped if she continued to defy his will. If reported accurately, which was not always the case, their fond reminiscences were atypical of the experiences of antebellum slaves and failed to recognize Jackson's periodic abrogation of his own paternalistic ideals.[10]

Jackson's influence also lingered in national politics. His protégé, James K. Polk, oversaw the successful prosecution of the 1846–1848 war with Mexico. This conflict exacerbated the debate over Manifest Destiny, in particular slavery's role in accompanying westward expansion. During the 1850s the intertwined fates of slavery and expansion produced crisis after crisis, increasingly splitting the Union that Jackson tried so hard to keep together. The Democratic party that he and Van Buren had built held together, but the Whigs fell apart following the presidential contest of 1852, replaced by the antislavery Republican party. By 1860 even Jackson's Democrats succumbed to the festering sectionalism gripping the nation; the party divided into northern and southern wings, allowing Republican Abraham Lincoln to win the presidential election. Secession followed quickly, and in April 1861 the war that Jackson had avoided in 1832–1833 commenced.

Americans remembered Old Hickory during the crucial fall and winter months of 1860–1861. Amos Kendall, Jackson's former advisor, denounced the extremism of the era, calling on southerners to "emulate WASHINGTON and JACKSON, and you will rally an irresistible force, who, by aid of the ballot-box only, will rescue your institutions from danger and firmly maintain every constitutional right." A satirical letter from one "Eefum Smoothe" encouraged "Old Uncle Abe" to treat the southern states like a team of horses. "The success of Old ABE," the anonymous humorist wrote, "makes us wonder whether 'Old Hickory' was a gen[i]us." Numerous newspaper editorials and speeches recounted Jackson's "energetic measures" to keep South Carolina in the Union during the nullification crisis. Following the Palmetto State's secession in December 1860, South Carolinians noted that the "acts and teachings" of the administrations of "Washington, Jefferson, Madison, Jackson, &c" agreed with the Supreme Court's 1857 decision that the United States was "a white man's Government."[11]

Many Americans then, as now, failed to understand that Jackson was a southerner shaped by the region's values. This foundation in turn enabled him to help create a new South, expansive in its desire for land, cotton, and slavery. His propensity for violence reflected the larger culture of the South in which he grew up and lived, a society that required elite white males, or those wishing to be accepted as such, to defend their honor. Jackson used violence not only to protect his reputation but also to take millions of acres of land from Native Americans. Ostensibly, these land seizures were for national security and to guarantee the survival of Indian culture, but they also benefited Jackson and his friends, as well as other white southerners looking to move up in society. Central to this social ascension was the ownership of slaves, an institution that Jackson embraced in all of its cruelty. Kinship ties, so necessary to success in the early republic South, provided him with a network of men who guaranteed his financial security and promoted his political career. By the time he died in 1845, Jackson was a southern planter, ensconced as a member of the gentry class to which he had aspired from an early age. While not solely responsible for creating the antebellum South, Old Hickory was a crucial figure in determining its influence on the nation's future.

NOTES

In citing works in the notes, short titles have generally been used. Works frequently cited have been identified by the following abbreviations:

AHR American Historical Review
AJ Andrew Jackson
AJH Andrew Jackson Hutchings
AJD Andrew Jackson Donelson
AJJr Andrew Jackson Jr.
AK Amos Kendall
BDP Bettie M. Donelson Papers, TSLA
BDTGA Biographical Directory of the Tennessee General Assembly
BDUSC Biographical Directory of the United States Congress
CAJ *Correspondence of Andrew Jackson,* ed. John Spencer Bassett and J. Franklin Jameson, 7 vols. (Washington, D.C.: Carnegie Institute of Washington, 1926–1935)
CJKP Correspondence of James K. Polk
DLC Andrew J. Donelson Papers, Library of Congress, Washington, D.C.
EGWB Edward G.W. Butler
ERD Elizabeth Randolph Donelson
ETHSP East Tennessee Historical Society Publications
ETD Emily Tennessee Donelson
FHS Filson Historical Society, Louisville, Ky.
FG Felix Grundy
FPB Francis P. Blair
GLC Gilder Lehrman Collection
HC Henry Clay
HLW Hugh Lawson White
JAH Journal of American History
JER Journal of the Early Republic
JCM John C. McLemore
JKP James K. Polk
JHE John Henry Eaton
JLC Andrew Jackson Papers, Library of Congress, Washington, D.C.
JSH Journal of Southern History
JSR Andrew Jackson Papers, Scholarly Resources, Wilmington, Del.
LC Library of Congress, Washington, D.C.
LHA Ladies' Hermitage Association
MVB Martin Van Buren

MVHR   *Mississippi Valley Historical Review*
NPT   Nicholas P. Trist
PAJ   *Papers of Andrew Jackson*
Parton, *Life of AJ*   James Parton, *Life of Andrew Jackson*, 3 vols. (New York: Mason Brothers, 1859–1861)
PHC   *Papers of Henry Clay*
PJCC   *Papers of John C. Calhoun*
RDC   Robert Dyas Collection, TLSA
Remini, *AJ*   Robert V. Remini, *Andrew Jackson*, 3 vols. (New York: Harper & Row, 1977–1984)
Richardson, *Messages and Papers*   *The Messages and Papers of the Presidents, 1789–1897*, ed. James D. Richardson, 10 vols. (Washington, D.C.: GPO, 1896–1899)
RJ   Rachel Jackson
RKC   Richard K. Call
SH   Sam Houston
SYJ   Sarah Yorke Jackson
TDH   Tennessee Documentary History, Hoskins Library, Univ. of Tennessee-Knoxville
TEHC   *Tennessee Encyclopedia of History and Culture*
THB   Thomas Hart Benton
THM   *Tennessee Historical Magazine*
THQ   *Tennessee Historical Quarterly*
TSLA   Tennessee State Library and Archives, Nashville, Tenn.
VBL   Martin Van Buren Papers, LC
WHC   William H. Crawford
WBL   William B. Lewis

INTRODUCTION

1. Frederick Jackson Turner, *The Frontier in American History* (1920; repr., New York: Dover, 1996), 252–253. Turner and his disciples seem to have embraced the characterization of Jackson that emerged from the War of 1812, which allowed "supposedly uncivilized [backcountry] settlers . . . [to be] transformed into hardy, courageous American frontiersmen" (Matthew Rainbow Hale, in "Interchange: The War of 1812," *JAH* 99 [September 2012]: 527).

2. John Spencer Bassett, *The Life of Andrew Jackson* (New York: Macmillan, 1911), xii; Frederic A. Ogg, *The Reign of Andrew Jackson: A Chronicle of the Frontier in Politics* (New Haven: Yale University Press, 1914), 114; Thomas P. Abernethy, *From Frontier to Plantation in Tennessee: A Study in Frontier Democracy* (1932; repr., Tuscaloosa: University of Alabama Press, 1967), 123–124; John William Ward, *Andrew Jackson: Symbol for an Age* (New York: Oxford University Press, 1955); Arthur M. Schlesinger Jr., *The Age of Jackson* (Boston: Little, Brown, 1945); Richard B. Latner, *The Presidency of Andrew Jackson* (Athens: University of Georgia Press, 1979), 5.

3. Lorman Ratner, *Andrew Jackson and His Tennessee Lieutenants: A Study in Political Culture* (Westport, Conn.: Greenwood Press, 1997); Andrew Burstein, *The Passions of*

Andrew Jackson (New York: Knopf, 2003); Jon Meacham, *American Lion: Andrew Jackson in the White House* (New York: Random House, 2008); Sean Wilentz, *The Rise of American Democracy: Jefferson to Lincoln* (New York: Norton, 2005); Daniel Walker Howe, *What Hath God Wrought: The Transformation of America, 1815–1848* (Oxford: Oxford University Press, 2007).

4. Robert V. Remini, *Andrew Jackson*, 3 vols. (New York: Harper & Row, 1977–1984); William J. Cooper Jr., *The South and the Politics of Slavery, 1828–1856* (Baton Rouge: Louisiana State University Press, 1978); William J. Cooper Jr., *Liberty and Slavery: Southern Politics to 1860* (1983; repr., Columbia: University of South Carolina Press, 2000); Bertram Wyatt-Brown, "Andrew Jackson's Honor," *JER* 17 (Spring 1997): 1–36; Bettina Drew, "Master Andrew Jackson: Indian Removal and the Culture of Slavery" (Ph.D. diss., Yale University, 2001), 2, 4; Matthew S. Warshauer "Andrew Jackson: Chivalric Slave Master," *THQ* 65 (Fall 2006): 202–229; Hendrik Booraem, *Young Hickory: The Making of Andrew Jackson* (Dallas: Taylor, 2001). Robert Remini also addressed Jackson's views on slavery in general terms in *The Legacy of Andrew Jackson: Essays on Democracy, Indian Removal, and Slavery* (Baton Rouge: Louisiana State University Press, 1988).

5. Aaron Scott Crawford, "Patriot Slaveholder: Andrew Jackson and the Winter of Secession," *Journal of East Tennessee History* 82 (2010): 10–32; Sean Wilentz, "Abraham Lincoln and Jacksonian Democracy," in *Our Lincoln: New Perspectives on Lincoln and His World,* ed. Eric Foner (New York: Norton, 2008), 76–77; Roy P. Basler, ed., *Abraham Lincoln: His Speeches and Writings* (Cleveland: World Publishing, 1946), 588–589; First Inaugural Address, 4 March 1861, in Richardson, *Messages and Papers,* 6:5–12.

I

"His Very Soul Was Grieved"

1. Remini, *AJ,* 1:2; John Reid and John Henry Eaton, *The Life of Andrew Jackson,* ed. Frank L. Owsley Jr. (Tuscaloosa: University of Alabama Press, 1974), 9; Henry Lee, *A Biography of Andrew Jackson, Late Major-General of the Army of the United States,* ed. Mark A. Mastromarino (Knoxville: Tennessee Presidents Trust, 1992), 1; Booraem, *Young Hickory,* 1–2, 217–218 n. 5; David E. Leslie, *The Leslie Family* (N.p., [1983]), 7, 10; A. J. McKelway, "The Scotch-Irish of North Carolina," *North Carolina Booklet* 4 (March 1905): 12; Robert J. Dickson, *Ulster Emigration to Colonial America, 1718–1775* (London: Routledge & Kegan Paul, 1966), 9–11.

2. Lee, *Biography of Andrew Jackson,* 1; Reid and Eaton, *Life of Andrew Jackson,* 9; James Parton, *Life of Andrew Jackson,* 3 vols. (New York: Mason Brothers, 1860), 1:46–47; Booraem, *Young Hickory,* 2–3.

The four sisters were Margaret Hutchinson McCamie, Sarah Hutchinson Leslie, Mary Hutchinson Leslie, and Jane Hutchinson Crawford.

3. Dickson, *Ulster Emigration,* 56.

4. James H. Merrell, *The Indians' New World: Catawbas and Their Neighbors from European Contact through the Era of Removal* (Chapel Hill: University of North Carolina Press, 1989), 13–14, 92–96, 103–104, 171–179, 195; diary entry, 25 January 1767, in Richard J. Hooker, ed., *The Carolina Backcountry on the Eve of the Revolution: The Journal and Other Writings of Charles Woodmason, Anglican Itinerant* (Chapel Hill: University of North Carolina Press, 1953), 14.

5. Merrell, *Indians' New World,* 181–191.

6. Ibid., 197–198.

7. Remini, *AJ,* 1:3–4; James G. Leyburn, *The Scotch-Irish: A Social History* (Chapel Hill: University of North Carolina Press, 1962), 221; Booraem, *Young Hickory,* 8–9; Reid and Eaton, *Life of Andrew Jackson,* 9; Parton, *Life of AJ,* 1:49–50. Jackson biographers, including those who wrote under the general's authority, disagree over when exactly when his father died. I agree with Remini's assessment that placing the elder Jackson's death before March 15 "makes sense in explaining the movements of Elizabeth Jackson at the time of Andrew's birth" (Remini, *AJ,* 1:427 n. 9).

8. AJ to James H. Witherspoon, 11 August 1824, in *CAJ,* 3:265; Reid and Eaton, *Life of Andrew Jackson,* 9; Remini, *AJ,* 1:4–5; Booraem, *Young Hickory,* 2–3, 10; Peter N. Moore, *World of Toil and Strife: Community Transformation in Backcountry South Carolina, 1750–1805* (Columbia: University of South Carolina Press, 2006), 56–58.

It would be an understatement to say that the actual place of Jackson's birth has been a serious point of contention between the two states of North Carolina and South Carolina, both of which have claimed him as a native son. For this question I have relied on A. S. Salley, "On the Birthplace of Andrew Jackson," in Cyrus T. Brady, *The True Andrew Jackson* (Philadelphia: J. B. Lippincott, 1906), 407–438; and Elmer Don Herd Jr., *Andrew Jackson, South Carolinian: A Study of the Enigma of His Birth* (Columbia, S.C.: Lancaster County Historical Commission, 1963).

9. Booraem, *Young Hickory,* 16–17; Drew, "Master Andrew Jackson," 16–27; Moore, *World of Toil and Strife,* 3, 4, 31, 38–42, 53, 56–58; S. Max Edelson, *Plantation Enterprise in Colonial South Carolina* (Cambridge: Harvard University Press, 2006), 255–268; Ira Berlin, *Generations of Captivity: A History of African-American Slaves* (Cambridge: Belknap Press of Harvard University Press, 2003), 67–71, 73–76; Peter N. Moore, "The Local Origins of Allegiance in Revolutionary South Carolina: The Waxhaws as a Case Study," *South Carolina Historical Magazine* 107 (January 2006): 26–41; François Furstenberg, "The Significance of the Trans-Appalachian Frontier in Atlantic History," *AHR* 95 (June 2008): 647–677; Kenneth E. Lewis, "Frontier Change, Institution Building, and the Archaeological Record in the South Carolina Backcountry," *Southeastern Archaeology* 28 (Winter 2009): 184–201; Ben Rubin, "Planters and Presbyterians: South Carolina from Atlantic Microcosm to the Eve of the American Revolution," *Journal of Backcountry Studies* 5 (Fall 2010): 1–16.

10. Affidavit of Thomas Stephenson, 30 July 1828, Certificate of Samuel Mayes, 31 July 1828, Statement of Nathaniel Stephenson, 1 August 1828, AJ to MVB, 4 December 1838, in *CAJ,* 3:416–417, 417, 417–418, 5:573; Reid and Eaton, *Life of Andrew Jackson,* 9–10; Lee, *Biography of Andrew Jackson,* 1.

11. *National Intelligencer* (Washington, D.C.), 29 August 1845; William A. Graham, *General Joseph Graham and His Papers on North Carolina Revolutionary History* (Raleigh, N.C.: Edwards & Broughton, 1904), 67–85. See also Hendrik Booraem's analysis of the accuracy of Alexander's recollections (*Young Hickory,* 205–209).

12. Leyburn, *Scotch-Irish,* 149, 268–269; Louise Pettus, *The Waxhaws* (Rock Hill, S.C.: Privately printed, 1993), 21; Lily Doyle Dunlap, "Old Waxhaw," *North Carolina Booklet* 19 (April 1920): 139.

13. Leyburn, *Scotch-Irish,* 149; Reid and Eaton, *Life of Andrew Jackson,* 10–11; Lee,

Biography of Andrew Jackson, 2; Pettus, *Waxhaws*, 30–32; Tracy M. Kegley, "James White Stephenson: Teacher of Andrew Jackson," *THQ* 7 (March 1948): 42–46; Booraem, *Young Hickory*, 27, 32–34, 230 n. 13; Chalmers G. Davidson, "Independent Mecklenburg," *North Carolina Historical Review* 46 (Spring 1969): 125; Daniel A. Tompkins, *History of Mecklenburg County and the City of Charlotte from 1740 to 1903*, 2 vols. (Charlotte: Observer Printing House, 1903), 1:72, 73.

14. Remini, *AJ*, 1:14–17; Booraem, *Young Hickory*, 85–88.

15. Moore, "Local Origins of Allegiance," 33–34, 38.

16. Reid and Eaton, *Life of Andrew Jackson*, 10–11; Lee, *Biography of Andrew Jackson*, 2; Remini, *AJ*, 1:14–17; Booraem, *Young Hickory*, 85–88.

17. Remini, *AJ*, 1:20–23; Reid and Eaton, *Life of Andrew Jackson*, 12–13; AJ to Amos Kendall, 9 January 1844, in *CAJ*, 6:253–254; and Document on AJ's capture, n.d., Document on AJ's imprisonment, n.d., and James McLaughlin to Amos Kendall, 2 January 1843, in *PAJ*, 1:5, 5–6, 7.

18. Remini, *AJ*, 1:24; AJ to James Hervey Witherspoon, 17 August 1824, James Hervey Witherspoon to AJ, 16 April 1825, in *PAJ*, 5:437–439, 6:60–61; Parton, *Life of AJ*, 1:94–95; Booraem, *Young Hickory*, 254.

19. Moore, *World of Toil and Strife*, 4, 92; Tom Hatley, *The Dividing Paths: Cherokees and South Carolinians through the Era of Revolution* (New York: Oxford University Press, 1993), 239–240.

II
"A Person of Unblemished Moral Character"

1. Booraem, *Young Hickory*, xii, 111–114; Editorial note, *PAJ*, 1:7.

2. Booraem, *Young Hickory*, 114–115; Barbara Stern Kupfer, "A Presidential Patron of the Sport of Kings: Andrew Jackson," *THQ* 29 (Fall 1970): 245–246; Charles C. Crittenden, "Overland Travel and Transportation in North Carolina, 1763–1789," *North Carolina Historical Review* 8 (July 1931): 252–253; Timothy H. Breen, "Horses and Gentlemen: The Cultural Significance of Gambling among the Gentry of Virginia," *William and Mary Quarterly* 34 (April 1977): 243, 246, 249.

3. Booraem, *Young Hickory*, 121–123; Reid and Eaton, *Life of Andrew Jackson*, 13–14; Parton, *Life of AJ*, 1:97–98; James A. McLaughlin to Amos Kendall, 14 February 1843, JLC.

4. Drew, "Master Andrew Jackson," 6–9; Moore, *World of Toil and Strife*, 38–42; Patrick S. Brady, "The Slave Trade in South Carolina, 1787–1808," *JSH* 38 (November 1972): 601–620; Philip D. Morgan, "Black Society in the Lowcountry, 1760–1810," in *Slavery and Freedom in the Age of the American Revolution*, ed. Ira Berlin and Ronald Hoffman (Charlottesville: University Press of Virginia, 1983), 86–87; Rachel N. Klein, *Unification of a Slave State: The Rise of the Planter Class in the South Carolina Backcountry, 1760–1808* (Chapel Hill: University of North Carolina Press, 1990), 250, 253; George C. Rogers, *Charleston in the Age of the Pinckneys* (Columbia: University of South Carolina Press, 1980), 71, 141; David L. Lightner, *Slavery and the Commerce Power: How the Struggle against the Interstate Slave Trade Led to the Civil War* (New Haven: Yale University Press, 2006), 17–18; Walter J. Fraser Jr., *Charleston! Charleston! The History of a Southern City*

(Columbia: University of South Carolina Press, 1989), 171; Drew, "Master Andrew Jackson," 6–8.

5. Parton, *Life of AJ*, 1:101; James W. Ely Jr., and Theodore Brown Jr., eds., *Legal Papers of Andrew Jackson* (Knoxville: University of Tennessee Press, 1987), xxxvi, 356–357; Booraem, *Young Hickory*, 139–147; Remini, *AJ*, 1:29; J. A. Hoskins, "The Most Distinguished Member of the Guilford Bar," *North Carolina Booklet* 19 (April–July 1920): 117–118; Archibald Henderson, "Jackson's Loose Living, Common Sin of His Period, but Records Show that He Has Been Much Libelled," *Raleigh (N.C.) News and Observer*, 17 October 1926; Archibald Henderson, "Richard Henderson and the Occupation of Kentucky, 1775," *MVHR* 1 (December 1941): 341–363; "Archibald Henderson," in *BDUSC*.

6. Booraem, *Young Hickory*, 141, 144–147; Ely and Brown, *Legal Papers of Andrew Jackson*, 378; Archibald Henderson, "Why Andrew Jackson Left North Carolina," *Raleigh News and Observer*, 31 October 1926.

7. Remini, *AJ*, 1:33; Law license, 26 September 1787, in *PAJ*, 1:10–11; Ely and Brown, *Legal Papers of Andrew Jackson*, xxxvi.

8. Parton, *Life of AJ*, 1:106–108; Booraem, *Young Hickory*, 163–164, 188; Recognizance bond, 28 October 1787, William Cupples to AJ, 19 August 1795, in *PAJ*, 1:11, 68.

9. Ely and Brown, *Legal Papers of Andrew Jackson*, xxxvi; Remini, *AJ*, 1:34–36; Mark R. Cheatham, "The State of Tennessee," in *The Uniting States: The Story of Statehood for the Fifty United States*, ed. Benjamin F. Shearer, 3 vols. (Westport, Conn.: Greenwood Press, 2004), 3:1133; Booraem, *Young Hickory*, 188–190; Charles D. Rodenbough, *Governor Alexander Martin: Biography of a North Carolina Revolutionary War Statesman* (Jefferson, N.C.: McFarland, 2004), 125; Lewis L. Laska, "'The Dam'st Situation Ever Man Was Placed In': Andrew Jackson, David Allison, and the Frontier Economy of 1795–96," *THQ* 54 (Winter 1995): 339.

Although misspelled, the Mero District was named for Spanish governor Don Esteban Miró (John R. Finger, *Tennessee Frontiers: Three Regions in Transition* [Bloomington: Indiana University Press, 2001], 126).

10. Cheatham, "The State of Tennessee," 3:1133–1135; Reid and Eaton, *Life of Andrew Jackson*, 15; John Allison, *Dropped Stitches in Tennessee History* (Nashville: Marshall & Bruce, 1897), 102–107; Abernethy, *From Frontier to Plantation*, 123–124; Kevin T. Barksdale, *The Lost State of Franklin: America's First Secession* (Lexington: University Press of Kentucky, 2009), 3–17; Henderson, "Why Andrew Jackson Left North Carolina"; Bill of sale, 17 November 1788, in *PAJ*, 1:15, 432.

11. Ratner, *Jackson and His Tennessee Lieutenants*, 9–14; Thomas P. Abernethy, *The South in the New Nation, 1789–1819* (Baton Rouge: Louisiana State University Press and the Littlefield Fund for Southern History of the University of Texas, 1961), 6–12; Bertram Wyatt-Brown, *Southern Honor: Ethics and Behavior in the Old South* (New York: Oxford University Press, 1982), 88–114.

12. Parton, *Life of AJ*, 1:161–162; Archibald Henderson, "Andrew Jackson and His Famous Duel with Col. Avery," *Raleigh News and Observer*, 7 November 1926; Paul M. Fink, "The Rebirth of Jonesboro," *THQ* 31 (Fall 1972): 225; James W. Ely Jr., "The Legal Practice of Andrew Jackson," *THQ* 38 (Winter 1979): 423; Ely and Brown, *Legal Papers of Andrew Jackson*, 357; AJ to Waightstill Avery, 12 August 1788, in *PAJ*, 1:12.

13. Wyatt-Brown, *Southern Honor*, 14, 355; Wyatt-Brown, "AJ's Honor," 8; Elliott J.

Gorn, "'Gouge and Bite, Pull Hair and Scratch': The Social Significance of Fighting in the Southern Backcountry," *AHR* 90 (February 1985): 22, 40; Douglas H. Yarn, "The Attorney as Duelist's Friend: Lessons from the Code Duello," *Case Western Reserve Law Review* 51 (Fall 2000): 84–85.

14. Parton, *Life of AJ,* 1:120–123; Remini, *AJ,* 1:40; Robert Weakley to James McLaughlin, 25 February 1843, JLC; Finger, *Tennessee Frontiers,* 109.

III
"Gentlemanly Satisfaction"

1. Abernethy, *From Frontier to Plantation,* 21–26; Henderson, "Richard Henderson," 352; Paul H. Bergeron, Stephen V. Ash, and Jeanette Keith, *Tennesseans and Their History* (Knoxville: University of Tennessee Press, 1999), 25–27; Harriet S. Arnow, *Seedtime on the Cumberland* (New York: Macmillan, 1960), 182–202; Ronald N. Satz, *Tennessee's Indian Peoples: From White Contact to Removal* (Knoxville: University of Tennessee Press and the Tennessee Historical Commission, 1979), 64–68.

2. Bergeron, Ash, and Keith, *Tennesseans,* 29–33; Pauline Wilcox Burke, *Emily Donelson of Tennessee,* 2 vols. (Richmond, Va.: Garrett & Massee, 1941), 1:3–11; Finger, *Tennessee Frontiers,* 80, 118; Henderson, "Richard Henderson," 358–361; Richard Douglas Spence, "John Donelson and the Opening of the Old Southwest," *THQ* 50 (Fall 1991): 162–165.

3. Burke, *Emily Donelson,* 1:11–15; Spence, "John Donelson," 165–169; Anita S. Goodstein, "Black History on the Nashville Frontier, 1780–1810," *THQ* 38 (Winter 1979): 403–404.

4. Frances Clifton, "John Overton as Andrew Jacksons Friend," *THQ* 11 (March 1952): 23; Remini, *AJ,* 1:41–42; Ann Toplovich, "Marriage, Mayhem, and Presidential Politics: The Robards-Jackson Backcountry Scandal," *Ohio Valley History* 5 (Winter 2005): 6.

Remini suggests that Robards was guilty of adultery and perhaps even violent behavior toward Rachel.

5. Parton, *Life of AJ,* 1:133, 110–112.

6. Parton, *Life of AJ,* 1:150, 168–169; Legislative permission to sue for divorce, 20 December 1790, Divorce decree, 27 September 1793, in *PAJ,* 1:424, 427–428.

7. Remini, *AJ,* 1:57–69; Robert V. Remini, "Andrew Jackson's Adventures," *Southern Quarterly* 29 (Summer 1991) 35–39; Harriet Chappell Owsley, "The Marriage of Rachel Donelson," *THQ* 36 (Winter 1977): 479–492; Burstein, *Passions of Andrew Jackson,* 29–33, 241–248; Toplovich, "Marriage, Mayhem, and Presidential Politics," 9; Marriage license, 18 January 1794, in *PAJ,* 1:44.

8. See the secondary sources listed in the previous note for these arguments.

9. Norma Basch, *Framing American Divorce: From the Revolutionary Generation to the Victorians* (Berkeley: University of California Press, 1999), 21–27; Richard Godbeer, *Sexual Revolution in Early America* (Baltimore: Johns Hopkins University Press, 2002), 128–132; Wyatt-Brown, *Southern Honor,* 244–246, 283–284, 300–305; Toplovich, "Marriage, Mayhem, and Presidential Politics," 12–15.

Andrew Burstein has argued that there "probably" was an economic deal struck by which Robards agreed to "sell" Rachel to Jackson via the divorce, while David Hackett Fischer has speculated, without evidentiary proof, that the Jackson marriage was an instance of voluntary bridal abduction. Burstein's claims need to be read in conjunction with Richard Godbeer's argument that wife sales, examples of which exist in England and colonial South Carolina, "generally took place in a public venue" and included a written agreement and witnesses, as well as Norma Basch's skepticism that wife sales were ubiquitous in the early republic. See Burstein, *Passions of Andrew Jackson*, 247; David Hackett Fischer, *Albion's Seed: Four British Folkways in America* (Oxford: Oxford University Press, 1989), 669–671; Godbeer, *Sexual Revolution*, 131–132; Basch, *Framing American Divorce*, 38.

10. Carolyn Earle Billingsley, *Communities of Kinship: Antebellum Planters and the Settlement of the Cotton Frontier* (Athens: University of Georgia Press, 2004), 15.

11. Ely, "Legal Practice of Andrew Jackson," 421–429; Appointment as district attorney, 15 February 1791, in *PAJ*, 1:26; Anita Goodstein, *Nashville, 1780–1860: From Frontier to City* (Gainesville: University of Florida Press, 1989), 24–25; *Hampton v. Boyd and Foster*, [c. January 1788–13 April 1790] and *Gilmore v. Williams*, [15 July 1791], in Ely and Brown, *Legal Papers of Andrew Jackson*, 28–31, 32–33.

12. Ely, "Legal Practice of Andrew Jackson," 429–435; Assignment of deed from Howell Tatum to AJ, 17 February 1790, Assignment of warrant from Howell Tatum, assignee of Malica White, to AJ, 11 May 1791, Bond acknowledged for AJ, Robert Hays, and Howell Tatum, 7 May 1792, Deed from Nicholas Perkins Hardeman to AJ, 8 December 1795, Memorandum, 14 June 1806, Deed from John Boyd to AJ, 17 October 1807, in *PAJ*, 1:432, 433, 434, 440, 2:538, 549; Ely and Brown, *Legal Papers of Andrew Jackson*, 374–375; Natalie Rishay Inman, "Friendship and Advancement: A Community of Lawyers in Nashville, Tennessee, 1788–1805" (M.A. thesis, Vanderbilt University, 2005), 1–24.

13. Walter T. Durham, *Daniel Smith: Frontier Statesman* (Gallatin, Tenn.: Sumner County Library Board, 1976), 64–77, 87–92; Arnow, *Seedtime on the Cumberland*, 311–312, 327; Remini, *AJ*, 1:86–87; Kristofer Ray, "Land Speculation, Popular Democracy, and Political Transformation on the Tennessee Frontier, 1780–1800," *THQ* 61 (Fall 2002): 175; Daniel Byron Dovenbarger, "Land Registration in Early Middle Tennessee: Laws and Practices" (M.A. thesis, Vanderbilt University, 1981), 76, 95; Abernethy, *From Frontier to Plantation*, 19, 51–53.

14. Clifton, "John Overton," 23–24; Arnow, *Seedtime on the Cumberland*, 339. The numbers for Jackson's land speculation are based on the recorded land transactions in *PAJ*, vol. 1. Some of the information is incomplete, and undoubtedly, these are not all of the land transactions in which Jackson participated. These data support Robert Remini's estimation that "at the age of thirty he was speculating in tens (maybe hundreds) of thousands of acres of land" (*AJ*, 1:87).

15. James A. McLaughlin to Amos Kendall, 13 March 1843, in *CAJ*, 6:213–214; John Buchanan, *Jackson's Way: Andrew Jackson and the People of the Western Waters* (New York: Wiley, 2001), 113–114, 127–136; AJ to John McKee, 30 January 1793, 16 May 1794, in *PAJ*, 1:40–41, 48–49.

16. George Cochran to AJ, 21 October 1791, Cato West to AJ, 26 June 1801, John Hutchings to AJ, 25 December 1801, William C. C. Claiborne to AJ, 9 December 1801,

23 December 1801, 9 January 1802, 20 March 1802, Jonathan Kearsley to AJ, 28 February 1802, AJ to Nathan Davidson, 18 April 1803, Boggs & Davidson to AJ, 2 August 1803, 19 September 1803, and 7 October 1803, AJ to Boggs & Davidson, 2 September 1803, Seth Lewis to AJ, 8 October 1803, in *PAJ,* 1:29–33, 245–247, 266, 260–262, 265, 269–270, 284–286, 280–281, 329, 350, 364–365, 370–371, 357, 371–372; Robert V. Remini, "Andrew Jackson Takes an Oath of Allegiance to Spain," *THQ* 55 (Spring 1995): 2–15; John D. W. Guice, "Old Hickory and the Natchez Trace," *Journal of Mississippi History* 69 (Spring 2007): 167–169.

17. Laska, "'The Dam'st Situation Ever Man Was Placed In," 337–338, 341, 343–345; Remini, *AJ,* 1:88, 132–133; John Overton to AJ, 8 March 1795, Financial statement, 26 April 1796, AJ to Samuel Donelson, [c. June 1796], Agreements with Thomas Watson and John Hutchings, 16 February 1802, Agreement with Thomas Watson, 6 August 1803, Agreement with John Hutchings, 23 August 1803, AJ to John Hutchings, 23 September 1803, in *PAJ,* 1:54, 90, 92, 94, 278–279, 280, 351–352, 355–356, 366–367, 2:6; Richard Douglas Spence, "Samuel Donelson: Young Andrew Jackson's Best Friend," *THQ* 69 (Summer 2010): 110–112; H. Phillip Bacon, "Nashville Trade at the Beginning of the Nineteenth Century," *THQ* 15 (March 1956): 32–33; Parton, *Life of AJ,* 1:250–251.

18. John Craig Hammond, "Slavery, Settlement, and Empire: The Expansion and Growth of Slavery in the Interior of the North American Continent, 1770–1820," *JER* 32 (Summer 2012): 175–206; Ellen Eslinger, "The Shape of Slavery on the Kentucky Frontier," *Register of the Kentucky Historical Society* 92 (Winter 1994): 1–23; Anita S. Goodstein, "Black History on the Nashville Frontier," 401–405; William Lloyd Imes, "The Legal Status of Free Negroes and Slaves in Tennessee," *Journal of Negro History* 4 (July 1919): 255–272.

19. Warshauer, "Chivalric Slave Master," 204-206; List of taxable property, [c. 1792–1797], Mark Mitchell to AJ, 21 November 1795, Tax assessment, 1 October 1798, in *PAJ,* 1:34, 77, 210-211. The data on slaves in this and subsequent paragraphs in this chapter, as well as the remainder of the book, are derived from an analysis of the bills of sales included in *PAJ,* as well as references to transactions contained in Jackson's correspondence but undocumented elsewhere. Specific sources are cited when appropriate to shed light on individual slaves or events.

20. Settlement of John Donelson's estate, 28 January 1791, Promissory note, 26 February 1791, Bill of sale, 21 December 1791, Tax assessment, [c. 1792–1797], AJ to Robert Hays, 16 December 1796, Tax assessment, 1 October 1798, AJ to John Overton, 30 November 1799, Samuel Jackson to AJ, 9 June 1802 and 25 October 1802, Agreement with Mark Mitchell, 12 December 1803, in *PAJ,* 1:425–426, 433, 26–27, 434, 34, 103–104, 210–211, 224–225, 298, 316, 409, 454.

21. James Cole Mountflorence to AJ, 23 July 1790, William C. C. Claiborne to AJ, 9 December 1801, 23 December 1801, 9 January 1802, John Hutchings to AJ, 25 December 1801, in *PAJ,* 1: 23, 260–262, 265, 269–270, 266; Remini, "Jackson's Adventures on the Natchez Trace," 35; Edward Michael McCormack, *Slavery on the Tennessee Frontier* (Nashville: Tennessee American Revolution Commission, 1977), 18; Eslinger, "Shape of Slavery," 10–11; John Lauritz Larson, *The Market Revolution in America* (Cambridge: Cambridge University Press, 2010), 1–38; Adam Rothman, *Slave Country: American Expansion and the Origins of the Deep South* (Cambridge: Harvard University Press, 2005),

19–20; Steven Deyle, *Carry Me Back: The Domestic Slave Trade in American Life* (Oxford: Oxford University Press, 2005), 1–11, 35–38.

IV
"As Members of Civilized Society"

1. Finger, *Tennessee Frontiers,* 99–106, 125–127; Remini, *AJ,* 1:51–52.
2. Finger, *Tennessee Frontiers,* 99–106, 125–127; Remini, *AJ,* 1:51–52.
3. Appointment as attorney general, 15 February 1791, Commission as judge advocate, 10 September 1792, in *PAJ,* 1:26, 37–38; Trevor A. Smith, "Pioneers, Patriots, and Politicians: The Tennessee Militia System, 1772–1857" (Ph.D. diss., University of Tennessee, 2003), 33–40; Remini, *AJ,* 1:15–16, 53–54; Goodstein, *Nashville,* 11; Kristofer Ray, *Middle Tennessee, 1775–1825: Progress and Popular Democracy on the Southwestern Frontier* (Knoxville: University of Tennessee Press, 2007), 42–44.

4. Appointment to board, 8 October 1791, AJ to William Cocke, 24 June 1798, in *PAJ,* 1:29, 200; Goodstein, *Nashville,* 50–51; Booraem, *Young Hickory,* 175–178; Marshall DeLancey Haywood, *The Beginnings of Freemasonry in North Carolina and Tennessee* (Raleigh, N.C.: Weaver & Lynch, 1906), 24–25, 29–31; Burstein, *Passions of Andrew Jackson,* 39; Editorial note, *CAJ,* 1:59; W. W. Clayton, *History of Davidson County,* 364; Gordon S. Wood, *Empire of Liberty: A History of the Early Republic, 1789–1815* (Oxford: Oxford University Press, 2009), 50–52; Steven C. Bullock, "A Pure and Sublime System: The Appeal of Post-Revolutionary Freemasonry," *JER* 9 (Fall 1989): 361.

5. Jacob E. Cooke, ed., *The Federalist* (Middletown, Conn.: Wesleyan University Press), 64; Lance Banning, *The Jeffersonian Persuasion: Evolution of a Party Ideology* (Ithaca: Cornell University Press, 1978); Drew R. McCoy, *The Elusive Republic: Political Economy in Jeffersonian America* (Chapel Hill: University of North Carolina Press for the Institute of Early American History and Culture, 1980); James Oakes, "From Republicanism to Liberalism: Ideological Change and the Crisis of the Old South," *American Quarterly* 37 (Fall 1985): 551–571; Steven J. Ross, "The Transformation of Republican Ideology," *JER* 10 (Fall 1990): 323–330.

6. Andrew R. L. Cayton, "'When Shall We Cease to Have Judases?' The Blount Conspiracy and the Limits of the 'Extended Republic," in *Launching the "Extended Republic": The Federalist Era,* ed. Ronald Hoffman and Peter J. Albert (Charlottesville: United States Capitol Historical Society by the University Press of Virginia, 1996), 168–169; Remini, *AJ,* 1:72–79.

7. Remini, *AJ,* 1:83–84; Joseph Anderson to AJ, 4 August 1796, AJ to Nathaniel Macon, 4 October 1795, AJ to Robert Hays, 16 December 1796, AJ to John Sevier, 18 January 1797, AJ to John Donelson, 24 February 1797, in *PAJ,* 1:97–98, 74–75, 103–104, 116–118, 167–168.

8. Burstein, *Passions of Andrew Jackson,* 34–35; Finger, *Tennessee Frontiers,* 144; John Sevier to AJ, William Blount, and William Cocke, 12 December 1796, AJ to John Sevier, 18 January 1797 and 24 February 1797, AJ to Robert Hays, 17 February 1797, in PAJ, 1:102, 116–118, 126–128, 124; *Annals of Congress,* House, 4th Cong., 2d sess., 1737–1739, 1742–1746, 2154–2155.

9. Remini, *Legacy of Andrew Jackson,* 7–13; Stephen J. Barry, "Nathaniel Macon: The Prophet of Pure Republicanism, 1758–1837" (Ph.D. diss., SUNY Buffalo, 1996), vii,

24, 34, 44–48; "Henry Tazewell," in *BDUSC;* Norman K. Risjord, *The Old Republicans: Southern Conservatism in the Age of Jefferson* (New York: Columbia University Press, 1965), 14; Stanley Elkins and Eric McKitrick, *The Age of Federalism* (New York: Oxford University Press, 1993), 403–449; Gordon Wood, *Empire of Liberty,* 197–199; Nathaniel Macon to AJ, 22 December 1794, AJ to Nathaniel Macon, 4 October 1795, Henry Tazewell to AJ, 20 July 1798, in *PAJ,* 1:52–53, 74–75, 205–209.

10. AJ to Nathaniel Macon, 4 October 1795, AJ to Robert Hays, 6 December [17]96, 16 December 1796, 8 January 1797, AJ to John Sevier, 18 January 1797, 24 February 1797, AJ to John Donelson, 18 January 1798, AJ to John Overton, 22 January 1798, 23 February 1798, AJ to Willie Blount, [21 February 1798], in *PAJ,* 1:74–75, 101–102, 103–104, 111–113, 116–118, 126–128, 167–168, 168–171, 183–184, 182–183.

For historians' views on Jackson's political theory, see Albert Somit, "Andrew Jackson as Political Theorist," *THQ* 8 (June 1949): 99–126; Remini, *Legacy of Andrew Jackson,* 7–44; and Harry L. Watson, *Liberty and Power: The Politics of Jacksonian America,* 2d ed. (New York: Hill & Wang, 1990, 2006), 7–12, 48–49.

11. Remini, *AJ,* 1:100–102; AJ to John Sevier, 8 May 1797 and 10 May 1797, John Sevier to AJ, 8 May 1797 and 11 May 1797, in *PAJ,* 1:136–137, 141–142, 137–138, 142.

12. John McNairy to AJ, 4 May 1797 and 12 May 1797, AJ to John McNairy, 9 May 1797 and 12 May 1797, in *PAJ,* 1:133–135, 143, 138, 139–141, 144.

13. Cayton, "'When Shall We Cease to Have Judases?'" 160–162; Abernethy, *South in the New Nation,* 172–173; Frederick Jackson Turner, ed., "Documents on the Blount Conspiracy, 1793–1797," *AHR* 10 (April 1905): 574–606; *Annals of Congress,* 5th Cong., 1st sess., 947–952; Remini, *AJ,* 1:103–106.

14. Remini, *AJ,* 1:106–107; AJ to William Cocke, 9 November 1797, 24 June 1798 (2 letters), 25 June 1798, William Cocke to AJ, 18 April 1797 and 25 June 1798, in *PAJ,* 1:60–61, 152–153, 199, 200, 204, 130–131, 203–204.

15. Laska, "'The Dam'st Situation Ever Man Was Placed In,'" 341–342, 346; Agreement with David Allison, 14 May 1795, Account, May–August 1795, Meeker, Cochran & Company to AJ, 11 August 1795, John B. Evans & Company, 4 January 1796, John Overton to AJ, 18 December 1796, AJ to Robert Hays, 8 January 1797, Statement, [c. 15 July 1801], in *PAJ,* 1:56–58, 58–59, 64, 79, 104–105, 111–113, 251–252.

16. Laska, "'The Dam'st Situation Ever Man Was Placed In,'" 343–345; Remini, *AJ,* 1:109–114; AJ to John Overton, 3 February 1798, AJ to William Blount, [24 June 1798], William Blount to John Sevier, 6 July 1798, John Sevier to AJ, 29 August 1798, Interim appointment, 20 September 1798, Commission, 22 December 1798, in *PAJ,* 1:174–175, 198–199, 199, 209, 210, 215–216; Paul Finkelman, *Millard Fillmore* (New York: Times Books, 2011), 12.

V
"You Cannot Mistake Me, or My Meaning"

1. Parton, *Life of AJ,* 1:166–168, 227–229.

2. AJ to Robert Hays, 24 August 1801 and 9 September 1801, in *PAJ,* 1:252–253, 254–255.

3. Ray, *Middle Tennessee,* 50–51; Smith, "Pioneers, Patriots, and Politicians," 65; Remini, *AJ,* 1:119; Commission, 1 April 1802, in *PAJ,* 1:291–292.

4. Remini, *AJ*, 1:117–119; Russell S. Koonts, "'An Angel Has Fallen': The Glasgow Land Frauds and the Establishment of the North Carolina Supreme Court" (M.A. thesis, North Carolina State University, 1995), 12; Editorial note, *PAJ*, 1:37; Stockley Donelson to AJ, 2 March 1794 and 2 October 1800, Statement regarding land frauds, 6 December 1797, AJ to John Overton, 22 January 1798, AJ to Samuel Ashe, 10 February 1798, in *PAJ*, 1:45–46, 236–237, 157–158, 168–171, 179–180.

Koonts's suggestion that historians believe that "Jackson blamed [Stockley] Donelson for informing him that Rachel Donelson's divorce from her first husband had been granted by the Virginia legislature" is unsubstantiated ("'An Angel Has Fallen,'" 12).

5. Remini, *AJ*, 1:119–120; Ray, *Middle Tennessee*, 51; Ray, "Land Speculation," 172–173; Robert E. Corlew, *Tennessee: A Short History*, 2d ed. (Knoxville: University of Tennessee Press, 1981), 134; Carl S. Driver, *John Sevier: Pioneer of the Old Southwest* (Chapel Hill: University of North Carolina Press, 1932), 155; AJ to Benjamin J. Bradford (with enclosures), 19 July 1803, Archibald Roane to AJ, 22 July 1803, *Knoxville Gazette*, 25 July 1803, in *PAJ*, 1:337–346, 347–348, 347–348.

6. AJ to John Sevier, [2 October 1803], 3 October 1803, 9 October 1803, 10 October 1803, 11 October 1803, John Sevier to AJ, [2 October 1803], 3 October 1803, 9 October 1803, [10 October 1803] (2 letters), AJ to the Public, [10 October 1803], AJ to David Campbell (with enclosure), 13 October 1803, AJ to Andrew White, 13 October 1803, in *PAJ*, 1:367–368, 368–369, 375–377, 379–380, 384–385, 368, 377, 379, 380–381, 378–379, 385, 388, 388–389; Parton, *Life of AJ*, 1:163–164; James W. Ely Jr., "Andrew Jackson as Tennessee State Court Judge, 1798–1804," *THQ* 40 (Summer 1981): 154.

7. Parton, *Life of AJ*, 1:234–235; Affidavit of Andrew White, 12 October 1803, Affidavit of Thomas J. Vandyke, 16 October 1803, Affidavit of Andrew Greer, 23 October 1803, Affidavit of Howell Tatum, 8 November 1803, "Knox County Citizen" to *Knoxville Gazette* printer, 10 November 1803, Affidavit of Robert Searcy, 22 November 1803, "Veritas" to *Tennessee Gazette* printer, [14 December 1803], Affidavits of Jesse Wharton, William Hall, and John K. Wynne, 21 December 1803, in *PAJ*, 1:503–505, 505, 489–490, 491–492, 492–496, 506, 496–502, 503.

8. Remini, *AJ*, 1:123–124; Driver, *John Sevier*, 187; Smith, "Pioneers, Patriots, and Politicians," 45; Samuel C. Williams, "Tennessee's First Military Expedition," *THM* 8 (October 1924): 171–190.

9. Kupfer, "Presidential Patron," 247–248; Memorandum, 11 May 1805, in *PAJ*, 2:57–58.

10. Kupfer, "Presidential Patron," 247–248; Editorial note, *PAJ*, 2:77–78; Remini, *AJ*, 1:136.

11. Thomas Swann to AJ, 3 January 1806, 12 January 1806, Affidavit of Joseph Erwin, [4 January 1806], AJ to Thomas Swann, 7 January 1806, in *PAJ*, 2:78, 82–83, 79, 79–81; *Impartial Review*, 1 February 1806, 15 February 1806, Affidavit of John Hutchings, 5 February 1806, Affidavit of John Coffee, n.d., in Parton, *Life of AJ*, 1:273–274, 276–285, 277–278, 278–281; Kenneth S. Greenberg, "The Nose, the Lie, and the Duel," *AHR* 95 (February 1990): 63; Wyatt-Brown, *Southern Honor*, 355–356; Kenneth S. Greenberg, *Honor & Slavery: Lies, Duels, Noses, Masks, Dressing as a Woman, Gifts, Strangers, Humanitarianism, Death, Slave Rebellions, the Proslavery Argument, Baseball, Hunting, and Gambling in the Old South* (Princeton: Princeton University Press, 1996), 58; Yarn, "Lessons from the Code Duello," 91; Steven M. Stowe, "The 'Touchiness' of the Gentle-

man Planter: The Sense of Esteem and Continuity in the Antebellum South," *Psychohistory Review* 8 (Winter 1979): 12; Williamjames Hull Hoffer, *The Caning of Charles Sumner: Honor, Idealism, and the Origins of the Civil War* (Baltimore: Johns Hopkins University Press, 2010), 13-15.

12. AJ to Thomas Swann, 7 January 1806, in *PAJ*, 2:79-81; Parton, *Life of AJ*, 1:268-269; Editorial note, *PAJ*, 2:78.

13. Charles Dickinson to AJ, 10 January 1806, John Brahan to John Overton, 8 March 1806, John Hutchings to AJ, 24 April 1806, in *PAJ*, 2:81-82, 90-91, 95-96; Parton, *Life of AJ*, 1:286-289.

14. Charles Dickinson to Thomas Eastin, 21 May 1806, AJ to Thomas Eastin, 10 February 1806, Arrangements for duel, 23-24 May 1806, in *PAJ*, 2:97-98, 84-89, 99-100; Remini, *AJ*, 1:140; Parton, *Life of AJ*, 1:298.

15. Remini, *AJ*, 1:140; AJ to Thomas Eastin, [c. June 1806], in *PAJ*, 2:106-107; Parton, *Life of AJ*, 1:298-299.

16. Parton, *Life of AJ*, 1:300, 303; Remini, *AJ*, 1:142-143; AJ to Thomas Eastin, 6 June 1806, [c. June 1806], William Harrison to AJ, 30 June 1806, AJ to Thomas G. Watkins, [c. 15 June 1806], Randal McGavock to AJ, 23 August 1806, Statements regarding duel, 20 June 1806, 25 June 1806, in *PAJ*, 2:101-102, 105-106, 106-107, 102-103, 107-108, 104-105; Burstein, *Passions of Andrew Jackson*, 57; Editorial note, *PAJ*, 2:104.

17. Samuel D. Jackson to Robert Hays, 9 March 1807, Stockley Donelson Hays to AJ, 20 April 1807, Minutes in *State v. AJ*, [9] November 1807, in *PAJ*, 2:172, 160-162, 173-174; Editorial note, *PAJ*, 2:172-173.

18. Wyatt-Brown, *Southern Honor*, 352-361; Dickson D. Bruce Jr., *Violence and Culture in the Antebellum South* (Austin: University of Texas Press, 1979), 29.

19. Joanne B. Freeman, "Dueling as Politics: Reinterpreting the Burr-Hamilton Duel," *William and Mary Quarterly* 53 (April 1996): 289-318; Wood, *Empire of Liberty*, 382-384; Remini, *AJ*, 1:146; Nancy Isenberg, *Fallen Founder: The Life of Aaron Burr* (New York: Viking, 2007), 272-365.

20. Ely, "Andrew Jackson as Tennessee State Court Judge," 152-156; AJ to RJ, 6 April 1804, in *PAJ*, 2:13; Remini, *AJ*, 1:127-129, 145; Parton, *Life of AJ*, 1:309; Editorial note, *PAJ*, 2:110.

21. William R. Shepherd, "Wilkinson and the Beginnings of the Spanish Conspiracy," *AHR* 9 (April 1904): 490-506; Isaac Joslin Cox, "General Wilkinson and His Later Intrigues with the Spaniards," *AHR* 19 (July 1914): 794-812; Marshall Smelser, *The Democratic Republic, 1801-1815* (New York: Harper & Row, 1968), 112-115; Remini, *AJ*, 1:147.

22. Remini, *AJ*, 1:147-148; AJ to [William Preston Anderson], 25 September 1806, AJ to James Winchester, 4 October 1806, Aaron Burr to AJ, 24 March 1806, Order to Brigadier Generals of the Second Division, [4 October 1806], Account, 6 October-3 December 1806, AJ to Thomas Jefferson, [c. 5 November 1806], Account, 9 December 1806, in *PAJ*, 2:110, 110-111, 91-93, 111-113, 113-114, 114-115, 122.

23. *PAJ*, 2:115-116; Remini, *AJ*, 1:149-151; AJ to William C. C. Claiborne, 12 November 1806, AJ to Daniel Smith, 12 November 1806, AJ to George Washington Campbell, 15 January 1807, in *PAJ*, 2:116-117, 117-120, 147-150.

24. Henry Dearborn to AJ, 19 December 1806, AJ to [William Preston Anderson], [3 January 1807], AJ to Brigadier Generals of the Second Division, 5 January 1807 and [10

January 1807], in *PAJ*, 2:125–126, 134–135, 137, 143–145; Remini, *AJ*, 1:154; Smelser, *Democratic Republic*, 115–117.

25. AJ to Henry Dearborn, 17 March 1807, AJ to [William Preston Anderson], 16 June 1807, Grand jury testimony, 25 June [1807], AJ to Thomas Monteagle Bayly, 27 June 1807, AJ to Daniel Smith, 28 November 1807, in *PAJ*, 2:155–158, 167–168, 168–169, 169–170, 174–177; Editorial note, *PAJ*, 2:164–166; Parton, *Life of AJ*, 1:333–335.

26. Wyatt-Brown, "Andrew Jackson's Honor," 8–13; Edward L. Ayers, *Vengeance and Justice: Crime and Punishment in the 19th-Century South* (New York: Oxford University Press, 1984), 9–33; Kenneth Greenberg, *Masters and Statesmen: The Political Culture of American Slavery* (Baltimore: Johns Hopkins University Press, 1985), 24, 27, 31–36; Bruce, *Violence and Culture in the Antebellum South*, 3–43, 67–88; Randolph Roth, *American Homicide* (Cambridge, Mass.: Belknap Press of Harvard University Press, 2009), 212–215.

VI
"Ten Dollars Extra, for Every Hundred Lashes"

1. Deed, 10 March 1796, Deed, 6 July 1804, Deed, 23 August 1804, AJ to Edward Ward, 10 June 1805, in *PAJ*, 1:84, 2:523, 525, 59–61; Editorial note, *PAJ*, 2:27; Rita Hiltenbrand Hall, "Colonel Edward Ward: The Life and Death of a Tennessee Senator," *West Tennessee Historical Society Papers* 64 (2011): 53; Remini, *AJ*, 1:131–132; Mary C. Dorris, *Preservation of the Hermitage, 1889–1915* (Nashville: Smith & Lamar, 1915), 8; Stanley Horn, *The Hermitage: Home of Old Hickory* (Richmond: Garrett & Massie, 1938), 17.

2. AJ to John Coffee, 3 May 1804, 13 May 1804, 21 June 1804, AJ to Thomas & Clifford, 24 July 1804, Jackson & Hutchings to Boggs & Davidson, 31 July 1804, in *PAJ*, 2:21–22, 22–23, 24–25, 27–29, 30–32; Remini, *AJ*, 1:132–133.

3. Remini, *AJ*, 1:132–133. Another fifteen slaves were purchased at a sheriff's sale and then conveyed to Jane Hays (Bill of sale, 7 March 1807, Davidson County, Tennessee, Wills and Inventories, 3:179, TSLA).

4. Bill of sale, 29 January 1806, JLC; Editorial note, *PAJ*, 2:56–57, 224; James W. Camp to William Purnell, 18 November 1809, William Purnell to AJ, 19 November 1809, AJ to Edward Ward, 26 October 1810, William Purnell to AJ, 14 December 1810, in *PAJ*, 2:224–225, 225, 253–254, 257–258.

5. Advertisement, [26 September 1804], Thomas Terry Davis to AJ, 20 February 1805, in *PAJ*, 2:40–41, 51; Robert P. Hay, "'And Ten Dollars Extra, for Every Hundred Lashes Any Person Will Give Him, to the Amount of Three Hundred': A Note on Andrew Jackson's Runaway Slave Ad of 1804 and on the Historian's Use of Evidence," *THQ* 36 (Winter 1977): 468–478.
Tom Gid was the name that the slave used upon running away. Two slaves named Tom appear in Jackson's records prior to this advertisement. One was Tom, formerly called Peter, who was twenty-seven years old when purchased in 1791. The other Tom was a fourteen-year-old purchased in 1794 (Bill of sale, 7 July 1791, 14 September 1794, in *PAJ*, 1:433–434, 437).

6. *Farmer's Library* (Louisville, Ky.), 12 September 1805, c. November 1805, Bullitt Family Papers–Oxmoor Collection, FHS; Memorandum, [1804–1806], Daniel Sayre to AJ, 30 November 1805, JLC; Estate inventory, appraisal, and division, 28 January–15

April 1791, Jesse Roach to AJ, 3 December 1805, John Williamson to AJ, 12 December 1805, AJ to John Hutchings, 7 April 1806, John Hutchings to AJ, 24 April 1806, in *PAJ*, 1:425–427, 2:73–74, 75–76, 93–95, 95–96.

I assume that this George was the one bequeathed as property in John Donelson's will and bitten by a snake (Benjamin Rawlings to AJ, [c. 1798], in *PAJ*, 1:160).

7. Eugene Genovese, *Roll, Jordan, Roll: The World the Slaves Made* (New York: Pantheon, 1974), 65, 648–657; John Hope Franklin and Loren Schweninger, *Runaway Slaves: Rebels on the Plantation* (New York: Oxford University Press, 1999), 209–233, 240–248, 251–252; Remini, *AJ*, 1:133; Tom Costa, "What Can We Learn from a Digital Database of Runaway Slave Advertisements?" *International Social Science Review* 76 (2001): 36–43; H. M. Henry, "The Slave Laws of Tennessee," *THM* 2 (1916): 180–181; Elizabeth Fortson Arroyo, "Poor Whites, Slaves, and Free Blacks in Tennessee, 1796–1861," *THQ* 55 (Spring 1996): 59–60; Michael P. Johnson, "Planters and Patriarchy: Charleston, 1800–1860," *JSH* 46 (February 1980): 45, 55.

8. Editorial note, *PAJ*, 2:261–262; Memorandum, 18 May 1811, AJ to Willie Blount, 25 January 1812, in *PAJ*, 2:262–263, 277–280.

9. Bette B. Tilly, "The Jackson-Dinsmoor Feud: A Paradox in a Minor Key," *Journal of Mississippi History* 39 (May 1977): 117–123; Ralph S. Cotterill, *The Southern Indians: The Story of the Civilized Tribes before Removal* (Norman: University of Oklahoma Press, 1954), 142, 170–171; Proclamation, April 1811, in Parton, *Life of AJ*, 1:350, 353.

10. AJ to Willie Blount, 25 January 1812, AJ to Robert Weakley, 5 August 1828, in *PAJ*, 2:277–280, 6:488–490; James A. McLaughlin to Amos Kendall, [30 January 1843], in *CAJ*, 6:186–187.

11. AJ to Willie Blount, 25 January 1812, in *PAJ*, 2:277–280.

12. AJ to Thomas Eastin, [c. June 1806], in *PAJ*, 2:106–107; Robert H. Gudmestad, *A Troublesome Commerce: The Transformation of the Interstate Slave Trade* (Baton Rouge: Louisiana State University Press, 2003), 166–167; Walter Johnson, *Soul by Soul: Life Inside the Antebellum Slave Market* (Cambridge: Harvard University Press, 1999), 24–25; Michael Tadman, "The Reputation of the Slave Trader in Southern History and the Social Memory of South," *American Nineteenth Century History* 8 (September 2007): 247–271.

13. The dependents discussed in this chapter are listed in Remini, *AJ*, 1:160–161.

14. Isabella Butler Vinson to AJ, 3 August 1803, 10 September 1810, Wade Hampton to AJ, 3 June 1810, in *PAJ*, 1:350–351, 2:251–252, 248–249.

15. Remini, *AJ*, 1:110–111; Donald R. Hickey, "Andrew Jackson and the Army Haircut: Individual Rights v. Military Discipline," *THQ* 35 (Winter 1976): 365–370; AJ, Joseph Anderson, and William C. C. Claiborne to John Adams, 5 March 1798, James McHenry to Joseph Anderson, AJ, and William C. C. Claiborne, 7 March 1798, John Sevier to Joseph Anderson, AJ, and William C. C. Claiborne, 5 April 1798, AJ to Thomas Jefferson, 7 August 1803, [3 August 1804], 23 September 1805, AJ to Thomas Butler, 25 August 1804, AJ, James Winchester, Edward Douglass, and William Hall to Thomas Jefferson, [c. December 1804], AJ to Henry Dearborn, 17 March 1807, in *PAJ*, 1:185–186, 187–188, 191, 353–354, 2:33–36, 36–37, 72–73, 45–46, 155–158; Petition to Congress, 30 January 1805, in Hickey, "AJ and the Army Haircut," 370–375; Editorial note, *PAJ*, 2:64–65.

16. AJ to Thomas Jefferson, [3 August 1804] and 23 September 1805, AJ to Thomas Butler, 25 August 1804, in *PAJ*, 2:33–36, 72–73, 36–37.

17. Thomas Butler to AJ, 4 March 1805, in *PAJ*, 2:51–53; Editorial note, *PAJ*, 2:53, 269.

18. Editorial note, *PAJ*, 2:6; Account, 28 May–9 July 1804, in *PAJ*, 2:24; Durham, *Daniel Smith*, 127, 185, 198; Spence, "Samuel Donelson," 113–114; Burke, *Emily Donelson*, 1:23–26.

19. Burke, *Emily Donelson*, 1:28; Robert B. Satterfield, *Andrew Jackson Donelson: Jackson's Confidant and Political Heir* (Bowling Green, Ky.: Hickory Tales, 2000), 2–3; Pauline Wilcox Burke, *Emily Donelson of Tennessee*, ed. Jonathan M. Atkins (Knoxville: University of Tennessee Press, 2001), 75–76; Durham, *Daniel Smith*, 89, 210, 235–236; AJ to James Sanders, [c. 13 January 1807], James Sanders to AJ, 13 January 1807, in *PAJ*, 2:145–146, 146–147.

20. James Sanders to AJ, 26 March 1809, in *PAJ*, 2:215; Mark R. Cheatham, *Old Hickory's Nephew: The Political and Private Struggles of Andrew Jackson Donelson* (Baton Rouge: Louisiana State University Press, 2007), 11.

21. Cheatham, *Old Hickory's Nephew*, 13–24, 27–29, 40–43; Editorial note, *PAJ*, 3:163; AJ to AJD, 29 April 1817, JLC.

22. Editorial note, *PAJ*, 2:218; Linda Bennett Galloway, "Andrew Jackson, Jr. [Part 1]," *THQ* 9 (September 1950): 195–199; Parton, *Life of AJ*, 1:339; Marquis James, *Andrew Jackson: The Border Captain* (Indianapolis: Bobbs-Merrill, 1933), 138; James C. Curtis, *Andrew Jackson and the Search for Vindication* (Boston: HarperCollins, 1976), 28; Remini, *AJ*, 1:161; E. Wayne Carp, "Introduction: A Historical Overview of American Adoption," in Carp, *Adoption in America: Historical Perspectives* (Ann Arbor: University of Michigan Press, 2002), 3–4.

23. AJ to RJ, 17 December 1811, 8 January 1813, 21 March 1813, 11 October 1813, 18 October 1813, 4 November 1813, in *PAJ*, 2:273, 353–355, 393–394, 436–437, 437–438, 444.

24. Lorri Glover, *All Our Relations: Blood Ties and Emotional Bonds among the Early South Carolina Gentry* (Baltimore: Johns Hopkins University Press, 2000), 32, 42.

VII
"We *Will Destroy Our Enemies*"

1. Address to Citizens of Nashville, [16 January 1809], in *PAJ*, 2:210–211.

2. Donald R. Hickey, *The War of 1812: A Short History* (Urbana: University of Illinois Press, 1995), 5–17; Frank L. Owsley Jr., and Gene A. Smith, *Filibusters and Expansionists: Jeffersonian Manifest Destiny, 1800–1821* (Tuscaloosa: University of Alabama Press, 1997), 83–84; Kenneth W. Porter, "Negroes and the Seminole War, 1817–1818," *Journal of Negro History* 36 (July 1951): 254.

3. Editorial notes, in *PAJ*, 2:194–195, 202, 207–208; AJ to the officers of the Second Division, 20 April 1808, AJ to Thomas Jefferson, 20 April 1808, 14 May 1808, Sampson Williams to AJ, 25 April 1808, AJ to Brigadier Generals of the Second Division, 19 December 1808, John Sevier to AJ, 12 January 1809, Resolutions of Second Division Officers, [16 January 1809], Address to Citizens of Nashville, [16 January 1809], in *PAJ*, 2:190–191, 191–194, 196–197, 195, 203–204, 205–207, 208–209, 210–211.

4. AJ to George W. Campbell, 10 April 1812, AJ to John Coffee, 25 March 1812, 26 March 1812, John Childress to AJ, 25 March 1812, Thomas Johnson to AJ, 27 May 1812,

AJ to Willie Blount, 4 June 1812, 5 June 1812, AJ to George Colbert, 5 June 1812, in *PAJ,* 2:295–296, 294–295, 296, 298–299, 300–301, 301–302, 302–303; Thomas Johnson to AJ, 8 June 1812, JSR; Tom Kanon, "The Kidnapping of Martha Crawley and Settler-Indian Relations prior to the War of 1812," *THQ* 64 (Spring 2005): 3–6; Deposition of Martha Crawley, 11 August 1812, in *CAJ,* 1:225–226; R. David Edmunds, *Tecumseh and the Quest for Indian Leadership* (New York: HarperCollins, 1984), 20, 124–125.

5. Kanon, "Kidnapping of Martha Crawley," 7–12; "The Massacre at the Mouth of the Duck River," [c. 7 July 1812], AJ to Willie Blount, 8 July 1812, in *PAJ,* 2:309–311; AJ to Willie Blount, 10 July 1812, in *CAJ,* 1:230–232; Hickey, *War of 1812,* 10, 16.

6. John Buchanan, *Jackson's Way: Andrew Jackson and the People of the Western Waters* (New York: Wiley & Sons, 2001), 6, 162, 302; Sean Michael O'Brien, *In Bitterness and in Tears: Andrew Jackson's Destruction of the Creeks and Seminoles* (Westport, Conn.: Praeger, 2003), 64; Orders to Second Division, 9 July 1812, 8 September 1812, Orders to Tennessee Volunteers, 31 July 1812, [14 November 1812], in *PAJ,* 2:313–315, 320–322, 317–318, 340–341.

7. William Eustis to Willie Blount, 21 October 1812, in *CAJ,* 1:240–241; AJ to Willie Blount, 8 September [1812], 11 November 1812, Willie Blount to AJ, 11 November 1812, in *PAJ,* 2:319–320, 336–338, 338–340; Remini, *AJ,* 1:170–172.

8. Remini, *AJ,* 1:173–180; James Wilkinson to AJ, 6 January 1813, 22 January 1813, 25 January 1813, 22 February 1813, 1 March 1813, 16 March 1813, John Armstrong to AJ, 6 February 1813, AJ to James Wilkinson, 16 February 1813, 20 February 1813, 8 March 1813, AJ to John Armstrong, 15 March 1813, in *PAJ,* 2:353, 358–359, 359–360, 371–372, 374–375, 389, 361, 365, 366–367, 379–381, 383–385.

9. AJ to Tennessee Volunteers, [16 March 1813], AJ to RJ, 15 March 1813, in *PAJ,* 2:390–392, 387; Remini, *AJ,* 1:178–180; Parton, *Life of AJ,* 1:381–382.

10. Editorial note, *PAJ,* 2:408–409, 410; Elbert B. Smith, *Magnificent Missourian: The Life of Thomas Hart Benton* (Philadelphia: J. B. Lippincott, 1958), 41–44; AJ to Tennessee Volunteers, [16 March 1813], AJ to Thomas H. Benton, 4 August 1813, Affidavit, 5 August 1813, AJ to John M. Armstrong (with Armstrong's responses), 9 August 1813, in *PAJ,* 2:390–392, 418–422, 422–423, 423–425; William Carroll to AJD, 4 October 1824, in *CAJ,* 1:322–312; Marquis James, *The Life of Andrew Jackson* (Indianapolis: Bobbs-Merrill, 1938), 530 n. 29.

11. Smith, *Magnificent Missourian,* 41–43; Burstein, *Passions of Andrew Jackson,* 94; Remini, *AJ,* 1:182; AJ to WBL, 4 March 1813 and [15 March 1813], AJ to John Armstrong, 10 May 1813, Memorandum, 13 July 1813, AJ to Felix Grundy, 15 July 1813, Andrew Hynes to AJ, 16 July 1813, AJ to Thomas H. Benton, 19 July 1813, 4 August 1813, Thomas H. Benton to AJ, 15 June 1813, 9 July 1813, 25 July 1813, in *PAJ,* 2:377–378, 388–389, 405, 411–413, 409–410, 410–411, 413, 418–422, 406–407, 409, 413–416.

12. Thomas H. Benton to the Public, 10 September 1813, in *PAJ,* 2:425–427; Deposition, 5 September 1813, in *CAJ,* 1:317; Parton, *Life of AJ,* 1:392–395.

13. Steven M. Stowe, *Intimacy and Power in the Old South: Ritual in the Lives of the Planters* (Baltimore: Johns Hopkins University Press, 1987), 15–30; Stowe, "'Touchiness' of the Gentleman Planter," 10–11; Bruce, *Violence and Culture,* 79–80.

14. Ross Hassig, "Internal Conflict in the Creek War of 1813–1814," *Ethnohistory* 21 (Summer 1974): 251–271; J.C.A. Stagg, *Mr. Madison's War: Politics, Diplomacy, and Warfare in the Early American Republic, 1783–1830* (Princeton: Princeton University Press,

1983), 348–355; Frank L. Owsley Jr., "The Fort Mims Massacre," *Alabama Review* 24 (July 1971): 196, 201; Daniel H. Usner Jr., "American Indians on the Cotton Frontier: Changing Economic Relations with Citizens and Slaves in the Mississippi Territory," *JAH* 72 (September 1985): 315; Porter, "Negroes and the Seminole War, 1817–1818," 258; John K. Mahon, "British Strategy and Southern Indians: War of 1812," *Florida Historical Quarterly* 44 (April 1966): 286.

15. Stagg, *Mr. Madison's War*, 355; Remini, *AJ*, 1:193; AJ to Willie Blount, 4 November 1813, 15 November 1813, in *CAJ*, 1:341, 348–350; AJ to RJ, 4 November 1813, AJ to Thomas Pinckney, 3 December 1813, in *PAJ*, 2:444, 465–467; Herbert J. Doherty Jr., *Richard Keith Call: Southern Unionist* (Gainesville: University of Florida Press, 1961), 6.

16. Frank L. Owsley Jr., *Struggle for the Gulf Borderlands: The Creek War and the Battle of New Orleans, 1812–1815* (Gainesville: University Press of Florida, 1981), 68–71; Remini, *AJ*, 1:202–205; AJ to Willie Blount, 29 December 1813, in *CAJ*, 1:416–420.

17. Remini, *AJ*, 1:206–207; Robert V. Remini, *Andrew Jackson and His Indian Wars* (New York: Viking Penguin, 2001), 73–79; Owsley, *Struggle for the Gulf Borderlands*, 79; AJ to Thomas Pinckney, 28 March 1814, AJ to RJ, 1 April 1814, John Coffee to AJ, 1 April 1814, in *PAJ*, 3:52–54, 54–55, 55–57; AJ to Willie Blount, 31 March 1814, in *CAJ*, 1:489–492.

18. Mahon, "British Strategy and Southern Indians," 287–290; Owsley, *Struggle for the Borderlands*, 7, 86–94; Remini, *Jackson and His Indian Wars*, 131–132, 86–93; AJ to the Cherokee and Creek Indians, [5 August 1814], Big Warrior to Benjamin Hawkins, [6 August 1814], AJ to Big Warrior, [7 August 1814], AJ to John Coffee, 10 August 1814, in *PAJ*, 3:103–104, 106–109, 109–111, 112–114; Reid and Eaton, *Life of AJ*, 183–193; Treaty of Fort Jackson, 9 August 1814, *U.S. Serial Set*, House, no. 4015, 56th Cong., 1st sess., 678–679; *American State Papers*, Indian Affairs, Senate, 13th Cong., 3d sess., 1:837–838; Editorial note, *PAJ*, 4:16–17; David S. Heidler and Jeanne T. Heidler, *Old Hickory's War: Andrew Jackson and the Quest for Empire* (Mechanicsburg, Pa.: Stackpole, 1996), 25–26.

19. Owsley and Smith, *Filibusters and Expansionists*, 95–97; AJ to John Armstrong, 27 June 1814, 24 July 1814, 25 August 1814, 10 October 1814, John Armstrong to AJ, 18 July 1814, THB to AJ, 11 September 1814, James Monroe to AJ, 21 October 1814, AJ to James Monroe, 26 October 1814, AJ to Mateo González Manrique, 6 November 1814, Mateo González Manrique to AJ, 7 November 1814, AJ to Willie Blount, 14 November 1814, in *PAJ*, 3:83–84, 92–93, 122–124, 155–156, 90, 132–133, 170–171, 173–175, 179–180, 181, 184–186; AJ to James Monroe, 14 November 1814, in *CAJ*, 2:96–99; Owsley, *Struggle for the Gulf Borderlands*, 118–119; Nathaniel Millett, "Defending Freedom in the Atlantic Borderlands of the Revolutionary Southeast," *Early American Studies* 5 (Fall 2007): 377–379; Nathaniel Millett, "Britain's 1814 Occupation of Pensacola and America's Response: An Episode of the War of 1812 in the Southeastern Borderlands," *Florida Historical Quarterly* 83 (Fall 2005): 233–243.

20. Robert V. Remini, *The Battle of New Orleans: Andrew Jackson and America's First Military Victory* (New York: Viking, 1999), 5–6, 37–39, 47–49, 79; William C. C. Claiborne to AJ, 12 August 1814, 17 October 1814, 4 November 1814, AJ to William C. C. Claiborne, 21 September 1814, 10 December 1814, AJ to Jacques Philippe Villeré, 19 December 1814, in *PAJ*, 3:115–117, 164–165, 176–179, 144–145, 201–203, 210–211; William C. C. Claiborne to AJ, 21 August 1814, Pierre Foucher et al. to AJ, 18 September 1814, AJ to Free Colored Inhabitants of Louisiana, 21 September 1814, AJ to William

C. C. Claiborne, 31 October 1814, in *CAJ,* 1:437–438, 2:51–54, 58–59, 87–88; William Buford to AJ, 19 September 1814, William C. C. Claiborne to AJ, 28 October 1814, 21 December 1814, James H. Gordon to AJ, 4 January 1815, JLC; Donald E. Everett, "Emigres and Militiamen: Free Persons of Color in New Orleans, 1803–1815," *Journal of Negro History* 38 (October 1953): 377–402; Millett, "Britain's 1814 Occupation of Pensacola," 229–243; Arsène Lacarrière Latour, *Historical Memoir of the War in West Florida and Louisiana in 1814–15, with an Atlas, Expanded Edition,* ed. Gene Allen Smith (Gainesville: Historic New Orleans Collection and University Press of Florida, 1999), 82–83.

21. Remini, *Battle of New Orleans,* 37–38, 135, 167; Owsley, *Struggle for the Gulf Borderlands,* 146, 157, 162; William C. C. Claiborne to AJ, 12 August 1814, AJ to James Monroe, 2 December 1814, 9 January 1815, AJ to James Winchester, 10 January 1815, AJ to David Holmes, 18 January 1815, in *PAJ,* 3:115–117, 199–200, 239–241, 242, 249–250; William C. C. Claiborne to AJ, 21 August 1814, AJ to James Monroe, 13 January 1815, in *CAJ,* 1:437–438, 2:51–54, 142–144.

22. Matthew S. Warshauer, *Andrew Jackson and the Politics of Martial Law: Nationalism, Civil Liberties, and Partisanship* (Knoxville: University of Tennessee Press, 2006), 19–45; AJ to John Wood, 14 March 1814, AJ to Philip Pipkin, 12 September 1814, William Lawrence to AJ, 15–16 September 1814, AJ to Willie Blount, 7 October 1814, Robert Butler to John Williams, 17 October 1814, Proclamation, 13 March 1815, AJ to the U.S. District Court, Louisiana, [27 March 1815], in *PAJ,* 3:48–49, 135–136, 137–139, 153–154, 166–168; *PAJ,* 3:47–48, 133–135, 310, 322–336.

23. William C. C. Claiborne to AJ, 28 January 1815, AJ to William C. C. Claiborne, 28 January 1815, JSR; William C. C. Claiborne to AJ, 31 January 1815, 3 February 1815, AJ to William C. C. Claiborne, 5 February 1815, AJ to Hughes Lavergne, 20 February 1815, John Lambert to AJ, 27 February 1815, 18 March 1815, AJ to John Lambert, 13 March 1815, AJ to Unknown, [c. 31 March 1815], Memorandum, [c. 27 April 1815], AJ to James Monroe, 28 April 1815, in *PAJ,* 3:263, 267–268, 270–271, 283–284, 290–291, 316–317, 309–310, 337–338, 349–351, 351; AJ to William C. C. Claiborne, 3 February 1815, William C. C. Claiborne to AJ, 6 February 1815, John Lambert to AJ, 8 February 1815, AJ to Alexander Cochrane, 20 February 1815, Maunsel White to AJ, 20 February 1815, Manley Powers to AJ, 30 March 1815, Edward Nicholls to Benjamin Hawkins, 2 April 1815, Benjamin Hawkins to AJ, 26 May 1815, in *CAJ,* 2:156–157, 159–161, 161–162, 175–176, 176–177, 200, 208–209n, 208–209; AJ to John Lambert, 24 March 1815, AJ to Alexander James Dallas, 16 May 1815, JLC.

24. Remini, *AJ,* 1:249, 316; Deppisch, "Andrew Jackson and American Medical Practice," 135; Hickey, *War of 1812,* 101.

VIII
"An End to All Indian Wars"

1. Editorial note, *CAJ,* 2:204n; *ASP,* Military Affairs, 14th Cong., 1st sess., 1:635; William S. Belko, "Epilogue to the War of 1812: The Monroe Administration, American Anglophobia, and the First Seminole War," in *America's Hundred Years' War: U.S. Expansion to the Gulf Coast and the Fate of the Seminole, 1763–1858,* ed. William S. Belko (Gainesville: University Press of Florida, 2011), 54–102.

2. Alexander J. Dallas to AJ, 22 May 1815, AJ to Edmund P. Gaines, 8 April 1816, in *CAJ,* 2:206, 238–239; AJ to Edmund P. Gaines, 24 June 1815, AJ to [Mauricio de Zuñiga], 23 April 1816, AJ to WHC, 24 April 1816, in *PAJ,* 3:365–366, 4:22–23, 25–26; Owsley and Smith, *Filibusters and Expansionists,* 103–117; James W. Covington, "The Negro Fort," *Gulf Coast Historical Review* 5 (Spring 1990): 78–91; Jane Landers, *Black Society in Spanish Florida* (Urbana: University of Illinois Press, 1999), 230; Millett, "Defining Freedom in the Atlantic Borderlands," 381–382, 386–393; Porter, "Negroes and the Seminole War, 1817–1818," 259–261.

3. Edmund Pendleton Gaines to AJ, 14 May 1816, in *PAJ,* 4:30–32; Receipts, 31 May 1816, D[uncan] L[amont] Clinch to AJ, 28 October 1816, Thomas P. Carnes to AJ, 8 November 1816, Thomas C. Clark to AJ, 8 November 1816, 25 February 1817, Alexander McCoy to AJ, 8 November 1816, Big Warrior to AJ, 24 January 1817, George Graham to AJ, 17 July 1817, José Masot to AJ, 16 February 1818 [translated copy], JLC; AJ to Duncan Lamont Clinch, 6 September 1816, JSR.

4. Alexander J. Dallas to AJ, 22 May 1815, in *CAJ,* 2:206; Owsley and Smith, *Filibusters and Expansionists,* 99–102; Remini, *Jackson and His Indian Wars,* 98–99; Gordon T. Chappell, "The Life and Activities of John Coffee," *THQ* 1 (June 1942): 131–133; Chappell, "John Coffee: Surveyor and Land Agent," *Alabama Review* 14 (July 1961): 188–195.

5. Remini, *Jackson and His Indian Wars,* 99–117, 182; AJ to Creek Chiefs, 4 September 1815, AJ to George Colbert, 13 February 1816, AJ to John Coffee, 19 September 1816, AJ to WHC, 20 September 1816, AJ to Eastern Cherokees, [c. 6 July 1817], AJ to Choctaw Indians, 3 October 1820, 17 October 1820, in *PAJ,* 3:382–383, 4:13–14, 63–64, 66–67, 124–125, 391–392, 393–397; Francis Paul Prucha, *The Great Father: The United States Government and the American Indians,* abr. ed. (Lincoln: University of Nebraska Press, 1986), 64–66; Bernard Sheehan, *Seeds of Extinction: Jefferson Philanthropy and the American Indian* (Chapel Hill: University of North Carolina Press, 1973), 244–249; George Foote to William Foote Sr., 2 October 1816, Philip Foote to William Foote Sr., 20 November 1816, Foote Family Papers, FHS.

6. Editorial note, *PAJ,* 3:381, 4:24–25, 32, 35–36; AJ to WHC, 4 September 1815, 17 December 1815, 24 April 1816, 4 June 1816, 16 June 1816, WHC to AJ, 20 May 1816, 1 July 1816, AJ to John Coffee, 26 December 1816, AJ to James Monroe, 9 July 1816, 15 November 1818, AJ to Richard Butler, 6 December 1817, in *PAJ,* 3:381–382, 395–397, 4:25–26, 36–39, 45–47, 77–78, 32–34, 48–50, 50–52, 246–248, 158–159; Heidler and Heidler, *Old Hickory's War,* 62; Samuel Watson, "Soldier, Expansionist, Politician: Eleazer Wheelock Ripley and the Dance of Ambition in the Early Republic," in *Nexus of Empire: Negotiating Loyalty and Identity in the Revolutionary Borderlands, 1760s–1820s,* ed. Gene Allen Smith and Sylvia L. Hilton (Gainesville: University Press of Florida, 2009), 325.

7. Kenneth Porter, *The Black Seminoles: History of a Freedom-Seeking People* (Gainesville: University Press of Florida, 1996), 18–19; Remini, *Jackson and His Indian Wars,* 144; Frank L. Owsley Jr., "Ambrister and Arbuthnot: Adventurers or Martyrs for British Honor?" *JER* 5 (Fall 1985): 291–300; Owsley and Smith, *Filibusters and Expansionists,* 95, 114–115, 145.

8. Edmund P. Gaines to Neamathla, [August 1817], Neamathla to Edmund P. Gaines, [August 1817], in *ASP,* Military Affairs, 15th Cong., 2d sess., 1:723; Edmund P.

Gaines to AJ, 1 October 1817, 21 November 1817, 2 December 1817, in *PAJ*, 4:140–142, 150–151, 153–155; Owsley, *Struggle for the Gulf Borderlands*, 150–151.

9. John C. Calhoun to AJ, 26 December 1817, AJ to James Monroe, 6 January 1818, in *PAJ*, 4:163–164, 166–168; Daniel Feller, "The Seminole Controversy Revisited: A New Look at Andrew Jackson's 1818 Florida Campaign," *Florida Historical Quarterly* 88 (Winter 2010): 309–325; Heidler and Heidler, *Old Hickory's War*, 117–118; David S. Heidler and Jeanne T. Heidler, "Mr. Rhea's Missing Letter and the First Seminole War," in Belko, *America's Hundred Years' War*, 103–127; Owsley, *Struggle for the Gulf Borderlands*, 151–153.

10. AJ to Francisco Caso y Luengo, 6 April 1818, Francisco Caso y Luengo to AJ, 7 April 1818, AJ to John C. Calhoun, 8 April 1818, AJ to RJ, 10 April 1818, in *PAJ*, 4:186–188, 188–189, 189–191, 191–192; Remini, *Jackson and His Indian Wars*, 147; Owsley and Smith, *Filibusters and Expansionists*, 153–155; Porter, "Negroes and the Seminole War, 1817–1818," 273–276; AJ to RJ, 8 April 1818, in *CAJ*, 2:367–358.

11. Alexander Arbuthnot to John Arbuthnot, 2 April 1818, General orders, 29 April 1818, in *ASP*, Military Affairs, 15th Cong., 2d sess., 1:722, 734; AJ to John C. Calhoun, 20 April 1818, 5 May 1818, in *CAJ*, 4:193–196, 197–201; Owsley, "Arbuthnot and Ambrister," 289–308.

12. AJ to William Davenport, 4 May 1818, José Masot to AJ, 2[3] May 1818, 24 May 1818, AJ to [Luis Piernas], 24 May 1818, AJ to José Masot, 25 May 1818, Proclamation, 29 May 1818, in *CAJ*, 2:364–365, 371, 372–373, 373–374, 374–375; AJ to John C. Calhoun, 5 May 1818, José Masot to AJ, 18 May 1818, AJ to James Monroe, 2 June 1818, in *PAJ*, 4:197–201, 203–205, 213–216; Owsley, *Struggle for the Gulf Borderlands*, 159–160; Remini, *Jackson and His Indian Wars*, 160–161.

13. Feller, "The Seminole Controversy Revisited," 309–325; Heidler and Heidler, *Old Hickory's War*, 177–186; John Niven, *John C. Calhoun and the Price of Union: A Biography* (Baton Rouge: Louisiana State University Press, 1988), 68–70; Lynn Hudson Parsons, *John Quincy Adams* (Madison, Wisc.: Madison House, 1998), 140–143; James Monroe to AJ, 19 July 1818, AJ to James Monroe, 19 August 1818, in *PAJ*, 4:224–228, 236–239.

14. Deborah A. Rosen, "Wartime Prisoners and the Rule of Law," *JER* 28 (Winter 2008): 559–595; Heidler and Heidler, *Old Hickory's War*, 204–221; David S. Heidler and Jeanne T. Heidler, *Henry Clay: The Essential American* (New York: Random House, 2010), 138–143; Robert V. Remini, *Henry Clay: Statesman for the Union* (New York: Norton, 1991), 162–168; Speech by Henry Clay, 20 January 1819, in *Annals of Congress*, 15th Cong., 2d sess., 654–655; Noble E. Cunningham Jr., *The Presidency of James Monroe* (Lawrence: University Press of Kansas, 1995), 60.

15. JHE to AJ, 14 December 1818, AJ to Francis Preston, 2 February 1819, in *CAJ*, 2:403, 409–410; AJ to WBL, 30 January 1819, AJ to AJD, 31 January 1819, AJ to RJ, 6 [February] 1819, John McCrea to AJ, 15 April 1819, AJ to William Williams, 25 September 1819, in *PAJ*, 4:268–270, 270–271, 271–272, 283–285, 325–329; *Annals of Congress*, 15th Cong., 2d sess., 1135–1138; Heidler and Heidler, *Old Hickory's War*, 217–218, 223–228.

16. Matthew Crocker, "The Missouri Compromise, the Monroe Doctrine, and the Southern Strategy," *Journal of the West* 43 (Summer 2004): 45–52; Glover Moore, *The*

Missouri Controversy, 1819–1821 (Lexington: University of Kentucky Press, 1966), 1–36; Robert P. Forbes, *The Missouri Compromise and Its Aftermath* (Chapel Hill: University of North Carolina Press, 2006), 1–140; Matthew Mason, *Slavery and Politics in the Early American Republic* (Chapel Hill: University of North Carolina Press, 2006), 177–212.

17. AJ to John Coffee, 23 February 1820, JHE to AJ, 11 March 1820, AJ to AJD, [16 April 1820], James Gadsden to AJ, 8 December 1820, AJ to James Monroe, 1 January 1821, in PAJ, 4:357–358, 359–363, 366–367, 403–404, 5:3–5; JHE to AJ, 27 January 1821, JLC.

18. Forbes, *Missouri Compromise*, 69–120; Michael S. Fitzgerald, "Rejecting Calhoun's Expansible Army Plan: The Army Reduction Act of 1821," *War in History* 3 (April 1996): 161–185; Harry Ammon, *James Monroe: The Quest for National Identity* (Newtown, Conn.: American Political Biography Press, 1971), 502; James Monroe to AJ, 24 January 1821, AJ to James Monroe, 11 February 1821, in *PAJ*, 5:9, 10–11; John C. Calhoun to AJ, 25 January 1821, in Clyde N. Wilson et al., eds., *The Papers of John C. Calhoun*, 28 vols. (Columbia: University of South Carolina Press, 1959–2003), 5:572–573; AJD to [unknown], n.d., qtd. in Herbert J. Doherty Jr., "The Governorship of Andrew Jackson," *Florida Historical Quarterly* 33 (July 1954): 9.

19. Commission, 10 March 1821, AJ to JQA, 1 May 1821, in *ASP*, Foreign Relations, 17th Cong., 1st sess., 4:751, 756–757; Owsley and Smith, *Filibusters and Expansionists*, 118–140; Editorial note, *PAJ*, 5:29; AJ to John Coffee, 1 May 1821, José Maria Callava to AJ, 10 June 1821, 19 June 1821, 22 June 1821, AJ to José Maria Callava, 12 June 1821, 12 July 1821, 15 July 1821, in *PAJ*, 5:34–35, 53–54, 59–60, 60–62, 54–57, 68–70, 72–73; AJD to REWE, 6 May 1821, in Andrew J. Donelson Papers, James D. Hoskins Library, University of Tennessee, Knoxville; Herbert J. Doherty Jr., "Andrew Jackson vs. the Spanish Governor," *Florida Historical Quarterly* 34 (October 1955): 142–151; Doherty, "Governorship of Andrew Jackson," 3–8, 17.

20. Doherty, "Governorship of AJ," 3–24; AJ to John C. Calhoun, 2 September 1821, 17 September 1821, *ASP*, Indian Affairs, House, 17th Cong., 2d sess., 2:414; AJ to James Monroe, 14 November 1821, John C. Calhoun to AJ, 16 November 1821, in *CAJ*, 3:131, 132; Editorial note, *PAJ*, 5:xxviii; RJ to Elizabeth Kingsley, 23 July 1821, RJ to John Donelson, 25 August 1821, in *PAJ*, 5:79–82, 99–100.

21. AJ to James Monroe, 5 October 1821, 29 January 1822, James Monroe to AJ, 31 December 1821, in *PAJ*, 5:110–112, 140–141, 126; AJ to James Monroe, 14 November 1821, in *CAJ*, 3:131; Editorial note, *PAJ*, 5:119, 126; Lynn Hudson Parsons, *The Birth of Modern Politics: Andrew Jackson, John Quincy Adams, and the Election of 1828* (Oxford: Oxford University Press, 2009), 54.

IX
"I Feel an Unusual Sympathy for Him"

1. Craig Thompson Friend and Lorri Glover, "Rethinking Southern Masculinity: An Introduction," in *Southern Manhood: Perspectives on Masculinity in the Old South*, ed. Craig Thompson Friend and Lorri Glover (Athens: University of Georgia Press, 2004), ix–xi.

2. AJ to RJ, 8 January 1813, 14 December 1813, 31 July 1814, RJ to AJ, 8 February

[1813], 5 April 1813, 10 February 1814, in *PAJ,* 2:353–355, 486–487, 400, 3:28–29, 101–102, 361–362.

3. AJ to RJ, 8 January 1813, 31 July 1814, 18 September 1816, AJ to AJD, 17 May 1819, 6 May 1820, in *PAJ,* 2:353–355, 3:361–362, 4:62–63, 299–300, 367–368.

4. AJ to RJ, 4 November 1813, 19 December 1813, 29 December 1813, 21 February 1814, 18 September 1816, RJ to AJ, 7 April 1814, AJJr to AJ, 8 April [1814], in *PAJ,* 2:444, 494–495, 515–516, 3:34–35, 59–60, 60, 4:62–63; AJ to RJ, 4 March 1814, JSR; AJ to RJ, 12 March 1814, RJ to AJ, 21 March 1814, in *CAJ,* 1:478, 482–483.

Michael Paul Rogin notes that "it was common for men involved in Indian relations to adopt Indian children" and gives two additional examples: John H. Eaton and Cherokee agent Thomas McKenney (Rogin, *Fathers and Children: Andrew Jackson and the Subjugation of the America Indian* [1975; repr., New Brunswick, N.J.: Transaction Publishers, 1991], 350 n. 74; Margaret Eaton, *The Autobiography of Peggy Eaton* [New York: Scribner, 1932], 165–169).

5. AJ to RJ, 29 December 1813, in *PAJ,* 2:515–516; Remini, *Jackson and His Indian Wars,* 64–65; *ASP,* Indian Affairs, Senate, 13th Cong., 3d sess., 1:837–838.

For scholarly discussion of Indian slavery in general and Jackson's participation specifically, see Drew, "Master Andrew Jackson"; Christina Snyder, *Slavery in Indian Country: The Changing Face of Captivity in Early America* (Cambridge: Harvard University Press, 2010); Dawn Peterson, "Unusual Sympathies: Settler Imperialism, Slavery, and the Politics of Adoption in the Early U.S. Republic" (Ph.D. diss., New York University, 2011).

6. Mark R. Cheathem, "'The High Minded Honourable Man': Honor, Kinship, and Conflict in the Life of Andrew Jackson Donelson," *JER* 27 (Summer 2007): 265–92; Wyatt-Brown, "Andrew Jackson's Honor," 14–16, 24, 33; Ratner, *Jackson and His Tennessee Lieutenants,* 1–34; Burstein, *Passions of Andrew Jackson,* xiii–xx.

7. Burstein, *Passions of Andrew Jackson,* 48, 218, 235; Wyatt-Brown, "Andrew Jackson's Honor," 33.

8. Ratner, *Jackson and His Tennessee Lieutenants,* 35–48; Clifton, "John Overton," 26–27; Mary T. Orr, "John Overton and Traveler's Rest," *THQ* 15 (September 1956): 222; Fletch Coke, "Profiles of John Overton: Judge, Friend, Family Man, and Master of Travellers' Rest," *THQ* 37 (Winter 1978): 393–409; Chappell, "Coffee: Surveyor and Land Agent," 180–195; Gordon T. Chappell, "John Coffee: Land Speculator and Planter," *Alabama Review* 22 (January 1969): 24–43; Chappell, "Life and Activities of John Coffee," 131–143.

9. Ratner, *Jackson and His Tennessee Lieutenants,* 49–55; AJ to GWC, 13 April 1804, AJ to HLW, 6 January 1814, WBL to AJ, 26 January 1814, JHE to AJ, 4 February 1817, AJ to John Coffee, 3 April 1819, AJ to James Jackson, 25 August 1819, in *PAJ,* 2:16, 3:9–12, 15–17, 4:87–89, 279–281, 316–318; HLW to AJ, 14 January 1814, in *CAJ,* 1:440–442; J. Roderick Heller III, *Democracy's Lawyer: Felix Grundy of the Old Southwest* (Baton Rouge: Louisiana State University Press, 2010), 85–86, 134–135, 140–143, 156–159; Editorial note, *PAJ,* 1:107, 2:260, 3:17.

10. Editorial note, *PAJ,* 2:254–255, 281; Smith, *Magnificent Missourian,* 33; Helen Reid Roberts, "Memoir of John Reid," in Reid and Eaton, *Life of Andrew Jackson,* app. Y; Reid and Eaton, *Life of Andrew Jackson,* v–ix; Burstein, *Passions of Andrew Jackson,* 108–114, 122–123; John McDonough, "Introduction," in *Index to the Andrew Jackson Papers*

(Washington, D.C.: Library of Congress, 1967), v–ix; John F. Marszalek, "John Henry Eaton," in *TEHC*, 275; "John Henry Eaton," in *BDTGA*, 98–99.

11. Editorial note, *PAJ*, 2:522; Ratner, *Jackson and His Tennessee Lieutenants*, 66–68, 99–102; Remini, *AJ*, 1:170–172; James L. Haley, *Sam Houston* (Norman: University of Oklahoma Press, 2002), 12–17; Louis R. Harlan, "Public Career of William Berkeley Lewis [Part 1]," *THQ* 7 (March 1948): 6–9; William Terrell Lewis, *Genealogy of the Lewis Family in America, from the Middle of the Seventeenth Century Down to the Present Time* (Louisville: Courier Journal, 1893), 62–117; AJ to John Hutchings, 7 April 1806, Agreement, [June 1809], in *PAJ*, 2:93–95, 217–218.

12. The kinship networks provided here were compiled from the biographical and genealogical data contained in *PAJ* and Lewis, *Genealogy of the Lewis Family*, 62–117. For the other family connections, see Burstein, *Passions of Andrew Jackson*, 108; Heller, *Democracy's Lawyer*, 84–85, 119; Ratner, *Jackson and His Tennessee Lieutenants*, 66; Edythe Rucker Whitley, *Marriages of Sumner County, Tennessee, 1787–1838* (Baltimore, Md.: Genealogical Publishing, 1981), 25; Louis Littleton Veazey, "George Washington Campbell," in *TEHC*, 119.

13. Remini, *AJ*, 1:379–380; Horn, *Hermitage*, 19–21.

14. AJ to AJJr, [c. 11 December 1823], 31 January 1827, 27 November 1827, in *PAJ*, 5:326–327, 6:272–273, 402–403; AJ to AJJr, 5 January 1824, 5 April 1824, in Samuel G. Heiskell, *Andrew Jackson and Early Tennessee History*, 2d ed., 2 vols. (Nashville: Ambrose, 1920–1921), 2:394, 400.

15. RJ to Elizabeth Kingsley, 23 July 1821, AJ to James Jackson, 2 August 1821, AJ to Horace Holley, 27 February 1822, AJ to James Gadsden, 2 May 1822, AJ to AJD, 6 August 1822, AJ to RJ, 20 February 1824, 16 March 1824, AJ to AJJr, 31 January 1827, in *PAJ*, 5:79–82, 91–93, 154, 179–182, 212–215, 359–360, 375–376, 6:272–273; AJ to AJJr, 25 January 1824, 5 April 1824, in Heiskell, *Andrew Jackson*, 2:400; AJ to RJ, 7 April 1824, in *CAJ*, 3:244–245; Galloway, "Andrew Jackson, Jr. [Part 1]," 209–210; Editorial note, *PAJ*, 5:472, 519, 568; Marquis James, *Andrew Jackson: Portrait of a President* (Indianapolis: Bobbs-Merrill, 1937), 139.

16. John H. DeWitt Jr., "Andrew Jackson and His Ward, Andrew Jackson Hutchings: A History Hitherto Unpublished," *THM* 1 (January 1931): 83–87; AJ to Horace Holley, 27 February 1822, AJ to James Gadsden, 2 May 1822, AJ to AJD, 6 August 1822, AJ to RJ, 20 February 1824, AJ to WBL, 21 January 1825, AJ to John Coffee, 8 April 1828, in *PAJ*, 5:154, 179–182, 212–215, 359–360, 6:17, 443–444; Editorial note, *PAJ*, 5:472, 515, 519, 559, 568, 573.

17. AJ to James Gadsden, 2 May 1822, AJ to RJ, 7 December 1823, in *PAJ*, 5:179–182, 322–323; Lyncoya to AJ, 29 December 1823, in Remini, *AJ*, 2:4; Parton, *Life of AJ*, 1:440; Remini, *AJ*, 2:144; *Raleigh Star and North Carolina Gazette*, 17 July 1828; *Portsmouth New-Hampshire Gazette*, 22 July 1828.

Remini notes the strong possibility that the Lyncoya letter may not be authentic, but the *PAJ* editors express no such reservations (Remini, *AJ*, 2:395–396 n. 12; Editorial note, *PAJ*, 5:552).

18. Anthony Wayne Butler to AJ, 21 December 1818, 10 March 1819, 6 May 1819, JLC; AJD to AJ, 5 May 1819, AJ to AJD, 17 May 1819, 23 July 1819, 31 January 1820, AJ to AWB, 2 June 1823, 10 November 1823, AJ to EGWB, 12 December 1824, 10 Novem-

ber 1825, in *PAJ,* 4:296–298, 299–300, 303–305, 354–355, 5:279–281, 317–319, 454–455, 6:120–121.

19. AJ to AJD, 17 May 1819, AJ to AJD, 31 March 1821, 26 April 1822, 6 August 1822, 11 October 1822, 23 December 1822, 21 January 1824, 26 February 1824, AJ to John C. Calhoun, 21 December 1820, AJ to Anthony Wayne Butler, 2 June 1823, in *PAJ,* 4:299–300, 409–411, 5:24–25, 176–177, 212–215, 220–221, 229–231, 279–281, 345–346, 366–368; John C. Calhoun to AJ, 19 May 1821, in *PJCC,* 6:130–131; AJ to AJD, 1 April 1822, 12 April 1822, 5 March 1823, DLC; AJ to AJD, 22 April 1822, 16 December 1822, [c. 30 December 1822], 8 January 1823, 21 January 1823, 22 February 1823, DSD to AJ, 20 November 1822, JSR; Sylvanus Thayer to AJ, 4 August 1823, DSD to AJ, 27 September 1823, 22 June 1824, JLC.

Daniel Donelson later served as a brigadier general in the Confederate army, losing his life near Knoxville in 1863 (Cheathem, *Old Hickory's Nephew,* 323).

20. AJ to Joseph G. Swift, 12 January 1817, AJD to AJ, 5 May 1819, AJ to Isabella Butler Vinson, 9 May 1817, EGWB to AJ, 5 June 1820, 14 July 1826, 11 January 1827, 27 April 1827, AJ to EGWB, 8 January 1822, 25 July 1825, 10 November 1825, in *PAJ,* 4:83–84, 114–115, 296–298, 360–370, 5:132–134, 6:94–95, 120–121, 184–185, 259–261, 312–314; EGWB to AJ, 17 December 1821, [September 1826], 4 September 1827, [February 1828], JLC; AJ to EGWB, 22 December 1826, JSR; Editorial note, *PAJ,* 6:261, 413.

21. Cheathem, *Old Hickory's Nephew,* 27–34, 37; AJ to AJD, 21 March 1822, 20 May 1822, in *PAJ,* 5:163–164, 188–189; AJ to AJD, 12 April 1822, 2 May 1822, DLC.

22. Cheathem, *Old Hickory's Nephew,* 40–43.

23. Michael P. Johnson, "Planters and Patriarchy: Charleston, 1800–1860," *Journal of Southern History* 46 (February 1980): 45–72; James Oakes, *The Ruling Race: A History of American Slaveholders* (New York: Random House, 1982), 201–204; Lorri Glover, *Southern Sons: Becoming Men in the New Nation* (Baltimore: Johns Hopkins University Press, 2007), 1–5, 89–91, 40–50, 107–111, 132–146; Wyatt-Brown, *Southern Honor,* 93–95; Wyatt-Brown, "Andrew Jackson's Honor," 18; Lorri Glover, "'Let Us Manufacture Men': Educating Elite Boys in the Early National South," in Friend and Glover, *Southern Manhood,* 22–48.

24. Wyatt-Brown, "Andrew Jackson's Honor," 14–16, 18, 27; Wyatt-Brown, *Southern Honor,* 59–61.

X
"A Great Field Is Now Open"

1. Genovese, *Roll, Jordan, Roll,* 10–12; J. Carlyle Sitterson, "The William J. Minor Plantations: A Study in Ante-Bellum Absentee Ownership," *JSH* 9 (February 1943): 59–74; J. Carlyle Sitterson, "Lewis Thompson, A Carolinian and His Louisiana Plantation, 1848–1888: A Study in Absentee Ownership," in *Essays in Southern History,* ed. Fletcher M. Green (Chapel Hill: University of North Carolina Press, 1949), 16–27.

2. AJ to RJ, 22 February 1813, 1 March 1813, 15 March 1813, 11 October 1813, 18 October 1813, 14 December 1813, 29 December 1813, 28 January 1814, 17 October 1814, 17 November 1814, 21 November 1814, 13 March 1816, 18 September 1816, 29

May 1817, 11 [June] 1817, 26 March 1818, 10 April 1818, 2 June 1818, 6 [February] 1819, 30 September 1820, RJ to AJ, 7 April 1814, in *PAJ*, 2:369–370, 372–373, 387, 436–437, 437–438, 486–487, 515–516, 3:17–22, 59–60, 162–163, 190–191, 194–195, 4:14, 62–63, 117, 117–118, 183–186, 191–192, 212–213, 271–272, 390–391; RJ to AJ, 12 April 1814, in *CAJ*, 1:499; James Douglas Anderson, *Making the American Thoroughbred; Especially in Tennessee, 1800–1845* (Norwood, Mass.: Plimpton Press, 1916), 48.

3. Editorial note, *PAJ*, 2:22; James Jackson to AJ, 27 November 1814, 13 January 1815, Robert Hays to AJ, 20 December 1814, Robert Butler to AJ, 2 November 1815, Richard Ivy Easter to AJ, 10 May 1821, in *PAJ*, 3:197–199, 244–246, 212–214, 390, 5:39–40; James Jackson to AJ, 16 December 1814, in *CAJ*, 6:444–445; Robert Butler to AJ, 12 March 1816, JLC.

4. List of AJ's taxable property, 1 January 1812, in *CAJ*, 1:212; Bill of sale, 7 September 1814 (2), 7 September 1814, 22 November 1816 (2), 14 December 1816, Edward Livingston to AJ, 2 February 1816, Gabriel William Perpall to AJ, 16 June 1818, Account, 18 January 1820, Bill of sale, 18 February 1820, JLC; AJ to Mr. Peal, 30 January 1819, Gilder Lehrman Collection (GLC06800), New-York Historical Society; James Jackson Hanna to AJ, 30 January 1820, in *PAJ*, 4:353–354.

One slave, Polydore, was a part of Jackson's household in 1818 but was not purchased until 1822. The value of the slaves was calculated using the inflation calculator at www .westegg.com/inflation/, accessed 22 November 2010. Because he was part of the transaction involving land, Jame was excluded from the calculation. Robert Forbes lists the average value of slaves in the United States in the 1820 census as four hundred dollars in year 2000 dollars (*Missouri Compromise,* 293). Jackson owned forty-four slaves at the Hermitage in 1820 (*Fourth Census of the United States: 1820* [Washington, D.C.: GPO, 1821]).

5. AJ to Mary Caffery, 8 February 1812, Robert Butler to AJ, 2 November 1815, James Jackson Hanna to AJ, 30 January 1820, James Jackson to AJ, 28 May 1821, in *PAJ*, 2:281–282, 3:390, 4:353–354, 5:48–51; Bill, 8 May 1812, AJ to Robert Sprigg, 4 October 1812, Robert Sprigg to AJ, 3 November 1812, Robert Butler to AJ, 12 March 1816, Bill of sale, 18 February 1820, Account, [18 February] 1821, Notice, [18 February] 1821, JLC; Advertisement for runaway slave, 12 September 1815, Bill of sale, 18 January 1820, JSR; *Richmond Enquirer,* 17 October 1820; James Jackson Hanna to AJ, 1 March 1821, in *CAJ*, 3:41–42; Notes on Ned (b. c. 1784) and Ned (b. c. 1798), Slave genealogy database, LHA.

6. Robert Hays to AJ, 20 December 1814, Robert Butler to AJ, 2 November 1815, AJ to James C. Bronaugh, 3 July 1821, in *PAJ*, 3:212–214, 390, 5:66–67; AJ to AJD, 3 July 1821, DLC; Sharla M. Fett, *Working Cures: Healing, Health, and Power on Southern Slave Plantations* (Chapel Hill: University of North Carolina Press, 2002), 37.

7. AJ to RJ, 28 January 1814, 17 November 1814, James Houston to AJ, 24 September 1819, in *PAJ*, 3:17–22, 190–191, 4:325; James Houston to AJ, 17 November 1819, *CAJ,* 2:440.

8. Lacy K. Ford Jr., *Deliver Us from Evil: The Slavery Question in the Old South* (Oxford: Oxford University Press, 2009), 162–165, 143–148, 173–174, 199–200; Johnson, "Planters and Patriarchy," 55; James Oakes, *The Ruling Race: A History of American Slaveholders* (New York: Vintage, 1983), xi–xii; Peter Kolchin, *American Slavery, 1619–1877* (New York: Hill & Wang, 1993), 111–112; Ayers, *Vengeance and Justice,* 133.

9. Editorial note, *PAJ,* 2:62–63, 296–297; Remini, *AJ,* 1:129–131; "Andrew Erwin," in Robert M. McBride and Dan M. Robison, eds., *Biographical Directory of the Tennessee General Assembly.* 6 vols. (Nashville: Tennessee State Library and Archives and Tennessee Historical Commission, 1975–1989), 1:233; "Joseph Anderson," *BDUSC;* AJ to John Strother, 1 May 1812, in *PAJ,* 2:297.

10. AJ to James Jackson, 19 September 1814, James Jackson to AJ, 10 October 1814, 27 November 1814, 13 January 1815, in *PAJ,* 3:141–142, 157–159, 197–199, 244–246.

11. Editorial note, *PAJ,* 4:89, 176–177; Daniel Parker to AJ, 10 February 1817, AJ to Francis Smith, 29 March 1817, AJ to RJ, 11 [June 1817], Arthur P. Hayne to AJ, 5 August 1817, AJ to John Coffee, 26 December 1816, 28 September 1817, 1 March 1821, 11 April 1821, 15 August 1823, James Jackson to AJ, 12 February 1818, 1 March 1821, 24 July 1822, James Gadsden to AJ, 28 September 1818, AJ to Isaac Shelby, 24 November 1818, John McCrea to AJ, 15 April 1819, AJ to James Gadsden, 1 August 1819, in *PAJ,* 4:89–90, 105–106, 117–118, 130–132, 77–78, 138–139, 177–179, 241–242, 250–251, 283–285, 307–312, 5:16–17, 204–205, 14–16, 27–29, 289–290.

12. Arda Walker, "Andrew Jackson: Planter," *ETHSP* 15 (1943): 19–34; AJ to RJ, 8 January 1813, 22 February 1813, 15 March 1813, 21 March 1813, 14 December 1813, 17 October 1814, 29 May 1817, James Jackson to AJ, 10 October 1814, Robert Butler to AJ, 2 November 1815, AJ to Robert Butler, 31 December 1815, AJ to William McIntosh, 8 July 1818, in *PAJ,* 2:353–355, 387, 393–394, 486–487, 3:162–163, 157–159, 390, 397–398, 4:117, 220–222; Lewis Cecil Gray, *History of Agriculture in the Southern United States to 1860* (Gloucester, Mass.: Peter Smith, 1958), 2:821–822; AJ to John Donelson, 3 September 1821, in *CAJ,* 3:116–117.

13. Jane Turner Censer, *North Carolina Planters and Their Children, 1800–1860* (Baton Rouge: Louisiana State University Press, 1984), 15; Gray, *History of Agriculture,* 2:854; Greenberg, *Honor & Slavery,* 138–139; Clement Eaton, *The Growth of Southern Civilization, 1790–1860* (New York: Harper & Row, 1961), 193; Anderson, *Making the American Thoroughbred,* 124–125, 238–242, 245; AJ to RJ, 29 December 1813, James Jackson to AJ, 27 November 1814, in *PAJ,* 2:515–516, 3:197–199; James, *Border Captain,* 289–290; [Louis Wallace, ed.], *The Horse and Its Heritage in Tennessee* (Nashville: Tennessee Department of Agriculture, 1945), 17–18; Editorial note, *PAJ,* 2:22; Tara Mitchell Mielnik, "Early Horseracing Tracks," in *TEHC,* 436–437; Wyatt-Brown, *Southern Honor,* 339–346; Marc R. Matrana, *Lost Plantations of the South* (Jackson: University Press of Mississippi, 2009), 118–119.

14. AJ to RJ, 11 [June] 1817, AJ to John Coffee, 28 September 1817, 4 January 1819, 26 July 1821, AJ to James Monroe, 15 November 1818, AJ to AJD, 31 January 1819, AJ to James Gadsden, 1 August 1819, John Coffee to AJ, 11 May 1821, James Jackson to AJ, 28 May 1821, AJ to James Jackson, 2 August 1821, Agreement, 20 September 1821, AJ to RKC, 27 November 1822, in *PAJ,* 4:117–118, 138–139, 266–267, 246–248, 270–271, 307–312, 5:41–43, 48–51, 82–84, 91–93, 507, 225–226; AJ to Eli Hammond, 21 November 1817, JSR; James Jackson Hanna to AJ, 1 March 1821, AJ to John Coffee, 26 August 1821, in *CAJ,* 3:41–42, 116.

15. Editorial note, *PAJ,* 4:267, 320–321; Harlan, "Public Career of William B. Lewis, [Pt. 1]," 9–12; AJ to Isaac Shelby, 7 July 1818, John McCrea to AJ, 15 April 1819, AJ to

William Williams, 25 September 1819, AJ to John Brown, 8 October 1819, AJ to JHE, 29 November 1819, Affidavit, [12 January 1820], AJ to John Coffee, 1 May 1821, in *PAJ*, 4:219–220, 283–285, 325–329, 339–342, 351, 5:34–35; Deposition, 20 August 1819, AJ to John Donelson, 3 July 1820, in *CAJ*, 2:443–444, 3:87–88.

16. George Dangerfield, *The Era of Good Feelings* (New York: Harcourt, Brace, 1952), 175–196; Murray N. Rothbard, *The Panic of 1819: Reactions and Policies* (New York: Columbia University Press, 1962), 28–29, 47–52, 56–58, 85–91; Larson, *Market Revolution*, 39–45; AJ to AJD, 24 February 1817, 23 July 1819, 17 September 1819, in *PAJ*, 4:91–92, 303–305, 322–323.

17. Editorial note, *PAJ*, 4:375–376; Thomas P. Abernethy, "The Early Development of Commerce and Banking in Tennessee," *MVHR* 14 (December 1927): 311–320; Charles G. Sellers Jr., "Banking and Politics in Jackson's Tennessee, 1817–1827," *MVHR* 41 (June 1954): 61–81; WBL to AJ, 15 July 1820, AJ to WBL, 16 July 1820, in *PAJ*, 4:376–377, 377–381.

18. Editorial note, *PAJ*, 4:281, 286–287, 329–330, 5:38, 122, 168, 224, 307, 433; AJ to John Clark, 20 April 1819, 18 [September] 1819, 6 January 1820, AJ to WBL, 17 August 1819, AJ to RKC, 9 September 1819, [c. 16 December 1820], 15 November 1821, AJ to James Monroe, 29 September 1819, AJ to JHE, 29 November 1819, AJ to Ellen Jackson Kirkman, 16 December 1820, in *PAJ*, 4:287, 323–325, 330–333, 349–351, 314–315, 319–320, 408–409, 339–342, 406–409, 5:114–117; John Clark to AJ, 18 August 1819, Robert Y. Hayne to AJ, 10 November 1819, in *CAJ*, 2:424–426, 6:474–475.

19. Editorial note, *PAJ*, 5:122, 168, 224, 307, 433; James C. Bronaugh and Henry M. Bronaugh to AJ, 7 May 1821, Robert Butler to AJ, 19 September 1821, AJ to John Overton, 9 December 1821, AJ to AJD, 6 September 1822, James Gadsden to AJ, 20 November 1822, AJ to Joseph Norvell and Patrick Henry Darby, 25 November 1822, Alfred Balch to AJ, 12 March 1823, 20 March 1823, AJ to John McNairy, [6 September 1823], James Jackson to AJ, 21 October 1823, 28 October 1823, AJ to JCM, 30 January 1824, AJ to John Coffee, 15 April 1823, 15 February 1824, 4 March 1824, 28 March 1824, 18 June 1824, in *PAJ*, 5:36–38, 101–102, 123–124, 217–218, 223–224, 224–225, 259–262, 262–263, 292–294, 307–309, 312–314, 350–351, 270–272, 357–359, 368–369, 382–384, 416–418; Heller, *Democracy's Lawyer*, 161–164.

20. Carter G. Baker, "John Patton Erwin" (MS in possession of author); Nancy N. Scott, *Memoir of Hugh Lawson White* (Philadelphia: J. B. Lippincott, 1856), 413–419; Editorial note, *PAJ*, 4:281, Remini, *AJ*, 2:42–43; Heidler and Heidler, *Henry Clay*, 155.

21. Sellers, "Banking and Politics," 76.

22. Sellers, "Banking and Politics," 81; Christopher Collier, *All Politics Is Local: Family, Friends, and Provincial Interests in the Creation of the Constitution* (Hanover, N.H.: University Press of New England, 2003), 5–8.

XI
"Pure & Uncontaminated by Bargain & Sale"

1. Editorial note, *PAJ*, 5:141; Felix Grundy to AJ, 27 June 1822, in *CAJ*, 3:163–164; Heller, *Democracy's Lawyer*, 155–161; AJ to RKC, 29 June 1822, in *PAJ*, 5:197–200;

Thomas M. Coens, "The Formation of the Jackson Party, 1822–1825" (Ph.D. diss., Harvard University, 2004), 10–13; Charles G. Sellers Jr., "Jackson Men with Feet of Clay," *AHR* 42 (April 1957): 537–551.

2. Coens, "Formation of the Jackson Party," chap. 1, 180.

3. James, *Portrait of a President,* chap. 1; James F. Hopkins, "Election of 1824," in *History of American Presidential Elections,* ed. Arthur M. Schlesinger and Fred L. Israel, 4 vols. (New York: Chelsea House, 1971), 1:366; Robert V. Remini, *The Election of Andrew Jackson* (New York: J. B. Lippincott, 1963), 64; Sellers, "Jackson Men with Feet of Clay," 537–551; Chappell, "Life and Activities of General John Coffee," 144–145; Heller, *Democracy's Lawyer,* 155–161; AJ to John Coffee, 15 August 1823, AJ to AJD, 18 January 1824, 21 January 1824, 11 April 1824, in *PAJ,* 5:289–290, 339–340, 343–344, 391–393.

Sam Houston is often included in the membership of the Nashville Junto, but neither his biographers nor his correspondence offer any convincing evidence of his activity on behalf of Jackson's campaign beyond his hope that the Tennessean won the election.

4. Sellers, "Jackson Men with Feet of Clay," 537–551; John Spencer Bassett, ed., "William B. Lewis on the Nomination of Andrew Jackson," *American Antiquarian Society* 33 (April 1923): 12–33; Harlan, "Public Career of William B. Lewis [Part 1]," 3–5, 12–21; Gabriel L. Lowe Jr., "John Eaton, Jackson's Campaign Manager," *THQ* 11 (June 1952): 99–117; Robert P. Hay, "The Case for Andrew Jackson in 1824: Eaton's *Wyoming Letters,*" *THQ* 29 (Summer 1970): 139–151.

5. Coens, "Formation of the Jackson Party," chaps. 1–3; Hay, "Case for Andrew Jackson," 139–151; Robert P. Hay, "'The Presidential Question': Letters to Southern Editors, 1823–24," *THQ* 31 (Summer 1972): 170–186; Warshauer, *Andrew Jackson and the Politics of Martial Law,* 56.

6. Coens, "Formation of the Jackson Party," 14; Hopkins, "Election of 1824," 349–376.

7. AJ to H. W. Peterson, 23 February 1823, Abram Maury to AJ, 20 September 1823, AJ to Abram Maury, 21 September 1823, AJ to William Bray and Thomas Williamson, 27 September 1823, AJ to John C. Calhoun, 4 October 1823, AJ to John Coffee, 5 October 1823, in *PAJ,* 5:252–253, 297–298, 298–299, 299–300, 300–302, 302–303.

8. Frances Tomlinson Gardner, "The Gentleman from Tennessee," *Surgery, Gynecology, and Obstetrics* 88 (February 1949): 408–409; Remini, *AJ,* 2:1–2; Otis [Ammedon?] to John Corlis, 4 February 1824, Corlis-Respess Family Papers, FHS.

For examples of Jackson's complaints about his health, see AJ to AJD, 26 April 1822, 2 May 1822, AJ to James Monroe, 26 July 1822, AJ to John Coffee, 24 October 1823, in *PAJ,* 5:176–177, 177–178, 207–208, 309–311.

9. Remini, *AJ,* 2:67–71; AJ to WBL, 7 May 1824, AJ to Littleton H. Coleman, 26 April 1824, in *PAJ,* 5:404, 398–400; Richard E. Ellis, *The Union at Risk: Jacksonian Democracy, States' Rights, and the Nullification Crisis* (New York: Oxford University Press, 1987), 41–42; *Niles' Weekly Register,* 12 June 1824; Dexter Perkins, "John Quincy Adams," in *The American Secretaries of State and Their Diplomacy,* ed. Samuel Flagg Bemis, 10 vols. (1928; repr., New York: Cooper Square, 1963), 4:104–107; Ammon, *James Monroe,* 520–527; William E. Ames and S. Dean Olson, "Washington's Political Press and the Election of 1824," *Journalism Quarterly* 40 (September 1963): 348–349; Donald J. Ratcliffe, "The Nullification Crisis, Southern Discontents, and the American Political

Process," *American Nineteenth Century History* 1 (Summer 2000): 4–5; Forbes, *Missouri Compromise*, 176–178.

Summaries of Jackson's senatorial votes are available in *PAJ*, 5:463–467.

10. AJ to James Monroe, [16 March 1824], in *PAJ*, 5:377; Remini, *Jackson and His Indian Wars*, 216–224; Robert P. Hay, "The American Revolution Twice Recalled: Lafayette's Visit and the Election of 1824," *Indiana Magazine of History* 69 (March 1973): 43–62.

11. Hopkins, "Election of 1824," 371–376.

12. AJ to John Overton, 19 December 1824, AJ to John Coffee, 27 December 1824, 23 January 1825, AJ to WBL, 11 January 1825, 21 January 1825, 24 January 1825, 29 January 1825, in *PAJ*, 5:455–456, 457–459, 6:18–19, 15, 17, 20, 22–24, 18–19.

13. AJ to John Overton, 10 February 1825, AJ to WBL, 14 February 1825, 20 February 1825, AJ to Squire Grant, 18 February 18[25], AJ to John Coffee, 19 February 1825, in *PAJ*, 6:28, 29–30, 36–38, 32, 35–36.

14. AJ to John Overton and the Citizens of Nashville, [16 April 1825], James Buchanan to AJ, 29 May 1825, Charles Pendleton Tutt, 1 June 1825, AJ to John Coffee, 23 July 1825, 12 October 1825, 30 October 1825, AJ to William Pope Duval, 25 July 1825, AJ to Robert Coleman Foster and William Brady, [12 October 1825], in *PAJ*, 6:62–63, 77–78, 78–80, 92–94, 106–108, 115–116, 95–96, 108–110.

XII
"The Old Hero Stands Heedless of the Pelting Storm"

1. Thomas J[efferson] Green to William Polk, 29 January 1825, Brown-Ewell Family Papers, FHS; George Kremer to AJ, 8 March 1825, AJ to Carter Beverley, 5 June 1827, AJ to Robert Y. Hayne, 9 July 1827, AJ to James Buchanan, 15 July 1827, AJ to the Public, 18 July 1827, AJ to John Coffee, 29 September 1827, in *PAJ*, 6:48–49, 330–332, 356–358, 359–360, 361–366, 394–395; Remini, *Legacy of Andrew Jackson*, 7–44.

2. John C. Niven, *Martin Van Buren: The Romantic Age of American Politics* (New York: Oxford University Press, 1983), 129–134, 140, 176–185, 191–193; Joel H. Silbey, *Martin Van Buren and the Emergence of American Popular Politics* (Lanham, Md.: Rowman & Littlefield, 2005), 46–49; James C. Curtis, *The Fox at Bay: Martin Van Buren and the Presidency, 1837–1841* (Lexington: University Press of Kentucky, 1970), 23–26; Niven, *John C. Calhoun*, 117–121, 126–127; Gretchen Garst Ewing, "Duff Green, John C. Calhoun, and the Election of 1828," *South Carolina Historical Magazine* 79 (April 1978): 132; John C. Calhoun to AJ, 4 June 1826, AJ to John C. Calhoun, [18 July 1826], SH to AJ, 13 January 1827, Henry Banks to AJ, 10 February 1826, FG to AJ, 20 November 1828, in *PAJ*, 6:177–178, 187–188, 261–263, 137–139, 534; Forbes, *Missouri Compromise*, 213–216; Paul H. Bergeron, *Antebellum Politics in Tennessee* (Lexington: University Press of Kentucky, 1982), 5; Charles G. Sellers Jr., *James K. Polk*, 2 vols. (Princeton: Princeton University Press, 1957, 1966), 1:137–138.

3. Coens, "Formation of the Jackson Party," 279–282; Niven, *John C. Calhoun*, 118–121; Forbes, *Missouri Compromise*, 214–228; W. Stephen Belko, *The Invincible Duff Green: Whig of the West* (Columbia: University of Missouri Press, 2006), 157–161; MVB to

Thomas Ritchie, 13 January 1827, VBL; Major L. Wilson, "Republicanism and the Idea of Party in the Jacksonian Period," *JER* 8 (Winter 1988): 432–440; Marc W. Kruman, "The Second American Party System and the Transformation of Revolutionary Republicanism," *JER* 12 (Winter 1992): 520–526; Silbey, *Martin Van Buren*, 22–27.

4. Forbes, *Missouri Compromise*, 211–215, 228–231.

5. Coens, "Formation of the Jackson Party," 241–282; Paul Goodman, *Of One Blood: Abolitionism and the Origins of Racial Equality* (Berkeley: University of California Press, 1998), 14–17; Ford, *Deliver Us from Evil*, 320–321; "Colonization Society: First Annual Report of the Colonization Society," p. 11, ser. 5, no. 1, ME Box (green), Papers of the American Colonization Society, LC; Douglas R. Egerton, "Averting a Crisis: The Proslavery Critique of the American Colonization Society," *Civil War History* 43 (June 1997): 155; Lynn Hudson Parsons, "'A Perpetual Harrow upon My Feelings': John Quincy Adams and the American Indian," *New England Quarterly* 46 (September 1973): 339–359; Nicholas Guyatt, "'The Outskirts of Our Happiness': Race and the Lure of Colonization in the Early Republic," *JAH* 96 (March 2009): 986–1011.

6. Remini, *AJ*, 2:409 n. 30; Editorial note, *PAJ*, 5:261, 6:19, 271, 577; Weymouth T. Jordan, *George Washington Campbell of Tennessee: Western Statesman* (Tallahassee: Florida State University, 1955), 21; McBride and Robison, *Biographical Directory*, 1:90–91, 145–146, 258–259, 667–668, 760–761, 773–774; Clayton, *History of Davidson County, Tennessee*, 198–199, 203, 99, 108–109.

The nineteen members of the Nashville Central Committee were Alfred Balch, William L. Brown, George W. Campbell, John Catron, Thomas H. Claiborne, Robert C. Foster, Daniel Graham, William B. Lewis, John McNairy, Josiah Nichol, John Overton, Nelson Patterson, Joseph Philips, Felix Robertson, John Shelby, Edward Ward, Jesse Wharton, William White, and Robert Whyte (Robert V. Remini, "Election of 1828," in Schlesinger and Israel, *History of American Presidential Elections*, 1:463).

7. Bassett, "William B. Lewis," 12–33; Lowe, "John Eaton," 117–145; Belko, *Invincible Duff Green*, 69–74; Heller, *Democracy's Lawyer*, 173–174; Sellers, *James K. Polk*, 129; JHE to John Coffee, 25 August 1826, RDC.

8. Llerena Friend, *Sam Houston: The Great Designer* (Austin: University of Texas Press, 1954), 7–16; Haley, *Sam Houston*, 34–35; "Sam Houston" and "James K. Polk," *BDUSC;* Charles G. Sellers Jr., "James K. Polk's Political Apprenticeship," *ETHSP* 25 (1953): 37–53; Joseph M. Pukl Jr., "James K. Polk's Early Congressional Campaigns of 1825 and 1827," *THQ* 39 (Winter 1980): 440–458; Sellers, *James K. Polk*, 1:128–131.

9. Mary Corlis to John Corlis, 17 June 1827, Corlis-Respess Family Papers, FHS; "The Coffin Handbill," in Remini, "Election of 1828," 485–491; Remini, *Election of Andrew Jackson*, 154–156.

10. Remini, *Election of Andrew Jackson*, 159–161; Donald B. Cole, *Vindicating Andrew Jackson: The 1828 Election and the Rise of the Two-Party System* (Lawrence: University Press of Kansas, 2009), 80–81; Michael Birkner, "The General, the Secretary, and the President: An Episode in the Presidential Campaign of 1828," *THQ* 42 (Fall 1983): 243–253; Editorial note, *PAJ*, 6:210; James Buchanan to AJ, 8 March 1826, AJ to John Coffee, 25 September 1826, AJ to SH, 5 January 1827, AJ to Samuel L. Southard, 5 June 1827, JHE to AJ, 4 March 1828, in *PAJ*, 6:146–148, 215–217, 254–255, 255–256, 427–432; JHE to AJ, 21 January 1828, HLW to AJ, 2 March 1828, in *CAJ*, 3:389–390, 6:496–497; "Jona-

than Roberts," *BDUSC;* M. Auge, *Lives of the Eminent Dead and Biographical Notes of Living Citizens of Montgomery County, PA* (Norristown, Pa.: Author, 1879), 96; Charles M. Wiltse, *John C. Calhoun: Nationalist, 1782–1828* (Indianapolis: Bobbs-Merrill, 1944), 363–364; Niven, *John C. Calhoun,* 131.

11. *Charleston (S.C.) Mercury,* 22 August 1828; *Daily National Journal,* 30 August 1828, 3 September 1828, 13 September 1828; Norma Basch, "Marriage, Morals, and Politics in the Election of 1828," *JAH* 80 (December 1993): 890–918; Francis P. Weisenburger, "Charles Hammond: The First Great Journalist of the Old Northwest," *Ohio History* 43 (October 1934): 386–387; "An Enquirer" to AJ, [November 1826], in *PAJ,* 6:236–238; HC to Charles Hammond, 23 December 1826, Charles Hammond to HC, 3 January 1827, in *PHC,* 5:1023–1024, 6:5–6; Toplovich, "Marriage, Mayhem, and Presidential Politics," 16–18; JHE to John Overton, 12 March 1824, Claybrooke Collection, TSLA; Editorial note, *PAJ,* 6:314–315; *Political Extracts from a Leading Adams Paper, The Massachusetts Journal, Edited and Published in Boston by David L. Child* (Boston, 1828), 10, 13, qtd. in Basch, "Marriage, Morals, and Politics," 904.

12. Clayton, *History of Davidson County,* 238; *National Banner and Nashville Whig,* 15 March 1828, 19 April 1828, 17 May 1828, 30 August 1828, 20 September 1828, 4 October 1828, 11 October 1828, 18 October 1828, 25 October 1828, 1 November 1828, 8 November 1828.

13. [Andrew Erwin], *Gen. Jackson's Negro Speculations, and His Traffic in Human Flesh, Examined and Established by Positive Proof* (N.p.p., 1828); [Andrew Erwin], *A Brief Account of General Jackson's Dealings in Negroes, in a Series of Letters and Documents by His Own Neighbors* (N.p.p., 1828); Editorial note, *PAJ,* 6:384–385; *National Banner and Nashville Whig,* 20 June 1828, 4 July 1828, 11 July 1828, 18 July 1828, 25 July 1828, 2 August 1828, 9 August 1828, 6 September 1828; *Genius of Universal Emancipation* (Mt. Pleasant, Ohio), 29 June 1828; *Daily National Journal* (Washington, D.C.), 2 July 1828, 16 July 1828; *Truth's Advocate and Monthly Anti-Jacksonian Expositor,* September 1828; A. W. Putnam to Peter Force, 14 September 1828, Hurja Collection, TSLA.

14. *National Banner and Nashville Whig,* 27 September 1828, 18 October 1828, 1 November 1828, 8 November 1828.

15. *Argus of Western America* (Frankfort, Ky.), 9 July 1828, Circular letter, October 1828, Andrew Jackson Papers, FHS.

16. AJ to Samuel L. Southard, 5 January 1827, SH to AJ, 13 January 1827, AJ to SH, 4 February 1827, 15 February 1827, Samuel L. Southard to AJ, 9 February 1827, AJ to WBL, 13 June 1827, AJ to John Overton, 15 August 1827, 18 August 1827, AJ to JKP, 23 March 1828, AJ to HLW, 30 March 1828, JKP to AJ, 13 April 1828, John C. Calhoun to AJ, 30 April 1828, 10 July 1828, AJ to John C. Calhoun, 25 May 1828, AJ to RKC, 14 August 1828, in *PAJ,* 6:255–256, 261–263, 274–275, 291–293, 288–290, 341–342, 377, 379, 436–439, 442–443, 444–447, 450–451, 480–482, 461–463, 493–494; *National Banner and Nashville Whig,* 17 May 1828; SH to Chapman Johnson, 20 February 1828, 14 May 1828, in Amelia W. Williams and Eugene C. Barker, eds., *The Writings of Sam Houston,* 8 vols. (Austin: University of Texas Press, 1938–43), 1:124–125, 125–128; Affidavit of Thomas Stephenson, 30 July 1828, Certificate of Samuel Mays, 31 July 1828, in *CAJ,* 3:416–417, 417; JKP, J. W. Egnew, Ben Reynolds, and M. D. Cooper to [AJ], 1 August

1828, in *CJKP*, 1:185–186; John B. Hays to AJ, 1 August 1828, Statement of Nathaniel Stephenson, 1 August 1828, JLC.

17. *A Letter from the Jackson Committee of Nashville, in Answer to One from a Similar Committee at Cincinnati, upon the Subject of Gen. Jackson's Marriage: Accompanied by Documents in an Appendix, Thereto Annexed* (Nashville: Hall & Fitzgerald, 1827), reprinted in Major L. Wilson, ed., *Mississippi Valley Collection Bulletin* 1 (Summer 1968); Statement of Elizabeth Craighead, 2 December 1826, Statement of Sally Smith, 10 December 1826, Statement of Mary H. Bowen, 21 December 1826, in *CAJ*, 3:319–321, 322–323, 325–326; "An Enquirer" to AJ, [November 1826], AJ to WBL, 12 December 1826, [SH] to AJ, 5 January 1827, 13 January 1827, EGWB to AJ, 11 January 1827, JHE to AJ, 27 January 1827, 4 February 1827, AJ to RKC, 3 May 1827, 2 October 1827, 14 August 1828, Richard G. Dunlap to AJ, 12 May 1827, John Overton to AJ, 14 May 1827, Anthony Butler to AJ, 17 May 1827, Henry Banks to AJ, 18 May 1827, AJ to William Douglass, 30 May 1827, "A Female Friend" to RJ, 10 June 1827, AJ to William B. Keene, 16 June 1827, AJ to [Peter Force et al.], [c. June 1827], Duff Green to AJ, 8 July 1827, RJ to Elizabeth Courts Love Watson, 18 July 182[7], AJ to Duff Green 13 August 1827, AJ to John McLean, 21 August 1827, AJ to William Robinson, 3 February 1828, AJ to John Coffee, 8 April 1828, in *PAJ*, 6:236–238, 240–241, 256–257, 261–263, 259–261, 267–269, 277–283, 315–317, 395–397, 493–495, 317–319, 319, 320–322, 322–324, 327–328, 340, 343–344, 351–352, 354–356, 367–369, 374–377, 379–380, 413, 443–444; WBL to [JCM], 9 April 1827, Robert Butler to AJ, 14 August 1827, John McLean to AJ, 22 September 1827, AJ to Henry Clay, [c. December 1826], JSR; Editorial note, *PAJ*, 6:580; Henry Banks to John Overton, 10 May 1827, Samuel R. Overton to AJ, 31 May 1827, JLC; "Obediah Penn" to HC, [c. 19] June 1827, in *PHC*, 6:696–699; Samuel Catlett to Henry M. Buckner, 23 May 1828, Buckner Family Papers, FHS.

18. AJ to Nathaniel W. Williams, 23 February 1828, Nathaniel W. Williams to AJ, 27 February 1828, Thomas Stuart to AJ, 1 March 1828, AJ to John Coffee, 12 May 1828, AJ to WBL, 16 July 1828, 28 July 1828, 13 August 1828, 15 August 1828, 16 August 1828, 19 August 1828, AJ to RKC, 14 August 1828, 18 October 1828, AJ to FG, 15 August 1828, James Shelby to AJ, 19 September 1828, JHE to AJ, 25 September 1828, 14 October 1828, AJ to John Coffee, 29 October 1828, 11 November 1828, AJ to Allen A. Hall and John Fitzgerald, 31 October 1828, in *PAJ*, 6:421–422, 423–424, 424–425, 457–459, 482–484, 485–486, 491–492, 496–498, 498–500, 500–501, 493–495, 515–516, 495–496, 505–506, 509–510, 511–512, 520–521, 529–530, 524–528; AJD to Boyd McNairy, 15 August 1828, 16 August 1828, Boyd McNairy to AJD, 16 August 1828, 19 August 1828, AJD to John Coffee, 15 November 1828, DLC; *National Banner and Nashville Whig*, 15 March 1828, 19 April 1828, 30 August 1828, 20 September 1828, 11 October 1828, 18 October 1828, 25 October 1828, 1 November 1828, 8 November 1828; Editorial note, *PAJ*, 6:492–493; JHE to John Coffee, 18 October 1828, 3 November 1828, 10 November 1828, AJD to John Coffee, 31 October 1828, RDC; AJ to John Coffee, 24 November 1828, in *CAJ*, 3:447; JHE to Aaron Ogden Dayton, 31 August 1828, John Henry Eaton Papers, FHS.

Gabriel L. Lowe Jr., misidentified AJD as John Donelson ("John Eaton," 143).

19. AJ to John Coffee, 20 June 1828, AJ to WBL, 22 June 1828, 28 June 1828, 16 July

1828, 5 August 1828, 1 September 1828, Ralph E. W. Earl to AJ, 17 July 1828, AJ to Robert Weakley, 5 August 1828, AJ to William Faulkner, 28 August 1828, AJ to Andrew Hays, 30 August 1827, Andrew Hays to AJ, 31 August 1827, JHE to AJ, 25 September 1828, in *PAJ,* 6:469–471, 471–473, 475–476, 482–484, 486–488, 387, 484, 488–490, 384, 385–386, 386–387, 509–510; AJ to WBL, 10 July 1828, in *CAJ,* 3:412–413; *United States' Telegraph* (Washington, D.C.), 26 July 1828, 23 August 1828; AJ to John Coffee, 4 August 1828, 11 August 1828, John Roane to AJ, 8 August 1828, JSR; *Nashville Republican and State Gazette,* 5 August 1828, 8 August 1828; *National Banner and Nashville Whig,* 5 August 1828, 9 August 1828, 16 August 1828, 23 August 1828, 20 September 1828, 23 September 1828; *Daily National Journal* (Washington, D.C.), 16 August 1828 and 28 August 1828; *Daily National Intelligencer* (Washington, D.C.), 23 August 1828; James Roane to AJ, 14 September 1828, JLC; *Nashville Republican,* 12 August 1828.

20. Cole, *Vindicating Andrew Jackson,* 137–139; Parsons, *Birth of Modern Politics,* 156–158; Niven, *Martin Van Buren,* 196–200; Robert V. Remini, "Martin Van Buren and the Tariff of Abominations," *AHR* 63 (July 1958): 903–917; William W. Freehling, *Prelude to the Civil War: The Nullification Controversy in South Carolina, 1816–1836* (New York: Harper & Row, 1966), 122–144; Niven, *John C. Calhoun,* 131–134; *Address of the Fayette County Correspondence Committee, . . . Supplement to the Kentucky Reporter* (Lexington: Thomas Smith, 1828), FHS.

21. John Branch to AJ, 23 May 1828, James Hamilton Jr., to AJ, 25 May 1828, Arthur P. Hayne to AJ, 3 November 1829, in *PAJ,* 6:459–461, 464–465, 7:532–535.

22. John C. Calhoun to AJ, 10 July 1828, AJ to John Branch, 24 June 1828, AJ to James Hamilton Jr., 29 June 1828, in *PAJ,* 6:480–482, 473–474, 476–477; Robert Y. Hayne to AJ, 3 September 1828, in *CAJ,* 3:432–436.

23. *Raleigh (N.C.) Register,* 26 September 1826; *New-Hampshire Statesman & Concord Register,* 12 July 1828; *Daily National Journal,* 28 June 1828, 17 July 1828, 18 July 1828, 18 July 1828, 21 July 1828, 28 July 1828, 29 July 1828, 1 August 1828, 4 August 1828, 5 August 1828, 8 August 1828, 27 August 1828, 2 September 1828, 6 September 1828, 27 September 1828, 29 September 1828, 8 October 1828, 15 October 1828, 13 November 1828, 14 November 1828, 17 November 1828; *Daily National Intelligencer,* 17 June 1828, 26 June 1828, 12 July 1828, 15 June 1828, 19 July 1828, 21 July 1828, 22 July 1828, 28 July 1828, 2 August 1828, 9 August 1828, 14 August 1828, 19 August 1828, 21 August 1828, 30 August 1828, 6 September 1828, 17 September 1828; Samuel Catlett to Henry M. Buckner, 12 March 1828, Buckner Family Papers, FHS; *Charleston (S.C.) Mercury,* 27 June 1828, 3 July 1828, 28 August 1828; James Hamilton Jr., qtd. in Robert Tinkler, *James Hamilton of South Carolina* (Baton Rouge: Louisiana State University Press, 2004), 95–98; Carl R. Osthaus, *Partisans of the Southern Press: Editorial Spokesmen of the Nineteenth Century* (Lexington: University Press of Kentucky, 1994), 76–77.

24. Cole, *Vindicating Andrew Jackson,* 149–150; Parsons, *Birth of Modern Politics,* 150–152.

25. Cole, *Vindicating Andrew Jackson,* 186–191, 195–197; Cooper, *The South and the Politics of Slavery*; *Presidential Elections since 1789,* 3d ed. (Washington, D.C.: Congressional Quarterly, 1983), 83; Derek L. A. Hackett, "Slavery, Ethnicity, and Sugar: An Analysis of Voting Behavior in Louisiana, 1828–1844," *Louisiana Studies* 13 (Summer 1974): 73–118.

26. John Breathitt, *Circular to the People of Kentucky, 26 June 1828* (N.p.: S. Penn Jr.,

1828), FHS; William W. Freehling, "Andrew Jackson: Great President (?)," in *Congress and the Emergence of Sectionalism: From the Missouri Compromise to the Age of Jackson*, ed. Paul Finkelman and Donald R. Kennon (Athens: Ohio University Press, 2008), 133–151; Inventory of Hermitage slaves and property, 5 January 1829, in *PAJ*, 7:8–11; Cooper, *Liberty and Slavery*, 170–171.

XIII
"Et Tu Brute"

1. Account, 21 October 1828–22 December 1828, RJ to Louise Moreau Davezac de Lassy Livingston, 1 December 1828, RJ to Mrs. L.A.W. Douglas, 3 December 18[28], JHE to RJ, 7 December 1828, AJ to Francis Preston, 18 December 1828, AJ to RKC, 22 December 1828, AJ to Jean Baptiste Plauché, 27 December 1828, in *PAJ*, 6:517, 536–537, 537–538, 543–544, 545–546, 546–547, 547; Remini, *AJ*, 2:148–155.

2. RJ to Elizabeth Courts Love Watson, 18 July 182[7], AJ to James Ronaldson, 4 January 1829, in *PAJ*, 6:367–369, 7:6–7; John F. Marszalek, *The Petticoat Affair: Manners, Mutiny, and Sex in Andrew Jackson's White House* (New York: Free Press, 1997), 20–21.

3. Donald B. Cole, *The Presidency of Andrew Jackson* (Lawrence: University Press of Kansas, 1993), 27–29; Richard B. Latner, "The Eaton Affair Reconsidered," *THQ* 36 (Fall 1977): 334–338.

4. Cole, *Presidency of AJ*, 27; Latner, "Eaton Affair Reconsidered," 334; Memorandum, [1831?], in *CAJ*, 6:504–505.

5. Simeon Kemper to Barnet Rogers, 5 August 1829, Rogers-Woodson Family Papers, FHS; Cole, *Presidency of AJ*, 27–29; Latner, "Eaton Affair Reconsidered," 334–338; Richard P. Longaker, "Was Jackson's Kitchen Cabinet a Kitchen Cabinet?" *MVHR* 44 (June 1957): 94–108; Richard B. Latner, "The Kitchen Cabinet and Andrew Jackson's Advisory System," *JAH* 65 (September 1978): 367–388; Donald B. Cole, *A Jackson Man: Amos Kendall and the Rise of American Democracy* (Baton Rouge: Louisiana State University Press, 2004), 115, 144–147.

6. Alfred Mordecai to Ellen Mordecai, 5 March 1829, in Sarah Agnes Wallace, ed., "Opening Days of Jackson's Presidency as Seen in Private Letters," *THQ* 9 (December 1950): 369–371; First Inaugural Address, 4 March 1829, in Richardson, *Messages and Papers*, 2:436–438; Cole, *Presidency of Andrew Jackson*, 32–34; AJ to MVB, 15 May 1830, in *PAJ*, 8:265.

7. Edwin A. Miles, "The First People's Inaugural–1829," *THQ* 37 (Fall 1978): 293–307; Margaret Bayard Smith, *The First Forty Years of Washington Society*, ed. Gaillard Hunt (New York: Scribner, 1906), 295–296; Remini, *AJ*, 2:178; ETD to Polly Coffee, 27 March 1829, in Burke, *Emily Donelson*, 1:177–179.

8. Marszalek, *Petticoat Affair*, 22–44, 72–74.

9. Marszalek, *Petticoat Affair*, 22–24; JHE to AJ, 7 December 1828, in *PAJ*, 6:541–542.

10. Marszalek, *Petticoat Affair*, 72–74; Cheathem, *Old Hickory's Nephew*, 60–61; ETD to Mary Donelson, 27 March 1829, in Burke, *Emily Donelson*, 1:177–179.

11. Niven, *John C. Calhoun*, 167–168; Marszalek, *Petticoat Affair*, 106–115; Editorial note, *PAJ*, 6:144.

12. AJ to Ezra Stiles Ely, 3 September 1829, Memorandum, 3 September 1829, State-

ment, 4 September 1829, AJ to AJD, [c. 3 September 1829], John N. Campbell to AJ, 5 September 1829 [2 letters], AJ to John N. Campbell, [5 September 1829], 10 September 1829, JHE to AJ, 7 September 1829, AJ to WBL, 10 September 1829, AJ to [JCM], [c. 15 September 1829] in *PAJ,* 7:403–405, 411–415, 405–411, 415, 415–416, 416, 423–424, 424–425, 420, 429–430; Curtis Dahl, "The Clergyman, the Hussy, and Old Hickory: Ezra Stiles Ely and the Peggy Eaton Affair," *Journal of Presbyterian History* 52 (Summer 1974): 137–155; Parton, *Life of AJ,* 3:203–205; MVB to James A. Hamilton, 24 September 1829, in James A. Hamilton, *Reminiscences of James A. Hamilton; Or, Men and Events, at Home and Abroad, during Three Quarters of a Century* (New York: Scribner, 1869), 147–148. William B. Lewis was almost certainly the source for Parton's description.

13. Cheathem, *Old Hickory's Nephew,* 57–77; JHE to ETD, 8 April 1829, 9 April 1829, AJD to JHE, 10 April 1829, Margaret Eaton to AJ, 9 June 1830, in *CAJ,* 4:29–30, 30, 145; Burke, *Emily Donelson,* 1:202–203, 205; ETD to JHE, 10 April 1829, in Burke, *Emily Donelson,* 1:186–187; AJ to Samuel Jackson Hays, [31 May] 1830, AJD to AJ, 25 October 1830, in *PAJ,* 8:332–333, 581–584.

14. Cheathem, *Old Hickory's Nephew,* 77–90; John Rogers to Edmund Rogers, 2 July 1830, Edmund Rogers Papers, FHS; AJ to WBL, 28 July 1830, AJ to Mary Eastin, 24 October 1830, AJ to AJD, 5 May 1831, in *CAJ,* 4:167, 186–188, 273–278.

15. Cheathem, "'High-Minded Honourable Man,'" 265–92; Johnson, "Planters and Patriarchy," 46, 49–50, 57, 60, 69.

16. William T. Barry to [Susan Barry], 25 February 1830, William T. Barry Papers, FHS; AJ to John Coffee, 19 March 1829, 22 March 1829, AJ to JCM, 24 November 1829, AJ to John Overton, 31 December 1829, in *PAJ,* 7:104–105, 108–109, 567–568, 655–658.

17. Freehling, *Prelude to Civil War,* 261–266; William W. Freehling, *The Road to Disunion,* vol. 1: *Secessionists at Bay, 1776–1854* (New York: Oxford University Press, 1990), 189–192.

18. Niven, *John C. Calhoun,* 137, 158–164; Freehling, *Prelude to Civil War,* 154–173.

19. Feller, "Seminole Controversy Revisited," 323–325; Cole, *Presidency of AJ,* 79–83; JHE to AJ, 4 March 1828, AJ to HLW, 30 March 1828, in *PAJ,* 6:427–432, 442–443; WHC to John Forsyth, 30 April 1830, AJ to James A. Hamilton, 3 May 1830, in *PAJ,* 8:257–259, 221.

20. AJ to John C. Calhoun, 13 May 1830, 30 May 1830, in *CAJ,* 4:136, 140–141; John C. Calhoun to AJ, 29 May 1830, in *PAJ,* 8:305–321.

21. Belko, *Invincible Duff Green,* 196–202; Niven, *John C. Calhoun,* 174–176; Cole, *Jackson Man,* 144–147; John C. Calhoun, *Correspondence between Gen. Andrew Jackson and John C. Calhoun, President and Vice-President of the U. States, on the Subject of the Course of the Latter, in the Deliberation of the Cabinet of Mr. Monroe, on the Occurrences in the Seminole War* (Washington, D.C.: Duff Green, 1831); Remini, *AJ,* 2:306–309; Statement, 21 November 1830, AJ to John Coffee, 28 December 1830, Memorandum, February 1831, AJ to Charles J. Love, 7 March 1831, in *CAJ,* 4:204–205, 215–217, 228–236, 245–246.

22. Cole, *Presidency of Andrew Jackson,* 84–86; Marszalek, *Petticoat Affair,* 158–176; John C. Fitzpatrick, ed., *The Autobiography of Martin Van Buren,* in *Annual Report of the American Historical Association for the Year 1918* (Washington, D.C.: GPO, 1920), 2:402–408; Meacham, *American Lion,* 101–102; JHE to AJ, 7 April 1831, in *CAJ,* 4:257–258.

In addition to Barry, the new cabinet included Edward Livingston in the State

Department, Lewis Cass as secretary of war, Levi Woodbury in the navy post, Louis McLane at the head of the Treasury, and Roger B. Taney as attorney general (Remini, *AJ*, 2:317–319).

23. Marszalek, *Petticoat Affair*, 183–185; Cheathem, *Old Hickory's Nephew*, 86–87; Cheathem, "'High-Minded Honourable Man,'" 265–282; AJ to AJD, 11 July 1831, JCM and John Bell to AJ, 29 July 1831, AJ to MVB, 5 September 1831, in *CAJ*, 4:311–312, 323, 346–348; AJD to [William Donelson], 17 September 1831, 20 October 1831, AJD to [John Coffee], 4 October 1831, 19 October 1831, DLC.

24. Parton, *Life of AJ*, 3:287; Marszalek, *Petticoat Affair;* Kirsten Wood, "'One Woman So Dangerous to Public Morals': Gender and Power in the Eaton Affair," *JER* 17 (Summer 1997): 237–276; Catherine Allgor, *Parlor Politics: In Which the Ladies of Washington Help Build a City and a New Government* (Charlottesville: University Press of Virginia, 2000); Joanne B. Freeman, *Affairs of Honor: National Politics in the New Republic* (New Haven: Yale University Press, 2001).

25. Cheathem, "'High-Minded Honourable Man,'" 265–282; AJ to John Coffee, 20 July 1830, AJ to WBL, 21 July 1830 and 28 July 1830, in *PAJ*, 8:435, 436, 455.

26. Latner, "Eaton Affair Reconsidered," 335–351.

XIV
"To the Brink of Insurrection and Treason"

1. Herman Belz, ed., *The Webster-Hayne Debate on the Nature of the Union* (Indianapolis: Liberty Fund, 2000), vii–xii, 144; Robert V. Remini, *Daniel Webster: The Man and His Times* (New York: Norton, 1997), 209, 316–317.

2. AJ to John Overton, 31 December 1829, in *PAJ*, 7:655–658; Fitzpatrick, *Autobiography of Martin Van Buren*, 2:413–414; Robert B. Satterfield, "Andrew Jackson Donelson: A Moderate Nationalist Jacksonian" (Ph.D. diss., Johns Hopkins University, 1961), 78; Remini, *AJ*, 2:234–235; Niven, *John C. Calhoun*, 172–173.

3. William T. Barry to [Susan Barry], 2 January 1831, William T. Barry Papers, [J.S. Johnston] to [Adam Beatty], Beatty-Quisenberry Family Papers, FHS; AJ to WBL, 25 August 1830, AJ to John Coffee, 28 December 1830, AJ to MVB, 23 July 1831, in *CAJ*, 4:176–178, 215–217, 316–317; "Gabriel Moore," *BDUSC;* Remini, *AJ*, 2:332, 349–350.

4. Niven, *John C. Calhoun*, 178–185; Ratcliffe, "Nullification Crisis," 22; Address, 26 July 1831, in Richard K. Crallé, ed., *The Works of John C. Calhoun*, 6 vols. (New York: D. Appleton, 1851–1856), 6:75.

5. Ellis, *Union at Risk*, 46–51; AJ to Robert Y. Hayne, 8 February 1831, AJ to MVB, 5 September 1831, 17 December 1831, in *CAJ*, 4:241–243, 346–348, 383–385; AJ to South Carolina Unionist Committee, 14 June 1831, in William W. Freehling, ed., *The Nullification Era: A Documentary Record* (New York: Harper & Row, 1967), 136–137.

6. Robert V. Remini, "Election of 1832," in Schlesinger and Israel, *History of American Presidential Elections*, 1:497–498, 507–508; Niven, *John C. Calhoun*, 186–188; AJ to John Coffee, 21 January 1832, 27 January 1832, AJ to James A. Hamilton, 27 January 1832, AJ to MVB, 17 December 1831, 12 February 1832, in *CAJ*, 4:400–401, 402, 402–403, 383–385, 404–405.

244 | Notes to Pages 136–141

7. Freehling, *Prelude to Civil War*, 247–250; Ratcliffe, "Nullification Crisis," 11–14; Ellis, *Union at Risk*, 45–46, 176.

8. Heidler and Heidler, *Henry Clay*, 241–242; *The Liberator*, 1 January 1831, in Henry Mayer, *All on Fire: William Lloyd Garrison and the Abolition of Slavery* (New York: St. Martin's Press, 1998), 111; Kenneth S. Greenberg, ed., *The Confessions of Nat Turner and Related Documents* (Boston: Bedford/St. Martin's, 1996); Kenneth S. Greenberg, ed., *Nat Turner: A Slave Rebellion in History and Memory* (Oxford: Oxford University Press, 2003); Louis P. Masur, *1831: Year of the Eclipse* (New York: Hill & Wang, 2001), 9–62; Ford, *Deliver Us from Evil*, 338–357; David Robertson, *Denmark Vesey: The Buried Story of America's Largest Slave Rebellion and the Man Who Led It* (New York: Knopf, 1999).

9. Robert J. Turnbull, *An Oration, Delivered in the City of Charleston, before the State Rights & Free Trade Party, the State Society of Cincinnati, the Revolution Society, the '76 Association, the Young Men's Free Trade Association, and Several Volunteer Companies of Militia on the 4th of July, 1832, Being the 56th Anniversary of American Independence* (Charleston: A. E. Miller, 1832), 42–45; Drew Gilpin Faust, *James Henry Hammond and the Old South: A Design for Mastery* (Baton Rouge: Louisiana State University Press, 1982), 137–141; William C. Davis, *Rhett: The Turbulent Life and Times of a Fire-Eater* (Columbia: University of South Carolina Press, 2001), 63–68; Tinkler, *James Hamilton*, 126–131.

10. Ellis, *Union at Risk*, 74–78; Freehling, *Road to Disunion*, 273–278; Ordinance of nullification, 24 November 1832, in Freehling, *Nullification Era*, 150–152; Niven, *John C. Calhoun*, 192–193.

11. AJ, qtd. in William H. Hurst to William S. Bodley, 14 October 1832, Bodley Family Papers, FHS; Fourth annual message, 4 December 1832, Nullification Proclamation, 10 December 1832, in Richardson, *Messages and Papers*, 2:591–606, 640–656; Cole, *Presidency of Andrew Jackson*, 160–161.

12. AJ to WBL, 23 August 1832, in *New York Times*, 11 January 1875; AJ to Edward Livingston, 11 September 1832, AJ to AJD, 17 September 1832, Joel R. Poinsett to AJ, 16 October 1832, 16 November 1832, 24 November 1832, 29 November 1832, AJ to Lewis Cass, 29 October 1832, AJ to George Breathitt, 7 November 1832 (2 letters), AJ to Joel R. Poinsett, 7 November 1832, 2 December 1832, 9 December 1832, in *CAJ*, 4:474–475, 475–476, 481–482, 486–488, 490–491, 491–492, 483, 484, 484–485, 485–486, 493–494, 497–498; Freehling, *Prelude to Civil War*, 265, 274–284; Ellis, *Union at Risk*, 79–80; Joshua Cain, "'We Will Strike at the Head and Demolish the Monster': The Impact of Joel R. Poinsett's Correspondence on President Andrew Jackson during the Nullification Crisis, 1832–1833," *Proceedings of the South Carolina Historical Association* (2011): 13–26.

13. Freehling, *Prelude to Civil War*, 284–286; Ellis, *Union at Risk*, 160–164, 97–98; Heller, *Democracy's Lawyer*, 205–206; Remini, *Daniel Webster*, 376–378; Henry Clay to Francis T. Brooke, 17 January 1833, Henry Clay Correspondence, FHS.

14. Heidler and Heidler, *Henry Clay*, 252–254; Remini, *Daniel Webster*, 382–386; Ellis, *Union at Risk*, 98–100, 166–177; Niven, *John C. Calhoun*, 193.

15. Heidler and Heidler, *Henry Clay*, 254–255; Scott, *Memoir of Hugh Lawson White*, 299–300; AJ to FG, 13 February 1833, in "Letters from Jackson, Clay, and Johnson," *American Historical Magazine* 5 (April 1900): 137–138.

16. Ellis, *Union at Risk*, 171–172, 175–177; Sol. Clark to FPB, 20 March 1833, Sol. Clark (?) Papers, FHS.

17. AJ to Andrew J. Crawford, 1 May 1833, in *CAJ,* 5:71–72; Howe, *What Hath God Wrought,* 409–410.

XV
"A Man Indebted Is a Slave"

1. Remini, *AJ,* 2:xiii–xvi, 3:xix–xxiii.
Jackson's trips back to Nashville were made on 17 June–30 October 1830, 22 July–19 October 1832, 8 July–30 September 1834, and 10 July–1 October 1836.

2. Editorial note, *PAJ,* 1:180, 3:21, 6:21, 146, 157, 368, 7:159, 201, 8:177; Charles J. Love to AJ, 15 April 1829, 15 January 1830, in *PAJ,* 7:159, 8:35–38; Robert Armstrong, to AJ, 14 October 1834, 20 October 1834, in *CAJ,* 5:295–296, 298.

3. Contract, 19 January 1829, AJ to John Donelson, 7 June 1829, Graves W. Steele to AJ, 30 December 1830, AJ to AJJr, 20 July 1829, 19 August 1829, in *PAJ,* 7:15, 268–270, 336–337, 384–385, 8:724–725; AJ to AJJr, 4 July 1829, in *CAJ,* 4:49–50; Cheathem, *Old Hickory's Nephew,* 116–117.

4. AJ to AJJr, 21 September 1829, AJ to William Donelson, 8 October 1829, 30 January 1830, AJ to Graves W. Steele, 7 November 1829, AJ to Charles J. Love, 17 December 1829, William Donelson to AJ, 20 December 1829, in *PAJ,* 7:446–447, 480–482, 539–541, 639–640, 643–645, 8:58–61; James G. Martin to AJD, 28 February 1829, TDH; William Donelson to AJD, 13 March 1829, BDP; John Coffee to AJD, [17?] September 1829, Dyas Collection.

5. Maunsel White to AJ, 29 January 1831, John Coffee to AJ, 28 April 1831, AJ to AJJr, 19 May 1832, 24 May 1832, 1 November 1833, Graves W. Steele to AJ, 25 May 1832, AJ to AJD, 19 August 1832, 13 September 1832, in *CAJ,* 4:227–228, 270–271, 441–442, 442–443, 443–444, 467–468, 475, 5:222–223; William Donelson to AJD, 23 October 1831, BDP; AJ to AJJr, 27 June 1832, JSR.

6. William K. Scarborough, *The Overseer: Plantation Management in the Old South* (Baton Rouge: Louisiana State University Press, 1966), 125–126.

7. Burnard W. Holtzclaw to AJ, 6 March 1833, 21 October 1833, AJ to AJJr, 8 April 1833, 1 November 1833, 13 November 1833, 8 December 1833, 22 December 1833, AJ to AJH, 18 April 1833, Miles B. McCorkle to AJ, 19 April 1833, WBL to AJ, 21 April 1833, AJ to WBL, 4 May 1833, AJ to Robert J. Chester, 8 August 1833, in *CAJ,* 5:29–30, 218, 224–225, 232–233, 234–235, 54, 222–223, 59–60, 61, 61–65, 73–74, 149–150.

8. AJ to AJD, 19 August 1832, 10 December 1836, AJ to AJJr, 30 October 1834, 15 November 1834, 1 May 1835, 12 September 1835, 25 March 1836, 5 November 1836, in *CAJ,* 4:467–468, 5:441–442, 303–304, 308–309, 342–343, 364, 393–394, 435–436.

9. Remini, *AJ,* 3:147.

10. AJ to AJJr, 14 July 1829, 20 July 1829, 22 July 1829, 18 August 1829, 19 August 1829, 20 August 1829, in *PAJ,* 7:333–334, 336–337, 340–341, 374, 384–385, 386–387; AJ to AJJr, [14 May 1831], 18 May 1831, 3 July 1831, 27 June 1832, 12 November 1832, 8 December 1832, AJ to SYJ, 10 October 1834, JSR.

11. Mary French Caldwell, *Andrew Jackson's Hermitage* (Nashville: Ladies' Hermitage Association, 1933), 83–84; Robert Armstrong to AJ, 14 October 1834, Stockley Donelson to AJ, 14 October 1834, AJ to AJJr, 23 October 1834, Memorandum, 1 January

1835, Statement of accounts, 2 August 1836, in *CAJ*, 5:295–296, 296–297, 302, 315–317, 414–415; AJ to AJJr, 10 July 1836, 23 July 1836, JLC.

12. AJ to AJJr, 3 July 1831, 24 September 1833, 19 October 1833, 20 October 1833, 11 January [1834], JSR; AJ to AJJr, 8 November 1832, JLC.

13. AJ to AJJr, 27 June 1832, 24 September 1833, JSR; Johnson, "Planters and Patriarchy," 55–60; Glover, *Southern Sons,* 84–86, 98–99, 107–111; Wyatt-Brown, *Southern Honor,* 345–346.

14. AJ to AJJr, 14 April 1835, 29 April 1835, 16 May 1835, in *CAJ,* 5:335–336, 341–342, 347–348; AJJr to SYJ, 25 April 1835, 10 April 1836, AJ to AJJr, 2 May 1835, 9 May 1835, JLC; W. J. Rorabaugh, *The Alcoholic Republic: An American Tradition* (Oxford: Oxford University Press, 1979).

15. AJ to AJJr, 22 July 1829, 26 July 1829, 20 August 1829, AJ to Francis Smith, 19 May 1830, AJ to Samuel J. Hays, 2 October 1830, in *PAJ,* 7:340–341, 345–346, 386–387, 446–447, 8:268–269, 538–539.

16. AJ to AJJr, 16 September 1831, JLC; Julia Ward Stickley, "Catholic Ceremonies in the White House, 1832–1833: Andrew Jackson's Forgotten Ward, Mary Lewis," *Catholic Historical Review* 51 (July 1965): 192–198; Marriage license, 25 November 1831, JSR; Galloway, "Andrew Jackson, Jr. [Part 1]," 215–216; Remini, *AJ,* 2:335.

17. AJ to AJJr, 30 September 1832, c. 1 November 1832, 8 November 1832, 12 November 1832, 16 November 1832, 8 December 1832, JSR; AJ to AJJr, 25 November 1832, JLC; AJ to AJJr, 15 April 1834, 20 April 1834, in *CAJ,* 5:261, 262; AJ to Mary Eastin Polk, 9 August 1834, Brown-Ewell Family Papers, FHS.

18. DeWitt, "Andrew Jackson Hutchings," 83–106; William Donelson to AJD, 13 March 1829, BDP; AJ to John Coffee, 19 March 1829, 22 March 1829, 21 July 1829, AJ to William Donelson, 22 March 1829, John Donelson to AJ, 19 May 1829, AJ to AJH, 13 June 1829, in *PAJ,* 7:104–105, 108–109, 337–338, 109–110, 229–231, 279–280.

19. Charles J. Love to AJ, 15 April 1829, AJ to Robert J. Chester, 14 February 1830, John Coffee to AJ, 2 March 1830, AJ to John Coffee, 10 April 1830, [8 May] 1830, in *PAJ,* 7:159, 8:73–74, 111–112, 183–184, 248–249; AJ to John Coffee, 26 May 1831, 6 September 1831, AJ to AJH, 3 November 1833, in *CAJ,* 4:285, 348–349, 5:223–224; AJ to AJH, 11 February 1832, AJ to John Coffee, 19 February 1832, JSR; DeWitt, "Andrew Jackson Hutchings," 90–96.

20. AJ to AJJr, 2 April 1833, 8 April 1833, 25 May 1834, 5 November 1836, in *CAJ,* 5:48–49, 54, 266, 435–436; AJ to AJJr, 16 April 1833, 24 March 1834, 18 June 1834, 1 October 1834, 6 November 1836, AJJr to AJ, 4 October 1833, JLC; AJ to AJJr, 8 December 1832, 2 September 1833, 6 October 1833, JSR.

21. Bill of sale, 2 January 1829, AJ to Sarah Bronaugh, 20 January 1830, Usher Skinner to AJ, 16 April 1830, 26 April 1830, AJ to Robert J. Chester, 7 November 1830, 25 November 1830, in *PAJ,* 7:4, 8:41–42, 199–200, 210, 611–612, 636–637; Check, 3 June 1830, AJ to AJJr, 5 February 1834, Bill of sale, 5 June 1834, JLC; AJD to ETD, 15 January 1831, AJ to AJJr, 22 December 1833, 12 February 1834, 16 February 1834, 9 March 1834, AJJr to AJ, 25 January 1834, in *CAJ,* 4:227, 5:234–235, 247–248, 248–249, 253–254, 240–242; AJD to [Lewis Jones], 7 March 1831, 21 June 1831, Arthur Holbrook Collection, Milwaukee Historical Society, Milwaukee; AJ to AJJr, 8 February 1834, 2 March 1834, Memorandum, 6 June 1834, JSR; Memorandum, 8 June 1843, DLC.

22. Deppisch, "Andrew Jackson and American Medical Practice," 137, 139–140, 142,

144; Remini, *AJ,* 2:321–322, 333, 3:84–85, 238, 333, 336; AJ to Maunsel White, 2 December 1836, in *CAJ,* 5:440–441; Cheathem, *Old Hickory's Nephew,* 121–124.

23. Jackson's will, 7 June 1843, in *CAJ,* 6:220–223.

XVI
"That My White and Red Children May Live in Peace"

1. Remini, *Jackson and His Indian Wars,* 84–85, 101, 114–116, 128–129, 193–194; AJ to John D. Terrell, 29 July 1826, AJ to John Coffee, [5 October 1826], AJ to Wilson Lumpkin, 15 February 1828, in *PAJ,* 6:192, 226–227, 417–418.

2. AJ to Creek Indians, 23 March 1829, in *PAJ,* 7:112–113.

3. Thomas P. Govan, "John M. Berrien and the Administration of Andrew Jackson," *JSH* 5 (November 1939): 448–449; Editorial note, *PAJ,* 7:113, 161.

4. Cole, *Presidency of Andrew Jackson,* 53–54, 71. The party affiliations of the committee members were determined from their entries in *BDUSC* and their regional representation from Perry Goldman and James S. Young, eds., *The United States Congressional Directories, 1789–1840* (New York: Columbia University Press, 1973), 222, 226.

5. Cole, *Presidency of Andrew Jackson,* 71–74; Ronald N. Satz, *American Indian Policy in the Age of Jackson* (Lincoln: University of Nebraska Press, 1974), 20–31; Speech, 7 April 1830, in *Speeches on the Passage of the Bill for the Removal of the Indians, Delivered in the Congress of the United States, April and May, 1830* (Boston: Perkins & Marvin, 1830), 27; William S. Bodley to Thomas Bodley, 19 July 1830, Bodley Family Papers, FHS; Editorial note, in *The Papers of Jefferson Davis,* ed. Lynda L. Crist et al., 12 vols. to date (Baton Rouge: Louisiana State University Press, 1971–), 2:155–156.

6. Cole, *Presidency of Andrew Jackson,* 71–74; Satz, *American Indian Policy,* 20–31; Speech, 7 April 1830, in *Speeches on the Passage of the Bill for the Removal of the Indians, Delivered in the Congress of the United States, April and May, 1830* (Boston: Perkins & Marvin, 1830), 27; *Register of Debates* 6 (1830): 328, 383. Vote percentages for the Senate were calculated from the roll call vote in the *Register.*

In "The American Indian and the Origin of the Second American Party System," *Wisconsin Magazine of History* 76 (Spring 1993): 180–203, Fred S. Rolater noted that while party affiliation was the strongest indicator of congressional voting on Indian removal, sectionalism also played a significant role, especially among U.S. senators.

7. Satz, *American Indian Policy,* 66–67; AJ to John M. Berrien, 16 June 1830, AJ to MVB, 12 July 1830, AJ to Samuel D. Ingham, 31 July 1830, 7 August 1830, AJ to John Pitchlynn, 5 August 1830, AJ to Chickasaw Indians, 22 August 1830, 26 August 1830, AJ to WBL, 25 August 1830, 31 August 1830, AJ to John Coffee and JHE, 27 August 1830, AJ to John Coffee, 16 October 1830, AJ to JHE, [c. 22 July 1830], 18 November 1830, in *PAJ,* 8:375, 423–424, 457–458, 467, 465–466, 495–499, 507–508, 500–501, 516, 511, 559–560, 439, 631–632; Prucha, *Great Father,* 82–83.

8. Satz, *American Indian Policy,* 67–87; Cole, *Presidency of Andrew Jackson,* 110–112; John Coffee to AJ, 29 September 1830, AJ to John Coffee, 16 October 1830, in *PAJ,* 8:531–532, 559–560; Arthur H. DeRosier Jr., *The Removal of the Choctaw Indians* (Knoxville: University of Tennessee Press, 1970), 162–163.

9. Michael D. Green, *The Politics of Indian Removal: Creek Government and Society in*

Crisis (Lincoln: University of Nebraska Press, 1982), 141, 155–186; J. Mills Thornton, *Politics and Power in a Slave Society: Alabama, 1800–1860* (Baton Rouge: Louisiana State University Press, 1978), 28–29; Editorial note, *PAJ*, 8:203; John Crowell to JHE, 30 June 1830, AJ to WBL, 25 August 1830, Memorandum, [c. August 1830], in *PAJ*, 8:404–405, 500–501, 518; AJ to John Coffee, 19 February 1832, 7 April 1832, Note, [November 1832], Wilson Lumpkin to AJ, 20 May 1835, in *CAJ*, 4:405–407, 429–430, 493, 5:349–351; Angela Pulley Hudson, *Creek Paths and Federal Roads: Indians, Settlers, and Slaves and the Making of the American South* (Chapel Hill: University of North Carolina Press, 2010), 169–171; Satz, *American Indian Policy*, 105–106.

10. Gary E. Moulton, *John Ross: Cherokee Chief* (Athens: University of Georgia Press, 1978), 31; Theda Perdue and Michael D. Green, eds., *The Cherokee Removal: A Brief History in Documents*, 2d ed. (Boston: Bedford/St. Martin's, 2005), 12–17; Memorial of protest, 22 June 1836, in Perdue and Green, *Cherokee Removal*, 90; Tiya Miles, *The House on Diamond Hill: A Cherokee Plantation Story* (Chapel Hill: University of North Carolina Press, 2010).

11. Remini, *Jackson and His Indian Wars*, 229–230; AJ to John Overton, 8 June 1829, in *PAJ*, 7:270–272.

12. AJ to WBL, 25 August 1830, in *PAJ*, 8:500–501; Tim Alan Garrison, *The Legal Ideology of Removal: The Southern Judiciary and the Sovereignty of Native American Nations* (Athens: University of Georgia Press, 2002), 125–150.

13. Garrison, *Legal Ideology of Removal*, 169–193.

14. Garrison, *Legal Ideology of Removal*, 193–197; Horace Greeley, *The American Conflict: A History of the Great Rebellion in the United States of America, 1860–'64: Its Causes, Incidents, and Results: Intended to Exhibit Especially Its Moral and Political Phases, with the Drift and Progress of American Opinion Respecting Human Slavery from 1776 to the Close of the War for the Union*, 2 vols. (Hartford, Conn.: O. D. Case, 1864), 1:106; AJ to John Coffee, 7 April 1832, in *CAJ*, 4:429–430.

For differing views on whether the Greeley quotation represented Jackson's position, even if the words were not his, see Garrison, *Legal Ideology of Removal*, 193; and Edwin A. Miles, "After John Marshall's Decision: *Worcester v. Georgia* and the Nullification Crisis," *JSH* 39 (November 1973): 528–529 n. 23.

15. AJ to WBL, 25 August 1830, in *PAJ*, 8:500–501; Second annual message, 6 December 1830, in Richardson, *Messages and Papers*, 2:519–523; E. Merton Coulter, "The Nullification Movement in Georgia," *Georgia Historical Quarterly* 5 (March 1921): 3–39; William S. Hoffman, "Andrew Jackson, State Rightist: The Case of the Georgia Indians," *THQ* 11 (December 1952): 329–345; Miles, "After John Marshall's Decision," 519–544; Garrison, *Legal Ideology of Removal*, 144–145.

16. Remini, *Jackson and His Indian Wars*, 261–268; James J. Trott to John Ross, 6 January 1836, John Ross to Lewis Cass, 9 February 1836, Memorial to the U.S. Senate, 8 March 1836, in Gary E. Moulton, ed., *The Papers of Chief John Ross*, 2 vols. (Norman: University of Oklahoma Press, 1985), 1:379–380, 385–386, 394–413; Satz, *American Indian Policy*, 117; Perdue and Green, *Cherokee Removal*, 167–168.

17. Kenneth W. Porter, "Florida Slaves and Free Negroes in the Seminole War, 1835–1842," *Journal of Negro History* 28 (October 1943): 390–397; Joe Knetsch, "Strategy, Operations, and Tactics in the Second Seminole War, 1835–1842"; Matthew Clavin, "'It

Is a Negro, Not an Indian War': Southampton, St. Domingo, and the Second Seminole War," in Belko, *America's Hundred Years' War*, 128–154, 181–208; John K. Mahon, *History of the Second Seminole War, 1835–1842* (Gainesville: University Press of Florida, 1985), 322, 325; John F. Marszalek, *Sherman: A Soldier's Passion for Order* (New York: Free Press, 1993), 31–39.

18. Tim Alan Garrison, "United States Indian Policy in Sectional Crisis: Georgia's Exploitation of the Compact of 1802," in Finkelman and Kennon, *Congress and the Emergence of Sectionalism*, 122–123; Mahon, *History of the Second Seminole War*, 321–327; AJ to Robert J. Chester, 14 February 1830, in *PAJ*, 8:73–74; Ratcliffe, "Nullification Crisis," 6.

XVII
"I Have Been Opposed Always to the Bank"

1. AJ to THB, [June 1832], in *CAJ*, 4:445–446.

2. Robert V. Remini, *Andrew Jackson and the Bank War* (New York: Norton, 1967), 49–55.

3. First annual message, 8 December 1829, second annual message, 7 December 1830, third annual message, 6 December 1831, in Richardson, *Messages and Papers*, 2:462, 528–529, 558; AJ to James A. Hamilton, 19 December 1829, in *PAJ*, 7:642–643.

4. Remini, *Bank War*, 70–74.

5. Thomas Hart Benton, *Thirty Years' View* (New York: Appleton, 1856), 1:235; Remini, *Bank War*, 77–80.

6. Remini, "Election of 1832," 507–508, 567–573.

7. Remini, *Bank War*, 80; *Register of Debates*, House, 22d Cong., 1st sess., 3851–3852; Thomas H. Benton, *Abridgement of the Debates of Congress, from 1789 to 1856*, 16 vols. (New York: D. Appleton, 1857–1861), 11:488, 753. Party and state affiliations for identifying southern congressmen were taken from the *BDUSC*.

8. Jackson to Amos Kendall, 23 July 1832, in *CAJ*, 4:465; Cole, *Jackson Man*, 165–171; Bank veto message, 10 July 1832, in Richardson, *Messages and Papers*, 2:581, 590–591.

9. Daniel Webster, *Works of Daniel Webster* (Boston: Little, Brown, 1857), 3:417, 435; Speech in Senate, 12 July 1832, Register of Debates, 22d Cong., 1st sess., 1265–1274; Nicholas Biddle to Henry Clay, 1 August 1832, in *PHC*, 8:556–557.

10. *Washington Globe*, 5 and 8 September and 17 October 1832, qtd. in Remini, *Bank War*, 99–100. The expenditure figure comes from Ralph C. H. Catterall, *The Second Bank of the United States* (Chicago: University of Chicago Press, 1903), 265.

11. *National Intelligencer*, 6 September 1832, qtd. in Remini, *Bank War*, 101; *National Intelligencer*, 9 August 1832, qtd. in George Rogers Taylor, ed., *Jackson versus Biddle: The Struggle over the Second Bank of the United States* (Boston: D. C. Heath, 1949), 31–32; E. A. Dudley to Sidney P. Clay, 7 August 1832, Clay, Green Papers, FHS.

12. [T. A. Marshall] to Eliza [Marshall], 26 February 1832, Marshall Family Papers, [J. S. Johnston] to Adam Beatty, 29 June 1832, Beatty-Quisenberry Family Papers, FHS.

13. Henry Clay to Robert P. Letcher, 1 April 1830, Isaac Shelby Papers–Jacobs Collection, Henry Clay to Norborne Beall, 27 January 1832, Beall-Booth Family Papers, FHS; Cole, *Presidency of Andrew Jackson*, 149–150.

14. William T. Barry to [Susan Barry], 4 July 1832, William T. Barry Papers, Wil-

liam H. Hurst to William S. Bodley, 19 November 1832, Bodley Family Papers, FHS; Samuel Rhea Gammon Jr., *The Presidential Campaign of 1832* (Baltimore: Johns Hopkins Press, 1922), 154; Remini, "Election of 1832," 515, 574; Remini, *AJ*, 2:389–391. Remini notes that "in Alabama, Georgia, and Mississippi, Jackson faced no opposition" (390). Clay's vote totals in Tennessee and Missouri are "inexact" but generally correct (574).

15. Remini, *Bank War*, 111; Remini, *AJ*, 2:315–330; Fourth annual message, 4 December 1832, in Richardson, *Messages and Papers*, 2:600; AJ to JKP, 16 December 1832, in *CJKP*, 1:575; Sellers, *James K. Polk*, 1:191–195.

16. Remini, *Bank War*, 112–115.

17. Remini, *Bank War*, 115–118; Remini, *AJ*, 3:57–58; Draft of paper read to the cabinet, 18 September 1833, in Bassett, *Correspondence*, 5:193. The final draft actually read to the cabinet is contained in Richardson, *Messages and Papers*, 3:5–19.

18. Remini, *AJ*, 3:99–102.

19. Remini, *Bank War*, 125–129.

20. Michael F. Holt, *The Rise and Fall of the American Whig Party: Jacksonian Politics and the Onset of the Civil War* (Oxford: Oxford University Press, 1999), 24–25; Jonathan M. Atkins, *Parties, Politics, and the Sectional Conflict in Tennessee, 1832–1861* (Knoxville: University of Tennessee Press, 1997), 34–35, 57–59; Cooper, *South and the Politics of Slavery*, 50–52; Peter Temin, *The Jacksonian Economy* (New York: Norton, 1969), 103; Donald J. Ratcliffe, "The Crisis of Commercialization: National Political Alignments and the Market Revolutions, 1819–1844," in *The Market Revolution in America: Social, Political, and Religious Expressions, 1800–1880*, ed. Melvyn Stokes and Stephen Conway (Charlottesville: University Press of Virginia, 1996), 185; John M. McFaul, *The Politics of Jacksonian Finance* (Ithaca, N.Y.: Cornell University Press, 1972), 18–24, 28, 45–48; Cole, *A Jackson Man; Register of Debates*, House, 23d Cong., 1st sess., 3074–3075.

21. Amos Kendall, *Autobiography of Amos Kendall* (Boston: Lee & Shepard, 1872), 416; Remini, *Bank War*, 131–135.

22. Remini, *Bank War*, 137–138; Cole, *Presidency of Andrew Jackson*, 201; HC to Francis T. Brooke, 16 December 1833, in *PHC*, 8:678–679.

23. Senate speech, 10 December 1833, in *Register of Debates*, 23d Cong., 1st sess., cols. 84–85, 94; Senate speech, 13 January 1834, in *The Papers of John C. Calhoun*, ed. Clyde N. Wilson et al., 28 vols. (Columbia: University of South Carolina Press, 1959–2003), 12:221–222; Philip Kearny to H. D. Smith, 19 January 1834, Philip Kearny Papers, FHS.

24. *Register of Debates*, 23d Cong., 1st sess., 1187; Cooper, *South and the Politics of Slavery*, 52; Veto protest message, 15 April 1834, in Richardson, *Messages and Papers*, 3:87.

25. Sellers, *James K. Polk*, 1:234–242; Joseph H. Parks, *John Bell of Tennessee* (Baton Rouge: Louisiana State University Press, 1950), 65–72; John Bell to William Polk, 1 February 1832, Brown-Ewell Family Papers, Lansford Yandell to Susan Yandell, 17 September 1832, Yandell Family Papers, FHS; James Walker to JKP, 22 October 1833, in *CJKP*, 2:119–121; Atkins, *Parties, Politics, and the Sectional Conflict in Tennessee*.

26. Remini, *Bank War*, 163–172.

27. Charles G. Sellers Jr., "Who Were the Southern Whigs?" *AHR* 59 (February 1954): 335–346; Glyndon G. Van Deusen, "Some Aspects of Whig Thought and Theory in the Jacksonian Period," *AHR* 63 (October 1957): 305–322; Lynn L. Marshall, "The

Strange Stillbirth of the Whig Party," *AHR* 72 (February 1967): 445–468; Glyndon G. Van Deusen, "The Whig Party," in Schlesinger, *History of U.S. Political Parties,* 1:333–363; Daniel Walker Howe, *The Political Culture of the American Whigs* (Chicago: University of Chicago Press, 1979), 88–90; Holt, *Rise and Fall of the American Whig Party,* 25–32; Cooper, *South and the Politics of Slavery,* 53–54.

28. Thomas P. Abernethy, "The Origin of the Whig Party in Tennessee," *MVHR* 12 (March 1926): 504–522; Powell Moore, "The Political Background of the Revolt against Jackson in Tennessee," *ETHSP* 4 (1932): 45–66; Jonathan M. Atkins, "The Whig Party versus the 'Spoilsmen' in Tennessee," *Historian* 57 (Winter 1995): 329–335; Atkins, *Parties, Politics, and Sectional Conflict,* 26–54; John C. McLemore to AJD, 5 April 1829, DLC; Megan Taylor Shockley, "King of the Wild Frontier vs. King Andrew I: Davy Crockett and the Election of 1831," *THQ* 57 (Fall 1997): 158–169; Michael Wallis, *David Crockett: Lion of the West,* 200–202, 221–224; Ratner, *Jackson and His Tennessee Lieutenants,* 68–71; Bergeron, *Antebellum Politics,* 35–38; Baker, "John Patton Erwin."

29. Sellers, *James K. Polk,* 1:234–242, 251, 253, 269, 289–290; Marszalek, *Petticoat Affair,* 206–210, 213–214; Louis R. Harlan, "Public Career of William Berkeley Lewis [Part 2]," *THQ* 7 (June 1948): 137–142; James Walker to JKP, 20 October 1833, 14 December 1833, 22 September 1834, William R. Rucker to JKP, 5 January 1835, JKP to Samuel H. Laughlin, 6 September 1835, AJD to JKP, 24 September 1835, in *CJKP,* 2:116–118, 175–176, 496–497, 3:12–14, 283–286, 307–308; WBL to AJ, 30 August 1839, in *CAJ,* 6:19–25.

30. Cooper, *Liberty and Slavery,* 175–178.

XVIII
"Firebrands of Anarchy and Bloodshed"

1. Leonard L. Richards, *"'Gentlemen of Property and Standing': Anti-Abolition Mobs in Jacksonian America* (Oxford: Oxford University Press, 1970); David Grimsted, *American Mobbing, 1828–1861: Toward Civil War* (New York: Oxford University Press, 1998); Robert E. Shalhope, *The Baltimore Bank Riot: Political Upheaval in Antebellum Maryland* (Urbana: University of Illinois Press, 2009); David Grimsted, "Rioting in Its Jacksonian Setting," *AHR* 77 (April 1972): 362.

2. Josephine Seaton, *William Winston Seaton of the National Intelligencer. A Biographical Sketch. With Passing Notices of His Associates and Friends* (Boston: Osgood, 1871), 217–219; William D. Hoyt Jr., "Washington's Living History: The Post Office Fire and Other Matters, 1834–39," *Records of the Columbia Historical Society* 46–47 (1944–1945): 60–65; Constance M. Green, *The Secret City: A History of Race Relations in the Nation's Capital* (Princeton: Princeton University Press, 1967), 35–37; John M. Werner, "Race Riots in the United States during the Age of Jackson, 1824–1849" (Ph.D. diss., Indiana University, 1972); Neil S. Kramer, "The Trial of Reuben Crandall," *Records of the Columbia Historical Society* 50 (1980): 123–139; Constance M. Green, *Washington: Village and Capital, 1800–1878* (Princeton: Princeton University Press, 1976), 140–142; Jean V. Berlin, "A Mistress and a Slave: Anna Maria Thornton and John Arthur Bowen," *Proceedings of the South Carolina Historical Association* (1990): 69–74; Stephanie Cole, "Changes for Mrs. Thornton's Arthur: Patterns of Domestic Service in Washington, D.C., 1800–1835," *Social Science History* 15 (Fall 1991): 367–379; G. Franklin Edwards and Michael R. Win-

ston, "Commentary: The Washington of Paul Jennings–White House Slave, Free Man, and Conspirator for Freedom," *White House History* 1 (Spring 1987): 52–63; Stanley Harrold, *Subversives: Antislavery Community in Washington, D.C., 1828–1865* (Baton Rouge: Louisiana State University Press, 2003), 32–35; Jefferson Morley, *Snow-Storm in August: Washington City, Francis Scott Key, and the Forgotten Race Riot of 1835* (New York: Nan A. Talese/Doubleday, 2012); Linda M. Maloney, *The Captain from Connecticut: The Life and Naval Times of Isaac Hull* (Boston: Northeastern University Press, 1986), 436–439; *Richmond Enquirer,* 18 August 1835; *Washington Globe,* 19 August 1835.

3. Memorandum, n.d., NPT Papers, LC; Parton, *Life of AJ,* 3:606–607; Remini, *AJ,* 3:268.

There is no record of an Augustus being owned by Jackson, so the man may have been a slave or free black hired in Washington or already serving on the White House staff.

4. *National Intelligencer,* 15 February 1836; Petition, 18 February 1836, JSR; John Arthur Bowen, qtd. in *Boston Courier,* 17 December 1835.

5. Memorial of George Gibson et al., c. 18 February 1836, Anna Maria Thornton to MVB, [21 February 1836], Anna Maria Thornton to AJD, [22 February 1836], Affidavit of William Cranch, 23 February 1836, Benjamin F. Butler to AJ, 25 February 1836, AJ to John Forsyth, 3 June 1836, Buckner Thruston to AJ, 16 June 1836, Petition, 18 February 1836, 17 June 1836, JSR; Berlin, "Mistress and a Slave," 72–73; Ludwig M. Deppisch, "Andrew Jackson and American Medical Practice: Old Hickory and His Physicians," *THQ* 62 (Summer 2003): 130–150; Morley, *Snow-Storm in August,* 193–196, 224–226, 233–234; Remini, *AJ,* 3:229; Respite, 25 February 1836, NAII, T967, reel 1; Pardon, 27 June 1836, National Archives II, College Park, Md., T967, reel 2; Arda S. Walker, "John Henry Eaton, Apostate," *ETHSP* 24 (1952): 36–37.

6. Frank Otto Gatell, ed., "Postmaster Huger and the Incendiary Publications," *South Carolina Historical Magazine* 64 (October 1963): 193–201; Bertram Wyatt-Brown, "The Abolitionists' Postal Campaign of 1835," *Journal of Negro History* 50 (October 1965): 227–238; Cole, *Jackson Man,* 199–201; Richard R. John, *Spreading the News: The American Postal System from Franklin to Morse* (Cambridge: Harvard University Press, 1995), 257–280; Ford, *Deliver Us from Evil,* 481–504; *Washington Globe,* 22 August 1835, 29 August 1835; *Richmond Enquirer,* 25 August 1835; AK to AJ, 7 August 1835, in *CAJ,* 5:359–360.

7. AJ to AK, 9 August 1835, in *CAJ,* 5:360–361.

8. Niven, *Martin Van Buren,* 386–400; William G. Shade, "'The Most Delicate and Exciting Topics': Martin Van Buren, Slavery, and the Election of 1836," *JER* 18 (Fall 1998): 465–466; Joel H. Silbey, "Election of 1836," in Schlesinger and Israel, *History of American Presidential Elections,* 1:584; Thomas Brown, "The Miscegenation of Richard Mentor Johnson as an Issue in the National Election Campaign of 1835–1836," *Civil War History* 39 (March 1993): 5–30; James A. Ramage and Andrea S. Watkins, *Kentucky Rising: Democracy, Slavery, and Culture from the Early Republic to the Civil War* (Lexington: University Press of Kentucky, 2011), 115–116, 118–122.

9. MVB to William T. Barry, 12 August 1829, Pirtle and Rogers Families Papers, William C. Preston to Sarah B. Preston, 27 December 1834, Preston Family Papers–Davie Collection, FHS; William Lee Miller, *Arguing about Slavery: The Great Battle in the United States Congress* (New York: Knopf, 1996), 27–62, 206–210; Thomas Brown, "From Old Hickory to Sly Fox: The Routinization of Charisma in the Early Democratic

Party," *JER* 11 (Fall 1991): 339–370; Joseph H. Harrison Jr., "Martin Van Buren and His Southern Supporters," *JSH* 22 (November 1956): 438–458; Shade, "Martin Van Buren, Slavery, and the Election of 1836," 459–484; MVB to Junis Amis et al., 4 March 1836, in William M. Holland, *The Life and Political Opinions of Martin Van Buren, Vice-President of the United States,* 2d ed. (Hartford, Conn.: Belknap & Hamersley, 1836), 348–355; Jonathan M. Atkins, "The Presidential Candidacy of Hugh Lawson White in Tennessee, 1832–1836," *JSH* 58 (February 1992): 27–56; Atkins, *Parties, Politics, and the Sectional Conflict,* 36–54, 290; Moore, "Political Background of the Revolt against Jackson," 45–66; Powell Moore, "The Revolt against Jackson in Tennessee, 1835–1836," *JSH* 2 (August 1936): 335–359.

10. Holt, *Rise and Fall of the American Whig Party,* 38–45; Moore, "Political Background of the Revolt against Jackson," 45–66; Moore, "Revolt against Jackson in Tennessee, 1835–1836," 335–359.

11. Smith, *Magnificent Missourian,* 152, 156; Remini, *AJ,* 3:376–377; AJ to JKP, 12 May 1835, 3 August 1835, 15 September 1835, AJ to FG, 24 September 1835, 5 October 1835, in *CAJ,* 5:345–346, 357–359, 365–366, 367, 371–372.

12. AJ to John C. Calhoun, 21 December 1820, in *PAJ,* 4:409–411; Crocker, "Missouri Compromise," 49–51; Randolph B. Campbell, *An Empire for Slavery: The Peculiar Institution in Texas, 1821–1865* (Baton Rouge: Louisiana State University Press, 1989), 18–34; David M. Pletcher, *The Diplomacy of Annexation: Texas, Oregon, and the Mexican War* (Columbia: University of Missouri Press, 1973), 66–69; Gregg Cantrell, *Stephen F. Austin: Empresario of Texas* (New Haven: Yale University Press, 1999), 176, 299; John H. Schroeder, "Annexation or Independence: The Texas Issue in American Politics, 1836–1845," *Southwestern Historical Quarterly* 89 (October 1985): 140.

13. Spencer Darwin Pettis to AJ, April 1831, Spencer Darwin Pettis Papers, FHS; Elizabeth Crook, "Sam Houston and Eliza Allen: The Marriage and the Mystery," *Southwestern Historical Quarterly* 94 (July 1990): 1:36; Daniel S. Donelson to AJD, [11 June 1829], in Stanley F. Horn, ed., "An Unpublished Photograph of Sam Houston," *THQ* 3 (December 1944): 350–351; AJ to JCM, [26] April 1829, 3 May 1829, Sam Houston to AJ, 11 May 1829, 18 May 1830, Memorandum, 21 May 1829, AJ to Sam Houston, 21 June 1829, Robert Mayo to AJ, 2 December 1830, AJ to William S. Fulton, 10 December 1830, in *PAJ,* 7:183–185, 200–201, 212–214, 193, 195, 294–295, 8:267–268, 643–647, 683–834, 683–684; AJ to William S. Fulton, 10 December 1830, in *CAJ,* 4:212–214.

Historian Richard Stenberg wrote several articles insisting that Jackson and Houston had a secret agreement to foment revolution in Texas. See "Jackson, Anthony Butler, and Texas," *Southwestern Social Science Quarterly* 13 (December 1932): 264–286; "The Texas Schemes of Jackson and Houston, 1829–1836," *Southwestern Social Science Quarterly* 15 (December 1834): 229–250; "Jackson's Neches Claim, 1829–1836," *Southwestern Historical Quarterly* 39 (April 1936): 255–274; "President Jackson and Anthony Butler," *Southwest Review* 22 (Summer 1937): 391–404; "Andrew Jackson and the Erving Affidavit," *Southwestern Historical Quarterly* 41 (October 1937): 142–153. See also Haley, *Sam Houston,* 62–63.

14. AJ to MVB, 12 August 1829, 13 August 1829, 14 August 1829, [c. 15 August 1829], [c. 10 October 1829], Notes for instructions to Joel R. Poinsett, [c. 13 August 1829], AJ to Joel R. Poinsett, 27 August 1829, AJ to Anthony Wayne Butler, 10 October 1829, in *CAJ,* 7:363–364, 364–365, 365–367, 367–368, 486–487, 370–371, 393, 487–490,

498–499; Joe Gibson, "A. Butler: What a Scamp!" *Journal of the West* 11 (April 1972): 235–237; Gerald D. Saxon, "Anthony Butler: A Flawed Diplomat," *East Texas Historical Journal* 24 (1986): 3–6; John M. Belohlavek, *"Let the Eagle Soar!": The Foreign Policy of Andrew Jackson* (Lincoln: University of Nebraska Press, 1985), 215–220. This Anthony Wayne Butler was not the ward taken in by the Jacksons.

15. AJ to Anthony Wayne Butler, 14 February 1833, 30 October 1833, 27 November 1833, Anthony Wayne Butler to AJ, 28 October 1833, 6 February 1834, in *CAJ*, 5:17, 221–222, 228–230, 219–220, 244–247; Gibson, "A. Butler," 237–247; Saxon, "Anthony Butler," 6–14; Belohlavek, *"Let the Eagle Soar,"* 220–229.

16. Haley, *Sam Houston,* 109; Eugene C. Barker, "President Jackson and the Texas Revolution," *AHR* 12 (1906–07): 788–809; Eugene C. Barker, "The United States and Mexico, 1835–1837," *MVHR* 1 (June 1914): 3–30; Sarah Brown McNiell, "Andrew Jackson and Texas Affairs, 1820–1845," *ETHSP* 28 (1956): 86–101; Curtis R. Reynolds, "The Deterioration of Mexican-American Diplomatic Relations," *Journal of the West* 11 (April 1972): 213–215; Pletcher, *Diplomacy of Annexation,* 69–70; Paul D. Lack, "Slavery and the Texas Revolution," *Southwestern Historical Quarterly* 89 (October 1985): 181–202; Schroeder, "Annexation or Independence," 137–145; John Catron to AJ, 8 June 1836, in *CAJ*, 5:401–402; William E. Channing, *The Works of William E. Channing,* 6 vols. (Boston: James Munroe, 1843), 2:219.

17. Richard P. McCormick, "Was There a 'Whig Strategy' in 1836?" *JER* 4 (Spring 1984): 65–66; Curtis, *Fox at Bay,* 152–156; Cooper, *South and Politics of Slavery,* 79–86; James C. Curtis, "In the Shadow of Old Hickory: The Political Travail of Martin Van Buren," *JER* 1 (Fall 1981): 256–257; Niven, *Martin Van Buren,* 384–400; AJ to Joseph C. Guild, 24 April 1835, Stephen F. Austin to AJ, 15 April 1836, AJ to Newton Cannon, 3 August 1836, 6 August 1836, AJ to AK, 12 August 1836, 8 December 1836, AJ to Edmund P. Gaines, 4 September 1836, in *CAJ*, 5:338–341, 397–398, 415–416, 416–418, 420–421, 441, 423–424; W. H. Bullock to William S. Bodley, 10 August 1836, Bodley Family Papers, FHS.

18. Silbey, "Election of 1836," 640; Atkins, *Parties, Politics, and the Sectional Conflict,* 51–52; Shade, "'The Most Delicate and Exciting Topics,'" 479–481; Cooper, *Liberty and Slavery,* 191; AJ to Maunsel White, 2 December 1836, in *CAJ*, 5:440–441.

19. Eighth annual message, 5 December 1836, Message regarding Texas, 21 December 1836, in Richardson, *Messages and Papers,* 3:238, 265–269; Pletcher, *Diplomacy of Annexation,* 72–73; William H. Wharton and Memucan Hunt to J. Pinckney Henderson, 3 March 1837, in *Diplomatic Correspondence of the Republic of Texas,* ed. George P. Garrison, 3 vols., in *Annual Report of the American Historical Association for the Years of 1907 and 1908* (Washington, D.C.: GPO, 1908, 1911), 2:201.

20. Cole, *Presidency of Andrew Jackson,* 264–266; Benton, *Thirty Years' View,* 1:730–731.

21. Farewell address, 4 March 1837, in Richardson, *Messages and Papers,* 3:292–308.

22. Edwin A. Miles, "The Whig Party and the Menace of Caesar," *THQ* 27 (Winter 1968): 361–379.

23. Remini, *AJ,* 2:164–165; Raymond T. Diamond, "James Moore Wayne," in *The Oxford Companion to the Supreme Court of the United States,* ed. Kermit L. Hall (Oxford: Oxford University Press, 1992), 920–921; Don E. Fehrenbacher, *The Dred Scott Case: Its Significance in American Law and Politics* (Oxford: Oxford University Press, 1978);

Timothy S. Huebner, *The Southern Judicial Tradition: State Judges and Sectional Distinctiveness, 1790–1890* (Athens: University of Georgia Press, 1999), 41, 60–66; Austin Allen, *Origins of the Dred Scott Case: Jacksonian Jurisprudence and the Supreme Court, 1837–1857* (Athens: University of Georgia Press, 2006), 10–12, 69–73, 98–99, 221–222; Gerard N. Magliocca, *Andrew Jackson and the Constitution: The Rise and Fall of Generational Regimes* (Lawrence: University Press of Kansas, 2007); Austin Allen, "Jacksonian Jurisprudence and the Obscurity of Justice John Catron," *Vanderbilt Law Review* 62 (2009): 491–517.

XIX
"There Would Be Great Risk"

1. Remini, *AJ,* 3:424.

2. AJ to MVB, 30 March 1837, in *CAJ,* 5:466–468; Cheathem, *Old Hickory's Nephew,* 120–124; Remini, *AJ,* 3:448–449; AJ to NPT, 19 September 1838, in *CAJ,* 5:565–566; e-mail, Marsha Mullin to author, 12 March 2012.

3. First auditor's report, 16 March 1837, AJJr to William Noland, 4 March 1837, c. 6 March 1837, 6 March 1837, [?] August 1837, 1 December 1837, JSR; National Park Service, "Administrative History: The White House and President's Park, Washington, D.C., 1791–1983, Epilogue, 1983–1997" (Washington, D.C.: Department of the Interior, 2001), 65; WBL to AJJr, 26 October 1837, JLC.

4. Editorial note, *CAJ,* 6:48; AJ to AJJr, 27 September 1835, 1 March 1836, Agreement for land purchase, 20 November 1838, in *CAJ,* 5:370, 388–389, 571; AJ to AJJr, 1 October 1835, JCM to AJJr, 7 July 1837, JLC; Jean-Marc Serme, "Stormy Weather at Andrew Jackson's Halcyon Plantation, in Coahoma County, Mississippi, 1838–1845," *Revue Française d'Études Américaines* 98 (September 2003): 34.

5. Peter Temin, *The Jacksonian Economy* (New York: Norton, 1969), 15–23; Peter L. Rousseau, "Jacksonian Monetary Policy, Specie Flows, and the Panic of 1837," *Journal of Economic History* 62 (June 2002): 457–488; Larson, *Market Revolution,* 92–97; Atkins, *Parties, Politics, and the Sectional Conflict,* 57–63, 88–97; Christopher J. Olsen, *Political Culture and Secession in Mississippi: Masculinity, Honor, and the Antiparty Tradition, 1830–1860* (Oxford: Oxford University Press, 2000), 34–37; Harold D. Woodman, *King Cotton and His Retainers: Financing and Marketing the Cotton Crop of the South, 1800–1925* (1968; repr., Columbia: University of South Carolina Press, 1990), 108; Serme, "Stormy Weather," 33–44; AJ to FPB, 23 April 1842, 29 August 1844, JSR; AJ to AJJr, 1 March 1836, James M. Parker to AJ, 21 July 1844, Memorandum, 20 August 1844, JLC; AJ to AJH, 7 September 1840, James M. Parker to AJ, 21 February 1841, 2 August 1844, James Howerton to AJ, 5 April 1841, James M. Parker to AJ and AJJr, 2 May 1841, AJ to FPB, 29 November 1844, in *CAJ,* 5:388–389, 6:74–75, 91–92, 308–309, 99–102, 108–109, 331–333.

6. James Howerton to Philip Howerton, 18 November 1839, James Howerton to Thomas Howerton, 15 December 1839, in J. D. Howerton, comp., "The Howerton Family as It Relates to Thomas Jefferson Howerton, His Ancestors and Descendants" (n.p., 1935), 12–13, 14–15, 49–51, LHA; AJ to AJH, 3 August 1840, James M. Parker to AJ, 21 February 1841, James Howerton to AJ, 5 April 1841, William J. Howerton to AJJr, 19 July 1841, in *CAJ,* 6:69–70, 91–92, 99–102, 116–117; James Howerton to AJJr, 21 Octo-

ber 1840, Memorandum, 3 November 1840–c. 8 March 1841, JLC.

7. DeWitt, "Andrew Jackson Hutchings," 103; AJ to AJH, 7 September 1840, 11 September 1840, James M. Parker to AJ, 21 February 1841, 2 August 1844, James Howerton to AJ, 5 April 1841, James M. Parker to AJ and AJJr, 2 May 1841, AJ to FPB, 3 February 1842, 9 October 1843, 29 November 1844, 3 March 1845, AJ to James M. Parker, 11 May 1844, in *CAJ,* 6:74–75, 77, 91–92, 308–309, 99–102, 108–109, 137–139, 233–234, 331–333, 376–377, 288–289; AJ to FPB, 7 September and 31 October 1843, 14 December 1844, JSR; James M. Parker to AJ, 21 July 1844, Memorandum, 20 August 1844, JLC.

8. AJ to AJJr, 3 January 1840, JSR; AJ to SYJ, 4 January 1840, AJ to FPB, 3 March 1845, in *CAJ,* 6:47, 376–377.

9. AJ to AJH, 11 September 1840, in *CAJ,* 6:77. Information on the court cases can be found in JLC, reel 51; and JSR, reels 34, 35, and 37.

10. Alcée Fortier, *A History of Louisiana,* 4 vols. (New York: Manzi, Joyant, 1904), 3:xi, 106; Jean Baptiste Plauché to AJ, 1 June 1841, Jean Baptiste Plauché and Company to AJ, 19 February 1843, in *CAJ,* 6:115–116, 210–211.

11. FPB to AJ, 18–23 January 1842, 21 February 1845, AJ to FPB, 3 February 1842, 24 February 1842, 29 March 1842, 3 March 1845, AJ to WBL, 3 March 1845, John C. Rives to AJ, 12 March 1845, in *CAJ,* 6:135–136, 370, 137–139, 140–141, 148–149, 376–377, 377–378, 379–380; AJ to FPB, 12 April 1843, JLC; AJ to FPB, 11 August 1843, 15 December 1843, 29 February 1844, 21 December 1844, FPB to AJ, 22 December 1844, FPB and John C. Rives to AJ, 11 May 1843, 12 March 1845, JSR.

12. Henry P. Dart, ed., "Andrew Jackson and Judge D. A. Hall," *Louisiana Historical Quarterly* 5 (October 1992): 509–570; Warshauer, *Politics of Martial Law,* 77–175; AJ and FPB correspondence, 1842–1844, JLC and JSR.

Warshauer downplays the personal financial crisis that Jackson faced, emphasizing instead his desire to repair his reputation and to reinforce the necessity of martial law in certain crises (*Politics of Martial Law,* 77–78).

13. AJ to AJJr, 31 December 1839, 28 September 1840, AJ to Fielding Davis, 13 May 1841, Deed of gift, 17 May 1843, AJ to AJD, 15 October 1843, in *CAJ,* 6:46–47, 79, 111, 111–112n, 219–220, 234; AJ to FPB, 23 April 1842, FPB to AJ, 3 May 1842, JSR.

14. Bills of sale, 1837–1845, Slave genealogy database, Hermitage Slave Files, LHA; *Sixth Census of the United States: 1840* (Washington, D.C.: GPO, 1841); Joel Tanner Hart to John Hart, 7 January 1839, Joel Tanner Hart Papers, FHS; AJ to FPB, 3 February 1842, in *CAJ,* 6:137–139; Walker, "Andrew Jackson: Planter," 30.

See also Sandra G. Craighead, "Genealogical History of the Slaves of President Andrew Jackson of Hermitage, Tennessee (1840–1877)," www.tngenweb.org/tncolor/ajack .htm, accessed 18 July 2007. Craighead incorrectly locates Halcyon in Holmes County, Mississippi. In the 1850 census Junior owned 137 slaves in Tennessee (*Seventh Census of the United States: 1850, Slave Inhabitants* [Washington, D.C.: GPO, 1853]).

15. Robert M. Burton to AJ, 1 February 1835, JLC; AJ to WBL, 23 January 1838, JSR; AJ to AJH, 3 August 1840, 12 August 1840, 7 September 1840, in *CAJ,* 6:69–70, 70–71, 74–75.

16. AJ to John A. Shute, 3 January 1839, AJ to JKP, 11 February 1839, AJ to AJH, 18 March 1839, 20 May 1839, in *CAJ,* 6:1–2, 4–5, 7, 13–14; AJ to AJH, 5 March 1839, JSR; Warshauer, "Chivalric Slave Master," 203, 216–218; Jeff Forret, "Conflict and the 'Slave

Community': Violence among Slaves in Upcountry South Carolina," *JSH* 74 (August 2008): 562; Rebecca Fraser, "Negotiating Their Manhood: Masculinity amongst the Enslaved in the Upper South, 1830–1861," in *Black and White Masculinity in the American South, 1800–2000,* ed. Lydia Plath and Sergio Lussana (Newcastle upon Tyne: Cambridge Scholars Publishing, 2009), 76–94; Sergio Lussana, "To See Who Was Best on the Plantation: Enslaved Fighting Contests and Masculinity in the Antebellum Plantation South," *JSH* 76 (November 2010): 901–922.

17. AJ to JKP, 11 February 1839, AJ to AJH, 18 March 1839, 20 May 1839, AJ to WBL, 30 September 1841, in *CAJ,* 6:4–5, 7, 13–14, 124–126; AJ to FG, 20 February 1839, AJ to AJH, 5 March 1839, JSR.

18. AJ to William Donelson and Stockley Donelson, 28 February 1839, Stockley Donelson to AJ, 5 March 1839, 9 March 1839, 14 July [1840], Agreement, 7 October 1844, *AJJr and Sarah Ward vs. Stockley Donelson,* 30 May 1845, *Stockley Donelson vs. Andrew Jackson Sr. and Jr.,* September 1845, JSR; Stockley Donelson to AJ, [n.d.], 2 March 1839, 24 August 1843, 22 August 1844, AJ to Stockley Donelson, 28 August 1843, JLC; AJ to ETD, 28 November 1830, in *PAJ,* 8:638–640; JCM to AJD, 20 December 1834, DLC; AJ to AJH, 5 August 1837, 20 May 1839, in *CAJ,* 5:502–503, 6:13–14; AJ to JKP, 6 August 1837, in *CJKP,* 4:199–201.

19. Eugene Genovese and Elizabeth Fox-Genovese, *Fatal Self-Deception: Slaveholding Paternalism in the Old South* (Cambridge: Cambridge University Press, 2011), 25–30; Johnson, "Planters and Patriarchy," 69–72; Forret, "Violence among Slaves," 568–570, 576–581, 582–583, 586–588; Bertram Wyatt-Brown, "The Mask of Obedience: Male Slave Psychology in the Old South," *AHR* 93 (December 1988): 1228–1252; AJ to John A. Shute, 3 January 1839, in *CAJ,* 6:1–2.

XX
"Texas Must, & Will Be Ours"

1. J. C. Beatty to Adam Beatty, 29 June 1837, Beatty-Quisenberry Family Papers, Henry Clay to Seth Wheatley, 18 August 1837, Henry Clay Correspondence, FHS.

2. Norma Lois Peterson, *The Presidencies of William Henry Harrison and John Tyler* (Lawrence: University Press of Kansas, 1989), 29; Broadside, 1840, Martin Van Buren, FHS; AJ to MVB, 31 July 1840, 12 November 1840, 24 November 1840, in *CAJ,* 6:68–69, 82–83, 83–84; Gail Collins, *William Henry Harrison* (New York: Times Books, 2012), 119–124.

3. Robert V. Remini, *John Quincy Adams* (New York: Times Books, 2002), 132; Parsons, *John Quincy Adams,* 224–229, 247–250; Miller, *Arguing about Slavery,* 387–395, 409–422; FPB to AJ, 26 April 1839, 30 November 1844, 19 January 1845, AJ to FPB, 24 October 1844, 29 November 1844, in *CAJ,* 6:10–11, 333–334, 365–366, 325–327, 331–333; AJ to WBL, 17 January 1843, 22 March 1844, JSR.

4. AJ to NPT, 6 February 1838, in *CAJ,* 5:536–537; Catharine Beecher, *An Essay on Slavery and Abolitionism, with Reference to the Duty of American Females* (Philadelphia: Perkins & Marvin, 1837), 53–54, 104–105; Kathryn Kish Sklar, *Catharine Beecher: A Study in American Domesticity* (New York: Norton, 1976), 237–238.

5. Alice Felt Tyler, *Freedom's Ferment: Phases of American Social History from the Colonial Period to the Outbreak of the Civil War* (New York: Harper & Row, 1962), 206–211; Mary P. Ryan, *Women in Public: Between Banners and Ballots, 1825–1880* (Baltimore: Johns Hopkins University Press, 1990), 134–135; Ronald G. Walters, *American Reformers, 1815–1860*, rev. ed. (New York: Hill & Wang, 1997), 74–75; AJ to Moses Dawson, 23 January 1844, in "The Jackson-Dawson Correspondence," ed. John J. Whealen, *Bulletin of the Historical and Philosophical Society of Ohio* 16 (January 1958): 28–29; Virginius C. Hall, "Moses Dawson, Chronic Belligerent," *Bulletin of the Historical and Philosophical Society of Ohio* 15 (July 1957): 189.

6. Major L. Wilson, *The Presidency of Martin Van Buren* (Lawrence: University Press of Kansas, 1984), 149–153; AJ to MVB, 23 January 1838, AJ to John Forsyth, 23 January 1838, 6 March 1838, AJ to William S. Fulton, 23 January 1838, William S. Fulton to John Forsyth, 13 February 1838, William S. Fulton to AJ, 10 July 1838, AJ to FPB, 19 July 1838, 9 August 1838, 14 August 1838, AJ to John Quincy Adams, 21 July 1838, FPB to AJ, 30 July 1838, 19 October 1838, AJ to Benjamin C. Howard, 2 August 1838, in *CAJ*, 5:529–530, 530–531, 540, 531–533, 540–541, 556–557, 557–558, 562–563, 563–564, 558–559, 559–560, 567–568, 560–561; AJ to William S. Fulton, 15 February 1839, Andrew Jackson, Presidential Papers, FHS; Leo Hershkowitz, "'The Land of Promise': Samuel Swartwout and Land Speculation in Texas, 1830–1838," *New York Historical Society Quarterly* 48 (October 1964): 307–325; FG to AJ, 13 November 1838, AJ to WBL, 10 December 1838, AJ to FPB, 23 December 1838, in *CAJ*, 5:569–570, 573–574, 575–576; *Niles' National Register,* 29 December 1838.

7. Schroeder, "Annexation or Independence," 148–154; David E. Narrett, "A Choice of Destiny: Immigration Policy, Slavery, and the Annexation of Texas," *Southwestern Historical Quarterly* 100 (January 1997): 288–292; Pletcher, *Diplomacy of Annexation,* 113–134; Cooper, *South and Politics of Slavery,* 184–188; Eugene C. Barker, "The Annexation of Texas," *Southwestern Historical Quarterly* 50 (July 1946): 63–64; Department of State circular, 29 February 1844, in Richardson, *Messages and Papers,* 4:333.

8. AJ to WBL, 22 March 1844, JSR; AJ to Aaron V. Brown, [12] April 1843, in *CAJ*, 6:201–202; Elbert B. Smith, *Francis Preston Blair* (New York: Free Press, 1980), 152. As noted in the footnote accompanying this letter in *CAJ*, the published version was edited into a more polished and detailed call for annexation. See *Niles' National Register,* 30 March 1844, 70, for this version.

9. Lelia M. Roeckell, "Bonds over Bondage: British Opposition to the Annexation of Texas," *JER* 19 (Summer 1999): 257–278; Edward B. Rugemer, "Robert Monroe Harrison, British Abolition, Southern Anglophobia, and Texas Annexation," *Slavery & Abolition* 28 (August 2007): 169–191; Edward B. Rugemer, "The Southern Response to British Abolitionism: The Maturation of Proslavery Apologetics," *JSH* 70 (May 2004): 221–248; Sam Haynes, *Unfinished Revolution: The Early American Republic in a British World* (Charlottesville: University of Virginian Press, 2010), 1–23; Sam Haynes, "Anglophobia and the Annexation of Texas: The Quest for National Security," in *Manifest Destiny and Empire: American Antebellum Expansion,* ed. Sam W. Haynes and Christopher Morris (College Station: Texas A&M University Press, 1997), 115–145; Kinley J. Brauer, "The United States and British Imperial Expansion, 1815–1860," *Diplomatic History* 12 (Winter 1988): 19–37; Thomas R. Hietala, *Manifest Design: Anxious Aggrandizement in*

Late Jacksonian America (Ithaca: Cornell University Press, 1985), 144–145; Lawrence A. Peskin, "Conspiratorial Anglophobia and the War of 1812," *JAH* 98 (December 2011): 668–669; D. McNaughtan to John Brunton, 24 March 1840, D. McNaughtan Papers, FHS; AJ to John Y. Mason, 5 March 1844, no. 03318, GLC.

10. Peterson, *Presidencies of Harrison and Tyler*, 201–203; Schroeder, "Annexation or Independence," 148–154; Narrett, "Choice of Destiny," 288–292; Pletcher, *Diplomacy of Annexation*, 134–138; Niven, *John C. Calhoun*, 270–274; AJ to WBL, 22 March 1844, JSR.

11. Niven, *John C. Calhoun*, 275–277; John C. Calhoun to Richard Pakenham, 18 April 1844, in *PJCC*, 18:273–278; Schroeder, "Annexation or Independence," 156; Pletcher, *Diplomacy of Annexation*, 147–149; AJ to FPB, 11 May 1844, FPB to AJ, 7 July 1844, in *CAJ*, 6:285–287, 299–302.

12. Remini, *Henry Clay*, 628–641; Heidler and Heidler, *Henry Clay*, 386–387; Niven, *Martin Van Buren*, 523–529; MVB to W. H. Hammet, 20 April 1844, in Charles G. Sellers Jr., "Election of 1844," in Schlesinger and Israel, *History of American Presidential Elections*, 1:822–828.

13. AJ to Benjamin F. Butler, 29 April 1844, no. 04915, GLC; AJ to FPB, 7 May 1844, 11 May 1844, JSR; AJ to FPB, 11 May 1844, 18 May 1844, AJ to editors of the *Nashville Union*, 13 May 1844, in *CAJ*, 6:285–287, 293–294, 289–291; JKP to Cave Johnson, 13 May 1844, 14 May 1844, in *CJKP*, 7:134–136, 136–138.

14. Cheathem, *Old Hickory's Nephew*, 161–164; AJ to Morven M. Jones, 25 June 1844, no. 01166, GLC.

15. AJ to William Russell, 8 July 1844, no. 04365, GLC; AJ to FPB, 7 June 1844, 25 June 1844, 12 July 1844, AJ to WBL, 26 July 1844, 27 September 1844, JSR; AJ to JKP, 29 June 1844, in *CJKP*, 7:299–300; Edward J. Crapol, *John Tyler: The Accidental President* (Chapel Hill: University of North Carolina Press, 2006), 218–219; AJ to WBL, 1 August 1844, in *CAJ*, 6:306–308.

16. Paul H. Bergeron, *The Presidency of James K. Polk* (Lawrence: University Press of Kansas, 1987), 19–20; AJ to AJD, 18 November 1844, in *CAJ*, 6:329–330; Reinhard O. Johnson, *The Liberty Party, 1840–1848: Antislavery Third-Party Politics in the United States* (Baton Rouge: Louisiana State University Press, 2009), 34–49; AJ to Thomas F. Marshall, 21 November 1844, in Bullitt Family Papers–Oxmoor Collection, Thomas F. Marshall Correspondence, 1817–1860, f. 563, FHS; Luke 2:25–26 (King James Version).

17. Cheathem, *Old Hickory's Nephew*, 125–139, 151–169; John Tyler to AJ, 17 September 1844, in *CAJ*, 6:318–320.

18. Gadsden to AJ, 1 August 1844, in St. George L. Sioussat, ed., "Selected Letters, 1844–1845, from the Donelson Papers," *THM* 3 (1917): 1844–45," 139–140; AJ to AJD, 2 December 1844, 11 December 1844, 28 December 1844, in *CAJ*, 6:334–336, 338–339, 349–350.

19. Peterson, *Presidencies of Harrison and Tyler*, 255–259; Pletcher, *Diplomacy of Annexation*, 180–182; Joel H. Silbey, *Storm over Texas: The Annexation Controversy and the Road to the Civil War* (Oxford: Oxford University Press, 2005), 3–5, 80–88; Bergeron, *Presidency of James K. Polk*, 54–55; AJ to FPB, 10 March 1845, in *CAJ*, 6:378–379.

20. Thomas J. Alsbury to AJ, 24 April 1839, H. G. Catlett to AJ, [4 November] 1839, John Claiborne to AJ, 9 December 1841, JLC; SH to Daniel D. Culp, 10 February 1843, in Williams and Barker, *Writings of Sam Houston*, 3:316; Thomas J. Alsbury to SH, 25

June 1843, Memorandum, n.d., Nelson Gresham Library, Sam Houston State University; SH to AJ, 16 February 1844, AJ to AJD, 18 November 1844, AJD to AJ, 24 December 1844, in *CAJ,* 6:260–264, 329–330, 348–349; SH to AJ, 24 July 1843, 17 February 1844, AJ to WBL, 22 March 1844, Affidavits, [c. May 1844], JSR; AJ to AJD, 12 March 1845, DLC; Lester G. Bugbee, "The Old Three Hundred: A List of the Settlers of Austin's First Colony," *Quarterly of the Texas State Historical Association* 1 (July 1897–April 1898): 108–117.

21. Smith, *Francis Preston Blair,* 150–168; Sellers, *James K. Polk,* 2:167, 272–278; AJ to JKP, 13 December 1844, 28 February 1845, 17 March 1845, 7 April 1845, 11 April 1845, in *CJKP,* 8:425–426, 9:148–149, 197–199, 263–264, 278–279; JKP to AJ, 26 March 1845, AJ to FPB, 26 May 1845, in *CAJ,* 6:389–390, 410–411.

22. AJ to FPB, 26 May 1845, in *CAJ,* 6:410–411.

CONCLUSION

1. Robert V. Remini, "The Final Days and Hours in the Life of General Andrew Jackson," *THQ* 39 (Summer 1980): 167–177; Gardner, "Gentleman from Tennessee," 405–411; Ludwig M. Deppisch, "Andrew Jackson and American Medical Practice: Old Hickory and His Physicians," *THQ* 62 (Summer 2003): 131, 139.

2. AJJr to Isaac Hill, 23 April 1845, AJJr to [William P. Hill], 4 June 1845, JSR; AJJr to A.O.P. Nicholson, 17 June 1845, in Joseph H. Parks, ed., "Letter Describes Andrew Jackson's Last Hours," *THQ* 6 (June 1947): 176–178; AJ to JKP, 6 June 1845, in *CJKP,* 9:432–433; ERD to AJD, 9 June 1845, LHA; Deppisch, "Old Hickory and His Physicians," 145–147.

3. AJD to ERD, 20 May 1845, DLC; ERD to AJD, 9 June 1845, LHA. Elizabeth's memory of her uncle's death was recorded on the back of her husband's May letter.

4. "'Old Hannah's Narrative' of Jackson's Last Days," [c. 1880], in *CAJ,* 6:415–416; Hannah, qtd. in "Reminiscences of the Hermitage," *Cincinnati Commercial,* 22 June 1880.

5. *Cincinnati Gazette,* [June 1845], LHA; *Nashville Union,* 12 June 1845; J. F. Schermerhorn to AJ, 27 October 1837, J. F. Schermerhorn Papers, FHS; Henry G. Rhodes, "REV. W. M. NORMENT. A Minister Sixty-Seven Years. Pastor of the Same Church since 1858," *Cumberland Presbyterian,* 26 February 1920, 9, www.cumberland.org/hfcpc/minister/NormentWilliamMenefee.htm, accessed 15 April 2012.

6. *Nashville Republican Banner,* 11 June 1845; *Nashville Whig,* 12 June 1845; James Pearce to Mrs. William S. Bodley, 11 June 1845, Bodley Family Papers; "Reminiscence of June 1845: Jacob's Wood, Louisville; Sham Funeral of Andrew Jackson; Also, An Account of the Combat between the Kearsarge and the Alabama, June 19, 1864," 19 December 1917, "Recollection of Jacob's Woods and the Sham Funeral of Andrew Jackson in Louisville," paper read to the Filson Club, 6 February 1922, Alfred Pirtle Papers, FHS.

7. Linda Bennett Galloway, "Andrew Jackson, Jr. [Part 2]," *THQ* 9 (December 1950): 327–337; Serme, "Stormy Weather," 43.

8. For masculinity in South Carolina, see Johnson, "Planters and Patriarchy"; for Mississippi, see Christopher J. Olsen, *Political Culture and Secession in Mississippi: Masculinity, Honor, and the Antiparty Tradition, 1830–1860* (Oxford: Oxford University Press, 2000).

9. Notice, [12 May 1855], LHA; *New York Times,* 24 September 1882; *Commercial Appeal* (Memphis, Tenn.), 3 June 1895. According to Marsha Mullin, the 1855 auction of the slaves did not take place. Correspondence with the author, 30 January 2012.

10. John Blassingame, *Slave Testimony: Two Centuries of Letters, Speeches, Interviews, and Autobiographies* (Baton Rouge: Louisiana State University Press, 1977), xxxii, lviii–lxii, 447–449; Leon Litwack, *Been in the Storm So Long: The Aftermath of Slavery* (New York: Knopf, 1979), 149–163; Litwack, *Trouble in Mind: Black Southerners in the Age of Jim Crow* (New York: Knopf, 1998), 184–196; David W. Blight, *Race and Reunion: The Civil War in American Memory* (Cambridge: Belknap Press of Harvard University Press, 2001), 286–288, 313–319; Fay A. Yarbrough, "Power, Perception, and Interracial Sex: Former Slaves Recall a Multiracial South," *JSH* 71 (August 2005): 559–588; Leslie A. Schwalm, "'Agonizing Groans of Mothers' and 'Slave-Scarred Veterans': The Commemoration of Slavery and Emancipation," *American Nineteenth Century History* 9 (September 2008): 289–304.

11. Crawford, "Patriot Slaveholder," 10–32; *New York Times,* 23 October 1860, 3 December 1860, 16 January 1861.

BIBLIOGRAPHY

PRIMARY SOURCES
Manuscript Collections

Filson Historical Society (Louisville, Ky.)
William T. Barry Papers
Beall-Booth Family Papers
Beatty-Quisenberry Family Papers
Bodley Family Papers
Brown-Ewell Family Papers
Buckner Family Papers
Bullitt Family Papers–Oxmoor Collection
Sol. Clark (?) Papers
Henry Clay Correspondence
Clay, Green Papers
Corliss-Respess Family Papers
John Henry Eaton Papers
Foote Family Papers
Joel Tanner Hart Papers
Andrew Jackson Papers
Philip Kearney Papers
Marshall Family Papers
D. McNaughtan Papers
Spencer Darwin Pettis Papers
Alfred Pirtle Papers
Pirtle and Rogers Families Papers
Presidential Papers–Andrew Jackson
Preston Family Papers–Davie Collection
Edmund Rogers Papers
Rogers-Woodson Family Papers
J. F. Schermerhorn Papers
Isaac Shelby-Jacobs Collection
Martin Van Buren

Yandell Family Papers
Ladies' Hermitage Association (Hermitage, Tenn.)

Jackson-Donelson Family Papers
Slave Genealogy Database

Library of Congress (Washington, D.C.)
American Colonization Society Papers
Andrew Jackson Donelson Papers
Andrew Jackson Papers
Nicholas P. Trist Papers
Martin Van Buren Papers
Martin Van Buren Papers, Chadwyck-Healey Collection

Milwaukee County Historical Society (Milwaukee, Wisc.)
Arthur Holbrook Collection

Scholarly Resources (Wilmington, Del.)
Andrew Jackson Papers

Tennessee State Library and Archives (Nashville)
Claybrooke and Overton Papers
Davidson County, Tennessee, Wills and Inventories
Bettie M. Donelson Papers
Robert Dyas Collection
Hurja Collection

University of Tennessee at Knoxville
Andrew Jackson Donelson Papers
Tennessee Documentary History

Newspapers

Argus of Western America (Frankfort, Ky.)
Commercial (Cincinnati, Ohio)
Daily National Journal (Washington, D.C.)
Enquirer (Richmond, Va.)
Gazette (Cincinnati)
Genius of Universal Emancipation (Mt. Pleasant, Ohio)
Globe (Washington, D.C.)
Mercury (Charleston, S.C.)
National Banner and Nashville Whig (Nashville)
National Intelligencer (Washington, D.C.)
New-Hampshire Statesman & Concord Register (Concord, N.H.)
New York Times
Niles' National Register (Washington, D.C.)

Niles' Weekly Register (Washington, D.C.)
Portsmouth New-Hampshire Gazette (Portsmouth, N.H.)
Raleigh Star and North Carolina Gazette (Raleigh, N.C.)
Register (Raleigh, N.C.)
Republican (Nashville)
Republican and State Gazette (Nashville)
Republican Banner (Nashville)
Truth's Advocate and Monthly Anti-Jackson Expositor (Cincinnati)
Union (Nashville)
United States' Telegraph (Washington, D.C.)
Whig (Nashville)

Government Documents

Department of the Interior. Washington, D.C.
National Park Service. "Administrative History: The White House and President's Park, Washington, D.C., 1791–1983, Epilogue, 1983–1997." Washington, D.C.: Department of the Interior, 2001.

Library of Congress. Washington, D.C.
American State Papers. Foreign Relations, 17th Cong., 1st sess.
———. Indian Affairs, House, 17th Cong., 2d sess.
———. Indian Affairs, Senate, 13th Cong., 3d sess.
———. Military Affairs, 14th Cong., 1st sess.
———. Military Affairs, 15th Cong., 2d sess.
Annals of Congress. House of Representatives. 4th Cong., 2d sess.
———. 15th Cong., 2d sess.
Register of Debates. Vol. 6. 1830.
———. 22d Cong., 1st sess.
———. 23d Cong., 1st sess.
U.S. Serial Set. No. 4015. 56th Cong., 1st sess.

United States Census Office. Washington, D.C.
Fourth Census of the United States: 1820. Washington, D.C.: GPO, 1821.
Sixth Census of the United States: 1840. Washington, D.C.: GPO, 1841.
Seventh Census of the United States: 1850. Slave Inhabitants. Washington, D.C.: GPO, 1853.

Published Correspondence, Memoirs, and Diaries

A Letter from the Jackson Committee of Nashville, in Answer to One from a Similar Committee at Cincinnati, upon the Subject of Gen. Jackson's Marriage: Accompanied by Documents in an Appendix, Thereto Annexed. Nashville: Hall &

Fitzgerald, 1827. Reprinted in Major L. Wilson, ed., *Mississippi Valley Collection Bulletin* 1 (Summer 1968).

Address of the Fayette County Correspondence Committee . . . Supplement to the Kentucky Reporter. Lexington, Ky.: Thomas Smith, 1828.

Basler, Roy P., ed. *Abraham Lincoln: His Speeches and Writings.* Cleveland: World Publishing, 1946.

Bassett, John Spencer, ed. "William B. Lewis on the Nomination of Andrew Jackson." *Proceedings of the American Antiquarian Society* 33 (April 1923): 12–33.

Bassett, John Spencer, and J. Franklin Jameson, eds. *Correspondence of Andrew Jackson.* 7 vols. Washington, D.C.: Carnegie Institute of Washington, 1926–1935.

Beecher, Catharine. *An Essay on Slavery and Abolitionism, with Reference to the Duty of American Females.* Philadelphia: Perkins & Marvin, 1837.

Belz, Herman, ed. *The Webster-Hayne Debate on the Nature of the Union.* Indianapolis: Liberty Fund, 2000.

Benton, Thomas Hart. *Abridgement of the Debates of Congress, from 1789 to 1856.* 16 vols. New York: D. Appleton, 1857–1861.

——. *Thirty Year's View, or, A History of the Workings of the American Government for Thirty Years, from 1820 to 1850.* 2 vols. New York: D. Appleton, 1857.

Breathitt, John. *Circular to the People of Kentucky,* 26 June 1828. N.p.: S. Penn Jr., 1828.

Calhoun, John C. *Correspondence between Gen. Andrew Jackson and John C. Calhoun, President and Vice-President of the U. States, on the Subject of the Course of the Latter, in the Deliberation of the Cabinet of Mr. Monroe, on the Occurrences in the Seminole War.* Washington, D.C.: Duff Green, 1831.

Channing, William E. *The Works of William E. Channing.* 6 vols. Boston: James Munroe, 1843.

Cooke, Jacob E., ed. *The Federalist.* Middletown, Conn.: Wesleyan University Press, 1961.

Crallé, Richard K., ed. *The Works of John C. Calhoun.* 6 vols. New York: D. Appleton, 1851–1856.

Crist, Lynda L., et al., eds. *The Papers of Jefferson Davis.* 12 vols. to date. Baton Rouge: Louisiana State University Press, 1971–.

Cutler, Wayne, et al., eds. *Correspondence of James K. Polk.* 11 vols. to date. Knoxville: University of Tennessee Press, 1969–.

Dart, Henry P., ed. "Andrew Jackson and Judge D. A. Hall." *Louisiana Historical Quarterly* 5 (October 1922): 509–570.

Eaton, Margaret. *The Autobiography of Peggy Eaton.* New York: Scribner, 1932.

Ely, James W., Jr., and Theodore Brown Jr., eds. *Legal Papers of Andrew Jackson.* Knoxville: University of Tennessee Press, 1987.

[Erwin, Andrew]. *Gen. Jackson's Negro Speculations, and His Traffic in Human Flesh, Examined and Established by Positive Proof.* N.p.p., 1828.

———. *A Brief Account of General Jackson's Dealings in Negroes, in a Series of Letters and Documents by His Own Neighbors.* N.p.p., 1828.

Feller, Daniel, et al., eds. *The Papers of Andrew Jackson.* 8 vols. to date. Knoxville: University of Tennessee Press, 1980–.

Fitzpatrick, John C., ed. *The Autobiography of Martin Van Buren. In Annual Report of the American Historical Association for the Year 1918.* Vol. 2. Washington, D.C.: GPO, 1920.

Freehling, William W., ed. *The Nullification Era: A Documentary Record.* New York: Harper & Row, 1967.

Garrison, George P., ed. *Diplomatic Correspondence of the Republic of Texas. 3 vols. In Annual Report of the American Historical Association for the Years of 1907 and 1908.* Washington, D.C.: GPO, 1908, 1911.

Gatell, Frank Otto, ed. "Postmaster Huger and the Incendiary Publications." *South Carolina Historical Magazine* 64 (October 1963): 193–201.

Greeley, Horace. *The American Conflict: A History of the Great Rebellion in the United States of America, 1860–'64: Its Causes, Incidents, and Results: Intended to Exhibit Especially Its Moral and Political Phases, with the Drift and Progress of American Opinion Respecting Human Slavery from 1776 to the Close of the War for the Union.* 2 vols. Hartford, Conn.: O. D. Case, 1864.

Greenberg, Kenneth S., ed. *The Confessions of Nat Turner and Related Documents.* Boston: Bedford/St. Martin's, 1996.

Hamilton, James A. *Reminiscences of James A. Hamilton; Or, Men and Events, at Home and Abroad, during Three Quarters of a Century.* New York: Scribner, 1869.

Holland, William M. *The Life and Political Opinions of Martin Van Buren, Vice-President of the United States,* 2d ed. Hartford, Conn.: Belknap & Hamersley, 1836.

Hooker, Richard J., ed. *The Carolina Backcountry on the Eve of the Revolution: The Journal and Other Writings of Charles Woodmason, Anglican Itinerant.* Chapel Hill: University of North Carolina Press, 1953.

Horn, Stanley F., ed. "An Unpublished Photograph of Sam Houston." *THQ* 3 (December 1944): 348–351.

Howerton, J. D., comp. "The Howerton Family as It Relates to Thomas Jefferson Howerton, His Ancestors and Descendants." N.p.p., 1935.

Kendall, Amos. *Autobiography of Amos Kendall.* Boston: Lee & Shepard, 1872.

Latour, Arsène Lacarrière. *Historical Memoir of the War in West Florida and Louisiana in 1814–15, with an Atlas, Expanded Edition.* Ed. Gene Allen Smith. Gainesville: Historic New Orleans Collection and University Press of Florida, 1999.

Lee, Henry. *A Biography of Andrew Jackson, Late Major-General of the Army of the United States.* Ed. Mark A. Mastromarino. Knoxville: Tennessee Presidents Trust, 1992.

"Letters from Jackson, Clay, and Johnson." *American Historical Magazine* 5 (April 1900): 132–144.

Moulton, Gary E., ed. *The Papers of Chief John Ross.* 2 vols. Norman: University of Oklahoma Press, 1985.

Parks, Joseph, ed. "Letter Describes Andrew Jackson's Last Hours." *THQ* 6 (June 1947): 176–178.

Perdue, Theda, and Michael D. Green, eds. *The Cherokee Removal: A Brief History in Documents,* 2d ed. Boston: Bedford/St. Martin's, 2005.

Reid, John, and John Henry Eaton. *The Life of Andrew Jackson.* Ed. Frank L. Owsley Jr. Tuscaloosa: University of Alabama Press, 1974.

Richardson, James D., ed. *The Messages and Papers of the Presidents, 1789–1897.* 10 vols. Washington, D.C.: GPO, 1896–1899.

Scott, Nancy N. *Memoir of Hugh Lawson White.* Philadelphia: J. B. Lippincott, 1856.

Seager, Robert, II, et al., eds. *The Papers of Henry Clay.* 11 vols. Lexington: University Press of Kentucky, 1959–1992.

Sioussat, St. George L., ed. "Selected Letters, 1844–1845, from the Donelson Papers." *THM* 3 (1917): 134–162.

Smith, Margaret Bayard. *The First Forty Years of Washington Society.* Ed. Gaillard Hunt. New York: Scribner, 1906.

Speeches on the Passage of the Bill for the Removal of the Indians, Delivered in the Congress of the United States, April and May, 1830. Boston: Perkins & Marvin, 1830.

Taylor, George Rogers, ed. *Jackson versus Biddle: The Struggle over the Second Bank of the United States.* Boston: D. C. Heath, 1949.

Turnbull, Robert J. *An Oration, Delivered in the City of Charleston, before the State Rights & Free Trade Party, the State Society of Cincinnati, the Revolution Society, the '76 Association, the Young Men's Free Trade Association, and Several Volunteer Companies of Militia on the 4th of July, 1832, Being the 56th Anniversary of American Independence.* Charleston: A. E. Miller, 1832.

Turner, Frederick Jackson, ed. "Documents on the Blount Conspiracy, 1793–1797." *AHR* 10 (April 1905): 574–606.

Wallace, Sarah Agnes, ed. "Opening Days of Jackson's Presidency as Seen in Private Letters." *THQ* 9 (December 1950): 367–371.

Webster, Daniel. *Works of Daniel Webster.* Boston: Little, Brown, 1857.

Whealen, John J., ed. "The Jackson-Dawson Correspondence." *Bulletin of the Historical and Philosophical Society of Ohio* 16 (January 1958): 3–30.

Whitley, Edythe Rucker. *Marriages of Sumner County, Tennessee, 1787–1838.* Baltimore: Genealogical Publishing, 1981.

Williams, Amelia W., and Eugene C. Barker, eds. *The Writings of Sam Houston.* 8 vols. Austin: University of Texas Press, 1938–1943.

Wilson, Clyde N., et al., eds., *The Papers of John C. Calhoun.* 28 vols. Columbia: University of South Carolina Press, 1959–2003.

Internet Sources

Biographical Directory of the United States Congress. http://bioguide.congress.gov/biosearch/biosearch.asp.

Craighead, Sandra G. "Genealogical History of the Slaves of President Andrew Jackson of Hermitage, Tennessee (1840–1877)." www.tngenweb.org/tncolor/ajack.htm.

Freidman, Steven Morgan. "The Inflation Calculator." www.westegg.com/inflation/.

Gilder Lehrman Collection. New-York Historical Society. New York City.

"Historic Papers by or Pertaining to Sam Houston, 1828–1863." East Texas Digital Archives and Collections. Ralph W. Steen Library. Stephen F. Austin University. Nacogdoches, Tex. http://digital.sfasu.edu/cdm/landingpage/collection/Newton.

Rhodes, Henry G. "REV. W. M. NORMENT. A Minister Sixty-Seven Years. Pastor of the Same Church since 1858." *Cumberland Presbyterian,* 26 February 1920, 9. www.cumberland.org/hfcpc/minister/NormentWilliamMenefee.htm.

SECONDARY SOURCES
Books

Abernethy, Thomas P. *From Frontier to Plantation in Tennessee: A Study in Frontier Democracy.* 1932. Reprint. Tuscaloosa: University of Alabama Press, 1967.

———. *The South in the New Nation, 1789–1819.* Baton Rouge: Louisiana State University Press and the Littlefield Fund for Southern History of the University of Texas, 1961.

Allen, Austin. *Origins of the Dred Scott Case: Jacksonian Jurisprudence and the Supreme Court, 1837–1857.* Athens: University of Georgia Press, 2006.

Allgor, Catherine. *Parlor Politics: In Which the Ladies of Washington Help Build a City and a New Government.* Charlottesville: University Press of Virginia, 2000.

Allison, John. *Dropped Stitches in Tennessee History.* Nashville: Marshall & Bruce, 1897.

Ammon, Harry. *James Monroe: The Quest for National Identity.* Newtown, Conn.: American Political Biography Press, 1971.

Anderson, James Douglas. *Making the American Thoroughbred; Especially in Tennessee, 1800–1845.* Norwood, Mass.: Plimpton Press, 1916.

Arnow, Harriet Simpson. *Seedtime on the Cumberland.* New York: Macmillan, 1960.

Atkins, Jonathan M. *Parties, Politics, and the Sectional Conflict in Tennessee, 1832–1861.* Knoxville: University of Tennessee Press, 1997.

Auge, M. *Lives of the Eminent Dead and Biographical Notes of Living Citizens of Montgomery County, PA.* Norristown, Pa.: By the author 1879.

Ayers, Edward L. *Vengeance and Justice: Crime and Punishment in the 19th-Century South.* New York: Oxford University Press, 1984.

Banning, Lance. *The Jeffersonian Persuasion: Evolution of a Party Ideology.* Ithaca: Cornell University Press, 1978.

Barksdale, Kevin T. *The Lost State of Franklin: America's First Secession.* Lexington: University Press of Kentucky, 2009.

Basch, Norma. *Framing American Divorce: From the Revolutionary Generation to the Victorians.* Berkeley: University of California Press, 1999.

Bassett, John Spencer. *The Life of Andrew Jackson.* New York: Macmillan, 1911.

Belko, W. Stephen. *The Invincible Duff Green: Whig of the West.* Columbia: University of Missouri Press, 2006.

Belohlavek, John M. *"Let the Eagle Soar!" The Foreign Policy of Andrew Jackson.* Lincoln: University of Nebraska Press, 1985.

Bergeron, Paul H. *Antebellum Politics in Tennessee.* Lexington: University Press of Kentucky, 1982.

———. *The Presidency of James K. Polk.* Lawrence: University Press of Kansas, 1987.

Bergeron, Paul H., Stephen V. Ash, and Jeanette Keith. *Tennesseans and Their History.* Knoxville: University of Tennessee Press, 1999.

Billingsley, Carolyn Earle. *Communities of Kinship: Antebellum Planters and the Settlement of the Cotton Frontier.* Athens: University of Georgia Press, 2004.

Blassingame, John. *Slave Testimony: Two Centuries of Letters, Speeches, Interviews, and Autobiographies.* Baton Rouge: Louisiana State University Press, 1977.

Blight, David W. *Race and Reunion: The Civil War in American Memory.* Cambridge: Belknap Press of Harvard University Press, 2001.

Booraem, Hendrik. *Young Hickory: The Making of Andrew Jackson.* Dallas: Taylor, 2001.

Brady, Cyrus T. *The True Andrew Jackson.* Philadelphia: J. B. Lippincott, 1906.

Bruce, Dickson D., Jr. *Violence and Culture in the Antebellum South.* Austin: University of Texas Press, 1979.

Buchanan, John. *Jackson's Way: Andrew Jackson and the People of the Western Waters.* New York: Wiley, 2001.

Burke, Pauline Wilcox. *Emily Donelson of Tennessee.* 2 vols. Richmond, Va.: Garrett & Massee, 1941.

————. *Emily Donelson of Tennessee*. Ed. Jonathan M. Atkins. Knoxville: University of Tennessee Press, 2001.

Burstein, Andrew. *The Passions of Andrew Jackson*. New York: Knopf, 2003.

Caldwell, Mary French. *Andrew Jackson's Hermitage*. Nashville: Ladies' Hermitage Association, 1933.

Campbell, Randolph B. *An Empire for Slavery: The Peculiar Institution in Texas, 1821–1865*. Baton Rouge: Louisiana State University Press, 1989.

Cantrell, Gregg. *Stephen F. Austin: Empresario of Texas*. New Haven: Yale University Press, 1999.

Catterall, Ralph C. H. *The Second Bank of the United States*. Chicago: University of Chicago Press, 1903.

Censer, Jane Turner. *North Carolina Planters and Their Children, 1800–1860*. Baton Rouge: Louisiana State University Press, 1984.

Cheathem, Mark R. *Old Hickory's Nephew: The Political and Private Struggles of Andrew Jackson Donelson*. Baton Rouge: Louisiana State University Press, 2007.

Clayton, W. W. *History of Davidson County, Tennessee*. Philadelphia: J. W. Lewis, 1880.

Cole, Donald B. *A Jackson Man: Amos Kendall and the Rise of American Democracy*. Baton Rouge: Louisiana State University Press, 2004.

————. *The Presidency of Andrew Jackson*. Lawrence: University Press of Kansas, 1993.

————. *Vindicating Andrew Jackson: The 1828 Election and the Rise of the Two-Party System*. Lawrence: University Press of Kansas, 2009.

Collier, Christopher. *All Politics Is Local: Family, Friends, and Provincial Interests in the Creation of the Constitution*. Hanover, N.H.: University Press of New England, 2003.

Collins, Gail. *William Henry Harrison*. New York: Times Books, 2012.

Cooper, William J. *Liberty and Slavery: Southern Politics to 1860*. 1983. Reprint. Columbia: University of South Carolina Press, 2000.

————. *The South and the Politics of Slavery, 1828–1856*. Baton Rouge: Louisiana State University Press, 1978.

Corlew, Robert E. *Tennessee: A Short History*, 2d ed. Knoxville: University of Tennessee Press, 1981.

Cotterill, Ralph S. *The Southern Indians: The Story of the Civilized Tribes before Removal*. Norman: University of Oklahoma Press, 1954.

Crapol, Edward J. *John Tyler: The Accidental President*. Chapel Hill: University of North Carolina Press, 2006.

Cunningham, Noble E., Jr. *The Presidency of James Monroe*. Lawrence: University Press of Kansas, 1995.

Curtis, James C. *Andrew Jackson and the Search for Vindication*. Boston: Harper-Collins, 1976.

————. *The Fox at Bay: Martin Van Buren and the Presidency, 1837–1841.* Lexington: University Press of Kentucky, 1970.

Dangerfield, George. *The Era of Good Feelings.* New York: Harcourt, Brace, 1952.

Davis, William C. *Rhett: The Turbulent Life and Times of a Fire-Eater.* Columbia: University of South Carolina Press, 2001.

DeRosier, Arthur H., Jr. *The Removal of the Choctaw Indians.* Knoxville: University of Tennessee Press, 1970.

Deyle, Steven. *Carry Me Back: The Domestic Slave Trade in American Life.* Oxford: Oxford University Press, 2005.

Dickson, Robert J. *Ulster Emigration to Colonial America, 1718–1775.* London: Routledge & Kegan Paul, 1966.

Doherty, Herbert J., Jr. *Richard Keith Call: Southern Unionist.* Gainesville: University of Florida Press, 1961.

Dorris, Mary C. *Preservation of the Hermitage, 1889–1915.* Nashville: Smith & Lamar, 1915.

Driver, Carl S. *John Sevier: Pioneer of the Old Southwest.* Chapel Hill: University of North Carolina Press, 1932.

Durham, Walter T. *Daniel Smith: Frontier Statesman.* Gallatin, Tenn.: Sumner County Library Board, 1976.

Eaton, Clement. *The Growth of Southern Civilization, 1790–1860.* New York: Harper & Row, 1961.

Edelson, S. Max. *Plantation Enterprise in Colonial South Carolina.* Cambridge: Harvard University Press, 2006.

Edmunds, R. David. *Tecumseh and the Quest for Indian Leadership.* New York: HarperCollins, 1984.

Elkins, Stanley, and Eric McKitrick. *The Age of Federalism.* New York: Oxford University Press, 1993.

Ellis, Richard E. *The Union at Risk: Jacksonian Democracy, States' Rights, and the Nullification Crisis.* New York: Oxford University Press, 1987.

Faust, Drew Gilpin. *James Henry Hammond and the Old South: A Design for Mastery.* Baton Rouge: Louisiana State University Press, 1982.

Fehrenbacher, Don E. *The Dred Scott Case: Its Significance in American Law and Politics.* Oxford: Oxford University Press, 1978.

Fett, Sharla M. *Working Cures: Healing, Health, and Power on Southern Slave Plantations.* Chapel Hill: University of North Carolina Press, 2002.

Finger, John R. *Tennessee Frontiers: Three Regions in Transition.* Bloomington: Indiana University Press, 2001.

Finkelman, Paul. *Millard Fillmore.* New York: Times Books, 2011.

Fischer, David Hackett. *Albion's Seed: Four British Folkways in America.* Oxford: Oxford University Press, 1989.

Forbes, Robert P. *The Missouri Compromise and Its Aftermath.* Chapel Hill: University of North Carolina Press, 2006.

Ford, Lacy K., Jr. *Deliver Us from Evil: The Slavery Question in the Old South.* Oxford: Oxford University Press, 2009.

Fortier, Alcée. *A History of Louisiana.* 4 vols. New York: Manzi, Joyant, 1904.

Franklin, John Hope, and Loren Schweninger. *Runaway Slaves: Rebels on the Plantation.* New York: Oxford University Press, 1999.

Fraser, Walter J., Jr., *Charleston! Charleston! The History of a Southern City.* Columbia: University of South Carolina Press, 1989.

Freehling, William W. *Prelude to the Civil War: The Nullification Controversy in South Carolina, 1816–1836.* New York: Harper & Row, 1966.

———. *The Road to Disunion.* Vol. 1: *Secessionists at Bay, 1776–1854.* New York: Oxford University Press, 1990.

Freeman, Joanne B. *Affairs of Honor: National Politics in the New Republic.* New Haven: Yale University Press, 2001.

Friend, Llerena. *Sam Houston: The Great Designer.* Austin: University of Texas Press, 1954.

Garrison, Tim Alan. *The Legal Ideology of Removal: The Southern Judiciary and the Sovereignty of Native American Nations.* Athens: University of Georgia Press, 2002.

Genovese, Eugene. *Roll, Jordan, Roll: The World the Slaves Made.* New York: Pantheon, 1974.

Genovese, Eugene, and Elizabeth Fox-Genovese. *Fatal Self-Deception: Slaveholding Paternalism in the Old South.* Cambridge: Cambridge University Press, 2011.

Glover, Lorri. *All Our Relations: Blood Ties and Emotional Bonds among the Early South Carolina Gentry.* Baltimore: Johns Hopkins University Press, 2000.

———. *Southern Sons: Becoming Men in the New Nation.* Baltimore: Johns Hopkins University Press, 2007.

Godbeer, Richard. *Sexual Revolution in Early America.* Baltimore: Johns Hopkins University Press, 2002.

Goodman, Paul. *Of One Blood: Abolitionism and the Origins of Racial Equality.* Berkeley: University of California Press, 1998.

Goodstein, Anita. *Nashville, 1780–1860: From Frontier to City.* Gainesville: University of Florida Press, 1989.

Graham, William A. *General Joseph Graham and His Papers on North Carolina Revolutionary History.* Raleigh, N.C.: Edwards & Broughton, 1904.

Gray, Lewis Cecil. *History of Agriculture in the Southern United States to 1860.* 2 vols. Gloucester, Mass.: Peter Smith, 1958.

Green, Constance M. *Washington: Village and Capital, 1800–1878.* Princeton: Princeton University Press, 1962.

Green, Michael D. *The Politics of Indian Removal: Creek Government and Society in Crisis.* Lincoln: University of Nebraska Press, 1982.

Greenberg, Kenneth S. *Honor & Slavery: Lies, Duels, Noses, Masks, Dressing as a Woman, Gifts, Strangers, Humanitarianism, Death, Slave Rebellions, the Pro-slavery Argument, Baseball, Hunting, and Gambling in the Old South.* Princeton: Princeton University Press, 1996.

———. *Masters and Statesmen: The Political Culture of American Slavery.* Baltimore: Johns Hopkins University Press, 1985.

———, ed. *Nat Turner: A Slave Rebellion in History and Memory.* Oxford: Oxford University Press, 2003.

Grimsted, David. *American Mobbing, 1828–1861: Toward Civil War.* New York: Oxford University Press, 1998.

Gudmestad, Robert H. *A Troublesome Commerce: The Transformation of the Interstate Slave Trade.* Baton Rouge: Louisiana State University Press, 2003.

Haley, James L. *Sam Houston.* Norman: University of Oklahoma Press, 2002.

Hatley, Tom. *The Dividing Paths: Cherokees and South Carolinians through the Era of Revolution.* New York: Oxford University Press, 1993.

Haynes, Sam. *Unfinished Revolution: The Early American Republic in a British World.* Charlottesville: University of Virginia Press, 2010.

Haywood, Marshall DeLancey. *The Beginnings of Freemasonry in North Carolina and Tennessee.* Raleigh, N.C.: Weaver & Lynch, 1906.

Heidler, David S., and Jeanne T. Heidler. *Henry Clay: The Essential American.* New York: Random House, 2010.

———. *Old Hickory's War: Andrew Jackson and the Quest for Empire.* Mechanicsburg, Pa.: Stackpole, 1996.

Heiskell, Samuel G. *Andrew Jackson and Early Tennessee History,* 2d ed. 2 vols. Nashville: Ambrose, 1920–1921.

Heller, J. Roderick, III. *Democracy's Lawyer: Felix Grundy of the Old Southwest.* Baton Rouge: Louisiana State University Press, 2010.

Herd, Elmer Don, Jr. *Andrew Jackson, South Carolinian: A Study of the Enigma of His Birth.* Columbia, S.C.: Lancaster County Historical Commission, 1963.

Hickey, Donald R. *The War of 1812: A Short History.* Urbana: University of Illinois Press, 1995.

Hietala, Thomas R. *Manifest Design: Anxious Aggrandizement in Late Jacksonian America.* Ithaca: Cornell University Press, 1985.

Hoffer, Williamjames. *The Caning of Charles Sumner: Honor, Idealism, and the Origins of the Civil War.* Baltimore: Johns Hopkins University Press, 2010.

Holt, Michael F. *The Rise and Fall of the American Whig Party: Jacksonian Politics and the Onset of the Civil War.* Oxford: Oxford University Press, 1999.

Horn, Stanley. *The Hermitage: Home of Old Hickory.* Richmond: Garrett & Massie, 1938.

Howe, Daniel Walker. *The Political Culture of the American Whigs*. Chicago: University of Chicago Press, 1979.

——. *What Hath God Wrought: The Transformation of America, 1815–1848*. New York: Oxford University Press, 2007.

Hudson, Angela Pulley. *Creek Paths and Federal Roads: Indians, Settlers, and Slaves and the Making of the American South*. Chapel Hill: University of North Carolina Press, 2010.

Huebner, Timothy S. *The Southern Judicial Tradition: State Judges and Sectional Distinctiveness, 1790–1890*. Athens: University of Georgia Press, 1999.

Isenberg, Nancy. *Fallen Founder: The Life of Aaron Burr*. New York: Viking, 2007.

James, Marquis. *Andrew Jackson: Portrait of a President*. Indianapolis: Bobbs-Merrill, 1937.

——. *Andrew Jackson: The Border Captain*. Indianapolis: Bobbs-Merrill, 1933.

——. *The Life of Andrew Jackson*. Indianapolis: Bobbs-Merrill, 1938.

John, Richard R. *Spreading the News: The American Postal System from Franklin to Morse*. Cambridge: Harvard University Press, 1995.

Johnson, Reinhard O. *The Liberty Party, 1840–1848: Antislavery Third-Party Politics in the United States*. Baton Rouge: Louisiana State University Press, 2009.

Johnson, Walter. *Soul by Soul: Life Inside the Antebellum Slave Market*. Cambridge: Harvard University Press, 1999.

Jordan, Weymouth T. *George Washington Campbell of Tennessee: Western Statesman*. Tallahassee: Florida State University, 1955.

Klein, Rachel N. *Unification of a Slave State: The Rise of the Planter Class in the South Carolina Backcountry, 1760–1808*. Chapel Hill: University of North Carolina Press, 1990.

Kolchin, Peter. *American Slavery, 1619–1877*. New York: Hill & Wang, 1993.

Landers, Jane. *Black Society in Spanish Florida*. Urbana: University of Illinois Press, 1999.

Larson, John Lauritz. *The Market Revolution in America: Liberty, Ambition, and the Eclipse of the Common Good*. Cambridge: Cambridge University Press, 2010.

Latner, Richard B. *The Presidency of Andrew Jackson*. Athens: University of Georgia Press, 1979.

Leslie, David E. *The Leslie Family*. N.p.p., [1983].

Lewis, William Terrell. *Genealogy of the Lewis Family in America, from the Middle of the Seventeenth Century Down to the Present Time*. Louisville: Courier Journal, 1893.

Leyburn, James G. *The Scotch-Irish: A Social History*. Chapel Hill: University of North Carolina Press, 1962.

Lightner, David L. *Slavery and the Commerce Power: How the Struggle against the Interstate Slave Trade Led to the Civil War*. New Haven: Yale University Press, 2006.

Litwack, Leon. *Been in the Storm So Long: The Aftermath of Slavery.* New York: Knopf, 1979.

———. *Trouble in Mind: Black Southerners in the Age of Jim Crow.* New York: Knopf, 1998.

Magliocca, Gerard N. *Andrew Jackson and the Constitution: The Rise and Fall of Generational Regimes.* Lawrence: University Press of Kansas, 2007.

Mahon, John K. *History of the Second Seminole War, 1835–1842.* Gainesville: University Press of Florida, 1985.

Marszalek, John F. *The Petticoat Affair: Manners, Mutiny, and Sex in Andrew Jackson's White House.* New York: Free Press, 1997.

———. *Sherman: A Soldier's Passion for Order.* New York: Vintage, 1994.

Mason, Matthew. *Slavery and Politics in the Early American Republic.* Chapel Hill: University of North Carolina Press, 2006.

Masur, Louis P. *1831: Year of the Eclipse.* New York: Hill & Wang, 2001.

Matrana, Marc R. *Lost Plantations of the South.* Jackson: University Press of Mississippi, 2009.

Mayer, Henry. *All on Fire: William Lloyd Garrison and the Abolition of Slavery.* New York: St. Martin's Press, 1998.

McCormack, Edward Michael. *Slavery on the Tennessee Frontier.* Nashville: Tennessee American Revolution Commission, 1977.

McCoy, Drew R. *The Elusive Republic: Political Economy in Jeffersonian America.* Chapel Hill: University of North Carolina Press for the Institute of Early American History and Culture, 1980.

Meacham, Jon. *American Lion: Andrew Jackson in the White House.* New York: Random House, 2008.

Merrell, James H. *The Indians' New World: Catawbas and Their Neighbors from European Contact through the Era of Removal.* Chapel Hill: University of North Carolina Press, 1989.

Miles, Tiya. *The House on Diamond Hill: A Cherokee Plantation Story.* Chapel Hill: University of North Carolina Press, 2010.

Miller, William Lee. *Arguing about Slavery: The Great Battle in the United States Congress.* New York: Knopf, 1996.

Moore, Glover. *The Missouri Controversy, 1819–1821.* Lexington: University of Kentucky Press, 1966.

Moore, Peter N. *World of Toil and Strife: Community Transformation in Backcountry South Carolina, 1750–1805.* Columbia: University of South Carolina Press, 2007.

Moulton, Gary E. *John Ross: Cherokee Chief.* Athens: University of Georgia Press, 1978.

Niven, John C. *John C. Calhoun and the Price of Union: A Biography.* Baton Rouge: Louisiana State University Press, 1988.

———. *Martin Van Buren: The Romantic Age of American Politics.* New York: Oxford University Press, 1983.

Oakes, James. *The Ruling Race: A History of American Slaveholders.* New York: Vintage, 1983.

Ogg, Frederic A. *The Reign of Andrew Jackson: A Chronicle of the Frontier in Politics.* New Haven: Yale University Press, 1914.

Olsen, Christopher J. *Political Culture and Secession in Mississippi: Masculinity, Honor, and the Antiparty Tradition, 1830–1860.* Oxford: Oxford University Press, 2000.

Osthaus, Carl R. *Partisans of the Southern Press: Editorial Spokesmen of the Nineteenth Century.* Lexington: University Press of Kentucky, 1994.

Owsley, Frank L., Jr. *Struggle for the Gulf Borderlands: The Creek War and the Battle of New Orleans, 1812–1815.* Gainesville: University Press of Florida, 1981.

Owsley, Frank L., Jr., and Gene A. Smith. *Filibusters and Expansionists: Jeffersonian Manifest Destiny, 1800–1821.* Tuscaloosa: University of Alabama Press, 1997.

Parks, Joseph H. *John Bell of Tennessee.* Baton Rouge: Louisiana State University Press, 1950.

Parsons, Lynn Hudson. *The Birth of Modern Politics: Andrew Jackson, John Quincy Adams, and the Election of 1828.* Oxford: Oxford University Press, 2009.

———. *John Quincy Adams.* Madison, Wisc.: Madison House, 1998.

Parton, James. *Life of Andrew Jackson.* 3 vols. New York: Mason Brothers, 1860.

Peterson, Norma Lois. *The Presidencies of William Henry Harrison and John Tyler.* Lawrence: University Press of Kansas, 1989.

Pettus, Louise. *The Waxhaws.* Rock Hill, S.C.: Privately printed, 1993.

Pletcher, David M. *The Diplomacy of Annexation: Texas, Oregon, and the Mexican War.* Columbia: University of Missouri Press, 1973.

Porter, Kenneth. *The Black Seminoles: History of a Freedom-Seeking People.* Gainesville: University Press of Florida, 1996.

Prucha, Francis Paul. *The Great Father: The United States Government and the American Indians,* abr. ed. Lincoln: University of Nebraska Press, 1986.

Ramage, James A., and Andrea S. Watkins. *Kentucky Rising: Democracy, Slavery, and Culture from the Early Republic to the Civil War.* Lexington: University Press of Kentucky, 2011.

Ratner, Lorman. *Andrew Jackson and His Tennessee Lieutenants: A Study in Political Culture.* Westport, Conn.: Greenwood Press, 1997.

Ray, Kristofer. *Middle Tennessee, 1775–1825: Progress and Popular Democracy on the Southwestern Frontier.* Knoxville: University of Tennessee Press, 2007.

Remini, Robert V. *Andrew Jackson.* 3 vols. New York: Harper & Row, 1977–1984.

———. *Andrew Jackson and the Bank War.* New York: Norton, 1967.

———. *Andrew Jackson and His Indian Wars.* New York: Viking Penguin, 2001.

———. *The Battle of New Orleans: Andrew Jackson and America's First Military Victory.* New York: Viking, 1999.

———. *Daniel Webster: The Man and His Time.* New York: Norton, 1997.

———. *The Election of Andrew Jackson.* New York: J. B. Lippincott, 1963.

———. *Henry Clay: Statesman for the Union.* New York: Norton, 1991.

———. *John Quincy Adams.* New York: Times Books, 2002.

———. *The Legacy of Andrew Jackson: Essays on Democracy, Indian Removal, and Slavery.* Baton Rouge: Louisiana State University Press, 1988.

Richards, Leonard L. *'"Gentlemen of Property and Standing": Anti-Abolition Mobs in Jacksonian America.* Oxford: Oxford University Press, 1970.

Risjord, Norman K. *The Old Republicans: Southern Conservatism in the Age of Jefferson.* New York: Columbia University Press, 1965.

Robertson, David. *Denmark Vesey: The Buried Story of America's Largest Slave Rebellion and the Man Who Led It.* New York: Knopf, 1999.

Rodenbough, Charles D. *Governor Alexander Martin: Biography of a North Carolina Revolutionary War Statesman.* Jefferson, N.C.: McFarland, 2004.

Rogers, George C. *Charleston in the Age of the Pinckneys.* Columbia: University of South Carolina Press, 1980.

Rogin, Michael Paul. *Fathers and Children: Andrew Jackson and the Subjugation of the America Indian.* 1975. Reprint. New Brunswick, N.J.: Transaction Publishers, 1991.

Rorabaugh, W. J. *The Alcoholic Republic: An American Tradition.* Oxford: Oxford University Press, 1979.

Roth, Randolph. *American Homicide.* Cambridge, Mass.: Belknap Press of Harvard University Press, 2009.

Rothbard, Murray N. *The Panic of 1819: Reactions and Policies.* New York: Columbia University Press, 1962.

Rothman, Adam. *Slave Country: American Expansion and the Origins of the Deep South.* Cambridge: Harvard University Press, 2005.

Ryan, Mary P. *Women in Public: Between Banners and Ballots, 1825–1880.* Baltimore: Johns Hopkins University Press, 1990.

Satterfield, Robert B. *Andrew Jackson Donelson: Jackson's Confidant and Political Heir.* Bowling Green, Ky.: Hickory Tales, 2000.

Satz, Ronald N. *American Indian Policy in the Age of Jackson.* Lincoln: University of Nebraska Press, 1974.

———. *Tennessee's Indian Peoples: From White Contact to Removal, 1540–1840.* Knoxville: University of Tennessee Press and the Tennessee Historical Commission, 1979.

Scarborough, William K. *The Overseer: Plantation Management in the Old South.* Baton Rouge: Louisiana State University Press, 1966.

Schlesinger, Arthur M., Jr. *The Age of Jackson*. Boston: Little, Brown, 1945.

Sellers, Charles G., Jr. *James K. Polk*. 2 vols. Princeton: Princeton University Press, 1957, 1966.

Shalhope, Robert E. *The Baltimore Bank Riot: Political Upheaval in Antebellum Maryland*. Urbana: University of Illinois Press, 2009.

Sheehan, Bernard. *Seeds of Extinction: Jefferson Philanthropy and the American Indian*. Chapel Hill: University of North Carolina Press, 1973.

Silbey, Joel H. *Martin Van Buren and the Emergence of American Popular Politics*. Lanham, Md.: Rowman & Littlefield, 2005.

———. *Storm over Texas: The Annexation Controversy and the Road to the Civil War*. Oxford: Oxford University Press, 2005.

Sklar, Kathryn Kish. *Catharine Beecher: A Study in American Domesticity*. New York: Norton, 1976.

Smelser, Marshall. *The Democratic Republic, 1801–1815*. New York: Harper & Row, 1968.

Smith, Elbert B. *Francis Preston Blair*. New York: Free Press, 1980.

———. *Magnificent Missourian: The Life of Thomas Hart Benton*. Philadelphia: J. B. Lippincott, 1958.

Snyder, Christina. *Slavery in Indian Country: The Changing Face of Captivity in Early America*. Cambridge: Harvard University Press, 2010.

Stagg, J.C.A. *Mr. Madison's War: Politics, Diplomacy, and Warfare in the Early American Republic, 1783–1830*. Princeton: Princeton University Press, 1983.

Stowe, Steven M. *Intimacy and Power in the Old South: Ritual in the Lives of the Planters*. Baltimore: Johns Hopkins University Press, 1987.

Temin, Peter. *The Jacksonian Economy*. New York: Norton, 1969.

Thornton, J. Mills, III. *Politics and Power in a Slave Society: Alabama, 1800–1860*. Baton Rouge: Louisiana State University Press, 1978.

Tinkler, Robert. *James Hamilton of South Carolina*. Baton Rouge: Louisiana State University Press, 2004.

Tompkins, Daniel A. *History of Mecklenburg County and the City of Charlotte from 1740 to 1903*. 2 vols. Charlotte: Observer Printing House, 1903.

Turner, Frederick Jackson. *The Frontier in American History*. 1920. Reprint. New York: Dover, 1996.

Tyler, Alice Felt. *Freedom's Ferment: Phases of American Social History from the Colonial Period to the Outbreak of the Civil War*. New York: Harper & Row, 1962.

[Wallace, Louis, ed.] *The Horse and Its Heritage in Tennessee*. Nashville: Tennessee Department of Agriculture, 1945.

Wallis, Michael. *David Crockett: Lion of the West*. New York: Norton, 2011.

Walters, Ronald G. *American Reformers, 1815–1860*, rev. ed. New York: Hill & Wang, 1997.

Ward, John William. *Andrew Jackson: Symbol for an Age.* New York: Oxford University Press, 1955.

Warshauer, Matthew S. *Andrew Jackson and the Politics of Martial Law: Nationalism, Civil Liberties, and Partisanship.* Knoxville: University of Tennessee Press, 2006.

Watson, Harry L. *Liberty and Power: The Politics of Jacksonian America,* 2d ed. New York: Hill & Wang, 2006.

Wilentz, Sean. *The Rise of American Democracy: Jefferson to Lincoln.* New York: Norton, 2005.

Wilson, Major L. *The Presidency of Martin Van Buren.* Lawrence: University Press of Kansas, 1984.

Wiltse, Charles M. *John C. Calhoun: Nationalist, 1782–1828.* Indianapolis: Bobbs-Merrill, 1944.

Wood, Gordon S. *Empire of Liberty: A History of the Early Republic, 1789–1815.* Oxford: Oxford University Press, 2009.

Woodman, Harold D. *King Cotton and His Retainers: Financing and Marketing the Cotton Crop of the South, 1800–1925.* 1968. Reprint. Columbia: University of South Carolina Press, 1990.

Wyatt-Brown, Bertram. *Southern Honor: Ethics and Behavior in the Old South.* New York: Oxford University Press, 1982.

Articles

Abernethy, Thomas P. "Andrew Jackson and the Rise of Southwestern Democracy." *AHR* 33 (October 1927): 64–77.

——. "The Early Development of Commerce and Banking in Tennessee." *MVHR* 14 (December 1927): 311–320.

——. "The Origin of the Whig Party in Tennessee." *MVHR* 12 (March 1926): 504–522.

Allen, Austin. "Jacksonian Jurisprudence and the Obscurity of Justice John Catron." *Vanderbilt Law Review* 62 (2009): 491–517.

Ames, William E., and S. Dean Olson. "Washington's Political Press and the Election of 1824." *Journalism Quarterly* 40 (Summer 1963): 343–350.

Arroyo, Elizabeth Fortson. "Poor Whites, Slaves, and Free Blacks in Tennessee, 1796–1861." *THQ* 55 (Spring 1996): 56–65.

Atkins, Jonathan M. "The Presidential Candidacy of Hugh Lawson White in Tennessee, 1832–1836." *JSH* 58 (February 1992): 27–56.

——. "The Whig Party versus the 'Spoilsmen' in Tennessee." *Historian* 57 (Winter 1995): 329–335.

Bacon, H. Phillip. "Nashville Trade at the Beginning of the Nineteenth Century." *THQ* 15 (March 1956): 30–36.

Barker, Eugene C. "The Annexation of Texas." *Southwestern Historical Quarterly* 50 (July 1946): 49–74.

———. "President Jackson and the Texas Revolution." *AHR* 12 (1906–1907): 788–809.

———. "The United States and Mexico, 1835–1837." *MVHR* 1 (June 1914): 3–30.

Basch, Norma. "Marriage, Morals, and Politics in the Election of 1828." *JAH* 80 (December 1993): 890–918.

Belko, William S. "Epilogue to the War of 1812: The Monroe Administration, American Anglophobia, and the First Seminole War." In *America's Hundred Years' War: U.S. Expansion to the Gulf Coast and the Fate of the Seminole, 1763–1858*. Ed. William S. Belko, 54–102. Gainesville: University Press of Florida, 2011.

Berlin, Jean V. "A Mistress and a Slave: Anna Maria Thornton and John Arthur Bowen." *Proceedings of the South Carolina Historical Association* (1990): 69–74.

Birkner, Michael. "The General, the Secretary, and the President: An Episode in the Presidential Campaign of 1828." *THQ* 42 (Fall 1983): 243–253.

Brady, Patrick S. "The Slave Trade and Sectionalism in South Carolina, 1787–1808." *JSH* 38 (November 1972): 601–620.

Brauer, Kinley J. "The United States and British Imperial Expansion, 1815–1860." *Diplomatic History* 12 (Winter 1988): 19–37.

Breen, Timothy H. "Horses and Gentlemen: The Cultural Significance of Gambling among the Gentry of Virginia." *William and Mary Quarterly* 34 (April 1977): 239–257.

Brown, Thomas. "From Old Hickory to Sly Fox: The Routinization of Charisma in the Early Democratic Party." *JER* 11 (Fall 1991): 339–370.

———. "The Miscegenation of Richard Mentor Johnson as an Issue in the National Election Campaign of 1835–1836." *Civil War History* 39 (March 1993): 5–30.

Bugbee, Lester G. "The Old Three Hundred: A List of the Settlers of Austin's First Colony." *Quarterly of the Texas State Historical Association* 1 (July 1897–April 1898): 108–117.

Bullock, Steven C. "A Pure and Sublime System: The Appeal of Post-Revolutionary Freemasonry." *JER* 9 (Fall 1989): 359–373.

Cain, Joshua. "'We Will Strike at the Head and Demolish the Monster': The Impact of Joel R. Poinsett's Correspondence on President Andrew Jackson during the Nullification Crisis, 1832–1833." *Proceedings of the South Carolina Historical Association* (2011): 13–26.

Carp, E. Wayne. "Introduction: A Historical Overview of American Adoption." In *Adoption in America: Historical Perspectives*. Ed. E. Wayne Carp, 1–26. Ann Arbor: University of Michigan Press, 2002.

Cayton, Andrew R. L. "'When Shall We Cease to Have Judases?' The Blount Conspiracy and the Limits of the 'Extended Republic.'" In *Launching the "Extended Republic": The Federalist Era*. Ed. Ronald Hoffman and Peter J. Albert, 156–189. Charlottesville: United States Capitol Historical Society by the University Press of Virginia, 1996.

Chappell, Gordon T. "John Coffee: Land Speculator and Planter." *Alabama Review* 22 (January 1969): 24–43.

———. "John Coffee: Surveyor and Land Agent." *Alabama Review* 14 (July 1961): 180–195.

———. "The Life and Activities of John Coffee." *THQ* 1 (June 1942): 126–146.

Cheathem, Mark R. "'The High Minded Honourable Man': Honor, Kinship, and Conflict in the Life of Andrew Jackson Donelson." *JER* 27 (Summer 2007): 265–292.

———. "The State of Tennessee." In *The Uniting States: The Story of Statehood for the Fifty United States*. Ed. Benjamin F. Shearer. 3 vols. Westport, Conn.: Greenwood Press, 2004.

Clavin, Matthew. "'It Is a Negro, Not an Indian War': Southampton, St. Domingo, and the Second Seminole War." In *America's Hundred Years' War: U.S. Expansion to the Gulf Coast and the Fate of the Seminole, 1763–1858*. Ed. William S. Belko, 181–208. Gainesville: University Press of Florida, 2011.

Cleves, Rachel Hope, et al. "Interchange: The War of 1812." *JAH* 99 (September 2012): 520–555.

Clifton, Frances. "John Overton as Andrew Jackson's Friend." *THQ* 11 (March 1952): 23–40.

Coke, Fletch. "Profiles of John Overton: Judge, Friend, Family Man, and Master of Travellers' Rest." *THQ* 37 (Winter 1978): 393–409.

Cole, Stephanie. "Changes for Mrs. Thornton's Arthur: Patterns of Domestic Service in Washington, D.C., 1800–1835." *Social Science History* 15 (Fall 1991): 367–379.

Costa, Tom. "What Can We Learn from a Digital Database of Runaway Slave Advertisements?" *International Social Science Review* 76 (2001): 36–43.

Coulter, E. Merton. "The Nullification Movement in Georgia." *Georgia Historical Quarterly* 5 (March 1921): 3–39.

Covington, James W. "The Negro Fort." *Gulf Coast Historical Review* 5 (Spring 1990): 78–91.

Cox, Isaac Joslin. "General Wilkinson and His Later Intrigues with the Spaniards." *AHR* 19 (July 1914): 794–812.

Crawford, Aaron Scott. "Patriot Slaveholder: Andrew Jackson and the Winter of Secession." *Journal of East Tennessee History* 82 (2010): 10–32.

Crittenden, Charles C. "Overland Travel and Transportation in North Carolina, 1763–1789." *North Carolina Historical Review* 8 (July 1931): 239–257.

Crocker, Matthew. "The Missouri Compromise, the Monroe Doctrine, and the Southern Strategy." *Journal of the West* 43 (Summer 2004): 45–52.

Crook, Elizabeth. "Sam Houston and Eliza Allen: The Marriage and the Mystery." *Southwestern Historical Quarterly* 94 (July 1990): 1–36.

Curtis, James C. "In the Shadow of Old Hickory: The Political Travail of Martin Van Buren." *JER* 1 (Fall 1981): 349–367.

Dahl, Curtis. "The Clergyman, the Hussy, and Old Hickory: Ezra Stiles Ely and the Peggy Eaton Affair." *Journal of Presbyterian History* 52 (Summer 1974): 137–155.

Davidson, Chalmers G. "Independent Mecklenburg." *North Carolina Historical Review* 46 (Spring 1969): 122–127.

Deppisch, Ludwig M. "Andrew Jackson and American Medical Practice: Old Hickory and His Physicians." *THQ* 62 (Summer 2003): 130–150.

DeWitt, John H., Jr. "Andrew Jackson and His Ward, Andrew Jackson Hutchings: A History Hitherto Unpublished." *THM* 1 (January 1931): 83–106.

Doherty, Herbert J., Jr. "Andrew Jackson vs. the Spanish Governor." *Florida Historical Quarterly* 34 (October 1955): 142–158.

———. "The Governorship of Andrew Jackson." *Florida Historical Quarterly* 33 (July 1954): 3–31.

Dunlap, Lily Doyle. "Old Waxhaw." *North Carolina Booklet* 19 (April 1920): 139–144.

Egerton, Douglas R. "Averting a Crisis: The Proslavery Critique of the American Colonization Society." *Civil War History* 43 (June 1997): 142–156.

Ely, James W., Jr. "Andrew Jackson as Tennessee State Court Judge, 1798–1804." *THQ* 40 (Summer 1981): 144–157.

———. "The Legal Practice of Andrew Jackson." *THQ* 38 (Winter 1979): 421–435.

Eslinger, Ellen. "The Shape of Slavery on the Kentucky Frontier." *Register of the Kentucky Historical Society* 92 (Winter 1994): 1–23.

Everett, Donald E. "Emigres and Militiamen: Free Persons of Color in New Orleans, 1803–1815." *Journal of Negro History* 38 (October 1953): 377–402.

Ewing, Gretchen Garst. "Duff Green, John C. Calhoun, and the Election of 1828." *South Carolina Historical Magazine* 79 (April 1978): 126–137.

Feller, Daniel. "The Seminole Controversy Revisited: A New Look at Andrew Jackson's 1818 Florida Campaign." *Florida Historical Quarterly* 88 (Winter 2010): 309–325.

Fink, Paul M. "The Rebirth of Jonesboro." *THQ* 31 (Fall 1972): 223–239.

Fitzgerald, Michael S. "Rejecting Calhoun's Expansible Army Plan: The Army Reduction Act of 1821." *War in History* 3 (April 1996): 161–185.

Forret, Jeff. "Conflict and the 'Slave Community': Violence among Slaves in Upcountry South Carolina." *JSH* 74 (August 2008): 551–588.

Fraser, Rebecca. "Negotiating Their Manhood: Masculinity amongst the En-slaved in the Upper South, 1830–1861." In *Black and White Masculinity in the American South, 1800–2000*. Ed. Lydia Plath and Sergio Lussana, 76–94. Newcastle upon Tyne: Cambridge Scholars Publishing, 2009.

Freehling, William W. "Andrew Jackson: Great President (?)." In *Congress and the Emergence of Sectionalism: From the Missouri Compromise to the Age of Jackson*. Ed. Paul Finkelman and Donald R. Kennon, 133–151. Athens: Ohio University Press, 2008.

Freeman, Joanne B. "Dueling as Politics: Reinterpreting the Burr-Hamilton Duel." *William and Mary Quarterly* 53 (April 1996): 289–318.

Friend, Craig Thompson, and Lorri Glover. "Rethinking Southern Masculin-ity: An Introduction." In *Southern Manhood: Perspectives on Masculinity in the Old South*. Ed. Craig Thompson Friend and Lorri Glover, vii–xxii. Athens: University of Georgia Press, 2004.

Furstenberg, François. "The Significance of the Trans-Appalachian Frontier in Atlantic History." *AHR* 95 (June 2008): 647–677.

Galloway, Linda Bennett. "Andrew Jackson, Jr. [Part 1]." *THQ* 9 (September 1950): 195–216.

———. "Andrew Jackson, Jr. [Part 2]." *THQ* 9 (December 1950): 306–343.

Gardner, Francis Tomlinson. "The Gentleman from Tennessee." *Surgery, Gyne-cology, and Obstetrics* 88 (February 1949): 405–411.

Garrison, Tim Alan. "United States Indian Policy in Sectional Crisis: Geor-gia's Exploitation of the Compact of 1802." In *Congress and the Emergence of Sectionalism: From the Missouri Compromise to the Age of Jackson*. Ed. Paul Finkelman and Donald R. Kennon, 97–124. Athens: Ohio University Press, 2008

Gibson, Joe. "A. Butler: What a Scamp!" *Journal of the West* 11 (April 1972): 235–247.

Glover, Lorri. "'Let Us Manufacture Men': Educating Elite Boys in the Early National South." In *Southern Manhood: Perspectives on Masculinity in the Old South*. Ed. Craig Thompson Friend and Lorri Glover, 22–48. Athens: University of Georgia Press, 2004.

Goff, Rheda C. "A Physical Profile of Andrew Jackson." *THQ* 28 (Fall 1969): 297–309.

Goodstein, Anita S. "Black History on the Nashville Frontier, 1780–1810." *THQ* 38 (Winter 1979): 401–420.

Gorn, Elliott J. "'Gouge and Bite, Pull Hair and Scratch': The Social Signif-icance of Fighting in the Southern Backcountry." *AHR* 90 (February 1985): 18–43.

Govan, Thomas P. "John M. Berrien and the Administration of Andrew Jack-son." *JSH* 5 (November 1939): 447–467.

Greenberg, Kenneth S. "The Nose, the Lie, and the Duel." *AHR* 95 (February 1990): 57–74.

Grimsted, David. "Rioting in Its Jacksonian Setting." *AHR* (April 1972): 361–97.

Guice, John D. W. "Old Hickory and the Natchez Trace." *Journal of Mississippi History* 69 (June 2007): 167–182.

Guyatt, Nicholas. "'The Outskirts of Our Happiness': Race and the Lure of Colonization in the Early Republic." *JAH* 96 (March 2009): 986–1011.

Hackett, Derek L. A. "Slavery, Ethnicity, and Sugar: An Analysis of Voting Behavior in Louisiana, 1828–1844." *Louisiana Studies* 13 (Summer 1974): 73–118.

Hall, Virginius C. "Moses Dawson, Chronic Belligerent." *Bulletin of the Historical and Philosophical Society of Ohio* 15 (July 1957): 175–189.

Hammond, John Craig. "Slavery, Settlement, and Empire: The Expansion and Growth of Slavery in the Interior of the North American Continent, 1770–1820." *JER* 32 (Summer 2012): 175–206.

Harlan, Louis R. "Public Career of William Berkeley Lewis [Part 1]." *THQ* 7 (March 1948): 3–37.

———. "Public Career of William Berkeley Lewis [Part 2]." *THQ* 7 (June 1948): 118–51.

Harrison, Joseph H., Jr. "Martin Van Buren and His Southern Supporters." *JSH* 22 (November 1956): 438–458.

Hassig, Ross. "Internal Conflict in the Creek War of 1813–1814." *Ethnohistory* 21 (Summer 1974): 251–271.

Hay, Robert P. "The American Revolution Twice Recalled: Lafayette's Visit and the Election of 1824." *Indiana Magazine of History* 69 (March 1973): 43–62.

———. "'And Ten Dollars Extra, for Every Hundred Lashes Any Person Will Give Him, to the Amount of Three Hundred': A Note on Andrew Jackson's Runaway Slave Ad of 1804 and on the Historian's Use of Evidence." *THQ* 36 (Winter 1977): 468–478.

———. "The Case for Andrew Jackson in 1824: Eaton's *Wyoming Letters*." *THQ* 29 (Summer 1970): 139–151.

———. "'The Presidential Question': Letters to Southern Editors, 1823–24." *THQ* 31 (Summer 1972): 170–186.

Haynes, Sam. "Anglophobia and the Annexation of Texas: The Quest for National Security." In *Manifest Destiny and Empire: American Antebellum Expansion.* Ed. Sam W. Haynes and Christopher Morris, 115–145. College Station: Texas A&M University Press, 1997.

Heidler, David S., and Jeanne T. Heidler. "Mr. Rhea's Missing Letter and the First Seminole War." In *America's Hundred Years' War: U.S. Expansion to the Gulf Coast and the Fate of the Seminole, 1763–1858.* Ed. William S. Belko, 103–127. Gainesville: University Press of Florida, 2011.

Henderson, Archibald. "Andrew Jackson and His Famous Duel with Col. Avery." *Raleigh News and Observer,* 7 November 1926.

———. "Jackson's Loose Living, Common Sin of His Period, but Records Show That He Has Been Much Libelled." *Raleigh (N.C.) News and Observer,* 17 October 1926.

———. "Richard Henderson and the Occupation of Kentucky, 1775." *MVHR* 1 (December 1941): 341–363.

———. "Why Andrew Jackson Left North Carolina." *Raleigh News and Observer,* 31 October 1926.

Henry, H. M. "The Slave Laws of Tennessee." *THM* 2 (1916): 175–203.

Hershkowitz, Leo. "'The Land of Promise': Samuel Swartwout and Land Speculation in Texas, 1830–1838." *New York Historical Society Quarterly* 48 (October 1964): 307–325.

Hickey, Donald R. "Andrew Jackson and the Army Haircut: Individual Rights v. Military Discipline." *THQ* 35 (Winter 1976): 365–375.

Hoffman, William S. "Andrew Jackson, State Rightist: The Case of the Georgia Indians." *THQ* 11 (December 1952): 329–345.

Hopkins, James F. "Election of 1824." In *History of American Presidential Elections.* Ed. Arthur M. Schlesinger and Fred L. Israel, 1:349–381. 4 vols. New York: Chelsea House, 1971.

Hoskins, J. A. "Andrew Jackson a Member of the Guilford, North Carolina Bar." *North Carolina Booklet* 19 (January 1920): 116–118.

Hoyt, William D., Jr. "Washington's Living History: The Post Office Fire and Other Matters, 1834–39." *Records of the Columbia Historical Society* 46–47 (1944–1945): 49–70.

Imes, William Lloyd. "The Legal Status of Free Negroes and Slaves in Tennessee." *Journal of Negro History* 4 (July 1919): 255–272.

Johnson, Michael P. "Planters and Patriarchy: Charleston, 1800–1860." *JSH* 46 (February 1980): 45–72.

Kanon, Tom. "The Kidnapping of Martha Crowley and Settler-Indian Relations prior to the War of 1812." *THQ* 64 (Spring 2005): 3–23.

Kegley, Tracy M. "James White Stephenson: Teacher of Andrew Jackson." *THQ* 7 (March 1948): 38–51.

Knetsch, Joe. "Strategy, Operations, and Tactics in the Second Seminole War, 1835–1842." In *America's Hundred Years' War: U.S. Expansion to the Gulf Coast and the Fate of the Seminole, 1763–1858.* Ed. William S. Belko, 128–154. Gainesville: University Press of Florida, 2011.

Kramer, Neil S. "The Trial of Reuben Crandall." *Records of the Columbia Historical Society* 50 (1980): 123–139.

Kruman, Marc W. "The Second American Party System and the Transformation of Revolutionary Republicanism." *JER* 12 (Winter 1992): 509–537.

Kupfer, Barbara Stern. "A Presidential Patron of the Sport of Kings: Andrew Jackson." *THQ* 29 (Fall 1970): 243–55.

Lack, Paul D. "Slavery and the Texas Revolution." *Southwestern Historical Quarterly* 89 (October 1985): 181–202.

Laska, Lewis L. "'The Dam'st Situation Ever Man Was Placed In': Andrew Jackson, David Allison, and the Frontier Economy of 1795–96." *THQ* 54 (Winter 1995): 336–347.

Latner, Richard B. "The Eaton Affair Reconsidered." *THQ* 36 (Fall 1977): 330–351.

———. "The Kitchen Cabinet and Andrew Jackson's Advisory System." *JAH* 65 (September 1978): 367–388.

Lewis, Kenneth E. "Frontier Change, Institution Building, and the Archaeological Record in the South Carolina Backcountry." *Southeastern Archaeology* 28 (Winter 2009): 184–201.

Longaker, Richard P. "Was Jackson's Kitchen Cabinet a Cabinet?" *MVHQ* 44 (June 1957): 94–108.

Lowe, Gabriel L., Jr. "John Eaton, Jackson's Campaign Manager." *THQ* 11 (June 1952): 99–147.

Lussana, Sergio. "To See Who Was Best on the Plantation: Enslaved Fighting Contests and Masculinity in the Antebellum Plantation South." *JSH* 76 (November 2010): 901–922.

Mahon, John K. "British Strategy and Southern Indians: War of 1812." *Florida Historical Quarterly* 44 (April 1966): 285–305.

Marshall, Lynn L. "The Strange Stillbirth of the Whig Party." *AHR* 72 (February 1967): 445–468.

McCormick, Richard P. "Was There a 'Whig Strategy' in 1836?" *JER* 4 (Spring 1984): 47–70.

McKelway, A. J. "The Scotch-Irish of North Carolina." *North Carolina Booklet* 4 (March 1905): 3–24.

McNiell, Sarah Brown. "Andrew Jackson and Texas Affairs, 1820–1845." *ETHSP* 28 (1956): 86–101.

Miles, Edwin A. "After John Marshall's Decision: *Worcester v. Georgia* and the Nullification Crisis." *JSH* 39 (November 1973): 519–544.

———. "The First People's Inaugural—1829." *THQ* 37 (Fall 1978): 293–307.

———. "The Whig Party and the Menace of Caesar." *THQ* 27 (Winter 1968): 361–379.

Millett, Nathaniel. "Britain's 1814 Occupation of Pensacola and America's Response: An Episode of the War of 1812 in the Southeastern Borderlands." *Florida Historical Quarterly* 83 (Fall 2005): 229–255.

———. "Defending Freedom in the Atlantic Borderlands of the Revolutionary Southeast." *Early American Studies* 5 (Fall 2007): 367–394.

Moore, Peter N. "The Local Origins of Allegiance in Revolutionary South Carolina: The Waxhaws as a Case Study." *South Carolina Historical Magazine* 107 (January 2006): 26–41.

Moore, Powell. "The Political Background of the Revolt against Jackson in Tennessee." *ETHSP* 4 (1930): 45–66.

———. "The Revolt against Jackson in Tennessee, 1835–1836." *JSH* 2 (August 1936): 335–359.

Morgan, Philip D. "Black Society in the Lowcountry, 1760–1810." In *Slavery and Freedom in the Age of the American Revolution*. Ed. Ira Berlin and Ronald Hoffman, 83–141. Charlottesville, Va.: Published for the United States Capitol Historical Society by the University Press of Virginia, 1983.

Narrett, David E. "A Choice of Destiny: Immigration Policy, Slavery, and the Annexation of Texas." *Southwestern Historical Quarterly* 100 (January 1997): 270–302.

Oakes, James. "From Republicanism to Liberalism: Ideological Change and the Crisis of the Old South." *American Quarterly* 37 (Fall 1985): 551–571.

Orr, Mary T. "John Overton and Traveler's Rest." *THQ* 15 (September 1956): 216–223.

Owsley, Frank L., Jr. "The Fort Mims Massacre." *Alabama Review* 24 (July 1971): 192–204.

Owsley, Frank L., Jr. "Ambrister and Arbuthnot: Adventurers or Martyrs for British Honor?" *JER* 5 (Fall 1985): 289–308.

Owsley, Harriet Chappell. "The Marriage of Rachel Donelson." *THQ* 36 (Winter 1977): 479–492.

Parsons, Lynn Hudson. "'A Perpetual Harrow upon My Feelings': John Quincy Adams and the American Indian." *New England Quarterly* 46 (September 1973): 339–379.

Perkins, Dexter. "John Quincy Adams." In *The American Secretaries of State and Their Diplomacy*. 16 vols. Ed. Samuel Flagg Bemis, 4:3–111. 1928. Reprint. New York: Cooper Square, 1963.

Peskin, Lawrence A. "Conspiratorial Anglophobia and the War of 1812." *JAH* 98 (December 2011): 647–669.

Porter, Kenneth W. "Florida Slaves and Free Negroes in the Seminole War, 1835–1842." *Journal of Negro History* 28 (October 1943): 390–421.

———. "Negroes and the Seminole War, 1817–1818." *Journal of Negro History* 36 (July 1951): 249–280.

Pukl, Joseph M., Jr. "James K. Polk's Early Congressional Campaigns of 1825 and 1827." *THQ* 39 (Winter 1980): 440–458.

Ratcliffe, Donald J. "The Nullification Crisis, Southern Discontents, and the American Political Process." *American Nineteenth Century History* 1 (Summer 2000): 1–30.

Ray, Kristofer. "Land Speculation, Popular Democracy, and Political Transformation on the Tennessee Frontier, 1780–1800." *THQ* 61 (Fall 2002): 160–181.

Remini, Robert V. "Andrew Jackson's Adventures on the Natchez Trace." *Southern Quarterly* 29 (Summer 1991): 35–42.

———. "Andrew Jackson Takes an Oath of Allegiance to Spain." *THQ* 55 (Spring 1995): 2–15.

———. "Election of 1828." In *History of American Presidential Elections*. Ed. Arthur M. Schlesinger and Fred L. Israel, 1:411–492. 4 vols. New York: Chelsea House, 1971.

———. "Election of 1832." In *History of American Presidential Elections*. Ed. Arthur M. Schlesinger and Fred L. Israel, 1:495–516. 4 vols. New York: Chelsea House, 1971.

———. "The Final Days and Hours in the Life of General Andrew Jackson." *THQ* 39 (Summer 1980): 167–177.

———. "Martin Van Buren and the Tariff of Abominations." *AHR* 63 (July 1958): 903–917.

Reynolds, Curtis R. "The Deterioration of Mexican-American Diplomatic Relations." *Journal of the West* 11 (April 1972): 213–224.

Roeckell, Lelia M. "Bonds over Bondage: British Opposition to the Annexation of Texas." *JER* 19 (Summer 1999): 257–278.

Rolater, Fred S. "The American Indian and the Origin of the Second American Party System." *Wisconsin Magazine of History* 76 (Spring 1993): 180–203.

Rosen, Deborah A. "Wartime Prisoners and the Rule of Law." *JER* 28 (Winter 2008): 559–595.

Ross, Steven J. "The Transformation of Republican Ideology." *JER* 10 (Fall 1990): 323–330.

Rousseau, Peter L. "Jacksonian Monetary Policy, Specie Flows, and the Panic of 1837." *Journal of Economic History* 62 (June 2002): 457–488.

Rubin, Ben. "Planters and Presbyterians: South Carolina from Atlantic Microcosm to the Eve of the American Revolution." *Journal of Backcountry Studies* 5 (Fall 2010): 1–16.

Rugemer, Edward B. "Robert Monroe Harrison, British Abolition, Southern Anglophobia, and Texas Annexation." *Slavery & Abolition* 28 (August 2007): 169–191.

———. "The Southern Response to British Abolitionism: The Maturation of Proslavery Apologetics." *JSH* 70 (May 2004): 221–248.

Salley, A. S. "On the Birthplace of Andrew Jackson." In Cyrus T. Brady, *The True Andrew Jackson,* 407–438. Philadelphia: J. B. Lippincott, 1906.

Saxon, Gerald D. "Anthony Butler: A Flawed Diplomat." *East Texas Historical Journal* 24 (1986): 3–14.

Schroeder, John H. "Annexation or Independence: The Texas Issue in American Politics, 1836–1845." *Southwestern Historical Quarterly* 89 (October 1985): 137–164.

Schwalm, Leslie A. "'Agonizing Groans of Mothers' and 'Slave-Scarred Veterans': The Commemoration of Slavery and Emancipation." *American Nineteenth Century History* 9 (September 2008): 289–304.

Sellers, Charles G., Jr. "Banking and Politics in Jackson's Tennessee, 1817–1827." *MVHR* 41 (June 1954): 61–84.

———. "Election of 1844." In *History of American Presidential Elections.* Ed. Arthur M. Schlesinger and Fred L. Israel, 1:745–861. 4 vols. New York: Chelsea House, 1971.

———. "Jackson Men with Feet of Clay." *AHR* 42 (April 1957): 537–551.

———. "James K. Polk's Political Apprenticeship." *ETHSP* 25 (1953): 37–53.

———. "Who Were the Southern Whigs?" *AHR* 59 (February 1954): 335–346.

Serme, Jean-Marc. "Stormy Weather at Andrew Jackson's Halcyon Plantation, in Coahoma County, Mississippi, 1838–1845." *Revue Française d'Études Américaines* 98 (September 2003): 32–47.

Shade, William G. "'The Most Delicate and Exciting Topics': Martin Van Buren, Slavery, and the Election of 1836." *JER* 18 (Fall 1998): 459–484.

Shepherd, William R. "Wilkinson and the Beginnings of the Spanish Conspiracy." *AHR* 9 (April 1904): 490–506.

Shockley, Megan Taylor. "King of the Wild Frontier vs. King Andrew I: Davy Crockett and the Election of 1831." *THQ* 57 (Fall 1997): 158–169.

Silbey, Joel H. "Election of 1836." In *History of American Presidential Elections.* Ed. Arthur M. Schlesinger and Fred L. Israel, 1:575–640. 4 vols. New York: Chelsea House, 1971.

Sitterson, J. Carlyle. "Lewis Thompson, a Carolinian, and His Louisiana Plantation, 1848–1888: A Study in Absentee Ownership." In *Essays in Southern History.* Ed. Fletcher M. Green, 16–22. Chapel Hill: University of North Carolina Press, 1949.

———. "The William J. Minor Plantations: A Study in Ante-Bellum Absentee Ownership." *JSH* 9 (February 1943): 59–74.

Somit, Albert. "Andrew Jackson as Political Theorist." *THQ* 8 (June 1949): 99–126.

Spence, Richard Douglas. "John Donelson and the Opening of the Old Southwest." *THQ* 50 (Fall 1991): 157–172.

———. "Samuel Donelson: Young Andrew Jackson's Best Friend." *THQ* 69 (Summer 2010): 106–123.

Stenberg, Richard. "Andrew Jackson and the Erving Affidavit." *Southwestern Historical Quarterly* 41 (October 1937): 142–153.

———. "Jackson, Anthony Butler, and Texas." *Southwestern Social Science Quarterly* 13 (December 1932): 264–286.

———. "Jackson's Neches Claim, 1829–1836." *Southwestern Historical Quarterly* 39 (April 1936): 255–274.

———. "President Jackson and Anthony Butler." *Southwest Review* 22 (Summer 1937): 391–404.

———. "The Texas Schemes of Jackson and Houston, 1829–1836." *Southwestern Social Science Quarterly* 15 (December 1834): 229–250.

Stickley, Julia Ward. "Catholic Ceremonies in the White House, 1832–1833: Andrew Jackson's Forgotten Ward, Mary Lewis." *Catholic Historical Review* 51 (July 1965): 192–198.

Stowe, Steven M. "The 'Touchiness' of the Gentleman Planter: The Sense of Esteem and Continuity in the Antebellum South." *Psychohistory Review* 8 (Winter 1979): 6–15.

Tadman, Michael. "The Reputation of the Slave Trader in Southern History and the Social Memory of South." *American Nineteenth Century History* 8 (September 2007): 247–271.

Tilly, Bette B. "The Jackson-Dinsmoor Feud: A Paradox in a Minor Key." *Journal of Mississippi History* 39 (May 1977): 117–131.

Toplovich, Ann. "Marriage, Mayhem, and Presidential Politics: The Robards-Jackson Backcountry Scandal." *Ohio Valley History* 5 (Winter 2005): 3–22.

Usner, Daniel H., Jr. "American Indians on the Cotton Frontier: Changing Economic Relations with Citizens and Slaves in the Mississippi Territory." *JAH* 72 (September 1985): 297–317.

Van Deusen, Glyndon G. "Some Aspects of Whig Thought and Theory in the Jacksonian Period." *AHR* 63 (October 1957): 305–322.

———. "The Whig Party." In *History of U.S. Political Parties.* 4 vols. Ed. Arthur M. Schlesinger Jr., 1:333–363. New York: Chelsea House, 1973.

Walker, Arda. "Andrew Jackson: Planter." *ETHSP* 15 (1943): 19–34.

Warshauer, Matthew S. "Andrew Jackson: Chivalric Slave Master." *THQ* 65 (Fall 2006): 202–228.

Watson, Samuel. "Soldier, Expansionist, Politician: Eleazer Wheelock Ripley and the Dance of Ambition in the Early Republic." In *Nexus of Empire: Negotiating Loyalty and Identity in the Revolutionary Borderlands, 1760s–1820s.* Ed. Gene Allen Smith and Sylvia L. Hilton, 321–346. Gainesville: University Press of Florida, 2009.

Weisenburger, Francis P. "Charles Hammond: The First Great Journalist of the Old Northwest." *Ohio History* 43 (October 1934): 338–427.

Williams, Samuel C. "Tennessee's First Military Expedition." *THM* 8 (October 1924): 171–190.

Wilson, Major L. "Republicanism and the Idea of Party in the Jacksonian Period." *JER* 8 (Winter 1988): 419–442.

Wilentz, Sean. "Abraham Lincoln and Jacksonian Democracy." In *Our Lincoln: New Perspectives on Lincoln and His World*. Ed. Eric Foner, 62–79. New York: Norton, 2008.

Wood, Kirsten. "'One Woman So Dangerous to Public Morals': Gender and Power in the Eaton Affair." *JER* 17 (Summer 1997): 237–276.

Wyatt-Brown, Bertram. "The Abolitionists' Postal Campaign of 1835." *Journal of Negro History* 50 (October 1965): 227–238.

———. "Andrew Jackson's Honor." *JER* 17 (Spring 1997): 1–36.

———. "The Mask of Obedience: Male Slave Psychology in the Old South." *AHR* 93 (December 1988): 1228–1252.

Yarbrough, Fay A. "Power, Perception, and Interracial Sex: Former Slaves Recall a Multiracial South." *JSH* 71 (August 2005): 559–588.

Yarn, Douglas H. "The Attorney as Duelist's Friend: Lessons from the Code Duello." *Case Western Reserve Law Review* 5 (Fall 2000): 69–113.

Dissertations, Theses, and Unpublished Papers

Baker, Carter G. "John Patton Erwin." MS in possession of author.

Barry, Stephen J. "Nathaniel Macon: The Prophet of Pure Republicanism, 1758–1837." Ph.D. diss., State University of New York at Buffalo, 1996.

Coens, Thomas M. "The Formation of the Jackson Party, 1822–1825." Ph.D. diss., Harvard University, 2004.

Dovenbarger, Daniel Byron. "Land Registration in Early Middle Tennessee: Laws and Practices." M.A. thesis, Vanderbilt University, 1981.

Drew, Bettina. "Master Andrew Jackson: Indian Removal and the Culture of Slavery." Ph.D. diss., Yale University, 2001.

Inman, Natalie Rishay. "Friendship and Advancement: A Community of Lawyers in Nashville, Tennessee, 1788–1805." M.A. thesis, Vanderbilt University, 2005.

Koonts, Russell S. "'An Angel Has Fallen': The Glasgow Land Frauds and the Establishment of the North Carolina Supreme Court." M.A. thesis, North Carolina State University, 1995.

Peterson, Dawn. "Unusual Sympathies: Settler Imperialism, Slavery, and the Politics of Adoption in the Early U.S. Republic." Ph.D. diss., New York University, 2011.

Satterfield, Robert B. "Andrew Jackson Donelson: A Moderate Nationalist Jacksonian." Ph.D. diss., Johns Hopkins University, 1961.

Sheidley, Nathaniel J. "Unruly Men: Indians, Settlers, and the Ethos of Frontier Patriarchy in the Upper Tennessee Watershed, 1763–1815." Ph.D. diss., Princeton University, 1999.

Smith, Trevor A. "Pioneers, Patriots, and Politicians: The Tennessee Militia System, 1772–1857." Ph.D. diss., University of Tennessee, 2003.

Werner, John Melvin. "Race Riots in the United States during the Age of Jackson, 1829–1849." Ph.D. diss., Indiana University, 1972.

Reference Works

Index to the Andrew Jackson Papers. Washington, D.C.: Library of Congress, 1967.

Goldman, Perry, and James S. Young, eds. *The United States Congressional Directories, 1789–1840.* New York: Columbia University Press, 1973.

McBride, Robert M., and Dan M. Robison. *Biographical Directory of the Tennessee General Assembly.* 6 vols. Nashville: Tennessee State Library and Archives and Tennessee Historical Commission, 1975–1989.

The Oxford Companion to the Supreme Court of the United States. Ed. Kermit L. Hall. Oxford: Oxford University Press, 1992.

Presidential Elections since 1789, 3d ed. Washington, D.C.: Congressional Quarterly, 1983.

West, Carroll Van, ed. *The Tennessee Encyclopedia of History and Culture.* Nashville: Rutledge Hill Press, 1998.

INDEX